T0230082

Lecture Notes in Computer Science 874

Edited by G. Goos, J. Hartmanis and J. van Leeuwen

Advisory Board: W. Brauer   D. Gries   J. Stoer

Alan Borning (Ed.)

Principles and Practice of Constraint Programming

Second International Workshop, PPCP '94
Rosario, Orcas Island, WA, USA, May 2-4, 1994
Proceedings

Springer-Verlag

Berlin Heidelberg New York
London Paris Tokyo
Hong Kong Barcelona
Budapest

Series Editors

Gerhard Goos
Universität Karlsruhe
Postfach 69 80, Vincenz-Priessnitz-Straße 1, D-76131 Karlsruhe, Germany

Juris Hartmanis
Department of Computer Science, Cornell University
4130 Upson Hall, Ithaka, NY 14853, USA

Jan van Leeuwen
Department of Computer Science, Utrecht University
Padualaan 14, 3584 CH Utrecht, The Netherlands

Volume Editor

Alan Borning
Department of Computer Science and Engineering, FR-35
University of Washington
Seattle, Washington 98195, USA

CR Subject Classification (1991): D.1.m, D.3.2-3, D.1.3, H.2.3, I.2.8

ISBN 3-540-58601-6 Springer-Verlag Berlin Heidelberg New York

CIP data applied for

© Springer-Verlag Berlin Heidelberg 1994
Printed in Germany

Typesetting: Camera-ready by author
SPIN: 10479196   45/3140-543210 - Printed on acid-free paper

Preface

PPCP'94, the Second Workshop on the Principles and Practice of Constraint Programming, was an interdisciplinary meeting focusing on constraint programming and constraint-based systems. The papers presented at the workshop covered a broad range of topics related to constraint programming, including constraint programming languages, algorithms for constraint satisfaction and entailment, and constraints and their relation to such fields as artificial intelligence, databases, operations research, and user interfaces. The workshop was held at Rosario, Orcas Island, Washington, USA, in May 1994.

The present volume contains revised versions of the papers presented at the workshop, as well as a summary of a panel session on commercial applications of constraint programming. The workshop was held in cooperation with the American Association for Artificial Intelligence and the Association for Logic Programming, and was sponsored in part by the U.S. Office of Naval Research.

An increasing number of researchers world-wide are now dealing with different aspects of constraints, and a new community of interest is growing around this notion. In the past, papers on such topics were presented at a variety of other conferences. We hope that PPCP'94, along with PPCP'93, and other recent constraint workshops and conferences, has helped to foster the growth of constraint programming as a subfield of computer science in its own right.

September 1994   Alan Borning
                                                  PPCP'94 Program Chair

Organizing Committee:

      Jean-Louis Lassez, Organizing Committee Chair (IBM Watson)
      Alan Borning (University of Washington)
      Jacques Cohen (Brandeis University)
      Alain Colmerauer (University of Marseilles)
      Herve Gallaire (Xerox Corporation)
      Paris Kanellakis (Brown University)
      Anil Nerode (Cornell University)
      Vijay Saraswat (Xerox Palo Alto Research Center)
      Ralph Wachter (Office of Naval Research)

Program Committee:

      Alan Borning, Program Chair (University of Washington)
      Colin Bell (University of Iowa)
      Frederic Benhamou (University of Marseilles)
      Rina Dechter (University of California, Irvine)
      Curtis Eaves (Stanford University)
      Bjorn Freeman-Benson (Carleton University)
      Eugene Freuder (University of New Hampshire)
      Martin Golumbic (Bar-Ilan University)
      Peter Hammer (Rutgers University)
      Deepak Kapur (SUNY Albany)
      Catherine Lassez (IBM Watson)
      Alan Mackworth (University of British Columbia)
      Satoshi Matsuoka (University of Tokyo)
      Raghu Ramakrishnan (University of Wisconsin)
      Francesca Rossi (University of Pisa)
      Gert Smolka (DFKI and University of Saarbrücken)
      Pascal Van Hentenryck (Brown University)
      Jennifer Widom (Stanford University)
      Richard Zippel (Cornell University)

Contents

Concurrent Constraint Languages

Databases

Artificial Intelligence

Other Topics

A Substitution Operation for Constraints

Peter Jeavons[1], David Cohen[1] and Martin Cooper[2]

[1] Department of Computer Science, Royal Holloway, University of London, UK
[2] IRIT, University of Toulouse III, France

Abstract. In order to reduce the search space in finite constraint satisfaction problems, a number of different preprocessing schemes have been proposed. This paper introduces a 'substitution' operation for constraints. This new operation generalizes both the idea of enforcing consistency and the notion of label substitution introduced by Freuder. We show that the constraints in a problem may be replaced by substitutable subsets in order to simplify the problem without affecting the existence of a solution. Furthermore, we show how substitutability may be established locally, by considering only a subproblem of the complete problem.

1 Introduction

The finite constraint satisfaction problem (or consistent labeling problem) is known to be NP-complete [7]. Such problems may always be solved by an exhaustive search strategy, but this is generally very inefficient.

The search space may be reduced by enforcing some level of 'consistency' [5] in the problem. This involves strengthening the given constraints by disallowing labels or combinations of labels which can be eliminated using other constraints. A number of efficient algorithms have been proposed for achieving various levels of consistency in a given problem [2, 8, 9].

For some applications of constraints, notably problems arising in machine vision [3, 10, 11], it is not necessary to calculate all possible solutions to a given problem, only to determine whether a solution exists, and if so to output a single possible solution. When only a single solution is required it is possible to generalize the notion of enforcing consistency to obtain a more powerful constraint simplification strategy, which will be called 'substitution'. The substitution operation simplifies the given constraints by removing labels or combinations of labels which can be shown to be unnecessary when seeking a single solution.

The idea that one label may be substituted for another in some problems, without affecting the existence of solutions was first proposed by Freuder in [6]. In this paper we generalize this idea to apply to arbitrary sets of labels for arbitrary sets of variables. This opens up a wider range of possible substitutions and allows us to apply substitution operations directly to the constraints in a problem.

The motivation for the work described here is to extend the range of simplification operations which may be applied to constraints, in order to identify more precisely the features of a constraint satisfaction problem which give rise to intractability [4].

2 Definitions

A *finite constraint satisfaction problem* (CSP) [7, 10] consists of a number of *variables* which must be assigned *labels* from associated *domains*, subject to a number of *constraints*. Each constraint specifies allowed combinations of labels for some subset of the variables, referred to as the *scope* of the constraint.

We now give a formal definition:

Definition 1. A *finite constraint satisfaction problem*, $\mathcal{P}$, consists of a pair (X, C), where:

- X is a finite set of variables.
- Each $x \in X$ is associated with a finite set of labels, $\delta(x)$, called the *domain* of x.
- C is a finite set of constraints.
- Each $c \in C$ is associated with a subset, $\Sigma(c)$, of X, called the *scope* of c.

A mapping t from $Y \subseteq X$ such that $t(x) \in \delta(x)$, for all $x \in Y$ is called a *labeling* of Y.

Each *constraint* $c \in C$ is a set of labelings of $\Sigma(c)$.

Definition 2. Let $\mathcal{P} = (X, C)$ be a constraint satisfaction problem.

- Given any constraint, $c \in C$, a labeling t of $\Sigma(c)$ is said to *"satisfy"* c if and only if $t \in c$.
- A labeling t of X is said to be a *"solution"* to $\mathcal{P}$ if and only if for every $c \in C$, the restriction of t to $\Sigma(c)$ satisfies c.

The set of all solutions to $\mathcal{P}$ is denoted $\mathrm{Sol}(\mathcal{P})$.

To illustrate these definitions, we now give an example of a specific constraint satisfaction problem which will be used as a running example.

Example 1. Let $\mathcal{P} = (X, C)$ be the constraint satisfaction problem illustrated in Figure 1, in which:

- $X = \{x_1, \ldots, x_5\}$
- $\delta(x_i) = \{a, b, c\}$, $i = 1, 2, \ldots, 5$
- $C = \{c_1, \ldots, c_4\}$
- The constraint scopes are as follows:

$$\Sigma(c_1) = \{x_1, x_2\}$$
$$\Sigma(c_2) = \{x_2, x_3, x_4\}$$
$$\Sigma(c_3) = \{x_3, x_5\}$$
$$\Sigma(c_4) = \{x_4, x_5\}$$

For this problem, a labeling is a mapping from a subset Y of X into the set $\{a, b, c\}$. For instance if $Y = \{x_1, x_4\}$, then the mapping $t : Y \rightarrow \{a, b, c\}$ with $t(x_1) = a$ and $t(x_4) = c$ is a labeling of Y. If we fix a nominal order for the variables in Y, then we can denote a labeling of Y by an n-tuple where n is the size of Y. Using the natural subscript ordering of the variables the labeling t can be written as (a, c).

From now on, for convenience, we shall assume that the variables of $\mathcal{P}$ have this natural subscript order. Using the notation just described, we define the constraints of $\mathcal{P}$ to be as follows:

$$c_1 = \{(a, a), (a, c)\}$$
$$c_2 = \{(a, a, a), (a, a, b), (a, b, b), (b, b, b), (c, c, c)\}$$
$$c_3 = \{(a, a), (a, b), (b, c), (c, c)\}$$
$$c_4 = \{(a, a), (b, b), (b, c), (c, c)\}$$

To complete this example we will compute $\mathrm{Sol}(\mathcal{P})$, the set of all solutions to $\mathcal{P}$. By a simple search we find that it is composed of four elements. As solutions are simply labelings of the complete set of variables X, we can write them as follows:

$$(a, a, a, a, a)$$
$$(a, a, a, b, b)$$
$$(a, a, b, b, c)$$
$$(a, c, c, c, c)$$

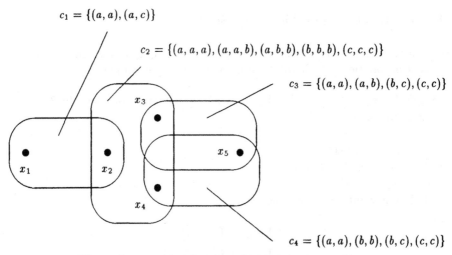

Fig. 1. An example of a constraint satisfaction problem

We will sometimes want to deal with *subproblems* of a given constraint satisfaction problem which arise from considering subsets of the set of constraints. We therefore make the following definition:

Definition 3. Let $\mathcal{P} = (X, C)$ be a constraint satisfaction problem and let D be any subset of C. The reduced *subproblem of $\mathcal{P}$ generated by D* is the constraint satisfaction problem $\mathcal{P}|_D = (X|_D, D)$, where:

$$X|_D = \bigcup_{c \in D} \Sigma(c)$$

We will make use of the following operations from relational algebra [1]:

Definition 4. Let Y, Z be sets of variables with $Z \subseteq Y$. For any labeling t of Y, the *projection* onto Z of t, denoted $t[Z]$, is the restriction of t to Z. Similarly, for any set S of labelings of Y, the *projection* onto Z of S, denoted $\pi_Z(S)$, is the set $\{t[Z] \mid t \in S\}$.

Definition 5. Let Y, Z be sets of variables with $Z \subseteq Y$. For any set T of labelings of Z, and any set S of labelings of Y, the *selection* by T from S, denoted $\sigma_T(S)$, is the set $\{t \in S \mid t[Z] \in T\}$.

3 Substitutability

Freuder [6] defined the concept of substitutability for labels in a CSP as follows: given two possible labels a and b for a variable x, a is *substitutable* for b iff substituting the value a for b at variable x in any solution yields another solution.

We now generalise Freuder's definition to apply to sets of labelings of arbitrary subsets, rather than just individual labels for single variables:

Definition 6. Let $\mathcal{P}$ be a constraint satisfaction problem with variables X, and let R be a subset of X.

Given any two sets T_1, T_2 of labelings of R, we say that T_2 is *substitutable* for T_1 in $\mathcal{P}$ if

$$\pi_{X-R}(\sigma_{T_1}(\mathrm{Sol}(\mathcal{P}))) \subseteq \pi_{X-R}(\sigma_{T_2}(\mathrm{Sol}(\mathcal{P})))$$

If T_2 is substitutable for T_1 in $\mathcal{P}$, then we will write $T_1 \overset{\mathcal{P}}{\preceq} T_2$.

In other words, given two sets of labelings, T_1 and T_2, for the same variables, we say that T_2 is substitutable for T_1 if the following condition holds: the elements of T_2 may be extended to complete solutions in all the same ways as the elements of T_1.

Note that for any problem $\mathcal{P}$ and any sets of labelings, T_1, T_2, we have

$$T_1 \subseteq T_2 \Rightarrow T_1 \overset{\mathcal{P}}{\preceq} T_2.$$

The following example illustrates the definition:

Example 2. Consider the constraint satisfaction problem $\mathcal{P}$ in Example 1. None of the possible labels for any of the individual variables is substitutable for any other in this example, according to Freuder's original notion of substitutability.

However, using Definition 6 and the list of solutions given in Example 1, we can show that the set of labelings $\{(a,a,a),(c,c,c)\}$ for the variables x_3, x_4 and x_5 is substitutable in $\mathcal{P}$ for $\{(a,b,b)\}$, i.e $\{(a,b,b)\} \overset{\mathcal{P}}{\preceq} \{(a,a,a),(c,c,c)\}$.

The next lemma indicates that a constraint in a constraint satisfaction problem may always be replaced by a substitutable set of labelings without eliminating all of the solutions:

Lemma 7. *Let $\mathcal{P} = (X, C)$ be a constraint satisfaction problem . If we replace any constraint $c \in C$ by a new constraint c' with the same scope, such that $c \overset{\mathcal{P}}{\preceq} c'$, then we obtain a new constraint satisfaction problem $\mathcal{P}'$ such that*

$$Sol(\mathcal{P}') = \emptyset \implies Sol(\mathcal{P}) = \emptyset$$

Proof. Note that $Sol(\mathcal{P}) = \sigma_c(Sol(P))$ and $Sol(\mathcal{P}') = \sigma_{c'}(Sol(P))$. Hence, if $Sol(\mathcal{P}) \neq \emptyset$ then $\sigma_c(Sol(\mathcal{P})) \neq \emptyset$, so if $c \overset{\mathcal{P}}{\preceq} c'$, then by Definition 6 we have $\sigma_{c'}(Sol(\mathcal{P})) \neq \emptyset$, hence $Sol(\mathcal{P}') \neq \emptyset$, and the result follows. $\square$

For the special case of substitutable *subsets* of a given constraint, Lemma 7 has the following important corollary:

Corollary 8. *Any constraint in a constraint satisfaction problem may be replaced by a substitutable subset without affecting the existence of solutions.*

Furthermore, in this case, the solutions to the new problem will simply be a subset of the solutions to the original problem.

Replacing a constraint with a substitutable subset will be called a 'substitution' operation. The following example illustrates how this substitution operation may be used to tighten the constraints in a constraint satisfaction problem.

Example 3. Reconsider the constraint satisfaction problem $\mathcal{P}$ defined in Example 1.

No proper subset of c_1 is substitutable for c_1 in $\mathcal{P}$,

The following proper subsets are substitutable for c_2 in $\mathcal{P}$:

$$\{(a,a,a),(a,a,b),(b,b,b),(c,c,c)\}$$
$$\{(a,a,a),(a,a,b),(b,b,b),(a,b,b)\}$$
$$\{(a,a,a),(a,a,b),(a,b,b),(c,c,c)\}$$
$$\{(a,a,a),(a,a,b),(a,b,b),\}$$
$$\{(a,a,a),(a,a,b),(c,c,c)\}$$

The following proper subsets are substitutable for c_3 in $\mathcal{P}$:

$$\{(a,a),(b,c),(c,c)\}$$
$$\{(a,a),(a,b),(c,c)\}$$

The following proper subsets are substitutable for c_4 in $\mathcal{P}$:

$$\{(b,b),(b,c),(c,c)\}$$
$$\{(a,a),(b,c),(c,c)\}$$

Definition 6 implies that if a set of labelings T_1 contains any labeling t which cannot be extended to a solution of $\mathcal{P}$, then $T_1 \overset{\mathcal{P}}{\preceq} (T_1 - t)$. This gives us the following result:

Proposition 9. *Any tuple which may be eliminated from a constraint in a constraint satisfaction problem by enforcing consistency may be removed by a substitution operation.*

This means that the substitution operation is a true generalization of the notion of enforcing consistency.

Calculating the smallest substitutable subset of a constraint is as difficult as solving the original problem. However, the next result shows that a sufficient condition for substitutability is substitutability within certain subproblems.

Definition 10. Let $\mathcal{P} = (X, C)$ be a constraint satisfaction problem.
For any $c \in C$ define the *closure* of c, $\bar{c}$, as follows:

$$\bar{c} = \{c' \in C \mid \Sigma(c') \cap \Sigma(c) \neq \emptyset\}$$

Lemma 11. *Let $\mathcal{P} = (X, C)$ be a constraint satisfaction problem.*
For any $c \in C$ and any set c' of labelings of $\Sigma(c)$, we have

$$c \overset{\mathcal{P}|_{\bar{c}}}{\preceq} c' \Rightarrow c \overset{\mathcal{P}}{\preceq} c'$$

Proof. Assume that $c \overset{\mathcal{P}}{\npreceq} c'$. By Definition 6, this means that

$$\pi_{X - \Sigma(c)}(\sigma_c(\mathrm{Sol}(\mathcal{P}))) \not\subseteq \pi_{X - \Sigma(c)}(\sigma_{c'}(\mathrm{Sol}(\mathcal{P})))$$

Hence, there is some $s \in \mathrm{Sol}(\mathcal{P})$ such that the restriction of s to $X - \Sigma(c)$ is not compatible with any element of c'. In other words, any labeling s' of X which satisfies c' and agrees with s on $X - \Sigma(c)$ must fail to satisfy some constraint in C.

By construction, s' satisfies c' and all elements of $C - \bar{c}$, so s' must fail to satisfy some element of $\bar{c} - c'$. Hence $c \overset{\mathcal{P}|_{\bar{c}}}{\npreceq} c'$. $\qquad\qquad\square$

Any labelling which is substitutable for a constraint c in $\mathcal{P}|_{\bar{c}}$ will be said to be 'locally' substitutable for c. Combining Lemma 11 with Corollary 8 shows that we may replace any constraint c in a constraint satisfaction problem $\mathcal{P}$ by a locally substitutable subset without affecting the existence of a solution. For many problems $\mathcal{P}$, local substitutability may be calculated much more efficiently than substitutability in $\mathcal{P}$, since it requires solutions to be calculated only for the subproblems generated by the constraint closures.

However, local substitutability is not implied by (global) substitutability, so using local substitutability is not guaranteed to find all possible constraint substitutions, as the following example shows:

Example 4. Reconsider the constraint satisfaction problem $\mathcal{P}$ defined in Example 1. The set $c_3' = \{(a,a),(a,b),(c,c)\}$ is substitutable in $\mathcal{P}$ for c_3 (Example 3).

However, if we consider the subproblem $\mathcal{P}|_{c_3}$, we find that $\mathrm{Sol}(\mathcal{P}|_{c_3})$ contains the element (b,b,b,c) so $c_3 \overset{\mathcal{P}|_{c_3}}{\npreceq} c_3'$.

4   Propagation of Substitution

Substitution operations may be propagated to obtain further reductions in the constraints, as the following example indicates. Note that in this example the use of substitution operations and propagation is sufficient to obtain a complete solution to the problem.

Example 5. Reconsider the constraint satisfaction problem $\mathcal{P}$ defined in Example 1. It was shown in Example 2 that the set of labelings

$$c_2' = \{(a,a,a),(a,a,b),(a,b,b)\}$$

is substitutable in $\mathcal{P}$ for c_2 (it is also locally substitutable).

If we replace c_2 with c_2' then we obtain a new constraint satisfaction problem $\mathcal{P}'$, and now we find that $c_1' = \{(a,a)\}$ is substitutable for c_1 in $\mathcal{P}'$.

If we replace c_1 with c_1' then we obtain a new constraint satisfaction problem $\mathcal{P}''$, and we find that $c_3' = \{(a,a),(a,b)\}$ is substitutable for c_3 in $\mathcal{P}''$.

If we replace c_3 with c_3' then we obtain a new constraint satisfaction problem $\mathcal{P}'''$, and we find that $c_4' = \{(a,a)\}$ is substitutable for c_4 in $\mathcal{P}'''$.

Finally, if we replace c_4 with c_4' then we obtain a new constraint satisfaction problem with only a single solution, (a,a,a,a,a). Further substitution operations may therefore be carried out on all of the constraints to reduce them to a single element, which is the projection of this solution.

As with the various methods for enforcing different levels of consistency, it is possible to organise the propagation of substitution operations according to a number of different schemes. One naive algorithm for repeatedly applying local substitutability and propagating the results is as follows:

Algorithm 12.

```
Repeat
      For each constraint c
          For each t ∈ c
                   P|c
              If c ≼ c − {t} then set c = c − {t}
      Until no further changes to constraints.
```

The complexity of this algorithm depends on the maximum size of a constraint closure, say k, and the maximum number of labelings permitted by a constraint, say m. The main repeat loop may be executed at most $m|C|$ times, since at least one element is removed from a constraint on each iteration. The complexity of checking for substitutability for each constraint element is $O(m^k)$, since each possible extension must be checked against each other element of c. Hence the overall complexity is $O(|C|^2 m^{k+2})$.

However, unlike operations which simply enforce consistency, the repeated application of substitution operations until no more substitution is possible does not always give an invariant result. More surprisingly, the *number of solutions* to the resulting problem is not always invariant either, as the following example shows:

Example 6. Reconsider the constraint satisfaction problem $\mathcal{P}$ defined in Example 1. It was shown in Example 2 that the set of labelings

$$c_2' = \{(a, a, a), (a, a, b), (c, c, c)\}$$

is substitutable in $\mathcal{P}$ for c_2 (note that this is a different substitutable set to the one considered in Example 5).

If we replace c_2 with c_2' then we obtain a new constraint satisfaction problem $\mathcal{P}'$, and now we find that $c_4' = \{(a, a), (c, c)\}$ is substitutable for c_4 in $\mathcal{P}'$.

If we replace c_4 with c_4' then we obtain a new constraint satisfaction problem $\mathcal{P}''$, and we find that $c_3' = \{(a, a), (c, c)\}$ is substitutable for c_3 in $\mathcal{P}''$.

If we replace c_3 with c_3' then we obtain a new constraint satisfaction problem $\mathcal{P}'''$, and we find that $c_2'' = \{(a, a, a), (c, c, c)\}$ is substitutable for c_2' in $\mathcal{P}'''$.

Finally, if we replace c_2' with c_2'' then we obtain a new constraint satisfaction problem with two solutions, (a, a, a, a, a) and (a, c, c, c, c). This constraint satisfaction problem cannot be further reduced using substitution operations.

The implication of this lack of invariance is that some sequences of substitution operations may be much more effective than others in reducing the search space. It is an open question whether an efficient algorithm exists for choosing the most effective sequence of substitution operations, although we strongly suspect that this problem is as difficult as solving the original problem.

5   Conclusion

We have presented a substitution operation which is a true generalization of Freuder's notion of label substitution, and also generalizes all forms of consistency enforcement.

Although this substitution operation is most useful when searching for a single solution, it may also be useful in the case where we want to find all solutions. In such cases, it can reduce search time by showing more quickly that a branch of the search tree leads to no solutions. Substitution operations may be worth applying to any constraint satisfaction problem that has a high probability of having no solutions.

References

1. Codd, E.F., "A Relational Model of Data for Large Shared Databanks", *Communications of the ACM* **13** (1970), pp. 377–387.
2. Cooper, M.C., "An optimal *k*-consistency algorithm", *Artificial Intelligence* **41** (1990), pp. 89–95.
3. Cooper, M.C., *Visual Occlusion and the Interpretation of Ambiguous Pictures*, Ellis Horwood, 1992.
4. Cooper, M.C., Cohen, D.A., and Jeavons, P.G., "Characterizing Tractable Constraints", *Artificial Intelligence* **66** (1994), pp. 347–361.
5. Freuder, E.C., "Synthesising Constraint Expressions", *Communications of the ACM* **21** (1978), pp. 958–966.
6. Freuder, E.C., "Eliminating interchangeable values in constraint satisfaction problems", Proceedings of AAAI-91, pp. 227–233.
7. Mackworth, A.K., "Consistency in Networks of Relations", *Artificial Intelligence* **8** (1977), pp. 99–118.
8. Mackworth, A.K., and Freuder, E.C., "The Complexity of Some Polynomial Network Consistency Algorithms for Constraint Satisfaction Problems", *Artificial Intelligence* **25** (1984), pp. 65–47.
9. Mohr, R., and Henderson, T.C., "Arc and Path Consistency Revisited", *Artificial Intelligence* **28** (1986), pp. 225-233.
10. Montanari, U., "Networks of Constraints: Fundamental Properties and Applications to Picture Processing", *Information Sciences* **7** (1974), pp. 95–132.
11. Waltz, D.L. "Understanding Line Drawings of Scenes with Shadows", in *The Psychology of Computer Vision*, Winston, P.H., (Ed.), McGraw-Hill, New York, (1975), pp. 19–91.

Contradicting Conventional Wisdom in Constraint Satisfaction

Daniel Sabin and Eugene C. Freuder

Department of Computer Science, University of New Hampshire, Durham NH 03824, USA

Abstract. Constraint satisfaction problems have wide application in artificial intelligence. They involve finding values for problem variables where the values must be consistent in that they satisfy restrictions on which combinations of values are allowed. Two standard techniques used in solving such problems are backtrack search and consistency inference. Conventional wisdom in the constraint satisfaction community suggests: 1) using consistency inference as preprocessing before search to prune values from consideration reduces subsequent search effort and 2) using consistency inference during search to prune values from consideration is best done at the limited level embodied in the forward checking algorithm. We present evidence contradicting both pieces of conventional wisdom, and suggesting renewed consideration of an approach which fully maintains arc consistency during backtrack search.

1 Introduction

Constraint satisfaction problems (*CSPs*) involve finding values for problem variables subject to constraints that are restrictions on which combinations of values are allowed [1]. They have many applications in artificial intelligence. (We restrict our attention here to *binary* CSPs, where the constraints involve two variables.)

The basic solution method is backtrack search. Often consistency inference (constraint propagation) techniques are used to prune values before or during search. The basic pruning technique involves establishing or restoring some form of arc consistency. If a value v for a variable V is not consistent with any value for some other variable U, then v is *arc inconsistent* and can be removed. *Full arc consistency* is achieved when all arc inconsistent values are removed.

One of the most successful forms of backtrack search has proven to be *forward checking* [2]. Forward checking combines backtrack search with a limited form of arc consistency maintenance. Some values are removed that become inconsistent when the problem is modified by the choices made during the search process.

This paper provides strong experimental evidence contradicting two well-established pieces of conventional wisdom in the CSP community:

- Conventional CSP wisdom says that using consistency inference in a preprocessing step, to prune values before search, will reduce the subsequent search effort. There has been some question as to the degree of consistency preprocessing that is desirable - additional preprocessing effort may outweigh subsequent search savings [3]. However, it seems an obvious article of faith that removing values from consideration during a preprocessing step will lead to savings during the subsequent search step - or at the very least do no harm. We demonstrate that there are circumstances in which pruning values by consistency preprocessing can in fact greatly *increase* subsequent search effort.

– Conventional CSP wisdom says that using consistency inference during search, to prune values that become inconsistent after making search choices, is best limited to the minimal inference embodied in the forward checking algorithm. The feeling is that additional search savings produced by pruning more values will be offset by the additional inference cost. We show that maintaining *full* arc consistency during search is often in fact very cost effective.

To contradict the first piece of conventional wisdom we tested the effects of arc consistency preprocessing on one of the most popular and successful CSP algorithms: forward checking combined with dynamic domain size variable ordering. *Dynamic domain size variable ordering* prefers to consider variables that have fewer values left to choose from. It is a popular ordering heuristic. In a probabilistic analysis, it was shown optimal under certain assumptions by Haralick and Elliott [2]. It has proven particularly useful in conjunction with forward checking search, and we believe it to be effective on our test problems.

Another counterintuitive demonstration that pruning values can increase search effort, was obtained recently by Prosser. He showed that pruning values can degrade performance for algorithms that employ "intelligent backtracking" (though the actual exhibited effects were small) [4]. However, even Prosser concluded that: "We should now assume that increased consistency, or the removal of redundancies, can only guarantee a reduction in search effort if that search is unintelligent (such as a chronological backtracker)."

Forward checking is a chronological backtracker. However, we found that removing values by arc consistency preprocessing made some problems an order of magnitude more difficult to solve by our ordered forward checking search. (In fairness to Prosser though one might argue that "unintelligent" should rule out dynamic search ordering.)

The explanation for this counterintuitive phenomenon is that arc consistency preprocessing is counterproductive when it interferes with the functioning of the search ordering heuristic. We interpret our results as implying that eliminating values can move a problem far enough away from the assumptions needed to demonstrate the "optimality" of dynamic domain size search ordering that the advantage of having fewer values is more than offset by the deterioration of the ordering heuristic's performance.

We believe this experience is a useful object lesson in the need to exercise some care in combining CSP methods: two rights may make a wrong. This lesson is particularly relevant now as new constraint programming environments are making it easier to combine techniques for customized algorithms.

To contradict the second piece of conventional wisdom we compared ordered forward checking with an algorithm that established and maintained full arc consistency. These two algorithms represent extreme points on a spectrum of algorithms that maintain various amounts of arc consistency during search.

The conventional wisdom expressed to us by some members of the constraint programming community already runs counter to the second piece of CSP conventional wisdom. Our experiments suggest that the constraint programming community has been conventionally wiser in this regard than the CSP community.

The combination of consistency pruning with backtrack search has a long history [5], [6], [7]. Various degrees of consistency processing interleaved with backtrack search were studied experimentally in [2], [8], [9]. A variety of algorithms were considered that alternate choosing a value for a variable with "looking ahead", via a constraint propagation process, to infer the consequences of that choice for pruning the values available for the as yet uninstantiated variables. The algorithms differed in how much constraint propagation they performed, and thus in the degree of arc consistency they achieved.

Forward checking is an algorithm which does a minimal amount of constraint propagation, in the sense that it performs the minimal amount of lookahead needed to avoid having to "look back", i.e. to avoid the need to check new choices against previous ones. In experimental studies forward checking repeatedly proved superior to algorithms interleaving more constraint propagation.

Of course, the limitations of these experiments were recognized. However, the repeated success of forward checking began to bias the conventional wisdom in the CSP community in the direction of "less is more". For example, in a recent survey of CSP algorithms [10], the section on "How Much Constraint Propagation Is Useful?" concludes: "Experiments by other researchers [in addition to Nadel] with a variety of problems also indicate that it is better to apply constraint propagation only in a limited form".

In our laboratory several studies began to suggest that "more could be more". Gevecker studied full arc consistency maintenance [11] and Freuder and Wallace studied a range of hybrid algorithms based on a notion of "selective" or "bounded" constraint propagation [12]. However, these results were still limited in their understanding of the random problem space. Also, they did not employ the powerful search ordering scheme we alluded to above.

We conduct here experiments on random problems, focusing on the "hard problem ridge" identified in recent studies of "really hard" random problems [13], [14]. Problems that contradict the conventional CSP wisdom appear to be pervasive, and orders of magnitude effects are found.

There are, of course, significant caveats to these experimental results. In particular, problems of different structure or size may behave differently. We assume individual constraint checks can be efficiently computed. (Each time we ask if a value v for a variable X and a value u for a variable Y satisfy the constraint between X and Y we are performing a *constraint check*.) If this were not the case, maintaining full arc consistency could conceivably require some very expensive constraint check computation that backtracking or forward checking avoided.

While we test two extremes of arc consistency processing, optimality may lie between these extremes. On the other hand, for difficult problems, maintaining even higher levels of consistency [15], may prove cost effective.

Section 2 describes the algorithms we compared. Section 3 describes our experimental objectives and how we generated test problems. Sections 4 and 5 present the experimental results and our summary observations.

2 Algorithms

Forward checking, which we implement here in an algorithm FC, combines backtrack search with a very limited form of arc consistency maintenance. The main idea is to project forward the consequences of variable assignments during search. When a variable X is assigned a value, v, from *domain(X)*, the set of available values for X, v is checked against the domains of each variable Y that is as yet unassigned and for which there is a constraint between X and Y. All values inconsistent with v are removed. This way a limited form of arc consistency is maintained. (If, during this process, the domain of some variable becomes empty, then no complete extension of the current assignment set to a solution is possible, and the current assignment for X must be discarded.) For details on forward checking consult [2].

The algorithm *MAC*, *Maintaining Arc Consistency*, is a combination of old ideas, which we give a new name because the combination is unique and the name is evocative. However, it is essentially a modern version of Gaschnig's CS2 [5].

MAC uses the same basic framework as forward checking, alternating search and consistency inference steps, but differs conceptually in two aspects:

- The constraint network is made arc consistent initially.
- When during the search a new variable X is instantiated to a value v, all the other values in the domain are eliminated and the effects of removing them are propagated through the constraint network as necessary to restore full arc consistency.

MAC takes an approach to arc consistency based on the AC–4 arc consistency algorithm [16]. This supports efficient maintenance of consistency during search.

We also combined arc consistency and search in a simpler manner than that embodied by FC and MAC. A single preprocessing pass to achieve some form of consistency has often been used before some form of subsequent search. Waltz's well-known scene labeling experiments [17] are an early example of the success of this basic approach. We will refer to the combination of arc consistency preprocessing followed by forward checking search as AC-FC. (The AC algorithm employed in AC-FC is also AC–4-based, though not identical in implementation to the arc consistency processing employed by MAC.)

The order in which variables are considered for instantiation during search has been found to be extremely important. We employ dynamic domain size variable ordering with FC, MAC and AC-FC. As we always use this ordering heuristic (except when we explicitly test the effect of eliminating it) we will not bother to repeatedly refer to "ordered FC" etc., but the ordering should be kept in mind.

3 Experimental Design

We addressed the problem of finding a single solution to a CSP (or determining that no solution exists). The test problems are random problems generated according to a (constant) probability of inclusion model, which we will describe briefly.

One way to represent CSPs is with *constraint graphs*, vertices corresponding to variables and edges to constraints. Since we want to deal only with connected constraint graphs (connected components of unconnected graphs can be solved independently), the number of edges for a graph with N vertices is at least N-1 (for a tree) and at most $\frac{N(N-1)}{2}$ (for a complete graph). As a consequence, we define constraint *density* as the fraction of the possible constraints, beyond the minimum N-1, that the problem has.

Constraint *tightness* is defined as the fraction of all possible pairs of values from the domains of two variables, that are not allowed by the constraint. For example, if the constraint between two variables with domains $\{a, b\}$ and $\{c, d\}$ does not allow the pairs *(a, c)* and *(a, d)* and *(b, c)*, then the constraint tightness is .75.

Basically, in our problems a specific constraint is present, or a specific pair of values is permitted by a constraint, with a probability based on the density and tightness specified for the problem. This problem generation method permits some variation in actual values for the density and tightness compared with the specified ones. Averaged over many constraints we expect the actual values to be close to the specified values, but it should be noted, in particular, that the tightness of an individual constraint within a problem can vary.

We do not allow problems to contain any null constraints (that do not allow any pair of values, and make the problem trivially unsolvable) or any trivial "constraints" (that allow all pairs of values, and are not usually represented by an edge in the constraint graph). We insure that constraint graphs are connected by initially randomly generating a tree of constraints.

The main experiments reported below used problems with 50 variables, each having a domain of 8 values. There is nothing magic about these numbers; we simply wanted problems of a size large enough to permit us to exhibit significant savings and small enough so that they would not require great amounts of processing time. We experimented some with different size problems, but a more systematic study is left for future work.

Based on recent research on really hard problems we expected to find that many random problems are easy, but that if we hold one of either tightness or density fixed, and vary the other sufficiently, that we will encounter a complexity "peak". Together these peaks form a complexity "ridge" in "tightness/density" space. We were particularly interested in performance on this ridge.

When we compared FC with AC-FC we used constraint checks as our measure of effort. Since constraint checks are not an appropriate measure for MAC (the only constraint checks are done during the initializing phase) we used CPU time to measure its performance and to compare it with FC and AC-FC.

4 On Pruning Considered Harmful

The data reported here are for problem parameter values chosen to exhibit the phenomenon dramatically. Our intuition, which requires further exploration, is that the phenomenon is more likely to occur at low densities and near, but not at, peak difficulty areas.

We used problems with 50 variables and an initial domain size of 8 values for each variable. For each of four density values .06, .07, .08 and .09 five random problems were generated with a tightness of .50. We measured constraint check effort for AC preprocessing, for FC search after AC preprocessing and for FC search without AC preprocessing. We also measured CPU time for AC-FC, FC and MAC (on a SPARCstation ELC). Table 1 and Table 2 present the results.

Table 1. Performance of AC-FC, FC, expressed in terms of constraint checks

			density			
			.06	.07	.08	.09
#1	AC + FC	P	15,370	16,352	18,465	16,640
		S	40,506	160,695	15,006	331,319
		T	55,876	177,047	33,471	347,959
	FC		1,078,271	1,421,487	79,245	7,998
#2	AC + FC	P	13,968	14,840	19,080	19,220
		S	847	119,886	150,656	18,287
		T	14,815	134,726	169,736	37,507
	FC		1,083	282,143	56,551	8,921
#3	AC + FC	P	15,526	15,664	16,971	21,899
		S	14,470	1,815,053	173,303	14,471
		T	29,996	1,830,717	190,274	36,370
	FC		10,006	1,574,023	14,659	8,396
#4	AC + FC	P	15,816	15,712	19,722	18,193
		S	1,461,280	1,118,572	13,519	5,477
		T	1,477,096	1,134,284	33,241	23,670
	FC		1,302,927	474,484	4,993	444,553
#5	AC + FC	P	14,752	14,104	18,146	17,857
		S	6,412	765	87,451	67,056
		T	21,164	14,869	105,597	84,913
	FC		2,349	910	50,137	100,312

P–preprocessing(AC)   S–search(FC)   T–total(AC–FC)

Table 2. Performance of AC-FC and FC expressed in terms of total CPU time

		density			
		.06	.07	.08	.09
#1	AC-FC	10	32	6	65
	FC	202	264	14	2
	MAC	1	2	1	3
#2	AC-FC	2	25	30	6
	FC	0	51	10	2
	MAC	1	2	3	1
#3	AC-FC	5	336	33	6
	FC	2	289	3	2
	MAC	1	4	3	1
#4	AC-FC	273	216	5	3
	FC	241	89	1	8
	MAC	5	7	1	1
#5	AC-FC	4	2	19	14
	FC	1	0	9	18
	MAC	1	1	2	2

Our main observations:

- AC-FC performed worse than FC on average for some problem sets and an order of magnitude worse on some problems. Pruning the search tree by eliminating some domain values can sometimes greatly increase subsequent search effort for the popular combination of forward checking and dynamic variable ordering based on minimal domain size.
- FC was sometimes superior to AC-FC because the preprocessing effort for the AC phase was larger than any possible savings in the FC phase, indeed larger than the entire FC effort with or without AC preprocessing.
- More significantly the FC search effort itself, after preprocessing, was sometimes much greater than the FC search effort without preprocessing.
- MAC, which employs the more extensive full arc consistency maintenance, was superior to both FC and AC-FC except on some very simple problems. (We will have further data on the comparison of MAC and FC in the next section.) Since MAC incorporates an AC preprocessing, we have a situation where adding some additional consistency processing, in the form of AC preprocessing alone, can decrease performance, but adding even more consistency processing, in the form of AC preprocessing plus full AC maintenance, can help.

In order to verify that it is indeed the ordering that is at issue, we took some other easy problems where AC-FC was inferior to FC, and ran AC-FC and FC on them without any variable ordering heuristic (in fact lexical ordering). Without the ordering heuristic the phenomenon of preprocessing making matters worse did indeed disappear. (Without the ordering, however, performance was much worse than either FC or AC-FC with the ordering.)

5   More Is More

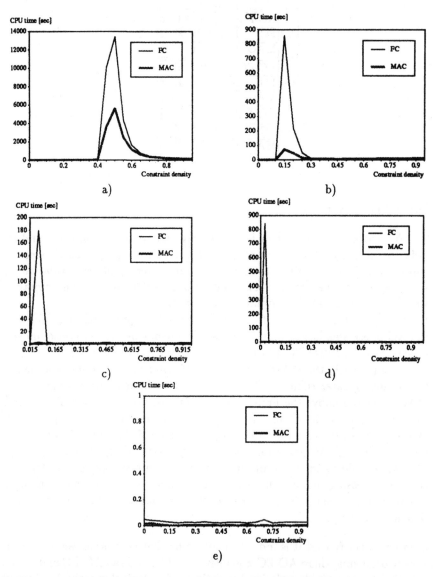

Fig. 1. Comparison FC-MAC on random problems with tightness .150 (a), .325 (b), .500 (c), .675 (d) and .850 (e), using CPU time to measure the performance

Again we used problems with 50 variables, each having a domain of 8 values. For this experiment, however, we used more combinations of density and tightness values to provide broad coverage of the "density/tightness space". For each combination of density and tightness values, we generated ten random problems, for a total of 1,200 problems.

Figure 2 presents the performance of FC and MAC, as average values over the ten problems generated for each pair (density, tightness). We used five values for the tightness parameter: .150, .325, .500, .675 and .850. For tightnesses .150, .325, .850, 20 equally distanced density values were taken throughout the entire range [0, 0.950]. For tightness .500, 20 equally distanced density values were taken throughout the entire range [0.015, 0.965]. For tightness .675, 40 equally distanced density values were taken throughout the entire range [0, 0.975]. The performance is expressed as seconds of CPU time (on a SPARCstation ELC) necessary either to find a solution or to discover that there is none.

Table 3. Performance of FC and MAC, expressed in terms of CPU time

	tightness	.150	.325	.500	.675
	density	.500	.150	.065	.018
#1	FC	19,545	115.5	30.0	45.2
	MAC	8,018	5.3	1.4	0.1
#2	FC	19,135	5.3	5.9	4.6
	MAC	8,217	1.0	3.3	0.1
#3	FC	2,881	7,346.2	95.7	1.4
	MAC	1,365	611.5	1.3	0.1
#4	FC	15,288	2.0	86.0	0.2
	MAC	6,213	2.8	0.5	0.1
#5	FC	16,281	750.2	6.5	28.6
	MAC	6,854	42.1	1.0	0.1
#6	FC	1,795	59.0	11.6	8356.0
	MAC	773	1.8	1.2	0.1
#7	FC	13,496	257.1	1,425.3	0.6
	MAC	5,871	32.4	0.6	0.1
#8	FC	25,541	40.6	0.3	0.8
	MAC	10,264	1.9	0.3	0.1
#9	FC	14,490	41.0	110.0	6.0
	MAC	5,849	6.7	7.8	0.1
#10	FC	5,915	3.4	29.4	0.8
	MAC	2,902	0.7	5.5	0.1

Just viewing averages can be misleading. For example, one problem in a set of ten can be so much harder than the others that it dominates the result. For each tightness value (except .850 for which all the problems were very easy to solve), Table 3 presents data on the ten individual problems in the problem set with the highest average difficulty.

Our main observations:

- Overall, establishing and maintaining full arc consistency during search was more efficient than limiting inconsistency removal to the partial arc consistency maintenance embodied in forward checking. MAC performed better than FC throughout the density/tightness space, except on some very easy problems.
- MAC was often at least an order of magnitude better than FC on the complexity peaks.
- The advantage of MAC along the complexity ridge exhibited in Table 3 increased as we moved toward the less dense, more tightly constrained end.

Acknowledgements: This material is based upon work supported by the National Science Foundation under Grant No. IRI-9207633. Richard Wallace and Gerard Verfaillie assisted us in obtaining appropriate test problems. This paper appeared in the proceedings volume of ECAI94, published by John Wiley and Sons Limited.

References

1. Tsang E.: Foundations of Constraint Satisfaction, Academic Press, London (1993).
2. Haralick R., Elliott G.: Increasing tree search efficiency for constraint satisfaction problems. Artificial Intelligence **14** (1980) 263–313.
3. Dechter R., Meiri I.: Experimental evaluation of preprocessing techniques in constraint satisfaction problems. Proceedings of the Eleventh International Joint Conference on Artificial Intelligence **1** (1989) 271–277.
4. Prosser P.: Domain filtering can degrade intelligent backtracking search. Proceedings of the Thirteenth International Joint Conference on Artificial Intelligence (1993) 262–267.
5. Gaschnig J.: A constraint satisfaction method for inference making. Proceedings of the Twelfth Annual Allerton Conference on Circuit and System Theory (1974) 866–874.
6. Golumb S., Baumert L.: Backtrack programming. Journal of the ACM **12** (1965) 516–524.
7. Mackworth A.: On reading sketch maps. Proceedings of the Fifth International Joint Conference on Artificial Intelligence (1977) 598–606.
8. McGregor J.: Relational consistency algorithms and their applications in finding subgraph and graph isomorphism. Information Science **19** (1979) 229–250.
9. Nadel B.: Constraint satisfaction algorithms. Computational Intelligence **5** (1989) 188–224.
10. Kumar V.: Algorithms for constraint-satisfaction problems: a survey. AI Magazine **13**, 1 (1992) 32–44.
11. Gevecker K.: Relating the utility of relaxation in costraint satisfaction algorithms to the structure of the problem. Master's thesis. Dept. of Comp. Sci., Univ. of New Hampshire (1991).

12. Freuder E., Wallace R.: Selective relaxation for constraint satisfaction problems. Proceedings of the Third International IEEE Computer Society Conference on Tools for Artificial Intelligence (1991) 332–339.
13. Cheeseman P., Kanefsky B., Taylor W.: Where the really hard problems are. Proceedings of the Twelfth International Joint Conference on Artificial Intelligence (1991) 331–337.
14. Williams C., Hogg T.: Using deep structure to locate hard problems. Proceedings of the Tenth National Conference on Artificial Intelligence (1992) 472–477.
15. Freuder E.: Synthesizing constraint expressions. Communications of the ACM **21** (1978) 958–966.
16. Mohr R., Henderson T.: Arc and path consistency revisited. Artificial Intelligence **25** (1986) 65–74.
17. Waltz D.: Understanding line drawings of scenes with shadows. The Psychology of Computer Vision, P. Winston editor, McGraw-Hill, Cambridge, MA. (1975) 19–91.

Nogood backmarking with min-conflict repair in constraint satisfaction and optimization

Yuejun Jiang[1], Thomas Richards[2] and Barry Richards

IC-Parc

Imperial College

London SW7 2BZ, England

{yj, etr, ebr}@uk.ac.ic.doc

Abstract

There are generally three approaches to constraint satisfaction and optimization: domain-filtering, tree-search labelling and solution repair. The main attractions of repair-based algorithms over domain-filtering and/or tree-search algorithms seem to be their *scalability, reactivity* and *applicability* to optimization problems. The main detraction of the repair-based algorithms appear to be their failure to *guarantee* optimality. In this paper, a repair-based algorithm, that guarantees to find an optimal solution if one exists, is presented. The search space of the algorithm is controlled by *no-good backmarking*, a learning process of *polynomial* complexity that records generic patterns of no-good *partial* labels[3]. These no-goods serve to avoid the repeated traversing of those failed paths of a search graph and to force the search process to jump out of a local optimum. Unlike some similar repair-based methods which usually work on *complete* (but possibly inconsistent) labels, the proposed algorithm works on partial (possibly inconsistent) labels by repairing those variables that contribute to the violation of constraints in the spirit of *dependency-directed backjumping*. In addition, the algorithm *will* accept a repair if it can minimise the conflicts of a label even if it does *not* eliminate them. To control the space of no-good patterns, we propose to generate the most generic no-good pattern as early as possible. To support dynamic constraint satisfaction, we introduce several strategies to maintain no-good patterns on the trade-offs between space, efficiency and overheads. In particular, through the comparisons with other works such as Dynamic Backtracking, weighted GSAT and Breakout, we suggest possible strategies to improve the proposed method.

Keywords : Constraint Satisfaction and Optimization, Backmarking, Learning, Backjumping, Repair-based Methods, Simulated Annealing, Tabu Search, No-good recording and No-good Justification, Dynamic Backtracking, GSAT and Breakout.

1 Introduction

The importance of constraint satisfaction and optimization is well-recognized in scheduling [Fox & Sadeh 93]. A *constraint satisfaction and optimization problem*

---

[1] EPSRC Advanced Fellow

[2] Supported by a British Telecom Scholarship

[3] That is a partial assignment to variables

(CSOP) can be specified as consisting of an (possibly empty) *objective function* and a set of constraints on n variables $(X_1, .., X_n)$ each of which can be assigned a value from its associated domain $(D_1, .., D_n)$. A *complete* (cf. *partial*) label for a CSOP is simply an assignment of a value for every (cf. some) variable from its associated domain. A *consistent* label is a label that satisfies all the constraints. *Labelling* is the process of finding a consistent label for a CSOP. A *solution* label is a complete and consistent label. An *optimal* label is a solution label that optimizes the objective function. *Constraint satisfaction* problems (CSP) aim to find a solution label; while *constraint optimization problems* (COP) try to look for an optimal label. The *objective constraint* of a CSOP is the constraint associated with the objective function. It is a *soft* constraint in the sense that the value of the function is *not* necessarily fixed and is intended to be optimized.

There are generally 3 classes of CSP techniques. Domain-filtering techniques seek to filter out elements of the domains of variables that do not participate in any solutions of a CSOP. They are generally *incomplete* in the sense that not all such elements are filtered out. For efficiency reasons, local consistency domain-filterings [Mackworth 77] such as arc-consistency and path-consistency are usually adopted. Domain-filtering techniques however do not produce a solution for a constraint problem. Even if it is complete, not every combination of the filtered domains of the variables is necessarily a solution. Domain-filtering is thus usually combined with a tree search labelling process such as dynamic arc-consistency with fail-first principle [Nadel 89].

Tree-search techniques follow the paths of a search tree in some *regular* fashion by constructing and extending *partial consistent* labels. They usually work in a backtracking fashion together with *backmarking* and/or *backjumping*. Backmarking marks the combination of values that have been proven to be satisfiable or unsatisfibale in order to reduce the redundant search (*thrashing*) and normally expensive constraint checks. Backjumping performs *dependency-directed backtracking* to the highest point of a search tree that contributes to the current failure in order to prune the search paths.

Repair-based techniques usually work on *complete* but possibly inconsistent labels by repairing them gradually towards a correct or optimal solution. It is naturally extensible to *reactive scheduling* [Minton et al 92] since it always repairs on a complete label or schedule. It is also easily extensible to *optimization* because the repair process is usually based on some estimated cost. Evaluation of constraints and optmization criteria are generally cheap with complete labels [Zweben et al 93]. Notable representatives of repair-based techniques are *hill-climbing, simulated annealling* and *genetic algorithms*. A key issue here is to avoid the trapping of a *local optimum* in a repair process.

Hill-climing generally involves repairing variables in conflict in such a fashion as to minimize the conflicts or to reduce the cost [Minton et al 92]. Dynamic hill-climing such as GSAT [Selman et al 92] improves on the trapping of local optimum by allowing multiple fresh runs of hill-climing. Simulated annealling [Kirkpatrick et al 83] on the other hand provides a temperature control to enable the repair method to jump out of a local optimum by allowing the possibility (which decreases with temperature) of a locally repaired label with a higher cost. Thresh-hold simulated annealing [Dueck & Scheuer 90] puts a deterministic footing on simulated annealing by accepting higher cost repairs within a thresh-hold which decreases with temperature.

To avoid cycles in the repair process, *tabu search* [Hertz & de Werra 87] keeps track of a buffer of forbidden moves between the best of neighbourhoods of a *complete* label and the label iself in a hill-climing process that always starts from a local optimum point. Reactive tabu search [Battiti & Techhhiolli 94] automates the size of tabu buffer by reacting to the occurence of cycles in a hill-climing process that may start from a random label if cycles are too excessive. To be on the safe side, genetic algorithms [Schraudolph 91] maintain a pool of potentially "healthy" and *complete* labels which can be jointly (via a *cross-over* operation) or individually (via a *mutation* operation) repaired to generate new healths labels. In particular, they can be combined with hill-climing in such a way that individual labels of the pool are first hill-climbed to local optimums before they are combined to generate new labels for further hill-climing [Aarts et al 94].

Unlike tree-search techniques which usually have a complete search space due to their systematic and constructive nature, repair-based techniques do not normally enjoy this luxury. This is of course *double-edged*. On one hand, the repair techniques *easily* jump around the search space and expect to find an *approximately* optimal solution in a fairly quick time for some large constraint problems[4]. On the other hand, the repair-based techniques regretably do not guarantee to find the optimal solution of a CSOP problem due to their stochastic nature of escaping local optimums.

The purpose of this paper is to present a repair-based technique called *NG-Backmarking* that combines the advantages of the three classes of techniques mentioned above. This technique performs an *indirect* domain filtering by no-good backmarking - a process that records the most generic partial labels that are known to have violated some constraints of a CSOP. Like tree-search techniques, the proposed technique also incorporates a backjumping strategy so that only culprit variables that contribute to the violation of some constraints are being repaired. However, unlike a tree-search backjump technique, the new technique does not deassign the variables that are jumped over. In particular, the technique attempts to produce the most generic no-good patterns as early as possible in order to reduce both the space and time overheads of the no-good patterns. Unlike a simple learning strategy (e.g. [Dechter 90]), the techqnique is also equiped with dynamic support of no-good patterns to deal with constraint maintenance. We propose several strategies to control such dynamic support.

Unlike the *no-good* justification method [Maruyama et al 91] that inspired the proposed technique here, the NG-Backmarking technique *can* accept a local repair if it minimises the conflicts (or the cost) of a label even if the resultant label does *not* eliminate all the conflicts. However unlike similar repair-based methods (eg. *min-conflict* Hill-climbing repair) which usually work on *complete*

---

[4]This is one reason why repair-based techniques are generally regarded as scalable.

(but possibly inconsistent) labels, the NG-Backmarking technique can repair *partial* and *inconsistent* labels. In particular, the no-good backmarking process can be seen as a generalization of the *tabu* search as it can forbid moves between the best neighbour of a partial (not just complete) label and the label itself. Furthermore, the repair process of NG-backmarking cannot be trapped in a local optimum as it can be forced out of the local optimum by no-goods. Similar to simulated annealling, it can also accept repair with higher cost than previous repairs since the repair process only chooses the best repair that does not satisfy any no-goods.

The proposed technique is in many ways similar to Ginsberg's dynamic backtracking technique [Ginsberg 93]. Both allows the backjump over assigned variables without deassigning these variables. Both learn generic no-good patterns that forces the escape of local optimum and avoid the repeated travesing of failed paths of a search graph. However it will be seen that there are some subtle differences between the two methods.

This paper is organized as follows. In Section 2, two CSOP problems are defined. They will be used to illustrate the ideas of the proposed method. In Section 3, the NG-Backmarking technique is presented. This is followed by some examples in Section 4. In Section 5, the control of the backmarking process in the NG-Backmarking technique is discussed. In Section 6, we propose several strategies to deal with the maintanance of no-good patterns in dynamic constraint satisfaction. In Section 7, comparisons with dynamic backtracking are made.

2   TSP and Capital Budget Problem

In this section, we define two CSOP problems; the Travelling Salesman Problem (TSP) and the Capital Budget Problem [Taha 92]. These problems are chosen purely for illustrative purposes. They are not intended as real-world applications or to be representative of the kind of problems best solved by the NG-Backmarking technique.

Problem 1 (n-city TSP) *The n-city TSP problem is to construct a least costly tour visiting each city exactly once in a n-city map.*

For reasons of clarity, we index the cities in a n-city TSP by numbers ranging from 0 to n-1 and we specify each tour/label of a n-city TSP by a sequence of n numbers ranging from 0 to n-1. For example, 01123 is a label (in this case, an inconsistent one) of a 5-city TSP. From a constraint satisfaction point of view, the variables are then the first city to be travelled to, the second city to be travelled to,.., and the nth city to be travelled to. If a variable is undefined in a partial label, we will use U to indicate its status, eg. 00U12.

Problem 2 (Capital Budget) *Five projects are being considered for execution over the next 3 years. The expected returns for each project and the annual expenditure (in £K) are tabulated below. The problem seeks to decide which of the five projects should be executed over the 3-year planning period. In this regard, the problem reduces to a* *"yes-no" decision for each project. We formalize the decision problem by treating each project as a variable whose domain is $\{0,1\}$ where the value 0 represents "no" and the value 1 represents "yes".*

Project	Expenditures			Returns
	Year 1	Year 2	Year 3	
1	5	1	8	20
2	4	7	10	40
3	3	9	2	20
4	7	4	1	15
5	8	6	10	30
Available funds	25	25	25	

The constraint satisfaction and optimization specification then become

$$\text{maximize } z = 20x_1 + 40x_2 + 20x_3 + 15x_4 + 30x_5$$

subject to the following resource constraints where $x_i \in \{0, 1\}$ for $i = 1, 2, .., 5$.

$$
\begin{array}{rrrrrr}
5x_1 + & 4x_2 + & 3x_3 + & 7x_4 + & 8x_5 & \leq 25 \\
x_1 + & 7x_2 + & 9x_3 + & 4x_4 + & 6x_5 & \leq 25 \\
8x_1 + & 10x_2 + & 2x_3 + & x_4 + & 10x_5 & \leq 25
\end{array}
$$

For simplicity, we represent a label for the capital budget problem as a sequence of integers in the set $\{0,1\}$, eg. 01011.

3   NG-Backmarking with min-conflict repair

NG-Backmarking is a complete repair-based method that works on partial and possibly inconsistent labels. Its architecture is based on the no-good justification algorithm which involves assigning and designing variables of a partial label until a complete and consistent label is generated. However instead of using a dynamically evolving and rather costly set of justifications (or constraints) as in the No-good Justification approach, the new algorithm works on a *fixed* set of initial constraints together with a *dynamically generated but simple* set of no-good patterns. *These patterns are partial labels (generated by no-good backmarking) to indicate that these partial labels violate some constraints and should be repaired.* They are used to prune the search space of a CSOP.

In the No-good Justification approach, the negation of each initial constraint is a no-good justification. If a variable X whose domain values *all* satisfy some existing no-good justifications given a partial label, then a new no-good justification is derived as a *conjunction* of these satisfying no-good justifications in which all variables *except* X are substituted according to the partial label. A no-good justification is not satisfied if its variables are not *all* assigned in the given partial label. The new no-good justifications can be regarded as redundant constraints learnt during the search process. Nevertheless, they can be used to prune the search space as they are more refined or specific than those constraints which derive them.

The major drawback of the No-good Justification approach is that the set of no-good justifications and the size of each no-good justification can grow combinatorially large. This point is supported by our implementation of the algorithm applied to the TSP problem and the Capital Budget problem. Since checking a no-good justification can be an expensive operation, the size of the no-good justification set has a significant impact on the performance of the algorithm. Although it is possible to remove some of them because they are subsumed by others, subsumption check can be very inefficient and the set can still be rather large at some intermediate stages of the search process.

In contrast, in the proposed NG-Backmarking approach, the size of each no-good pattern stays the same (if not smaller). In addition, the no-good patterns are simple to check and the subsumption check is also a straightforward operation. For example, given {01UU2, 01UU4} in the database of no-good patterns , if a new no-good pattern 01UUU is generated, the subsumption check will remove {01UU2, 01UU4} before inserting 01UUU into the database. It is important to note that no-good patterns are *not* permutations of all the labels that violate some constraints. They are generic patterns that correspond to the most general partial labels that so far violate some constraints. The objective is to reduce both the spatial and temporal overheads of the no-good patterns where the minimum partial labels that violate some constraints are created.

Although it is claimed in [Maruyama et al 91] that no-good justifications provide more generic constraints than no-good patterns in some cases, the extra efforts in checking the satisfiability of these justifications appear to far outweigh their advantage of generality. For example, when a partial label L is firstly known to be no good, L will be generated as a no-good pattern. So if the label L pops up again in later repairs, it will be immediately eliminated by the no-good pattern for L. On the other hand, the no-good justification approach will generate a no-good justification J for L when it is firstly detected to be no-good. So if L pops up again in later repairs, the No-good Justification approach still has to *re-evaluate* J which can be a rather lengthy conjunction of several previously generated no-good justifications. Even if one such lengthy no-good justification prunes some other labels, we still have to search through this possibly large set of no-good justifications and evaluate each of them. In contrast, the NG-Backmarking approach maintains a static set of constraints. If several other labels are also meant to be pruned by one lengthy no-good justification, it will be picked out in the NG-Backmarking approach by checking this fixed set of constraints.

Unlike the no-good justification approach which randomly chooses any defined variable to repair, the NG-Backmarking algorithm only randomly repairs a defined variable that contributes to the violation of some constraints in the spirit of dependency-directed backjumping. For example, to repair the tour 01123 in a 5-city TSP problem, the proposed algorithm will choose either the 2nd or 3rd variable to repair. In the case of choosing the second variable, it can assign the value 4 to the variable if it does not violate any constraints and does not match any no-good patterns.

In addition, the NG-Backmarking algorithm can be regarded as a genuine repair algorithm. Instead of looking for a value that makes the locally repaired label satisfy all the constraints, the proposed algorithm simply chooses an alternative value that minimizes the number of constraint violations given that the resultant label does not match any no-good patterns. For example, to repair the tour 0112233 in a 7-city TSP problem, if the second variable is chosen to repair, we can assign a new value, say 4. Although this value does not eliminate all the constraint violations, it is the best possible repair. This approach of repairing (in the spirit of min-conflict repair [Minton et al 92]) is very useful for reactive scheduling applications where the repair of a schedule should be the minimum possible repair to the original schedule when new circumstances arise.

Although randomness is often a virtue in constraint solving as evidenced by some simulated annealing applications [Kirkpatrick et al 83], it is still commonly recognized that constrained heuristics [Fox & Sadeh 92] can greatly improve the performance of many real-world applications. This point is also noted in Zweben et al's anytime scheduling algorithm [90] where a heuristically controlled simulated annealing is shown to be more effective. For these reasons, we have not indicated in the following specification of the proposed algorithm the particular selection strategies of defined variables, undefined variables and domain values. Since we are trying to provide the principles in this paper, we have therefore not elaborated any particular heuristics here which are generally application dependendent. To name a few, we can choose the defined variable to be the most conjested in an application or the one that is most likely to reduce the cost of the objective function. The point to note however is that the NG-Backmarking algorithm is *complete* whatever selection strategies are adopted.

Definition 1 (NG-Backmarking with Min-Conflict Repair) *Given a partial label (which can be complete or inconsistent) and an initial bound on the objective function.*

1. *Check if there is any no-good pattern matched by the label. If there is, go to the Repair Process in 3; else check if there is any constraint violated by the label. If there is, generate a no-good pattern for the label and go to the Repair Process in 3; else go to the Labelling Process in 2.*

2. *Labelling Process*

   - *If there is no undefined variable, the current label is a solution and go to the Optimization Process in 4;*

   - *Else select an undefined variable and check if it is possible to assign a value to it that satisfies all the constraints and the resultant label does not match any no-good patterns. If it is, choose such a value and go back to the Labelling Process in 2; Else generate a no-good from the label and go to the Repair Process in 3.*

3. *Repair Process*

(a) If there is no defined variable left, the algorithm terminates with no solution.

(b) Else examine all defined variables of the label that are defined in the newly generated/matched no-good pattern and check if it is possible to assign an alternative value for one of these variables that minimizes the number (or cost) of constraint violations given that the resultant label does not match any of the no-good patterns.

> *i. If it is possible, choose such a variable and a value that minimizes the number (or cost) of constraint violations given that the resultant label does not match any of the no-good patterns. If the value can eliminate all the conflicts, go to the Labelling Process in 2; else generate a no-good pattern for the label and go back to the Repair Process in 3;*
>
> *ii. Else make all these variables undefined and generate a no-good pattern for the resultant label that involves the rest of the defined variables; go back to the Repair Process in 3.*

4. Optimization Process

- *If optimization is not required, then terminate with the current label as a solution.*

- *Else calculate the new cost of the objective function against the current label and reset the bound of the constraint on the objective function to the new cost; generate a no-good pattern for the current label and go to the Repair Process in 3.*

The major advantages of the no-good backmarking algorithm are

1. Evaluation of a constraint and optimization criteria is cheap since any constraint whose variables are not all instantiated by the partial label is considered to be satisfied.

2. It can repair a partial (including complete) label that is inconsistent. This can be constrasted with a systematic method which always extends partial consistent label to a solution label.

3. If a partial label is trapped or surrounded by no-good patterns in its repair on some defined variables, it makes all these variables undefined and generate a no-good pattern for the resultant label whose other defined variables are then repaired. This ensures that the repair method is not trapped by no-good neighbours.

4. It can accept a repair of a label with higher cost since the old label might be a no-good pattern. Note that the repair is to achieve the minimum number of conflicts on the repaired variables *given that the resultant label does not satisfy any no-good patterns.*

5. It randomly jumps around the search space in assigning and deassigning values of variables. The choice of variable for repair is essentially random and so is not confined to chronological backtracking or dependency-directed backtracking along some regular search structure.

6. It is *complete* in satisfaction and optimization while the search space is controlled by no-good patterns. It is guaranteed to find an optimal solution (if one exists) for a constraint problem. No-good patterns in a way force or direct the search process towards solutions. If the neighbourhood labels of a repair on some defined variables of a label are all no-goods, the repair process makes all these variables undefined and start repair on the resultant label. This allows the repair process to bypass the trap or surroundings of no-goods barriers.

7. No-good patterns are simple to generate and to check. Subsumption checking of no-good patterns is easy to perform.

Theorem 1 *The algorithm is sound and complete for finite domain constraint satisfaction problems (CSP). That is, for any finite domain CSP, every complete label that is generated on the termination of the algorithm is a solution label of the CSP and the algorithm will find a solution label if one exists for the CSP.*

The algorithm however does not find all solutions of a constraint problem. This can be easily amended by iteratively backmarking every current solution label as a no-good pattern. This will trigger the algorithm to find alternative solutions until no more solution can be found.

Theorem 2 *The algorithm is sound and complete for finite domain constraint optimization problems (COP). That is, for any COP, the last complete label that is generated on the termination of the algorithm is an optimal solution of the COP and the algorithm will find an optimal solution if one exists for the COP.*

Finally, it is important to note that the set of no-goods generated during search is always polynomial. The main reason is due to subsumption check.

Theorem 3 *The space complexity of no-goods in NG-backmarking is polynomial.*

Consider for example the CSP problem of n=100 variables (X1 to X100) where the minimum conflict sets are any 50 (ie. n/2) variables have the same value and the maximum domain size of all variables is D. Then the space complexity of generic no-goods will be in the order of $D * C_{100}^{50}$, ie. $D * C_n^{n/2}$.

4 Examples

Example 1 Consider the following 3-colour graph-colouring CSP which falls into the region of hard problems [Cheeseman et al 91] due to its loose connectivity. Given the graph's initial complete label which is a local minimum that often traps simple hill-climing based algorithm such as Min-conflict repair [Minton et al 93] or GSAT [Selman et al 92], the NG-Backmarking can move out of the local minimum via no-goods.

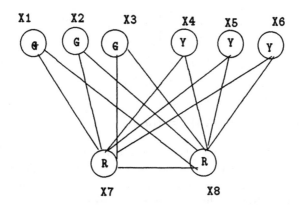

Initially, the no-good pattern UUUUUURR is generated because X7 and X8 are neighbour nodes with the same colour. This means that we need to repair X7 and X8 which are the variables contributing to some violations. Given that UUUUUURR is a no-good pattern, the best we can do is to change X7 or X8 to a non-red colour. This point illustrates the advantage that NG-Backmarking can move to a repair with a higher cost than an old label since the old label is a no-good pattern.

Suppose X7's colour is now changed to G. Then there are three conflicts between X7 and X1, between X7 and X2, and between X7 and X3. We choose one such conflict, say between X1 and X7 and make it a no-good, ie. GUUUUUGU and then repair it. Changing X1's colour to Y is the minimum number of conflicts the label can be repaired without satisfying any no-good patterns. Since there are still conflicts left, we go on to generate no-good patterns for other conflicts and repair them while bypassing no-goods. This process is repeated until we have X1, X2 and X3 all coloured Y.

This example also illustates the way how NG-Backmarking escapes from local optimum. In Breakout [Morris 93], a local optimum is escaped by adding weight incrementally to conflicts. This allows the repair gradually moving up the local optimum to reach another local optimum. Similar idea is also applied in Weighted GSAT [Selman & Kautz 93] except that a new starting point is chosen when a local optimum is reached and each time a conflict is reached, its weight is incremented by one. While these methods can be seen as gradually filling up a local valley in a cost graph in order to move to another local valley, NG-Backmarking can be seen as a forced jump to move out of a local valley to move to another valley. This advantage is more evident if we change Example 1 involving 4 by 4 instead of 3 by 3 nodes green-colooured and yellow-coloured respectively. It will then take the weighted repair 4 times repair to move out of the local valley.

Example 2 Consider the following CSP problem where the conflict sets for each subset of variables are defined as follows and all variables take the constant domain {a,b}

$$\{X1, X2\} = \{(a, b), (b, a), (b, b)\}$$
$$\{X1, X3\} = \{(a, b)\}$$
$$\{X1, X4\} = \{(b, b)\}$$
$$\{X3, X4\} = \{(a, b)\}$$
$$\{X3, X5\} = \{(a, b)\}$$
$$\{X3, X6\} = \{(a, b)\}$$

Clearly, the label aaaaaa is a solution. But suppose we start off with an initial complete label abbbbb, then the repair path and nogoods will be processed as follows. The underlines of variables indicate conflicts in a label. The crossed no-good labels indicate that they are subsumed by other no-goods.

	Repair path	No-good database
1	abbbbb	~~abUUUU~~
2	aabbbb	~~aUbUUU~~
3	babbbb	~~baUUUU~~
4	bbbbbb	~~bbUUUU~~
		bUUUUU
		UbUUUU
5	UUbbbb	~~UUbbbb~~
6	UUbabb	~~UUbabb~~
7	UUbaab	~~UUbaab~~
8	UUbaaa	~~UUbaaa~~
9	Uabaaa	UUbUUU
10	Uaaaaa	
11	aaaaaa	

Initially, X1=a and X2=b are in conflict, so we generate the no-good abU-UUU and produce the best repair aabbbb. Next X1=a and X3=b are in conflict, we generate the no-good pattern aUbUUU and produce the best repair babbbb which has two conflicts while the other repair aaabbb has three conflicts. Next we randomly choose the conflict X1=b and X2=a and generate the no-good baU-UUU. The best repair now is bbbbbb given that aabbbb will match a no-good. Recall that NG-backmarking only accepts a repair that does not match any no-goods. We now choose the conflict X1=b and X2=b and generate the no-good bbUUUU. Since all variables take the constant domain {a,b}, combined with the previous no-good abUUUU and baUUUU, we generate two more generic no-goods bUUUUU and UbUUUU respectively and remove abUUUU, bbUUUU and baUUUU from the no-good database. Since the repair of X1=b and X2=b are all trapped by no-goods, the next label becomes UUbbbb which is also a no-good to be repaired. This point illustrates the way how NG-Backmarking jumps over the no-good barriers by making undefined all the variables to be repaired but trapped by no-goods.

Note here the complete label becomes a partial label (ie. UUbbbb) to be repaired. Repairing further, we generate UUbabb, UUbaab and UUbaaa which all then become no-goods. Although the partial label UUbaaa itself has no conflicts, however we cannot label X1 any further since X1=a and X3=b will match a no-good. This generates a more generic no-good UUbUUU which removes aUbUUU, UUbabb, UUbaab and UUbaaa from the no-good database. Repair further we generate UUaaaa, aUaaaa and aaaaaa which is a solution.

5 Generation of no-good patterns

As noted in the last section, *NG-Backmarking* simply records partial labels that violate constraints. Despite their simplicity to check and the polynomial space of no-goods, it is still essential to maintain only the most generic no-good patterns. This raises the question of *subsumption checking*. Even if we allow subsumption checking it is still important to generate more generic no-good patterns as early as possible in order to avoid the accumulation of the database of no-good patterns during the intermediate repair process of the proposed method. For example, for a 10 city TSP, the space complexity can be in the order of 1000 no-goods. As we have experienced from our implementation, a large set of no-good patterns can significantly hinder the performance of the NG-Backmarking method.

First let us address the subsumption checking process. Every time a partial label is found to be no-good, we first perform a retract operation from the no-good database of those patterns that unify with the partial label whose undefined values are viewed as "don't care" variables. We then simply insert the partial label where an undefined value is replaced by a "don't care" variable. To check if a partial label matches a no-good pattern, we simply treat the partial label as a goal against the no-good database. Note here that the undefined value U in the partial label is *not* treated as a variable in the goal; otherwise a partial label, say, 1UU1U will match a no-good pattern such as 11111.

To generate more generic no-good patterns as early on as possible, the generation process should be related to specific applications. Here we use the TSP and Capital Budget problems to illustrate the point.

Consider for example a solution tour 02341 in a 5-city TSP problem where the cost of the tour is C. Suppose we try to find the optimal solution, then the bound associated with the constraint on the objective function will be reset to C. The solution label 02341 is no longer a good tour. Normally we will simply add 02341 as a no-good pattern and repair the label. However for the TSP problem, we can generate n no-good generic patterns with one value of the last solution label to be undefined. For the above example, we would immediately generate five generic no-good patterns {U2341, 0U341, 02U41, 023U1, 0234U } since there is no alternative value for repair for any variable given that the other variables' values remain the same. In particular, we can choose any one of the partial labels to repair.

Consider another example in the Capital Budget Problem where a partial label L = 10UUU is to be repaired. Suppose previously, we have already found a solution label 01111 with the benefit of the objective function as 95. Normally, we would simiply continue to label L. However for this particular problem, we can immediately treat L as a no-good pattern since whatever values we assign to the undefined variables, the objective function of the resultant label cannot be more than 95, ie. the objective constraint is always violated.

The generation of generic no-good patterns is dependent on the domain values of variables. Consider for example a 3-variables (X1,X2,X3) CSP. Suppose X1's domain is {a,b}, then if we have two no-good patterns acU and bUd, then we can generate another no-good pattern Ucd, ie. the union of the variables that are different from X1 and X1 is undefined in the resultant no-good pattern. Of course if the two no-good patterns are acU and bcU, then the union will become UcU which subsumes the two no-good patterns.

The generation of generic no-good patterns is also dependent on the kind of constraint being violated in a specific application. Consider the Capital Budget problem again. Given an initial label 11001, although the objective constraint is not violated, a resource constraint (the third one) is violated. Instead of simply generating 11001 as a no-good pattern, we produce the more generic label 11UU1 as a no-good pattern since the only alternative values (ie. 1) to repair the variables with 0 values would only increase the violation of the label. Consider another label 00111. This is a solution label, but not an optimal one. During the optimizatin process, although this label satisfies all the resource constraints, it no longer satisfies the objective constraint with the current cost. Instead of making the label to be no-good, we generate the more generic no-good pattern 00UUU since whatever values chosen for U will not improve the benefit of the objective function. To summerize, in the Capital Budget problem, if a label violates a resource constraint, we make all the 0 values in the label to be undefined and then generate the resultant label as a no-good pattern; if a label violates an objective constraint, we make the 1 values in the label to be undefined and then generate the resultant label as a no-good pattern. This shows that the generation of no-good patterns can be controlled by exploring the characteristics of the problem.

6 Dynamic Support of no-good patterns

No-good patterns express knowledge learnt during a search process. They can be used in subsequent search and new constraint problems. In a dynamic environment, such knowledge is still valid when new constraints (eg. new jobs, new machine restrictions) are added or old constraints (eg. dealine is put forward) are tightened. This is because we do not create good patterns. However, they may no longer be valid when some old constraints (eg. cancellations of jobs, deadline is delayed) are removed (eg. cancellations of jobs) or relaxed (eg. deadline is delayed).

To incorporate constraint relaxation and removal, we propose to support every no-good pattern by an approximation of the minimum set of constraints for which the pattern causes a violation in the spirit of Schiex & Verfaillie's No-good Recording algorithm [93] for dynamic constraint satisfaction. Subsumption checking in this case will also involve checking if the supporting set of set of constraints is also subsumed. In this way, if a constraint is removed, then any set in the supporting set of a no-good pattern that contains the constraint is removed from the support set. If a constraint is relaxed, then any set in the supporting set of a no-good pattern that contains the constraint relaxed will be rechecked by the no-good pattern. If the no-good pattern is no longer supported by the relaxed set, relaxed set is removed from the support set. If the support set is empty, then the no-good pattern is removed.

Like the generation of no-good patterns, uncontrolled generation of the supporting set of a no-good pattern can also be very costly. To control this problem, we suggest several strategies to approximate the supporting set. One is to build the supporting set by the total number of constraints that the no-good pattern is involved with. If any constraint is removed or relaxed from the set, the no-good pattern will be withdrawn. The other strategy is to simply remove a pattern if a constraint that involves the variables of the pattern is removed/relaxed. The advantage of this strategy is that it does not require any space to store the supporting set of a no-good pattern. Subsumption check is just like that in a static environment. Both strategies do not affect the completeness of the no-good backmarking method, but may remove some knowledge (or no-good patterns) even though the constraint relaxation or removal does not affect the knowledge. However this trade-off between the overheads of maintaining no-good patterns and the loss of no-good patterns is often necessary in practice.

7 Comparison with dynamic backtracking

The proposed technique is similar to Ginsberg's dynamic backtracking technique [93] with the obvious difference that the dynamic support of no-good patterns for constraint relaxation is not addressed in dynamic backtracking. Like NG-backmarking, dynamic backtrackng also records generic no-goods for combinations of variable assignments. In particular, it performs repair of culprit variables without deassigning those assigned variables that are not contributing to the culprit. At each step of repair, dynamic backtracking records the explanation for each variable and each value eliminated by the minimum set of previously assigned variables. Such explanations roughly correspond to no-goods in our terminology. In a particular instantiation order, if an assigned variable is jumped over in a repair, then all the eliminating explanations for the variable that involves the variable to be repaired will be removed because they are no longer justified. Like NG-backmarking, dynamic backtracking is also complete and ensures a polynoimal space of complexity of no-goods.

However there are some subtle differences between dynamic backtracking and NG-backmarking. First, the repair of NG-backmarking involves examing all culprit variables and chooses the best repair for a variable given that it does not satisfy any no-goods; while dynamic backtracking examines only one culprit variable at a time.

Example 3 Consider the following graph colouring problem in dynamic back-tracking and NG-Backmarking repsectively.

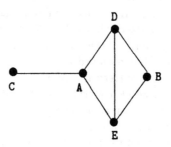

Dynamic backtracking

A	B	C	D	E	No − goods
r	g	r			$rUrUU$
r	g	b	r		$rUUrU$
r	g	b	g		$rUUgU$
r	g	b	b	r	$rUUUr$
r	g	b	b	g	$UgUUg$
r	g	b	b	b	$UUUbb$
r	g	b	b		$rgUbU$
r	g	b			$rgUUU$

NG-backmarking

A	B	C	D	E	No − goods
r	g	r			$rUrUU$
r	g	b	b		$rgUbU$
r	r	b	b		
r	r	b	b	g	

It can be seen that when repairing the initial partial label rgrUU, dynamic back-tracking produces rgbrU, rgbgU and their no-goods before moving on to rgbbU; while NG-backmarking jumps directly to rgbbU since it only tries to assign an undefined variable by a value that does not violate any constraints (note here that no-goods are considered as simple constraints). When repairing the culprit variables of rgbbU, ie. involving the no-good rbUbU, NG-backmarking examines all the culprit variables, ie. A, B and D while dynamic backtracking only looks at the variable D. NG-backmarking thus sets B's colour to r (it is also possible to set A's colour to g) and then labels E's colour by g to obtain a solution of the graph colouring problem.

Another subtle difference between dynamic backtracking and NG-backmarking is the way how they deal with the situation where the repair of a label is all surrounded by no-good barriers. In dynamic backtracking, it can eliminate these previously generated no-goods to allow the repair to proceed onto the culprit variables that lead to the situation. While in NG-backmarking, the repair makes undefined of all the variables to be repaired and proceeds to repair the culprit variables that lead to the situation. Consider Example 2 again. When repairing the label bbbbbb on the culprit variables X1=b and X2=b, NG-backmarking makes both variables undefined and proceeds to repair the resultant label UUbbbb because the paths of repairing X1 or X2 are all blocked by no-good barriers. In contrast, dynamic backtracking will first generate the no-good $X1 \neq b$ and then generates the no-good $X3 \neq b$ from the no-good $X1 \neq b$ and the no-good $X3 = b- > X1 \neq a$. This then repairs X3 to a. In this way, dynamic backtracking can be used to repair complete labels without ever making them *partial* [Ginsberg & McAllester 94] in the same spirit as traditional repair-based algorithms.

To adapt NG-backmarking to allow repairing of a label without ever making assigned variables undefined, we propose to modify the step 3.b.ii of the NG-backmarking as follows. The basic idea is to remove those no-good barriers on the variables to be repaired and repair instead on the rest of the defined variables.

> 3.b.ii Else generate a no-good pattern from the rest of the defined variables in the label and remove all no-goods that involve the variables that cannot be repaired; go back to the Repair Process in 3.

Return to Example 2 on the repair of bbbbbb. Since we cannot repair X1 and X2 without being trapped by a no-good pattern, we generate a no-good from the rest of defined variables, ie. X3, X4, X5 and X6. From the no-good pattern aUbUUU, we derive the new no-good pattern UUbUUU. We then remove aUbUUU, bUUUUU and UbUUUU from the no-good database. Repair bbbbbb on X3 yields bbabbb. Repairing bbabbb on the conflict X1=b and X2=b yields ababbb. Repairing ababbb on the no-good pattern abUUUU yields aaabbb. Repairing aaabbb on the conflicts between X3 and X4, X5 or X6 three times yields the solution aaaaaa.

Another way to adapt NG-backmarking to avoid deassigning variables during the repair process is based on the weighting concepts from Breakout and Weighted GSAT. The basic idea is to associate a weight each time a no-good pattern is matched during the repair process. When a new no-good patterns is generated, its weight is assigned a unit weight 1. During the repair process, if the variables to be repaired are all trapped by no-good barriers, then the repair chooses the no-good pattern with the lowest weight to continue repair. In this way, the repair process can walk over a no-good barrier with the weakest resistance.

Perhaps the most fundamental difference between dynamic backtracking and NG-backmarking is between subsumption and no-good dropping process. This is because a no-good in dynamic backtracking is usually in the form of

$$X1 = a \wedge .. \wedge Xn = b \rightarrow Y \neq c$$

where $Y \neq c$ denote the value to be repaired; while such a no-good will be logically equivalent to the form of

$$X1 = a \wedge .. \wedge Xn = b \wedge Y = c \rightarrow nogood$$

in NG-backmarking. Consider for example, the no-good database contains the nogood N $X1 = a \wedge X2 = b \rightarrow X3 \neq c$ in dynamaic backtracking. Suppose a new no-good $X1 = a \rightarrow X3 \neq c$ is generated in a search process, then N cannot be dropped in dynamic backtracking as X3=c is not in the condition part of N. In contrast, NG-backmarking will remove N via subsumption check. Consider another example where the no-good database contains the no-good M $X1 = a \rightarrow X2 \neq b$ in dynamic backtracking. Suppose a new no-good $X3 = c \rightarrow X1 \neq a$ is generated, then M will be dropped because X1=a will be repaired. In contrast, subsumption check in NG-backmarking cannot remove M via subsumption check.

Finally, no-goods that are dropped can come back in dynamic backtracking; while no-goods that are removed via subsumption can never become no-goods again in NG-backmarking although this is not the case for the modified NG-backmarking algorithm.

8   Conclusions and future directions

In this paper, we have proposed a new repair-based technique that guarantees to find the global optimum of a CSOP or a solution of a CSP. The repair path is controlled by no-goods which are generic patterns indicating the failure of some search paths. These no-goods barriers can force the search process to jump out of a local optimum. In the case where a repair process is surrounded by no-good barriers, the proposed technique can jump over the barriers by making undefined all the variables to be repaired or by removing those no-goods on these variables. We have compared the technique with dynamic backtracking.

The proposed technique has been implemented and tested against the TSP and the Capital Budget problem. For these problems, the performance of our no-good backmarking methods compares about 100 times faster than the no-good justification approach. When compared with a pure simulated annealling implementation of TSP, the method also fares much better for 10 city TSP problem. For larger TSPs, it is observed that the method performs still better than simulated annealling if we compare the times of the two methods in obtaining the best cost of the simulated annealling method. This is partly expected as the no-good backmarking method also incorporates an element of randomness. Since the NG-Backmarking method adopts a min-max strategy in optimization, it performs a great deal better if the initial cost of a problem is set low.

However to test the effectiveness of NG-backmarking, much more experientations on real-world problems and benchmarks are required. We are currently conducting such process with comparative studies against dynamic backtracking, GSAT, weighted GSAT and Breakout. We hope to report these results in due time.

Acknowledgement

The authors would like to thank helpful discussions with Nader Azarmi, Hani El-Sakkout, Bob Kowalski and Francesa Toni. The first author would also like to thank Tara-san, Yugami-san, Oto-san and Maruyama-san for their stimulating discussions during his visit in Japan.

References

E. Aarts, P. van Laarhoven, J. Lenstra & N. Ulder (1994) *A computational study of local search algorithms for job-shop scheduling* ORSA Journal on Computing, Vol 6, No 2.

R. Battiti & G. Techiolli (1994) *The reactive tabu search* ORSA Journal on Computing Vol 6, No 2.

P. Cheesman, B. Kenesky & M. Taylor (1991) *Where the really hard problems are* IJCAI 91.

R. Dechter (1990) *Learning while searching in constraint satisfaction problems* AAAI 90.

G. Dueck & T. Scheuer (1990) *Threshold accepting - a general purpose optimization algorithm* Journal of computational physics 90.

M. Fox & N. Sadeh (1992) *Why is scheduling difficult - a CSP perspective* ECAI 92.

M. Ginsberg (1993) *Dynamic backtracking* Electronic Journal of AI Research 1.

M. Ginsberg & D. McAllester (1994) *Dynamic backtracking and GSAT* KR'94.

A. Hertz & D. de Werra (1987) *Using tabu search techniques for graph colouring* Computing 39.

S. Kirkpatrick, C.D. Gelatt & M.P. Vecchi (1983) *Optimization by simulated annealing* Science 220

A. Mackworth (1977) *Consistency in networks of relations* AI 8.

F. Maruyama, Y. Minoda, S. Sawada, Y. Takizawa & N. Kawato (1991) *Solving combinatorial constraint satisfaction and optimization problems using sufficient conditions for constraint violation* ISAI 4.

P. Morris (1993) *The breakout method for escaping from local minima* AAAI 93.

S. Minton, M. Johnson, A. Philips & P. Laird (1992) *Minimizing conflicts: a heuristic repair method for constraint satisfaction and scheduling problems*, Artificial Intelligence 58.

B. Nadel (1989) *Constraint satisfaction algorithms* Computational Intelligence Vol 8, No 4.

T. Schiex & G. Verfaillie (1993) *No-good recording for static and dynamic constraint satisfaction problems.*

N. Schraudolph (1991) *Genetic algorithms software survey - overview* Genetic Algorithm Digest 5 (34).

B. Selman, H. Levesque & D. Mitchell (1992) *A new method for solving hard satisfiability problem* AAAI 92.

B. Selman & H. Kautz (1993) *Domain independent extensions to GSAT* IJCAI 93.

H. Taha (1992) *Operations Research - an introduction* Macmillan Publishing Company.

M. Zweben,E. Davis, B. Daun & M. Deale (1993) *Scheduling and rescheduling with iterative repair* IEEE transactions on Systems, MAN and Cybernetics, Vol 23 No 6.

Global Consistency for Continuous Constraints

D. Haroud and B. Faltings

Swiss Federal Institute of Technology, Ecublens 1015-Lausanne, Switzerland

Abstract. This paper provides a technique for solving general constraint satisfaction problems (CSPs) with continuous variables. Constraints are represented by a hierarchical binary decomposition of the space of feasible values. We propose algorithms for path- and higher degrees of consistency based on logical operations defined on this representation and demonstrate that the algorithms terminate in polynomial time. We show that, in analogy to convex temporal problems and discrete row-convex problems, convexity properties of the solution spaces can be exploited to compute minimal and decomposable networks using path consistency algorithms. Based on these properties, we also show that a certain class of non binary CSPs can be solved using strong 5-consistency.

1 Introduction

In the general case, constraint satisfaction problems (CSPs) are NP-complete. Trying to solve them by search algorithms, even if theoretically feasible, often results in prohibitive computational cost. One approach to overcome this complexity consists of pre-processing the initial problem using *propagation algorithms*. These algorithms establish various degrees of local consistency which narrow the initial feasible domain of the variables, thus reducing the subsequent search effort. Traditional consistency techniques and propagation algorithms — such as the Waltz propagation algorithm— provide relatively poor results when applied to continuous CSPs: they ensure neither completeness nor convergence in the general case (a good insight into the problems encountered can be found in [1]). However, Faltings [5] has shown that some undesirable features of propagation algorithms with interval labels must be attributed to the inadequacy of the propagation rule and to a lack of precision in the solution space description. He has also demonstrated that the problem with local propagation could be resolved by using *total constraints* on pairs of variables. Lhomme [10] has identified similar problems and proposed an interval propagation formalism based on bound propagation.

Van Beek's work on temporal reasoning [14] using Helly's theorem has shown the importance of path-consistency for achieving globally consistent labellings. In certain cases, path-consistency algorithms are difficult to implement in continuous domains because they require intersection and composition operations on constraints. We propose a constraint representation by recursive decomposition which allows implementation of these operations. This allows us to apply Helly's theorem to general continuous constraint satisfaction problems. The results obtained for temporal CSPs could therefore be extended to more general classes of continuous CSPs.

In the following, a continuous CSP (CCSP),($P = (V, D, R)$), is defined as a set V of *variables* $x_1, x_2, \ldots x_n$ taking their values respectively from a set D of continuous domains $D_1, D_2, \ldots, D_n$ and constrained by a set of *relations* $R_1, \ldots, R_m$. A *domain*

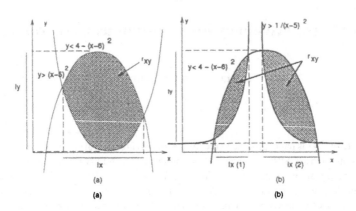

Fig. 1. *Figure (a) illustrates a binary relation R_{xy} given intensionally by the two inequalities $y > (x-5)^2$ and $y < 4 - (x-6)^2$. R_{xy} determines the region r_{xy} and is both y- and x-convex: the projection of r_{xy} respectively over the x and y axes yields single bounded intervals (resp. I_x and I_y). In Figure (b), the relation R_{xy} is given intensionally by the constraints $y > 1/(x-5)^2$ and $y < 4 - (x-6)^2$. In this last case, the relation is only y-convex since its projection over the x-axis yields two distinct intervals I_{x1} and I_{x2}.*

is an interval of $\mathcal{R}$. A *relation* is defined intensionally by a set of algebraic equalities and inequalities (see figure 1). A relation R_{ij} is a total constraint: it takes into account the whole set of algebraic constraints involving the variables i and j. Each variable has a *label* defining the set of possible consistent values. The label L_x of a variable x is represented as a set of intervals $\{I_{x,1} = [x_{min,1} \ldots x_{max,1}], \ldots\}$.

2   Constraint and Label Representation

Constraints on continuous variables are most naturally represented by algebraic or transcendental equations and inequalities. However, as Faltings [5] has shown, this leads to incomplete local propagation when there are several simultaneous constraints between the same variables. More importantly, making a network path-consistent requires computing the intersection and union of constraints, operations which cannot be performed on (in)equalities. It is therefore necessary to represent and manipulate the sets of feasible value combinations explicitly.

Providing each variable with an interval label implicitly represents feasible regions by enclosing rectangles or hypercubes. As shown in Figure 2, this is not powerful enough for region intersection operations. To define a more precise and yet efficient representation, we observe that most applications satisfy the following two assumptions:

- each variable takes its values in a bounded domain (bounded interval)
- there often exists a maximum precision with which results can be used.

Provided that these two assumptions are verified, a relation $R_{x_1 \ldots x_k}$ can be approximated by carrying out a hierarchical binary decomposition of its solution space into 2^k-trees (quadtrees for binary relations, octrees for ternary ones etc. . .)(see Figure 3). A

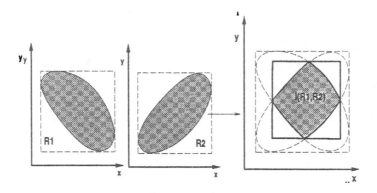

Fig. 2. *The enclosing rectangle of an intersection of regions R_1 and R_2 is in general different from the intersection of the enclosing rectangles of R_1 and R_2.*

similar representation has recently been proposed by Tanimoto for representing spatial constraints [13]. When a relation is determined by *inequalities*, it can be approximated by a 2^k-tree where each node represents a k-dimensional cubic sub-region of the original domain (i.e. the domain over which the decomposition is carried out). A node has one of three possible states:

- *white*: if the region it defines is completely legal
- *gray*: if the region is partially legal and partially illegal
- *black*: if the region is completely illegal

When a black or white node is identified, the recursive division stops. Each gray k-dimensional cube is decomposed into 2^k smaller ones whose sides are half as long. Unless the boundaries of a region are parallel to the coordinates axes, infinitely many levels of representation would be required to precisely represent a region. However, since the minimum granularity is fixed, any gray node with a smaller size than the minimum granularity can be declared black and the decomposition stops.

Equalities In the case of equality constraints, a strict application of the binary decomposition into a 2^k-tree as described would amount to pursuing the decomposition to infinity since an infinite degree of precision is required to represent single point solutions. We can avoid this problem by exploiting the fact that many practical applications require a limited degree of precision and it is thus admissible to treat equalities with a certain error range. Presently, our system translates strict equalities $f(x_1, \ldots x_k) = C$ into a weaker form, $f(x_1, \ldots x_k) = C \pm \varepsilon/2$, where ε is the fixed maximum precision, as defined for inequalities. This amounts to replacing each equality by two inequalities.

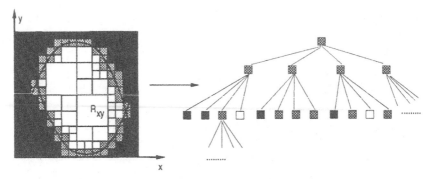

Fig. 3. *A binary relation R_{xy} can be approximated by carrying out a hierarchical binary decomposition of its solution space into a quadtree*

3 Consistency Algorithms Using 2^k-Trees

Path consistency algorithms, such as PC-1 [12] and PC-2 [11] require the application of the following update rule defined on constraints:

$$C'_{ij} = C_{ij} \oplus \prod^k (C_{ik} \otimes C_{kj}) \tag{1}$$

This relaxation operation uses two binary operators (intersection and composition, denoted respectively by $\oplus$ and $\otimes$) and a unary one (projection, denoted by $\prod$), which can be defined on 2^k-trees. Since all variables are decomposed within the same interval, *intersection* is simply the logical intersection of the corresponding quadtrees and can be carried out efficiently. *Composition* can be implemented by first extending the k-dimensional constraints into $k + 1$-dimensional space and then projecting back the result into k-dimension, as shown in Figure 4. Given an ordering $white < gray < black$, rules for determining the feasibility of a node obtained by one of these operators can be expressed as follows:

    i. $color(node_1 \oplus node_2) = Max(color(node_1), color(node_2))$
    ii. $color(node_1 \otimes node_2) = Max(color(node_1), color(node_2))$
    iii. $color(\prod^x(node_1)) = Min(color(node_i))$
        where $node_i$ are the nodes having $node_1$ as facet.

The operators required for path consistency algorithms (and their generalization for higher degrees of consistency) can therefore be implemented as straightforward logical rather than numerical operations.

    At each relaxation step described by eq. 1 using operations on 2^k-trees, the intervals contained in the involved labels are constructed by an implicit binary search: each successive relaxation step refines the interval bounds to an interval half the size of the previous one until maximum granularity is reached. Consequently, the decomposition into 2^k-trees has the important advantage of ruling out infinite cycling of the propagation algorithm as observed for the Waltz algorithm applied to continuous domains. While the Waltz algorithm performs slow and unstable fixed point iterations, the binary search method using the 2^k-tree decomposition guarantees stability and convergence.

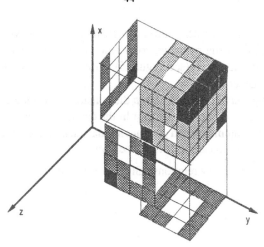

Fig. 4. *Information on a 3-dimensional node can be simply derived by composing its facets (2-dimensional nodes), and vice versa, information on a 2-dimensional node can be obtained by projecting the 3-dimensional node over one of its facets*

N-ary CSPs In many realistic problems, the constraints are not binary, but n-ary. However, each n-ary constraint can be reduced to a set of ternary constraints without loss of information. An n-ary algebraic relation, $C(x_1, \ldots x_n)$, can be transformed into a set of ternary algebraic expressions by:

> i. replacing iteratively in C each sub-expression $< x_i$ operator
> $x_j >$ by a new variable x_{n+1}
> ii. adding a ternary equality constraint $x_{n+1} = < x_i$ operator $x_j >$

The process stops when C itself becomes ternary. This transformation is only based on symbolic manipulations and consequently, no information is lost in the solution space description. For example, the 5-ary CSP with one constraint, $(x - y)^2 + \frac{(z+t)}{u} > 2$, can be translated into a ternary one with three constraints: $w_1^2 + (w_2/u) > 2$, $w_1 = x - y$, $w_2 = z + t$. Hence, addressing n-ary continuous CSPs amounts to giving the ternary counterparts of the algorithms and representation used for solving binary continuous CSPs.

Constructing 2^k-tree representations A total binary constraint R_{xy} is given intensionally by a set of algebraic equations $(C_1 \ldots C_l)$. The quadtree approximation T_{xy} of a binary relation R_{xy} can be obtained as follows:

> For each $C_i \in (C_1 \ldots C_l)$ Do
> 1. build a quadtree representation T_{xy}^i for the basic constraint C_i
> 2. $T_{xy} = T_{xy} \oplus T_{xy}^i$

Constructing the quadtree representation of an individual algebraic constraint, requires a procedure for determining the color of each sub-region (rectangle) created by the recursive decomposition. Two cases have to be considered:

i. If the constraint curve determines a *transverse segment* within the considered rectangle, testing for the rectangle color amounts to finding an intersection of its boundaries with the curve (see Figure 5). This test requires iterative numerical analysis in the general case.

ii. If not (i.e. the curve is *closed* within the considered rectangle), a pre-processing phase must be carried out in order to split the curve into transverse segments. This can be done for example by carrying out a binary search for determining a division which intersects the constraint curve. (see Figure 5)).

Computing octrees for ternary relations can be carried out in a similar manner.

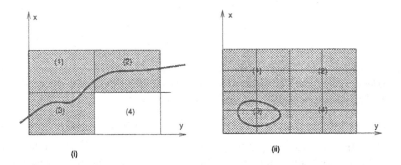

Fig. 5. *In case (i), the constraint curve determines a transverse segment: if the boundaries of a rectangle intersect the curve , the rectangle is gray (rectangle(1)). If not it suffices to test if one vertex of the rectangle satisfies the constraint to know if it is white or black (rectangle (4)). In case ii, a rectangle might be gray even if all of its vertices satisfy (or do not satisfy) the constraint (rectangle(3)). A preliminary search must be carried out to determine the divisions where the constraint curve is transverse.*

4 Global Consistency in Constraint Networks

In a *minimal* network, all the constraints are as explicit as possible and any value of the labels can be extended to a solution. In a *decomposable* network, the search for a solution is *backtrack-free* (the search process can generally be carried out in linear time). We show that certain convexity properties of the solution space make it possible to compute minimal and decomposable networks in polynomial time for continuous CSPs.

Encouraging results have been obtained for continuous CSPs in the domain of temporal reasoning: Dechter, Meiri and Pearl [2] have shown that for simple temporal problems (STP), where labels have to be convex intervals (i.e: disjunctive constraints are not allowed), the minimal constraint network can be constructed in polynomial time by ensuring path consistency. Similar results have been obtained by Van Beek [14] on a subset of the Allen's interval algebra excluding the binary relation $\neq$. Recently, Van Beek [15] has generalized the convexity property to the case of discrete CSPs: *row-convexity* guarantees the minimality and the decomposability of a path-consistent constraint network.

Although the convexity properties exploited in temporal and row-convex discrete problems derive mainly from results in the continuous domain (see Helly's theorem for convex sets [14]), no framework has been defined to exploit them in the case of general continuous CSPs. This is because the restriction imposed by the convexity condition on algebraic continuous solution spaces is too strong. In this work, we show that the *axis-convexity* property (a weaker condition) is sufficient for generalizing the results obtained in simple temporal [2] and row-convex discrete [15] domains to continuous CSPs.

In simple temporal problems (STPs) constraints take the form of bounded differences $b_1 < x_i - x_j < b_2$ where $[b_1 b_2]$ has to be a *single* interval. This condition amounts to saying that each variable takes its value within a single interval (convex interval). Path consistent STPs can be solved by backtrack-free search. The key observation is that this solution requires the convexity property *only* for each individual variable domain. Hence, generalizing to non-temporal continuous CSPs would amount to imposing convexity conditions only on the *projections* of the solution space over the different axes involved (the convexity condition is required only on projected intervals).

Consequently, to generalize the results obtained for STPs, it is sufficient that the solution space verifies partial convexity properties (convex projections). The weaker form of partial convexity that can be used is arcwise connectivity. A region R is arcwise connected if for any pair of points x and y of R, there exists a path connecting x and y which is entirely within R. An arcwise connected region yields convex outer projections over the axes involved. Convex outer projections aid in determining a tighter consistent approximation of the solution space but are not sufficient to guarantee that the resulting bounds are minimal. This is due to the fact that even if the outer projection is convex, this property is not necessarily preserved for a subprojection of the solution space. For this reason, we define a new category of partial convexity called *axis-convexity*. This property is more restrictive than arcwise connectivity but guarantees the convexity of any subprojection. We show in the next sections how this property can be used to determine minimal approximations of the solution space in polynomial time complexity.

Definition 1 : **Axis-Convex Region**
Let r be a region defined by a set of algebraic or transcendental constraints on n variables $x_1 \ldots x_n$. r is said to be x_k-convex in the domain D_{x_k} if, for any two points q_1 and q_2 in r such that the segment $q_1 q_2$ is orthogonal to x_k, $q_1 q_2$ is entirely contained in r.

The *axis-convexity* requirement is clearly weaker than convexity: a k-ary relation, defined on a set of k variables $V = x_1, \ldots, x_k$ and determining a convex region has convex projections for each variable x_i of V for any value of x_i. However, the converse is not true, a region may have convex projections for each involved variable x without being convex.

4.1 Convex binary CCSPs

Let us first describe how convexity properties can be exploited in the case of binary constraints. The case of n-ary constraints will be dealt with later on. We define:

Definition 2 : **Axis-Convex Relation**

A binary relation R_{x_i,x_j} is x_k-convex (where $k \in \{i,j\}$) if it determines a x_k-convex region in the domain D_{x_k}.

Definition 3 : **x-Intersection**

The x_i-intersection of two bi-dimensional regions, $r^1_{x_i,x_u}$ and $r^2_{x_i,x_v}$, is the intersection of their projection over the x_i axis.

Definition 4 : **Convex constraint network**

A constraint network representing a CCSP (V,D,R) is convex if for all relation R_{x_i,x_j} in R, Rx_i, x_j is x_k-convex for each k in $\{i,j\}$.

Continuous constraint satisfaction problems (CCSPs) having convex constraint network representations are the generalized counterparts of simple temporal problems (STP) as defined in [2]. Note finally that CCSPs including disjunctive or non-linear constraints may admit no convex constraint network representation since these types of constraints often create splits in the solution space.

Now we are in position to extend the theorems of Van Beek (theorem 1 and 4 of [15]) to the case of CCSPs. We first have to extend the lemma on which his proofs are based. This can be done as follows:

Lemma 1 *Let F be a finite collection of x-convex regions in R^2. If F is such that every pair of regions has a non null x-intersection, then the x-intersection of all these regions is not null (i.e: there exists at least one value v for x so that each region $r_{x,y}$ contains a point (v, y_i), where y_i is a possible value for y)*

Proof. This lemma is a direct application of Helly's theorem to the case of R^2.
We can generalize the results given in [15] as follows:

Theorem 1 *Let N be a path consistent binary constraint network. If the network is convex, it is also minimal and decomposable. If it is not convex, a consistent instantiation can be found without backtracking if there exists an ordering of the variables $x_1, \ldots x_n$ such that each relation of N R_{x_i,x_j}, $1 \le j \le i$, is x_i-convex.*

Proof. Analogous to the ones given in [15] (and based on the generalization of the backtrack-free instantiation algorithm proposed in this work).

4.2 Convex n-ary CCSPs

As stated before, generalizing to n-ary CCSPs the results described before for binary CCSPs amounts to giving the ternary counterpart of theorem 1.

Global consistency for ternary CCSPs The x-convexity property generalizes straightforwardly to the case of non binary CCSPs. In the case of ternary constraints, the generalization of lemma 1 can be used to prove the decomposability of the constraint network only if each pair of ternary relations has a non null x-intersection. Two ternary relations $R_{i_1,j_1,k}$ and $R_{i_2,j_2,k}$ have a non null k-intersection when each subset of *five* variables (i_1, i_2, j_1, j_2, k) are consistently labelled. In the particular case where each pair of ternary constraints has two variables in common,(i.e: $i_1 = i_2$ or j_1 or j_2), the number of variables that must be consistently labelled reduces to four and strong 4-consistency guarantees that the network is decomposable. Hence, theorem 1 generalizes to ternary constraints as follows:

Theorem 2 *A ternary constraint network which is convex and strongly 5-consistent is minimal and decomposable. Furthermore, in the particular case where each pair of relations share two variables, strong 4-consistency is enough to ensure that a convex ternary constraint network is minimal and decomposable.*

Since the translation of an n-ary network into a ternary one is done at the cost of increasing the number of variables, the practicality of 5-consistency for n-ary CCSPs is still an open question. This result is mainly intended to provide a theoretical bound for solving certain classes of n-ary CCSPs in a complexity better than exponential.

4.3 Non-convex CCSPs

A general CCSP may admit no convex constraint network representation. Moreover, even if the initial problem is convex, consistency algorithms may not preserve this property since intersecting two non convex — even if axis-convex— regions may result in an arbitrary number of distinct sub-regions. We can distinguish three classes of CCSPs:

  i. CCSPs where all the relations determine convex regions
  ii. CCSP where each relation determining a non arcwise connected
        solution space is constituted by a set of convex regions.
  iii. CCSPs where there exist non convex regions

In case *i*, since the intersection of two convex regions is necessarily convex (and hence axis-convex), consistency algorithms will preserve the convexity of the constraint network representation. Hence, problems of this first category can be solved, with no further search, using partial consistency algorithms (as stated in theorems 1 and 2). In case *ii*, the problem can be decomposed into convex sub-problems (one for each possible combination of convex sub-region), for which each sub-problem is of type *i*. A solution to the whole problem can be determined by solving each sub-problem individually and then combining their solutions. Even if the complexity is, in this case, exponential in the number of disjoint convex sub-regions, the computational effort can be bounded *a priori* since consistency algorithms cannot create new case splits in the individual sub-problems. In the last case, the splitting problem (similar to the one described in [9]) may occur and the complexity is difficult to estimate. In the best case, the consistency algorithm may create a convex constraint network from a set of non-convex relations. In the worst case however, the intersection of each pair of non convex regions may result in an unbounded number of disjoint new sub-regions which can in turn split again. Practical solutions (such as stopping the splitting process when the maximum precision is reached) can be used to bound the combinatorial explosion, but in general the complexity remains exponential for CCSPs of type *iii*.

5 Complexity of Consistency Algorithms

The complexity of the intersection, composition and projection operators on 2^k-trees can be roughly estimated in terms of the number of nodes generated by each operation. $O(2^{k*s/\epsilon})$ (where s is the maximum domain size and ϵ the tightest interval size accepted for variables) gives a rough approximation of the complexity. This measure assumes that, in the worst case, a 2^k-tree resulting from a given operation is complete. A more realistic measure can be done in terms of the number of gray nodes generated, since the recursive quartering stops as soon as a node color is set to white or black. We can show that this measure is a function of the boundary size of the solution space. Furthermore, 2^k-tree structures are by nature well-adapted to parallel processing. Parallel implementation of the intersection, composition and projection are likely to be very efficient.

Convex Binary CCSPs The algorithm PC-2 can be implemented using eq. 1 by way of the revise function. According to the definitions of $\oplus$ and $\otimes$ for 2^k-trees, the relaxation operation described by eq. 1 is monotonic. Moreover, since the region decomposition into 2^k-trees discretizes the solution space, the fact that PC-1 (and hence PC-2) terminates and computes a path-consistent network using the relaxation operation $C'_{ij} = C_{ij} \oplus \prod^k (C_{ik} \otimes C_{kj})$ can be shown in a manner similar to the case for discrete-domain CSPs (see [12]). The worst case running time of PC-2 occurs when each revision step suppresses only one node from the considered relation (i.e. the node becomes black), hence:

Theorem 3 *PC-2 computes the path consistent network representation of binary CC-SPs, (V, D, R), in $O(2^{(2*s/\epsilon)}n^3)$ where s is the largest interval size in D and ϵ the tightest interval size accepted for variables of V.*

According to theorem 1, when the path consistent network computed by PC-2 is convex, it is also minimal and decomposable. Similarly, we can demonstrate that strong 5-consistency can be ensured for a ternary CCSP in $O(2^{(3*s/\epsilon)}n^5)$.

Non convex CCSPs During the construction and propagation of 2^k-trees, the case in which a single region is split into several can be reliably detected. At this point the algorithm branches and explores both regions separately (a new CCSP is generated). The pathological case where an infinite number of sub-regions are generated is avoided in practice, since regions smaller than the maximum precision are not explored. However, the worst case complexity is clearly exponential.

6 Conclusion

In this paper we present a generalization of the results obtained for convex temporal problems and discrete row-convex problems to more general classes of continuous CSPs (convex CCSPs). The main contributions is to show that *partial convexity* properties of continuous solutions spaces can be exploited to compute solutions to CCSPs in polynomial time. A recursive decomposition scheme is proposed that solves the problem of representing total constraints for path consistency algorithms. The 2^k-tree decomposition amounts to performing the stable binary-search method which guarantees convergence according to numerical analysis results. The cycling problems, generally posed by fixed point iteration methods (such as those observed by Davis for the Waltz algorithm [1]) are consequently avoided. Finally, we show that solving non-convex CCSPs remains inherently costly, but decomposition methods can be proposed and might be of practical interest for many particular applications.

7 Acknowledgments

We thank the Swiss National Science Foundation for sponsoring this research under contract No.5003-034269

References

1. Davis E. : *"Constraint propagation with interval labels"*, Artificial Intelligence 32 (1987)
2. Dechter R., Meiri I., Pearl J. : *"Temporal constraint networks"*, Artificial Intelligence 49(1-3) (1990)
3. Dechter R.: *"From local to global consistency"*, Proceedings of the 8th Canadian Conference on AI (1990)
4. Deville Y., Van Hetenryck P.: *"An efficient arc consistency algorithm for a class of CSP problems"*, Proceedings of the 12th International Joint Conference on AI (1991)
5. Faltings B.: *"Arc consistency for continuous variables"*, Artificial Intelligence 65 (2) (1994)
6. Freuder E.C.: *"Synthesizing constraint expressions"*, Comm. ACM 21 (1978)
7. Freuder E.C.: *"A sufficient condition for backtrack-free search"*, J. ACM 29 (1982)
8. Freuder E.C.: *"A sufficient condition for backtrack-bounded search"*, J. ACM 32 (1985)
9. Hyvönen E.: *"Constraint reasoning based on interval arithmetic: the tolerance propagation approach"*, Artificial Intelligence 58(1-3) (1992)
10. Lhomme O.: *"Consistency techniques for numeric CSPs"*, Proceedings of the 13th International Joint Conference on AI (1993)
11. Mackworth A.: *"Consistency in networks of relations"*, Artificial Intelligence 8 (1977)
12. Montanari U.: *"Networks of constraints: fundamental properties and applications to picture processing"*, Inform. Scie. 7 (1974)
13. Tanimoto T.: *"A constraint decomposition method for spatio-temporal configurations problems"*, Proceedings of the the 11th National Conference on AI (1993)
14. Van Beek P.: *"Approximation algorithms for temporal reasoning"*, Proceedings of the 11th International Joint Conference on AI (1989)
15. Van Beek P.: *"On the minimality and decomposability of constraint networks"*, Proceedings of the 10th National Conference on AI (1992)

Locally Simultaneous Constraint Satisfaction

Hiroshi Hosobe,[1]* Ken Miyashita,[1] Shin Takahashi,[1]
Satoshi Matsuoka,[2] and Akinori Yonezawa[1]

[1] Department of Information Science, University of Tokyo
[2] Department of Mathematical Engineering, University of Tokyo
7-3-1 Hongo, Bunkyo-ku, Tokyo 113, Japan

Abstract. Local propagation is often used in graphical user interfaces to solve constraint systems that describe structures and layouts of figures. However, algorithms based on local propagation cannot solve simultaneous constraint systems because local propagation must solve constraints individually. We propose the '*DETAIL*' algorithm, which efficiently solves systems of constraints with strengths, even if they must be solved simultaneously, by 'dividing' them as much as possible. In addition to multi-way constraints, it handles various other types of constraints, for example, constraints solved with the least squares method. Furthermore, it unifies the treatment of different types of constraints in a single system. We implemented a prototype constraint solver based on this algorithm, and evaluated its performance.

1   Introduction

Local propagation is an efficient constraint satisfaction algorithm that takes advantage of potential locality of constraint systems. It is often used in graphical user interfaces (GUIs) to solve constraint systems that describe structures and layouts of figures.

Recent constraint solvers based on local propagation handle *multi-way constraints* [4]. A multi-way constraint can be solved for any one of its variables. For example, the constraint $x = y + z$ is multi-way because it can be transformed into $x \leftarrow y + z$, $y \leftarrow x - z$, and $z \leftarrow x - y$. Local propagation satisfies systems of multi-way constraints by solving each constraint at most once in some order. For example, consider a constraint system with the constraints $v = w \times x$, $w = y$, and $x = y + z$. Figure 1a shows a *constraint graph* representing this system, where circles and squares represent variables and constraints respectively. This system can be satisfied by solving $x \leftarrow y + z$, $w \leftarrow y$, and $v \leftarrow w \times x$ in this order. This case is illustrated by the *correct solution graph* in Fig. 1b, where arrows from constraints point to variables to which the constraints output values. A solution graph is a constraint graph that dictates how each constraint will be solved, and a correct solution graph satisfies the following two properties: (1) the value of each variable must be determined by at most one constraint, that is, the graph should have no *conflicts*, and (2) all the constraints must be partially ordered, that is, the graph must have no *cycles*.

---

* E-mail: detail@is.s.u-tokyo.ac.jp

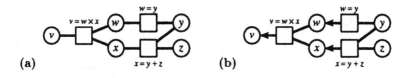

Fig. 1. (a) A constraint graph and (b) its correct solution graph

Multi-way constraints embody a problem that correct solution graphs are not determined uniquely. Borning et al. proposed *constraint hierarchies* to cope with this problem [7]. A constraint hierarchy is a system of constraints with hierarchical *strengths*. If the system is over-constrained, it is solved so that there are as many satisfied strong constraints as possible, which allows programmers to implicitly specify solution graphs. In Fig. 2a, for example, the constraints $x = 1$ and $x = 3$ conflict. However, if $x = 1$ and $x = 3$ are associated with **strong** and **weak** respectively, the constraint system is solved by satisfying only $x = 1$ as shown in Fig. 2b. DeltaBlue is the first proposed algorithm that efficiently solves hierarchies of multi-way constraints [2, 5]. It determines output variables of constraints incrementally when a constraint is added or removed, and realizes constraint satisfaction without spoiling the efficiency of local propagation.

Fig. 2. (a) A solution graph for an over-constrained system and (b) one for a constraint hierarchy

Local propagation has a serious problem that constraint systems employed in real applications often result in solution graphs with cycles or conflicts. For example, consider a constraint system with the constraints $a - b = l$, $(a+b)/2 = m$, stay(l), and edit(m). This system represents a typical situation where the midpoint of two points is moved with a mouse, but its solution graphs contain cycles by necessity, e.g. as illustrated in Fig. 3a. As another example, suppose a constraint hierarchy with the constraints strong $x = 1$ and strong $x = 3$. Even if one wants to apply the least squares method to these constraints and to obtain the solution $x = 2$, the resulting solution graph contains a conflict as shown in Fig. 3b. Generally, in constraint systems that result in solution graphs with cycles or conflicts, constraints need to be solved simultaneously.

We propose the '*DETAIL*' algorithm, which efficiently solves constraint hierarchies, even if constraints must be solved simultaneously, by 'dividing' them as

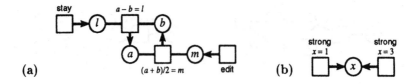

Fig. 3. (a) A solution graph with a cycle and (b) one with a conflict

much as possible. This algorithm is efficient enough to be applied to constraint-based GUIs since it incrementally finds parts of constraint systems that must be solved simultaneously. In addition to multi-way constraints, it handles various other kinds of constraints, for example, constraints solved with the least squares method. Furthermore, it unifies the treatment of different types of constraints in a single hierarchy. We implemented a prototype constraint solver based on this algorithm, and evaluated its performance.

2 Locally Simultaneous Constraint Satisfaction

In this section, we present an extended theory of constraint hierarchies and the *DETAIL* algorithm.

2.1 Constraints

In our extended constraint hierarchy theory, constraints are categorized into *solution types*, which are determined by how the constraints are solved. For example, there is a solution type of constraints that will be ignored if they cannot be solved exactly, as with the DeltaBlue algorithm. Also, there is another solution type of constraints that must be solved even in such a case by minimizing their errors with the least squares method.

All constraints with an equal strength must belong to a single solution type. Intuitively, this requirement is necessary because it is difficult to equally treat constraints of different solution types.

Based on this theory, the *DETAIL* algorithm solves hierarchies of multi-way constraints where all constraints are independent. For example, a hierarchy must not contain the constraints **strong** $x + y = 1$ and **weak** $x + y = 1$.

2.2 Theory

By extending the theory described in [7], we formulated constraint hierarchies that contain multiple solution types of constraints. A constraint hierarchy H is a pair (V, C), where V is a set of variables that range over some domain $\mathcal{D}$, and C is a set of constraints on variables in V. Each constraint is associated with a strength i where $0 \leq i \leq n$. Strength 0 represents the strength of required constraints, and the larger the number of a strength, the weaker it is. All constraints with an equal strength i are categorized into a solution type τ_i. C is divided into a set of lists $\{C_0, C_1, \ldots, C_n\}$, where C_i contains constraints with strength i in some arbitrary order.

Solutions to a constraint hierarchy are defined as a set of valuations. A valuation θ is a function that maps variables in V to their values in $\mathcal{D}$. An error function e_τ returns a non-negative real by evaluating the error for θ of a constraint c of a solution type τ. The error $e_\tau(c\theta) = 0$ if and only if c is exactly satisfied by θ. The function E_{τ_i} returns the list of errors of a list of constraints $C_i = [c_1, c_2, \ldots, c_k]$, i.e.,

$$E_{\tau_i}(C_i\theta) = [e_{\tau_i}(c_1\theta), e_{\tau_i}(c_2\theta), \ldots, e_{\tau_i}(c_k\theta)] \ .$$

Each element $e_{\tau_i}(c_i\theta)$ can be weighted by a positive real w_i. An error sequence $R(C\theta)$ is the error of C except C_0:

$$R(C\theta) = [E_{\tau_1}(C_1\theta), E_{\tau_2}(C_2\theta), \ldots, E_{\tau_n}(C_n\theta)] \ .$$

A combining function g_{τ_i} combines $E_{\tau_i}(C_i\theta)$ into a value of a domain where elements are comparable. Two combined errors $g_{\tau_i}(E_{\tau_i}(C_i\theta))$ and $g_{\tau_i}(E_{\tau_i}(C_i\varphi))$ are compared by a reflexive and symmetric relation $<>_{g_{\tau_i}}$, and an irreflexive, antisymmetric, and transitive relation $<_{g_{\tau_i}}$. The function G combines an error sequence $R(C\theta)$:

$$G(R(C\theta)) = [g_{\tau_1}(E_{\tau_1}(C_1\theta)), g_{\tau_2}(E_{\tau_2}(C_2\theta)), \ldots, g_{\tau_n}(E_{\tau_n}(C_n\theta))] \ .$$

Two combined error sequences $G(R(C\theta))$ and $G(R(C\varphi))$ are compared by a lexicographic ordering $<_G$:

$$G(R(C\theta)) <_G G(R(C\varphi)) \equiv \exists k \in \{1, 2, \ldots, n\}.$$
$$\forall i \in \{1, 2, \ldots, k-1\}. \ g_{\tau_i}(E_{\tau_i}(C_i\theta)) <>_{g_{\tau_i}} g_{\tau_i}(E_{\tau_i}(C_i\varphi)) \ \wedge$$
$$g_{\tau_k}(E_{\tau_k}(C_k\theta)) <_{g_{\tau_k}} g_{\tau_k}(E_{\tau_k}(C_k\varphi)) \ .$$

We say that θ is *better* than φ if and only if $G(R(C\theta)) <_G G(R(C\varphi))$.

The set S of solutions to H is defined as follows:

$$S_0 = \{\theta \mid \forall c \in C_0. \ e_{\tau_0}(c\theta) = 0\}$$
$$S = \{\varphi \in S_0 \mid \forall \theta \in S_0. \neg(G(R(C\theta)) <_G G(R(C\varphi)))\} \ .$$

The main difference from the original formulation in [7] is existence of solution types. In [7], all constraints in a constraint hierarchy are categorized into some single solution type, and therefore, for each strength i, e_{τ_i} and g_{τ_i} are some e and g respectively. Since errors of constraints with different strengths are never compared directly, we can safely assign various solution types to each strength.

Two error functions are presented in [7]: Given a constraint c and a valuation θ, the *metric* error function returns c's metric, e.g. for the constraint $x = y$, the distance between x and y. Also, the *predicate* error function returns 0 if c is exactly satisfied for θ, and 1 otherwise.

Also in [7], several combining functions and associated relations are provided. Since it does not introduce multiple solution types in a constraint hierarchy, an instance of $<_G$ is determined by single instances of e and g. For an instance of $<_G$ called *least-squares-better*, given lists of errors $\mathbf{v} = [v_1, v_2, \ldots, v_k]$ obtained with the metric error function, $g(\mathbf{v}) = \sum_{i=1}^{k} w_i v_i^2$, $<_g$ is $<$ and $<>_g$ is $=$ for reals. For instances of $<_G$ called *locally-better*, given $\mathbf{v} = [v_1, v_2, \ldots, v_k]$ and $\mathbf{u} = [u_1, u_2, \ldots, u_k]$, $g(\mathbf{v}) = \mathbf{v}$ and $<_g$ and $<>_g$ are defined as follows:

$$\mathbf{v} <_g \mathbf{u} \equiv \forall i.\ v_i \leq u_i\ \wedge\ \exists j.\ v_j < u_j$$
$$\mathbf{v} <>_g \mathbf{u} \equiv \forall i.\ v_i = u_i\ .$$

Locally-predicate-better is the locally-better using the predicate error function, and *locally-metric-better* is the one employing the metric error function.

In the rest of this paper, we refer to the solution type associated with least-squares-better as τ_{LSB} and constraints of τ_{LSB} as least-squares-better constraints, and correspondingly locally-predicate-better as τ_{LPB} and locally-predicate-better constraints.[3]

2.3 Solution Graphs

Local propagation cannot solve conventional solution graphs with cycles or conflicts. To cope with this problem, we propose a new definition of solution graphs. Before presenting it, we define constraint graphs of constraint hierarchies.

Definition 1 (Constraint graph). Given a constraint hierarchy $H = (V, C)$, a bipartite graph $B = (V, C, E)$, where V and C are sets of nodes and E is a set of edges, is a constraint graph of H if and only if

$$E = \{(v, c) \in V \times C \mid v \text{ is constrained by } c\}\ .$$

We say that v and c are *adjacent* if and only if $(v, c) \in E$.

We define solution graphs using *constraint cells* to overcome the defects of conventional solution graphs.

Definition 2 (Constraint cell). Let $H = (V, C)$ be a constraint hierarchy, and $B = (V, C, E)$ a constraint graph of H. For $X \subseteq V$, define Γ as follows:

$$\Gamma(X) = \{c \mid (v, c) \in E\ \wedge\ v \in X\}\ .$$

A pair $p = (V_p, C_p)$ is a constraint cell in B if and only if:

1. $V_p \subseteq V$, $C_p = \emptyset$, and $|V_p| = 1$, or
2. $V_p \subseteq V$, $C_p \subseteq C$, the subgraph of B induced by V_p and C_p is connected, and

$$\forall X \subseteq V_p.\ |X| \leq |\Gamma(X) \cap C_p|\ .$$

---

[3] These names may sound strange because 'better' is associated with $<_G$ (not $<_g$), but we use them to avoid introducing new terminologies.

We say that p is *over-constrained* if and only if $|V_p| < |C_p|$.

Values of variables in a constraint cell are obtained by evaluating constraints in the cell. Because of Definition 2, this is always possible for constraints that we handle. Definition 2 is based on Hall's theorem, known in graph theory, which describes the condition on existence of perfect matchings of bipartite graphs. Intuitively, Definition 2 means that given a constraint cell $p = (V_p, C_p)$, the value of each variable in V_p can be determined by at least one constraint in C_p.

Definition 3 (Solution graph). Given a constraint graph $B = (V, C, E)$ and a set P of constraint cells in B, a quadruple $B_S = (V, C, E, P)$ is a solution graph for B if and only if:

1. each variable in V belongs to only one constraint cell in P,
2. each constraint in C belongs to only one constraint cell in P, and
3. there are no cyclic dependencies among constraint cells in P.

For example, Fig. 4 shows a solution graph equivalent to the one in Fig. 1b, where boxes with round corners illustrate constraint cells.[4]

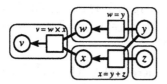

Fig. 4. A solution graph with constraint cells

Constraint cells are created so that they contain cycles and conflicts. In addition, over-constrained cells are sometimes merged with other cells to produce a 'better' solution graph, i.e. the corresponding valuation is better, because the new cells may acquire more freedom to determine the values of their variables. For example, consider a constraint hierarchy with the constraints $\alpha, \beta, \gamma, \delta, \epsilon, \zeta, \eta$, and θ. Let α be required $t = 0$, β weak $t = u$, γ weak $v = 1$, δ strong $t + v = w$, ϵ weak $w = x$, ζ strong $x + y = z$, η required $x + 1 = y$, and θ medium $z = 7$, where strong and medium constraints are locally-predicate-better, and weak constraints are least-squares-better. Figure 5a shows a solution graph of this hierarchy. Satisfying constraints locally in these cells, the corresponding valuation Θ is obtained as $\{t \mapsto 0, u \mapsto 0, v \mapsto 1, w \mapsto 1, x \mapsto 3, y \mapsto 4, z \mapsto 7\}$, and the combined error sequence is $[g_{T_{\mathrm{LPB}}}(E_{T_{\mathrm{LPB}}}([\delta, \zeta]\Theta)), g_{T_{\mathrm{LPB}}}(E_{T_{\mathrm{LPB}}}([\theta]\Theta)), g_{T_{\mathrm{LSB}}}(E_{T_{\mathrm{LSB}}}([\beta, \gamma, \epsilon]\Theta))]$ $= [[0, 0], [0], 4]$. By contrast, merging the over-constrained cell W and the cell V

---

[4] For readability, we often draw arrowheads in constraint cells although they are not essential.

into the new cell W', we obtain the solution graph in Fig. 5b,[5] and then, the corresponding valuation Φ is $\{t \mapsto 0,\ u \mapsto 0,\ v \mapsto 2,\ w \mapsto 2,\ x \mapsto 3,\ y \mapsto 4,\ z \mapsto 7\}$, and the combined error sequence is $[[0, 0], [0], 2]$. This indicates that Φ is better than Θ.

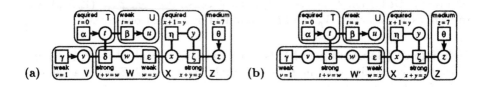

(a)   (b)

Fig. 5. Merging an over-constrained cell with another constraint cell

We define correct solution graphs using *internal strengths* and *walkabout strengths* of constraint cells so that the graphs can produce solutions to constraint hierarchies. Walkabout strengths were first introduced in the DeltaBlue algorithm, but for our purpose, we extend its definition:

Definition 4 (Internal strength). The internal strength of a constraint cell $p = (V_p, C_p)$ is (1) **weakest** if $C_p = \emptyset$, or (2) the weakest among strengths of constraints in C_p, otherwise.

Definition 5 (Walkabout strength). The walkabout strength of a constraint cell p is the weakest among p's internal strength and walkabout strengths of constraint cells with variables adjacent to the constraints in p.

Definition 6 (Correct solution graph). A solution graph is correct if and only if:

1. for each constraint cell with multiple constraints, the pair of the set of its variables and the set of its non-weakest constraints does not constitute a constraint cell, i.e. does not satisfy Definition 2, and
2. for each over-constrained cell, its internal strength is weaker than the walkabout strengths of any other constraint cells with the variables adjacent to the constraints in the over-constrained cell.

Intuitively, Condition 1 of Definition 6 makes constraint cells use the weakest constraints to determine the values of their variables, and Condition 2 guarantees that constraints in over-constrained cells cannot override constraints in other cells even if they are merged.

---

[5] Note that constraint cells are *not* merged simply because they contain constraints of similar solution types or constraints with equal strengths. For example, W' in Fig. 5b contains multiple solution types of constraints with multiple strengths

2.4 Algorithm

It is desirable that sizes of constraint cells in correct solution graphs are minimized since local propagation can be efficiently applied to such graphs. The *DETAIL* algorithm creates such solution graphs incrementally when invoked with the following five operations: adding a variable, removing a variable, adding a constraint, removing a constraint, and updating a variable value. The former four operations cause the corresponding solution graph to be modified, and the last operation applies local propagation to the solution graph as described earlier. We call the former *planning* and the latter *execution*.

The algorithm for adding or removing a variable is quite straightforward: to add a variable, *DETAIL* only creates a new constraint cell with the variable, and to remove a variable, it deletes the constraint cell with the variable after verifying that the variable is not adjacent to any constraints. In the rest of this section, we describe the algorithm for adding or removing a constraint to a hierarchy.

Adding a Constraint. Initially, there is a correct solution graph whose constraint cells are minimized. When a new constraint is added to this hierarchy, one or more constraints with an equal or weaker strength may be 'victimized,' that is, their associated errors will be increased. In such a case, *DETAIL* reconstructs the solution graph incrementally to keep it correct and its constraint cells minimal by modifying the necessary set of cells.

DETAIL treats locally-predicate-better constraints specially by permitting 'equal to' as well as 'weaker than' in Condition 2 of Definition 6, because these constraints can be ignored if they cannot be exactly satisfied, and resulting solution graphs may be solved more efficiently.

Figure 6 shows the algorithm that adds a constraint *con* to a constraint hierarchy, and Fig. 7 describes the algorithm to decompose a constraint cell at lines 12 and 17 in Fig. 6. The former algorithm works as follows: First, it creates a constraint cell with *con* at line 1. Second, it finds the strength of the 'victim' constraint at line 2. Next, it follows the path from *con* to the victim at lines 4–19, reversing the dependency between the cells along the path. After this process, *con* becomes active. Then, it eliminates cycles of constraint cells generated in the previous process at line 20, and updates walkabout strengths correctly at line 21. Finally, it merges over-constrained cells with others at line 23 so that they can minimize the errors of their constraints.

Figure 8 shows an example of the execution of this algorithm. Initially, there is a correct solution graph illustrated in Fig. 8a. When a constraint θ is added to the constraint hierarchy, this algorithm works as follows:

1. A constraint cell H with θ is created (Fig. 8b). The strength of the victim is found to be **weak**.
2. After the variable z is removed from the cell G, it is added to H (Fig. 8c).
3. The variable x is deleted from the cell E, and is added to G (Fig. 8d). The **weak** constraint ϵ in E is found to be the victim.
4. The constraint cells G and F are merged because they form a cycle.

1   $cl \leftarrow$ a new cell with con;
2   $wastr \leftarrow$ the weakest of walkabout strengths of
         cells with variables adjacent to con;
3   $str \leftarrow con$'s strength;
4   **while** str is stronger than $wastr$ **do**
5     $nextcl \leftarrow$ a cell with a variable adjacent to a constraint in cl and
           with walkabout strength $wastr$;
6     $var \leftarrow$ a variable in $nextcl$ that connects to cl;
7   remove var from $nextcl$;
8   add var to cl;
9   **if** $nextcl$ is empty **then**
10      $str \leftarrow$ **weakest**;
11   **else if** $nextcl$'s internal strength is $wastr$ **then**
12      $cl \leftarrow$ an over-constrained cell generated by decomposing $nextcl$;
13      $str \leftarrow cl$'s internal strength;
14   **else**
15      $bordercon \leftarrow$ a constraint in $nextcl$ and
             adjacent to a variable in a cell with walkabout strength $wastr$;
16   remove $bordercon$ from $nextcl$;
17   decompose $nextcl$;
18      $cl \leftarrow$ a new cell with $bordercon$;
19      $str \leftarrow cl$'s internal strength; /* end of **while** */
20   merge cyclic cells dependent on con;
21   update walkabout strengths of cells dependent on con;
22   **if** $wastr$ is not **weakest** and constraints with strength $wastr$ are
         not locally-predicate-better constraints **then**
23   merge cells that cl depends on and
           that have the same walkabout strength as cl;

Fig. 6. Adding a constraint con to a constraint hierarchy.

1   **for** each variable var in cl **do**
2   remove var from cl;
3   create a cell with var;
4   **for** each constraint con stronger than $wastr$ in cl **do**
5   remove con from cl;
6     $var \leftarrow$ a variable initially in cl that forms a cell alone and
           that con depends on;
7   reverse the dependency between con and var;
8   **for** each constraint con with strength $wastr$ in cl **do**
9   remove con from cl;
10   **if** there is a variable initially in cl that forms a cell alone and
           that con depends on **then**
11      $var \leftarrow$ the variable found above;
12   reverse the dependency between con and var;
13   **else**
14   create a cell with con;

Fig. 7. Decomposing a constraint cell cl with walkabout strength $wastr$

5. Walkabout strengths are updated (Fig. 8e).

6. Since E is over-constrained, it is joined with the constraint cells D and C, which have the same walkabout strength weak as E (Fig. 8f).

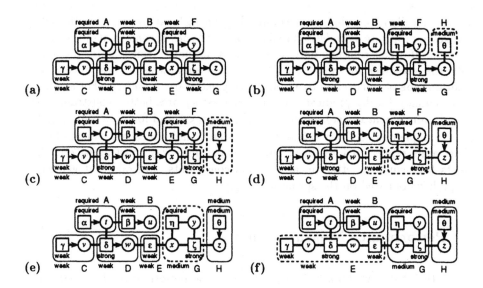

Fig. 8. Adding a constraint

It is sometimes necessary to decompose 'large' constraint cells that contain multiple constraints. Figure 7 describes the algorithm that decomposes 'large' cells into 'small' ones. Basically, it matches variables with constraints, employing a perfect matching algorithm for bipartite graphs. In addition, since the weakest constraints sometimes need to remain unsatisfied, it later tries to match the weakest constraints at lines 8–14. Definition 2 of constraint cells guarantees that there are no undetermined variables after decomposing cells with one or more constraints. Even if constraint cells that do not satisfy Condition 3 in Definition 3 or Condition 2 in Definition 6 are generated, they will be merged by the caller algorithm in Fig. 6.

Removing a Constraint. Removing a constraint from a constraint hierarchy may cause one or more constraints with an equal or weaker strength to decrease their errors, because it or they may acquire more freedom to determine the value of variables instead of the removed constraint. In the similar way to adding a constraint, the algorithm reverses the dependency between the cell with such constraints and the cell that has been contained the removed constraint.

3   Implementation

Based on the algorithm presented in the previous section, we implemented the
DETAIL constraint solver in Objective-C. It consists of two layers, a *solver*
and *subsolvers*. A *solver* produces correct solution graphs, to which it applies
local propagation. *Subsolvers* obtain values of variables by solving constraint
systems locally in individual constraint cells. During local propagation, the *solver*
invokes appropriate *subsolvers* based on solution types of constraints in cells. For
example, if a cell contains only locally-predicate-better constraints, the *solver*
calls the *subsolver* for τ_{LPB}. This architecture enables us to introduce a new
solution type of constraints by implementing necessary *subsolvers*. For example,
if we employ locally-predicate-better and least-squares-better constraints, we
have to implement the subsolvers for τ_{LPB}, for τ_{LSB}, and for τ_{LPB} and τ_{LSB}.[6]

We implemented three *subsolvers*: one that handles locally-predicate-better
constraints represented as linear equations or multi-way constraints, one that
treats least-squares-better linear-equation constraints, and one that generates
graph layouts based on the spring model [1].

4   Performance Measurements

Using the chain benchmark [5], we compared the performance of the *DETAIL*
constraint solver implemented in Objective-C with that of the DeltaBlue constraint solver implemented in C. Initially, the constraint hierarchy contains the
required constraints $x_0 = x_1$, $x_1 = x_2, \ldots, x_{n-2} = x_{n-1}$ and the constraint
weak stay(x_0). The chain benchmark measures the planning time to add the
constraint strong edit(x_{n-1}) to the hierarchy, and also measures the execution
time to compute values of variables when the value of x_{n-1} is changed through
edit(x_{n-1}). Both of the planning and the execution are the worst cases where
the overall solution graph must be processed.

Table 1 shows the result:[7] while the planning time of *DETAIL* is almost four
times as long as that of DeltaBlue, the execution time is nearly twenty times as
long. The main handicaps of *DETAIL* are the complex data structure of constraint cells, and dynamic binding of methods in Objective-C.[8] We believe that
dynamic binding caused slowdown in performance because the source program
involves numerous message sendings with dynamic binding. If we re-implement
the *DETAIL* constraint solver in C++, its performance is expected to approach
that of DeltaBlue.

---

[6] However, since the *DETAIL* algorithm tries to divide constraint hierarchies as much
as possible, the subsolver for τ_{LPB} and τ_{LSB} may never be invoked.

[7] Precisely speaking, the separation of planning and execution is slightly different from
the description presented in Sect. 2.4. In both *DETAIL* and DeltaBlue, the planning
time includes the time of topological sort for local propagation.

[8] Objective-C does not support static binding like C++.

Table 1. Results of the chain benchmark

n		1000	2000	3000	4000	5000
Planning (ms)	DETAIL	283	617	933	1183	1817
	DeltaBlue	67	166	250	350	434
Execution (ms)	DETAIL	36.7	68.3	105.0	140.0	176.7
	DeltaBlue	2.5	4.3	6.7	8.7	10.8

On NeXTstation *TurboColor* (33 MHz 68040)

5 Conclusions and Status

We proposed the *DETAIL* algorithm, which incrementally solves multiple solution types of constraints in a single constraint hierarchy by grouping together cyclic or conflicting constraints into constraint cells. We implemented the *DETAIL* constraint solver, which exhibited promising performance results.

Using this solver, we developed the IMAGE system, which generates GUIs by generalizing multiple visual examples [3]. This system takes advantage of the ability of *DETAIL* to handle hierarchies of simultaneous constraints. Also, we are planning on applying *DETAIL* to our algorithm animation system based on declarative specification [6].

References

1. Kamada, T., *Visualizing Abstract Objects and Relations, A Constraint-Based Approach*. Singapore: World Scientific, 1989.
2. Maloney, J. H., A. Borning, and B. N. Freeman-Benson, "Constraint Technology for User-Interface Construction in ThingLab II," in *Proc. of the ACM Conference on Object-Oriented Programming Systems, Languages, and Applications*, Oct. 1989, pp. 381–388.
3. Miyashita, K., S. Matsuoka, S. Takahashi, and A. Yonezawa, "Interactive Generation of Graphical User Interfaces by Multiple Visual Examples," in *Proc. of the ACM Symposium on User Interface Software and Technology*, Nov. 1994 (to appear).
4. Myers, B. A., D. A. Giuse, R. B. Dannenberg, B. Vander Zanden, D. S. Kosbie, E. Pervin, A. Mickish, and P. Marchal, "Garnet: Comprehensive Support for Graphical, Highly Interactive User Interfaces," *IEEE Computer*, vol. 23, no. 11, Nov. 1990, pp. 71–85.
5. Sannella, M., B. Freeman-Benson, J. Maloney, and A. Borning, "Multi-way versus One-way Constraints in User Interfaces: Experience with the DeltaBlue Algorithm," Technical Report 92-07-05, Department of Computer Science and Engineering, University of Washington, July 1992.
6. Takahashi, S., K. Miyashita, S. Matsuoka, and A. Yonezawa, "A Framework for Constructing Animations via Declarative Mapping Rules," in *Proc. of the IEEE Symposium on Visual Languages*, Oct. 1994 (to appear).
7. Wilson, M. and A. Borning, "Hierarchical Constraint Logic Programming," Technical Report 93-01-02a, Department of Computer Science and Engineering, University of Washington, May 1993.

Analyzing and Debugging Hierarchies of Multi-Way Local Propagation Constraints

Michael Sannella

Department of Computer Science
and Engineering, FR-35
University of Washington
Seattle, Washington 98195

Abstract. Multi-way local propagation constraints are a powerful and flexible tool for implementing applications such as graphical user interfaces. SkyBlue is an incremental constraint solver that uses local propagation to maintain a set of constraints as individual constraints are added and removed. If all of the constraints cannot be satisfied, SkyBlue leaves weaker constraints unsatisfied in order to satisfy stronger constraints (maintaining a constraint hierarchy). Our experience has indicated that large constraint networks can be difficult to construct and understand. To investigate this problem, we have developed the CNV system for interactively constructing constraint-based user interfaces, integrated with tools for displaying and analyzing constraint networks. This paper describes the debugging facilities of CNV, and presents a new algorithm for enumerating all of the ways that SkyBlue could maintain a set of constraints.

1 Introduction

A multi-way local propagation constraint is represented by a set of *method* procedures that read the values of some of the constrained variables, and calculate values for the remaining constrained variables that satisfy the constraint. A set of such constraints can be maintained by a constraint solver that chooses one method for each constraint such that no variable is set by more than one selected method (i.e., there no *method conflicts*). If there are no cycles in the selected methods, the solver can sort and execute them to satisfy all of the constraints. For example, given the constraint $A + B = C$ (represented by three methods $C := A + B$, $A := C - B$, and $B := C - A$) and the constraint $C + D = E$ (represented by three similar methods), the two constraints could be satisfied by executing the methods $C := A + B$ and $E := C + D$ in order.

For a given set of constraints, it may not be possible to choose methods for all constraints so there are no method conflicts, or there may be multiple ways to select methods. The theory of constraint hierarchies [1] offers a way to control the behavior of a constraint solver in these situations. Given a constraint hierarchy, a set of constraints where each constraint has an associated *strength*, a constraint solver can leave weaker constraints unsatisfied in order to solve stronger constraints. If there are multiple ways to select methods, the programmer can control the solver by adding weak *stay* constraints to variables whose values should not be changed. Different strength stay constraints can be used to specify relative preferences for which variables should be constant.

SkyBlue is an incremental constraint solver that uses local propagation to maintain a set of constraints as individual constraints are added and removed [8, 7]. If all of the constraints cannot be satisfied, SkyBlue leaves weaker constraints unsatisfied in order to satisfy stronger constraints (maintaining a constraint hierarchy). SkyBlue is a successor to DeltaBlue [5, 10] that supports two additional features: (1) SkyBlue maintains cycles of constraints by calling external solvers, and (2) SkyBlue supports multi-output methods (methods that set multiple output variables). These features make SkyBlue more useful for constructing user interfaces, since cycles of constraints can occur frequently in user interface applications and multi-output methods are necessary to represent certain constraints. The Multi-Garnet package [9] uses the SkyBlue solver to add support for multi-way constraints and constraint hierarchies to the Garnet user interface toolkit [6].

SkyBlue maintains a set of constraints by constructing a *method graph* (or *mgraph*) consisting of a set of constraints along with the selected method for each of the constraints. If a constraint has a selected method in an mgraph, it is *enforced* in the mgraph, otherwise it is *unenforced*. When a constraint is added or removed, SkyBlue incrementally updates the mgraph by enforcing stronger constraints and unenforcing weaker constraints. More formally, SkyBlue constructs a *method-graph-better* (or *MGB*) mgraph, where *mg* is an MGB mgraph if it has no method conflicts and for each unenforced constraint *cn* in *mg* there exists no conflict-free mgraph for the same constraints where *cn* is enforced and all of the enforced constraints of *mg* with the same or stronger strength as *cn* are enforced. By constructing MGB mgraphs, SkyBlue ensures that weaker constraints are left unenforced if necessary to enforce stronger constraints. However, weaker constraints can influence which selected methods are used to enforce stronger constraints. SkyBlue can handle any number of different constraint strengths. Examples in this paper use the strengths *max, strong, medium, weak* (strongest to weakest).

As constraint solvers have been applied to larger problems it has become clear that there is a need for constraint network debugging tools. In order to debug a constraint network, the programmer needs tools to examine the constraint network, determine why a given solution is produced, and change the network to produce the desired solution. The CNV system allows the programmer to constructing graphical user interfaces based on constraints (maintained by SkyBlue), and debug the constraint networks. The remainder of this paper describes the debugging facilities provided by CNV, and presents a new algorithm for generating all MGB mgraphs for a set of constraints.

2 Debugging Constraint Networks

Figure 1 shows two pictures of a simple user interface constructed using CNV. In Fig. 1a, the two horizontal lines are lined up. In Fig. 1b, the mouse has moved the left endpoint of the bottom line, and the right endpoint is moved by the same amount. This figure also displays the constraints relating the variables $x1$ and $x2$, the X-coordinates of the two ends of the bottom horizontal line, to the variable *width*, the difference between the two X-coordinates. The constraint $x1=mouse.X$ sets $x1$ to the X-coordinate of the mouse position. The *medium* stay constraint (displayed with an anchor symbol) on *width* prevents the solver from changing this variable. The *weak* stay constraint on $x2$ is not enforced, since the solver cannot enforce this constraint without unenforcing a stronger constraint. As the mouse is moved, the width of the line is kept constant.

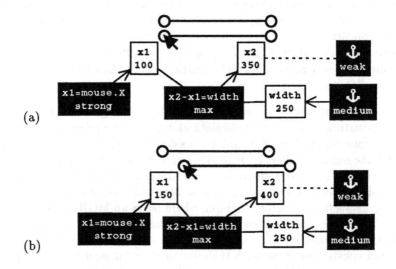

Fig. 1. Moving the left endpoint of a constant-width horizontal line.

The constraint diagrams present information about the constraints (black boxes) and variables (white boxes) including names, constraint strengths and variable values. The connection between the graphic objects and the variables specifying their positions (such as $x1$) is shown by positioning the variables next to their graphics. These diagrams also show how each variable value is calculated: the arrows indicate the variables currently determined by the selected method of each constraint. If the constraint is not enforced by any method, the lines to its variables are dashed (i.e., the stay constraint on $x2$). It is possible to explain the derivation of a variable value by examining all of constraints and variables *upstream* of the given variable.

CNV can be used to construct complex constraint graphs, and experiment with the behavior of the user interface as constraints are added and removed.

This system includes a set of debugging tools that analyze the constraint network, and present information about disjoint subgraphs, directed cycles, or directed paths between two variables. A more sophisticated tool determines why a particular constraint is unenforced, identifying those stronger constraints that prevent the given constraint from being enforced. Similar tools have been developed for the QOCA toolkit [2] and the Geometric Constraint Engine [4]. The following sections describe a tool for examining the different possible MGB mgraphs that SkyBlye may produce, and presents a new algorithm for generating these mgraphs.

3   Examining Multiple MGB Method Graphs

When debugging a constraint network, the programmer may want to know whether the constraints specify a unique solution, or whether SkyBlue might produce different solutions at different times. Some constraint solvers can produce different possible solutions for a set of constraints, such as the CLP($\mathcal{R}$) system that generates symbolic expressions representing sets of multiple solutions, and produces alternate solutions upon backtracking [3]. Examining the different solutions can help the programmer understand the constraint network, and determine what constraints should be added to control the solver.

Given a hierarchy of multi-way local propagation constraints, there may be more than one possible MGB mgraph that SkyBlue could use to maintain the constraints. For example, consider the constraint network shown in Fig. 2a. In this situation, there are three ways for the solver to maintain the constraints: by keeping *width* constant and moving the line (2a), keeping $x2$ constant and moving the two endpoints inward (2b), or keeping $x3$ constant and solving the cycle of linear constraints to position $x2$ between $x1$ and $x3$ (2c). The solver can be forced to choose one of these behaviors by adding stay constraints to variables that the user would prefer stay constant (2d).

In this example, it is easy to manually generate the possible MGB mgraphs. This is much more difficult for large constraint networks: it may not be clear whether there are *any* alternate MGB mgraphs. The following sections present an algorithm that enumerates all possible MGB mgraphs that SkyBlue could produce for a set of constraints. This algorithm systematically calls the SkyBlue solver to increase the strength of unenforced constraints, searching for alternate mgraphs where these constraints are enforced. SkyBlue incrementally updates the current MGB mgraph as a constraint is added, removed, or has its strength changed, so it is practical to change constraint strengths repeatedly. The following sections present this algorithm in stages. First, an algorithm is presented for generating all sets of constraints that can be simultaneously enforced in an MGB mgraph. Then, this algorithm is extended to generate all MGB mgraphs.

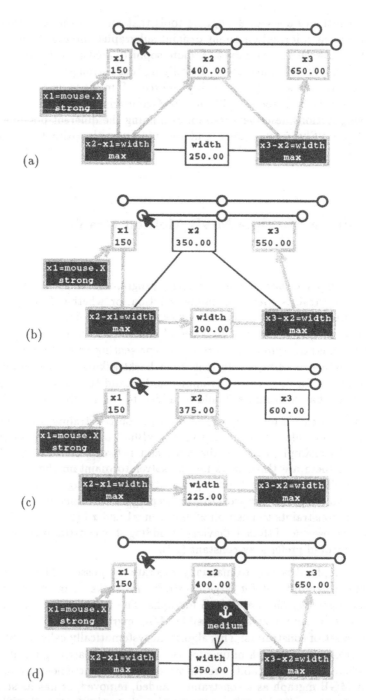

Fig. 2. Moving the left endpoint of a horizontal line with a midpoint. The top line shows the initial positions of the three points. Constraints and variables downstream of the mouse constraint are highlighted.

4 MGB Enforced Sets

The *enforced set* (or *E-set*) of an mgraph is the set of constraints that are enforced in the mgraph. The E-set of an MGB mgraph are known as an MGB E-set. For example, Fig. 3 shows the two possible MGB mgraphs for three constraints. These mgraphs have E-sets of $\{C1, C2\}$ and $\{C2, C3\}$ respectively. Sometimes it is useful to speak of the E-set for the constraints with a particular strength. For example, Fig. 3a has a *strong* E-set of $\{C2\}$, and a *weak* E-set of $\{C1\}$.

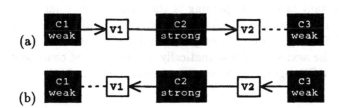

Fig. 3. Two MGB mgraphs with different MGB E-sets.

Note that no MGB E-set for a set of constraints can be a proper subset of another MGB E-set. Suppose that e_1 and e_2 are the E-sets for two MGB mgraphs mg_1 and mg_2 for the same set of constraints. If e_1 were a proper subset of e_2, this would imply that every constraint enforced in mg_1 is enforced in mg_2, and mg_1 contains at least one unenforced constraint that is enforced in mg_2, hence mg_1 would not be an MGB mgraph.

5 Pinning Constraints

Consider an MGB mgraph for a set of constraints. If all of the constraints are enforced, then there is only one possible MGB E-set for these constraints. If some of the constraints are unenforced, then there may be other MGB mgraphs for the constraints where some of the currently-unenforced constraints are enforced and other currently-enforced constraints are unenforced. The question is how to generate these mgraphs.

Suppose that we start with the MGB mgraph of Fig. 3a. All of the *strong* constraints are enforced, so all MGB mgraphs for these constraints will have a strong E-set of $\{C2\}$. Consider the unenforced *weak* constraint $C3$. Suppose that we changed the strength of $C3$ to be slightly stronger than *weak*. In this case, $C3$ would be enforced and $C1$ would be unenforced, leading to the mgraph in Fig. 4 (the only MGB mgraph for the modified constraints). This mgraph has an E-set of $\{C2, C3\}$, the same as Fig. 3b.

For each constraint strength *str*, define the *pin-strength* of *str* as another strength that is slightly stronger than *str* and weaker than the next stronger

Fig. 4. Increasing the strength of $C3$ to produce a different E-set.

constraint strength. The act of changing the strength of a constraint to its pin-strength is called "pinning" the constraint. Pinning different constraints can produce MGB mgraphs with different E-sets, as in Fig. 4.

An important fact about pinning is that, no matter what combination of constraints are pinned, the selected methods in the resulting MGB mgraph will specify an MGB mgraph for the original (unpinned) constraints. The algorithm described in the next section systematically pins unenforced constraints to generate different MGB mgraphs for the original constraints, and collects their E-sets.

6 Generating All MGB E-Sets

Figure 5 presents pseudocode that generates all of the MGB E-sets for a set of constraints. All global variables in the pseudocode begin and end with an asterisk. All other variables are local to their procedures. The procedure **get_esets** initializes global variables containing a list of the constraints we are interested in (***cns***), a list of the collected E-sets (***esets***), and a procedure to be called to save each E-set (***save_proc***). In this case ***save_proc*** is set to the procedure **save_eset**, which adds the E-set for the current mgraph to ***esets*** if it isn't there already. After setting the global variables, **get_esets** calls **pin_cns**, which pins different combinations of constraints, calling ***save_proc*** to process each of the resulting MGB mgraphs.

Most of the work happens in the recursive procedure **pin_cns**. During any call to **pin_cns**, it is processing the set of constraints at a single strength level. The arguments **pinned**, **unpinned** and **cns** are the sets of constraints at the current strength level that have been pinned, left unpinned, and have not been processed. The argument **weaker_cns** contains weaker constraints to be processed later. If **cns** contains any unenforced constraints, one is chosen (**cn**) and **pin_cns** recurses to investigate mgraphs where **cn** is not pinned. When that recursive call returns, **cn** is pinned. If **cn** can be enforced along with all of the other pinned constraints, then **pin_cns** recurses to investigate mgraphs where **cn** is pinned. Finally we unpin **cn**, restoring its original strength.

If there are no unenforced constraints in **cns**, then we have finished processing the constraints at this strength level. Now we are ready to processes the weaker constraints. To ensure that the current strength E-set doesn't change, all of the enforced constraints that haven't been pinned (**enforced_unpinned**) are pinned. Then **pin_cns** recurses, extracting the constraints with the next-weaker strength from **weaker_cns**. Note that when **pin_cns** is initially called from **get_esets** the first three arguments are all empty sets, so **pin_cns** just extracts the strongest constraints from **weaker_cns** and recurses.

```
get_esets(cns)
   *cns* := cns
   *esets* := {}
   *save_proc* := save_eset
   pin_cns({}, {}, {}, cns)
   return *esets*

save_eset()
   eset := collect list of all enforced constraints in *cns*
   add eset to *esets* if it is not already there

pin_cns(pinned, unpinned, cns, weaker_cns)
   If cns contains any unenforced constraints then
      cn := choose any unenforced cn in cns
      ;; generate e-sets with cn unpinned
      pin_cns(pinned, unpinned ∪ {cn}, cns - {cn}, weaker_cns)
      ;; generate e-sets with cn pinned
      pin(cn)
      If pinned ∪ {cn} are all enforced then
         pin_cns(pinned ∪ {cn}, unpinned, cns - {cn}, weaker_cns)
      unpin(cn)
   Else If weaker_cns is not empty then
      ;; pin all unpinned enforced constraints at current strength
      enforced_unpinned := all enforced constraints in unpinned ∪ cns
      For cn in enforced_unpinned do pin(cn)
      ;; process next weaker constraints
      next_strength := strongest strength of constraints in weaker_cns
      next_cns := collect list of all constraints in weaker_cns whose
                  strength is equal to next_strength
      pin_cns({}, {}, next_cns, weaker_cns - next_cns)
      ;; unpin constraints
      For cn in enforced_unpinned do unpin(cn)
   Else
      ;; all constraints processed: save current state
      call the procedure *save_proc*

pin(cn)
   cn.original_strength := cn.strength
   change_constraint_strength(cn, get_pin_strength(cn.strength))

unpin(cn)
   change_constraint_strength(cn, cn.original_strength)
```

Fig. 5. Pseudocode to generate all MGB E-sets for cns.

When all of the constraints have been processed, *save_proc* is called to save information about the current MGB mgraph. The procedure get_esets sets this to save_eset, which saves the current MGB E-set.

7   Why get_esets Generates All E-Sets

Since get_esets only modifies the mgraph by pinning constraints, every E-set collected is a correct MGB E-set for the original constraints. To show that get_esets is correct, it is necessary to show that every possible E-set is generated. Suppose that this were not true, and there was a set of constraints cns with an MGB E-set E that was not generated by get_esets(cns). Consider the tree of recursive calls to pin_cns caused by get_esets(cns). Figure 6 shows part of such a tree, where first C1, and then C2, are found to be unenforced, and then either left unpinned or pinned during different recursive calls.

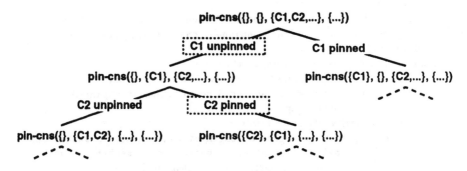

Fig. 6. Partial tree of recursive calls to pin_cns.

Consider tracing down this tree, following each branch that pins a constraint in E, and each branch that leaves unpinned a constraint that is not in E. For example, if E contained C2 and did not contain C1, one would follow the branches with boxed labels in Fig. 6. Note that every time a constraint in E is pinned it *must* be possible to enforce it along with the other pinned constraints, since E is the E-set for an MGB mgraph, so all of the constraints in E must be simultaneously enforcible. Eventually, you will reach a leaf of the tree, and *save_proc* will be called to process the current mgraph, call it mg.

We claim that the E-set of mg is exactly E. First, all of the constraints in E that were found unenforced in cns and pinned must be enforced in mg. Consider some other constraint cn that is in E but was not found unenforced in cns. It must not have been removed from cns, since the only way constraints are removed from cns is when they are considered for pinning, and if this had happened then cn would have been explicitly pinned. Since it wasn't removed from cns, then it must have been enforced when that strength level was processed, and hence it was pinned when going to the next strength level. Therefore, it must be enforced in the final mgraph mg, and all of the constraints in E must be enforced in mg. Finally, consider some constraint cn' that is not in E. If it was enforced in mg, then this would be an MGB mgraph where all of the constraints in E plus another constraint cn' are enforced, in which case E would not be the E-set of an MGB mgraph. Thus, we have shown that exactly those constraints in E are enforced in mg.

8   Generating E-Sets Multiple Times

The procedure **save_eset** adds the current E-set to the list ***esets*** only if it is not there already. This is necessary because **get_esets** may generate the same E-set multiple times if constraints have multi-output methods. For example, suppose **get_esets** is called on the three *strong* constraints $C1$, $C2$, and $C3$, whose current mgraph is shown in Fig. 7a. The clock diagram indicates that $C1$ has a single method which outputs to both $V1$ and $V2$ (this diagram is not shown for constraints with a single-output method outputting to each of their variables). If **get_esets** pins $C2$ and not $C3$, it produces the mgraph of Fig. 7b, and collects its E-set. On backtracking, if $C2$ is left unpinned, and $C3$ is pinned, it produces Fig. 7c, which has the same E-set.

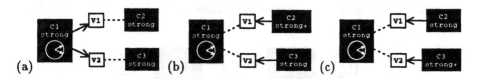

Fig. 7. get_esets may collect the same E-set multiple times.

9   Collecting Some MGB Method Graphs by Adding Stay Constraints

It would be possible to modify **save_eset** to collect the enforced constraints along with their current selected methods when it is called within **get_esets**. If the given set of constraints had exactly one MGB mgraph for each MGB E-set, this would collect all of the MGB mgraphs. However, if there are multiple MGB mgraphs that have the same E-set (Fig. 8), there is no guarantee that they would all be generated by **get_esets**.

One thing that distinguishes different MGB mgraphs with the same E-set is the sets of variables that are determined and undetermined. This observation can be used to generate these different MGB mgraphs: Given a set of constraints cns, let $v\text{-}weak$ be a strength weaker than any of these constraints. For each of the variables that can be determined by any of the constraints' methods (the

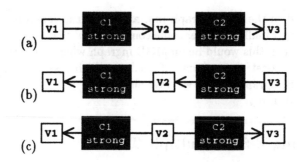

Fig. 8. Three possible MGB mgraphs for $\{C1, C2\}$.

potential outputs of the constraints), add a new stay constraint with strength *v-weak*. Consider an MGB mgraph for this extended set of constraints, *cns'*. The selected methods for *cns* in the extended mgraph define an MGB mgraph for *cns* alone, since none of the *v-weak* stay constraints can affect which stronger constraints are enforced, but they can affect the selected methods used to enforce stronger constraints. Calling `pin_cns(`*cns'*`)` will pin all of the constraints including the *v-weak* stay constraints, generating different MGB mgraphs for *cns*. For example, Fig. 9 shows how extra *v-weak* stay constraints added to the constraints from Fig. 8 can be pinned to generate the mgraphs in Fig. 8a and 8c.

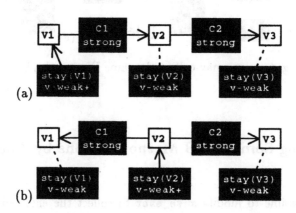

Fig. 9. Pinning extra stay constraints to generate different MGB mgraphs.

Figure 10 presents pseudocode that creates the extra variable stay constraints and passes all of these constraints to `pin_cns`, which will generate different MGB mgraphs for `cns`. Note that `*save_proc*` is set to the procedure `save_mgraph`, so it will be called to save the current mgraph (including selected methods) within `pin_cns`. The set `*cns*` does not include the extra variable stay constraints, since we are only concerned with collecting the mgraphs for the original constraints.

```
get_some_mgb_mgraphs(cns)
    *cns* := cns
    *mgraphs* := {}
    *save_proc* := save_mgraph
    ;; add stays to output variables
    var_stay_strength := any strength weaker than all constraints in cns
    potential_outputs := a list of all potential output variables for cns
    output_var_stays := a stay constraint with strength var_stay_strength
                        for each var in potential_outputs
    For cn in output_var_stays do add_constraint(cn)
    ;; generate mgraphs for constraints, including extra stays
    pin_cns({}, {}, {}, cns ∪ output_var_stays)
    ;; remove added stays
    For cn in output_var_stays do remove_constraint(cn)
    return *mgraphs*

save_mgraph()
    mgraph := For cn in *cns* collect cn and its current selected mt
    add mgraph to *mgraphs* if it is not already there
```

Fig. 10. Pseudocode to generate some MGB mgraphs for cns.

10   Collecting All MGB Method Graphs by Adding Method Variables

There are two situations where **get_some_mgb_mgraphs** may not generate all possible MGB mgraphs for a set of constraints: (1) There are constraints with "subset methods," where the outputs of one constraint method are a subset of the outputs of another method for the same constraint. This is rare, but it is not prohibited by the definition of multi-way local propagation constraints. For example, the constraint in Fig. 11a has one method that outputs to $V7$ and $V8$, and another method that outputs to $V8$. If the constraint solver always chooses the second method, **get_some_mgb_mgraphs** will never generate an mgraph containing the first method. (2) There are directed cycles of methods. The constraints in Fig. 11b have two MGB mgraphs, one with a directed cycle in each direction. Pinning extra stay constraints on the variables will not choose one mgraph over the other.

Given cycles or subset methods, it is possible to generate all possible mgraphs using the pseudocode of Fig. 12. This code modifies every constraint that has more than one method, creating an extra variable for each constraint method, and adding it as an output to all of the *other* methods of the constraint. Applying this to Fig. 11b produces Fig. 11c, where the new variable $X1$ is only set when $C1$ is enforced with a method other than its second method (setting $V2$ and $X2$). When the modified constraints are passed to **get_some_mgb_mgraphs**, and *v-weak* stays are added to these extra variables, pinning these extra stays will

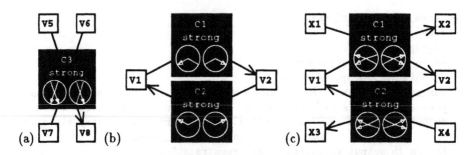

Fig. 11. (a) A constraint with subset methods. (b) A method graph with a directed method cycle. (c) Adding extra variables to (b).

try all of the methods of each constraint, if they are allowed in an MGB mgraph. Note that constraints with only a single method do not need to have any extra variables added, since such a constraint's single method must be used whenever the constraint is enforced.

```
get_all_mgb_mgraphs(cns)
   ;; add extra variables to methods
   For all constraints cn in cns with more than one method do
      remove_constraint(cn)
      For mt in cn.methods do
         v := create a new variable
         add v to cn.variables
         add v to the outputs of all of cn's methods except mt
      add_constraint(cn)
   ;; add extra stays to variables, and generate mgraphs
   mgraphs := get_some_mgb_mgraphs(cns)
   ;; remove extra variables from constraints and methods
   For all constraints cn in cns with more than one method do
      remove_constraint(cn)
      restore cn.variables
      restore outputs for all of cn's methods
      add_constraint(cn)
   return mgraphs
```

Fig. 12. Pseudocode to generate all MGB mgraphs for cns.

The pseudocode removes all of the constraints before adding the additional variables to the methods, and then re-adds the constraints. Likewise, the constraints are removed before removing these additional variables. This would not be necessary if the constraint solver had an entry for incrementally modifying methods.

11 Conclusions

This paper has described some of the debugging tools included within the CNV system for interactively constructing constraint-based user interfaces, and presented a new algorithm for generating all of the MGB mgraphs for a set of constraints. The different algorithms described in this paper may be useful at different points during debugging. The procedure `get_esets` can be used to determine whether a given constraint is always enforced, or never enforced. If there are no subset methods and the programmer doesn't care about the directions of cycles, `get_some_mgb_mgraphs` can be called instead of `get_all_mgb_mgraphs`.

These algorithms call the SkyBlue constraint solver to manipulate the constraints. Therefore, any future performance improvements to SkyBlue (or other algorithms that maintain MGB mgraphs) will directly improve the performance of these algorithms.

In the future we want to continue developing new debugging tools, improving the facilities for invoking them and presenting the results of their analyses. One area of interest is finding better ways of examining a set of MGB method graphs, such as automatically partitioning them into subclasses depending on which variables are constant. Given two mgraphs, it may not be obvious how they differ. Tools have been created for comparing two or more mgraphs, highlighting the similarities and differences.

Acknowledgements

This work was supported in part by National Science Foundation grants IRI-9102938, IRI-9302249, and CCR-9402551, and by Academic Equipment Grants from Sun Microsystems.

References

1. Alan Borning, Bjorn Freeman-Benson, and Molly Wilson. Constraint Hierarchies. *Lisp and Symbolic Computation*, 5(3):223–270, September 1992.
2. Richard Helm, Tien Huynh, Kim Marriott, and John Vlissides. An Object-Oriented Architecture for Constraint-Based Graphical Editing. In *Proceedings of the Third Eurographics Workshop on Object-oriented Graphics*, Champery, Switzerland, October 1992. Also will be published in *Advances in Object-Oriented Graphics II*, Springer-Verlag, 1993.
3. Joxan Jaffar, Spiro Michaylov, Peter Stuckey, and Roland Yap. The CLP($\mathcal{R}$) Language and System. *ACM Transactions on Programming Languages and Systems*, 14(3):339–395, July 1992.
4. Walid T. Keirouz, Glenn A. Kramer, and Jahir Pabon. Exploiting Constraint Dependency Information for Debugging and Explanation. In Saraswat and van Hentenryck, editors, *Proceedings of the 1993 Workshop on Principles and Practice of Constraint Programming*. MIT Press, 1994. To appear.
5. John Maloney. *Using Constraints for User Interface Construction*. PhD thesis, Department of Computer Science and Engineering, University of Washington, August 1991. Published as UW CSE Technical Report 91-08-12.

6. Brad A. Myers, Dario A. Giuse, Roger B. Dannenberg, Brad Vander Zanden, David S. Kosbie, Ed Pervin, Andrew Mickish, and Philippe Marchal. Garnet: Comprehensive Support for Graphical, Highly-Interactive User Interfaces. *IEEE Computer*, 23(11):71–85, November 1990.

7. Michael Sannella. *Constraint Satisfaction and Debugging for Interactive User Interfaces*. PhD thesis, Department of Computer Science and Engineering, University of Washington, 1994.

8. Michael Sannella. The SkyBlue Constraint Solver and Its Applications. In Saraswat and van Hentenryck, editors, *Proceedings of the 1993 Workshop on Principles and Practice of Constraint Programming*. MIT Press, 1994. To appear.

9. Michael Sannella and Alan Borning. Multi-Garnet: Integrating Multi-Way Constraints with Garnet. Technical Report 92-07-01, Department of Computer Science and Engineering, University of Washington, September 1992.

10. Michael Sannella, John Maloney, Bjorn Freeman-Benson, and Alan Borning. Multi-way versus One-way Constraints in User Interfaces: Experience with the DeltaBlue Algorithm. *Software—Practice and Experience*, 23(5):529–566, May 1993.

Inferring 3-dimensional constraints with DEVI

Suresh Thennarangam
suresh@iss.nus.sg
Institute of Systems Science
National University of Singapore,
Heng Mui Keng terrace,
Singapore 0511

Gurminder Singh
gsingh@iss.nus.sg
Institute of Systems Science
National University of Singapore,
Heng Mui Keng terrace,
Singapore 0511

Abstract

Constraints can be used to specify and maintain spatial relationships among objects in a geometric design. In the 3-D geometric design domain, the diversity of possible relationships among objects makes it difficult for the designer to specify useful or intended relationships in a productive and intuitive manner. We have built a constraint-based 3D geometric editor called DEVI that infers possible or intended relationships among objects in a design. DEVI's database of relationships between design primitives can be extended using a descriptive language which enables the developer to specify a set of rules made up of conditions to be satisfied and inferences to be made. Each rule has two parts; the first is a boolean condition wherein a certain situation is described; the second part is an instruction to the system to infer the specified constraint (or set of constraints) if the boolean condition is true.

1 Introduction

Constraints have proven useful in automatically keeping spatial relationships satisfied among geometric objects in a geometric design. They alleviate much of the tedium involved in making small changes and then propagating their effect.

Constraint-based geometric-design is not a new area. Nelson's Juno [Nelson85] is a 2D drawing system that integrated a hierarchical constraint-based geometric specification language with a WYSIWYG drawing editor; modifying a design interactively, implicitly changes the text of the program describing the design. Rossignac's CSG system [Rossignac86] allows the user to specify models in terms of unevaluated constraints that are evaluated sequentially during the construction process in a user-specified order. Constraints are evaluated by performing rigid-body motions. In their paper, Nguyen *et.al.* [Nguyen91] describe a generic model for representing polyhedra as a network of nodes and constraints. Van Emmerik's solid modeling system [vanEmmerik90] is an example of a constraint-based modeling system with a graphical front-end that allows the specification of constraints via popup and cascading menus.

Constraints thus represent a significant advantage in geometric-design systems. To gain this advantage, designers have to invest extra effort to specify constraints. Geometric-design systems usually allow a fixed number of pre-defined relationships among the geometric objects. In a typical interactive geometric design environment, the designer would create the geometric objects using menus, positioning and alignment tools, and tell the system how he wants them constrained to each other. The designer normally knows, in advance, where the new geometric object that he is creating should be located and how it should be related to its' neighbours. He therefore tends to create a situation close to the end-result that he has in mind.

To make the process of specifying relationships simpler, earlier systems have used some of the following approaches. VanWyk's automatic drawing beautifier [vanWyk85] looks at a design to check if any predefined relationships exist and makes them persistent. This approach is not interactive. Converge [Sistare90] provides a "locus" input mode for constraints wherein newly created geometric objects are automatically constrained in a desired way to a specified existing geometric object. It is an improvement over the previous approach but is still rather limiting because it forces the user to switch modes constantly and is not a general solution. A more general approach is to use geometry context, users' actions and knowledge of geometric objects and their possible relationships to infer what the user is trying to do. Variations of this approach have been used successfully by a few systems, primarily in the two-dimensional domain. Peridot [Myers86] uses the 'demonstration' metaphor to help specify constraints. It infers the relationships of the users' actions to user-interface elements during a demonstration sequence, and generates code to handle this action in a real situation. Chimera [Kurlander93] infers constraints from multiple snapshots of scenes — snapshots are taken of an initial scene configuration and additional snapshots are taken after the scene has been edited into other valid configurations; the constraints that are satisfied in all of the snapshots are then applied to scene objects. Metamouse is a 2-D drawing program [Maulsby89] that induces picture-editing procedures from execution traces of the users actions at work — it performs a localized analysis of changes in spatial relationships to isolate constraints and matches action sequences to build a state graph that describes what it has learned. On detecting a repetition, it uses the state graph to predict further actions. Briar [Gleicher92] augments snap-dragging [Bier86] by making the relationships persistent. Rockit [Karsenty92] also uses augmented snap-dragging and maintains a database of relationships and a static inference-rule base — it allows the user to dynamically change the conditions that determine which rules to execute.

The last approach has a limitation: it is difficult to extend and customize. We propose to extend this method by allowing the designer to write inference rules in a descriptive language. Each rule has two parts; the first is a boolean condition wherein a certain situation is described in terms of geometric objects and the geometric constraints relating them; the second part of the rule is an instruction to the system to infer a specified constraint (or set of constraints) if the boolean condition is satisfied. These rules are applied in response to interactive events like creation or perturbation of geometric objects.

In this paper we describe in detail how DEVI infers constraints using it's knowledge database and how we have augmented it with our inference-rule approach. For a general introduction to DEVI, please see [Thennarangam93].

2 DEVI's Approach

DEVI is a constraint-based, interactive 3D geometric editing environment that uses flexible user-interface techniques to simplify the task of editing 3D geometry (see Figure 1). DEVI provides an interpretive language to specify geometric objects and the constraints between them. It infers constraints among geometric objects as they are created and manipulated. These inferred constraints subsequently become persistent and are maintained by the system. In order to help understand and debug the design in a graphical fashion, DEVI presents the network of constraints and geometry in a constraint-network browser that is useful in determining relationships and debugging the constraint network (see Figure 1).

DEVI organizes its' constraint network as a partitioned directed graph. When an event occurs in the interactive geometry editor, DEVI quickly isolates the portion of the design that will be affected by the event. By default, DEVI only tries to infer constraints between selected objects and newly created or newly perturbed objects — a newly created object is added to the current selection. This limits the number of inferences the system has to consider. Experience with the Druid UIMS [Singh90] shows that designers tend to create designs incrementally — they usually create related parts of the design one after the other, rather than randomly. DEVI exploits this fact. In case it makes more than one inference, it prompts the user to make a choice. This scheme also serves as an aid in case the designer forgets to specify some relationships that he had intended to.

Consider the process of solving a network of constraints. DEVI's hybrid solver propagates known values about the constraint graph until it satisfies each constraint node. Failing to do so, it resorts to an iterative approach, using Newton-Raphson's iteration to solve the set of algebraic functions that describe the constraint network.

A minimization function is defined for each constraint. When this function has a value close to zero, that instance of the constraint is considered satisfied. In fact, DEVI calls the algebraic solver with a single constraint as an argument, demanding only a single iteration of the solver, when it is propagating values in the constraint network; the solver tells DEVI whether the constraint is satisfied or not. DEVI uses this property to infer constraints. Consider a scenario where we want to infer a constraint between geometric objects A and B. Assume that constraints of type C_1 and C_2 can exist between the geometric classes of A and B. We compute the minimization function values for those two classes of constraints i.e. $f_{C_1}(A, B)$ and $f_{C_2}(A, B)$. We choose those values that are smaller than some threshold value. If there is more than one such value then the user is asked to make a choice.

For the sake of generality and robustness of the solving process, one can have the minimization function return an euclidean value that is representative of the constraint. See [Sutherland80] and [Sistare90] for further discussion on this point. For example, to constrain a point to lie on a plane, one measures the distance of the point to the plane. Algebraically, this can be expressed by substituting the point in the equation of the plane. With more complicated constraints, it is not easy to see this relationship.

Consider another constraint that fixes the angle between two planes A and B to be θ. Let $k_A = |n_A|, k_B = |n_B|$, where n_A and n_B are unit normal vectors to planes A and B respectively. We could express the function we want to minimize as follows:

$$f_\theta = \sqrt{k_A^2 + k_B^2 - 2k_A k_B \cos\theta} - |n_A - n_B|$$

The geometrical interpretation of this equation is as follows:

$\sqrt{k_A^2 + k_B^2 - 2k_A k_B \cos\theta}$ is the desired length between the tips of the vectors n_A and n_B, when they are constrained at an angle θ, and $|n_A - n_B|$ is the current length. Obviously, when this value reaches zero, the constraint is satisfied.

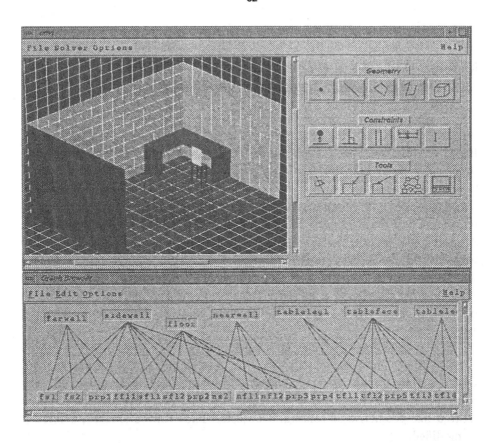

Figure 1: DEVI's User-Interface - The top-left window is the design work-area. To the right are the geometry, constraint and tools palettes. The window at the bottom depicts the constraint-network browser. The user can edit and manipulate constraints using the browser.

The problem with this approach is how to choose an appropriate threshold value, which is essentially a real number. This number might not have much intuitive value. Since the designer may not be able to relate too well to these seemingly obscure numbers, he might find it difficult to customize the inferencing process. All he has are a set of real numbers that he can manipulate back and forth. The significance of this number is determined by how the system translates geometric constraints into algebraic equations that can be minimized.

Our method uses familiar terminology like distance, angle etc. Although the solver eventually works with vectors and real numbers, the designer thinks in terms of concepts like angles, adjacencies, equalities and distances. He might want, for example, to specify that angles close to 45° should become 45° angles because, presumably, he has a lot of 45° angle situations in his design and he does not want to go through all the trouble of explicitly constraining them each time.

Here is an example of a rule written in this language:

```
RULE Rp( POLYGON p1, POLYGON p2)
   IF  ( (ABS ( ANGLE ( p1, p2 ) - 45 )) <= 5 )
   THEN
       INFER CONSTRAINT FIXANGLE ( p1, p2, 45 );
```

Based on this rule, the system automatically constrains the planes of two polygons to lie at 45° to each other if it detects that the angle between them is anywhere between 40° and 50°. The magic number 5 here represents the desired angular tolerance and it is easy to understand exactly what it represents and the consequences of changing this number to suit preferences. A significant advantage of this approach is that it provides a way to limit the problem of "over-generalization" [Bos92] with inferencing systems — that they insist on making inferences that the user did not intend.

The syntax of DEVI's inference rules is simple and the effort involved in creating new rules is well worth the effort in terms of the productivity gained from it.

DEVI stores inference rules in memory; for each inference rule, a record is maintained that consists of it's name, it's parameter types and a parse tree that is evaluated each time the rule is triggered. A rule is triggered if it's parameters match with that of the current event. Inference rules are thus treated like geometric or constraint objects. They can be created, deleted or modified.

3   Implementation

DEVI has been implemented in the C++3.0 programming language. It runs on a Silicon Graphics Indigo Elan workstation running IRIX 4.0.5F and the X11R4 Windows system. It uses the Motif 1.1 toolkit and IrisGL graphics libraries.

4   Discussion

We have presented a system that enhances the ease and functionality of using constraints in a geometric-design environment. DEVI uses constraint-inferencing to ease the effort involved in specifying constraints in the 3-D geometry domain. It achieves this by using it's knowledge of geometric objects and their possible relationships. It also provides a powerful means to extend the inferencing process by allowing the user to write inference rules. To our knowledge, DEVI is the first system that infers spatial constraints in the 3-D geometric domain and provides the user with the means to extend and customize the system's constraint-inferencing capability.

Future work on DEVI will concentrate on making it more conversational, especially offering advice on the degree of constraint to the designer and detecting and warning of redundant and circular constraints. Another interesting use of inference rules would be to describe unwanted, perhaps overconstrained or circular situations. The system could use these rules to block the creation of new constraints that would cause such undesirable situations. We would also like to provide a graphical way to compose and edit inference rules. At present, they have to be written by hand and do represent some effort.

References

[Bos92]   Edwin Bos. Some virtues and limitations of action inferring interfaces. In *UIST 92*, pages 79–88. UIST, ACM, November 1992.

[Bier86]   Eric Bier and Maureen Stone. Snap-dragging. In *Computer Graphics*, pages 234–240, 1986.

[Gleicher92] Michael Gleicher. Integrating constraints and direct manipulation. In *1992 Symposium on Interactive 3D Graphics*, pages 171–174, March 1992.

[Kurlander93] David Kurlander and Steven Feiner. Inferring constraints from multpile snapshots. *ACM Transactions on Graphics*, 12(4):277–304, October 1993.

[Myers86] Brad A. Myers and William Buxton. Creating highly interactive and graphical user interfaces by demonstration. In *SIGGRAPH '86*, volume 20, pages 249–258. ACM, 1986.

[Maulsby89] David L. Maulsby, Ian H. Witten, and Kenneth A. Kittlitz. Metamouse: specifying graphical procedures by example. In *Computer Graphics*, volume 23, pages 127–136. ACM, July 1989.

[Nelson85] G. Nelson. Juno:a constraint-based graphics system. In *SIGGRAPH'85*, number 3. ACM, 1985.

[Nguyen91]   Van-Duc Nguyen, Joseph L. Mundy, and Deepak Kapur.
                  Modeling generic polyhedral objects with constraints. In
                  Computer vision and pattern recognition, pages 479–485,
                  Hawaii, 1991. IEEE.

[Rossignac86]   Jaroslaw R. Rossignac. Constraints in constructive solid
                  geometry. In *Workshop on interactive 3D graphics*, pages
                  93–110, Chapel Hill, North Carolina, 1986. ACM SIG-
                  GRAPH.

[Sistare90]   Steven Sistare. *A Graphical Editor for Three-Dimensional
                  Constraint-Based Geometric Modeling*. PhD thesis, Har-
                  vard University, Cambridge,Massachusetts, 1990.

[Karsenty92]   C Weikart S. Karsenty, J Landay. Inferring graphical con-
                  straints with rockit. PRL Research report 17, Digital Cor-
                  poration, March 1992.

[Singh90]   Gurminder Singh, ChunHong Kok, and TengYe Ngan.
                  Druid: A system for demonstrational rapid user interface
                  development. In *UIST 90*, pages 167–177. UIST, ACM,
                  October 1990.

[Sutherland80]   Ivan Sutherland. Sketchpad: A man-machine graphical
                  communication system. In *Tutorial and selected readings
                  in interactive computer graphics*, pages 2–19. IEEE Com-
                  puter Society, 1980.

[Thennarangam93] Suresh Thennarangam and Gurminder Singh. Devi:
                  A 3-d constraint-based geometry editor that infers con-
                  straints. In Tat-Seng Chua and Tosiyasu L. Kunii, editors,
                  First International Conference on Multi-Media Modeling,
                  volume 1, pages 45–56. World Scientific Pte. Ltd, Novem-
                  ber 1993.

[vanEmmerik90]   Maarten van Emmerik. A system for interactive graphi-
                  cal moedling with three-dimensional constraints. In *Eu-
                  rographics '90*, pages 361–376, 1990.

[vanWyk85]   C. van Wyk. An automatic beautifier for drawings and
                  illustrationss. In *SIGGRAPH'85*, number 3, pages 225–
                  234. ACM, 1985.

Beyond Finite Domains

Joxan Jaffar[1], Michael J. Maher[1],
Peter J. Stuckey[2] and Roland H.C. Yap[2,3]

[1] IBM T.J. Watson Research Center, P.O. Box 704,
Yorktown Heights, NY 10598, USA
[2] Dept. of Computer Science, Univ. of Melbourne,
Parkville, Vic 3052, Australia
[3] Dept. of Computer Science, Monash Univ.,
Clayton, Vic 3168, Australia

1   Introduction

A finite domain constraint system can be viewed as an linear integer constraint system in which each variable has an upper and lower bound. Finite domains have been used successfully in Constraint Logic Programming (CLP) languages, for example CHIP [4], to attack combinatorial problems such as resource allocation, digital circuit verification, etc. In these problems, finite domains allow a natural expression of the problem constraints because bounds on the problem variables are explicit in the problem. In other problems however, for example in temporal reasoning and some scheduling problems, there may not be natural bounds.

For these problems, a standard approach has been to use ad hoc bounds, giving rise to a two-fold problem. If a bound is too tight, then important solutions could be lost. If a bound is too loose, then significant inefficiency may result. This is because the algorithms used in finite domains work by propagating bounds on variables[4] until certain local consistency conditions (for example, arc-consistency [6, 14]) are achieved. These algorithms have the disadvantage that they reason about transitivity of inequalities in an iterative manner; for example, detecting that $x + 1 \leq y \leq x$, $0 \leq x \leq k$, $0 \leq y \leq k$ is unsatisfiable will require a cost proportional to k.

We thus suggest that it is worthwhile to go beyond finite domains to more general integer constraints. The issue then becomes the trade-off between greater expressiveness and potentially exponential-cost constraint solving. In this abstract, we propose a restricted class of integer constraints which can be solved more efficiently than in the general case, but which remains reasonably expressive. Furthermore, our algorithm can be extended easily to accommodate more general integer constraints, and it also combines well with traditional propagation-based methods. In this abstract, our presentation level is restricted to high-level algorithmic issues, and we do not address specific implementation considerations.

---

[4] And other domain information, in general.

2 Integer Constraints

What are the features we desire of an integer constraint domain and solver for a CLP system? Clearly soundness is essential. Completeness is obviously attractive, but there is no known sufficiently efficient solver. In fact, the satisfiability problem for nonlinear integer constraints is undecidable, so completeness is impossible to achieve. The problem is decidable for linear integer constraints, but it is NP-complete. Thus it appears that, in the context of a CLP system, a constraint solver that handles linear integer constraints will necessarily be either incomplete or inefficient. In practice, the choice taken by implementations is incompleteness and efficiency.

Given an incomplete solver, it is highly desirable to be able to characterize classes of constraints for which the solver is complete. On the practical front, the algorithm should be efficient, incremental and should support backtracking. Other operations that may be required are: the ability to detect groundness, implicit equalities and constraint entailment, the ability to extract constraints from disjunctive information, and the ability to eliminate variables (projection).

Propagation-based solvers (e.g. [6, 7]) are a prime example of the choice of an efficient algorithm which is relatively incomplete. These solvers are complete when each of the constraints they handle involves only a single variable. Call this the class of (linear) single-variable-per-inequality (SVPI) integer constraints [5]. In general, these propagation-based solvers handle constraints by extracting SVPI information from the interaction of non-SVPI constraints with SVPI constraints. These solvers satisfy most of the efficiency criteria mentioned above, but are incomplete and/or inefficient when handling problems with variables which are unbounded or have very large domains.

An obvious generalization of SVPI is the class of (linear) two-variable-per-inequality (TVPI) integer constraints. This class appears to be strictly simpler than the general problem (unlike the three-variable-per-inequality problem). There is a strong analogy here with the corresponding problem over the real numbers. There, current algorithms for deciding real TVPI constraints (e.g. [3]) are more efficient than current algorithms for arbitrary real linear constraint solving. Certainly integer TVPI constraints are far more expressive than SVPI constraints: for example we can encode constraints such as $x \bmod 11 \in \{1, 5\}$ by $x \geq 11y + 1, x \leq 11y + 5, x \geq 11z + 5, x \leq 11z + 12$. Surprisingly, solving integer TVPI constraints is also NP-complete [11]. However TVPI constraints seem more directly amenable to transitivity-based methods similar to those used for real constraints [1, 3, 20].

A class of constraints intermediate between SVPI and TVPI is the class of TVPI constraints $ax + by \leq d$ with unit coefficients, that is, $a, b \in \{-1, 0, 1\}$. We call these *unit TVPI constraints*. This class is considerably less expressive than the general class of TVPI constraints (for example, it cannot express mod-

---

[5] In this abstract we ignore disequality ($\neq$) constraints. However we note that the addition of disequalities such as $x \neq y$ to the class of SVPI constraints results in an NP-complete satisfiability problem (see, for example, [19]).

ulo constraints). However, the constraints are sufficient for many problems in temporal reasoning and scheduling.

Much earlier, Pratt [17] had considered a restricted class of unit TVPI constraints, those of the form $ax + d \leq by$, $a, b \in \{0, 1\}$, and presented an efficient algorithm for their solution. (Essentially, the integer and real satisfiability problems for these constraints are equivalent, and hence real-based methods are applicable.) However, unlike unit TVPI constraints, this class is not expressive enough for many problems. For example it cannot express the mutual exclusion $\neg(x \wedge y)$ which has a unit TVPI representation $x + y \leq 1, x \geq 0, y \geq 0$.

A generalization of this problem is due to Le Pape. He showed that for any totally ordered Abelian group on this class of constraints, a transitivity-based algorithm is complete [13]. The generalization of Pratt's class to permit any positive a, b can be solved using arc-consistency techniques, provided all variables have finite domains [6]. A subclass of Pratt's class is addressed in [18] and modulo constraints are added in [22].

Finally, we note several algorithms for linear integer constraints based, directly or indirectly, on projection. The relationship between this approach and transitivity-based methods is quite close, since transitive closure can be thought of as a cumulative form of projection with redundancy elimination. The SUP-INF method [2, 20] is complete over the real numbers, but the class of integer constraints on which it is complete is not clearly defined. The Omega test [15, 16] and the algorithm of [10] adapt Fourier's projection algorithm for real numbers to integers. The former computes a disjunction of constraints, whereas the latter accumulates additional conditions that must be satisfied. All these algorithms have essentially theorem-proving applications, and have proven useful in practice. However these applications involve small sets of constraints and it is not clear that the algorithms scale up to the size of problems expected in a CLP system. Furthermore, the algorithms are not incremental.

3 Unit TVPI Constraints

At the heart of our algorithm is a general framework for implementing transitive-closure in real TVPI inequalities. This is described in the next subsection, together with an adaptation of the framework to deal with integers. In the next section we present our algorithm as an instance of the (modified) transitive-closure algorithm.

3.1 A Transitive-Closure Algorithm

Shostak [20] gave an algorithm for satisfiability of real TVPI problems, not restricted to unit coefficients. In this algorithm every single variable inequality (i.e. bound) is converted to a two variable inequality by adding a dummy variable v_0 as follows: $x \leq 10$ becomes $x + 0v_0 \leq 10$. We give an incremental formulation of this algorithm, which maintains integer coefficients for integer problems, as follows.

A singleton set of TVPI constraints is *transitively closed*. Assume we are given a transitively closed set of TVPI constraints C and new TVPI constraint $c \equiv ax + by \leq d$. Let $C_x^a = \{c' : c' \equiv a'x + b'z \leq d', a \times a' < 0, c' \in C\}$ and let $C_{x,y}^a = \{c' : c' \equiv a'x + b'y \leq d', a \times a' < 0, c' \in C\}$. Define C_y^b and $C_{y,x}^b$ similarly. The *transitive closure* of $C \cup \{c\}$ is as follows (where $|x|$ denotes absolute value of x):

$$C \cup \{c\} \cup \{|a'|by + |a|ez \leq |a'|d + |a|d' : a'x + ez \leq d' \in C_x^a\}$$
$$\cup \{|b'|ax + |f|bt \leq |b|d'' + |f|d : b''y + ft \leq d'' \in C_y^b\}$$

$$\cup \{|ab''|ez + |a'b|ft \leq |a'b|d'' + |a'b''|d + |ab''|d' :$$
$$a'x + ez \leq d' \in C_x^a, b''y + ft \leq d'' \in C_y^b, (z \neq y \vee t \neq x)\}$$

$$\cup \{|(|a'|b + |a|b')|ft \leq |a'b''|d + |ab''|d' + |(|a'|b + |a|b')|d'' :$$
$$a'x + b'y \leq d' \in C_{x,y}^a, b''y + ft \leq d'' \in C_y^{|a'|b+|a|b'}, t \neq x\}$$

$$\cup \{|(|b''|a + |b|a'')|ez \leq |b''a'|d + |ba'|d'' + |(|b''|a + |b|a'')|d' :$$
$$b''y + a''x \leq d'' \in C_{y,x}^b, a'x + ez \leq d' \in C_x^{|b''|a+|b|a''}, z \neq y\}$$

The system $C \cup \{c\}$ is satisfiable (in the reals) iff the transitive closure does not contain a constraint of the form $0 \leq d$ where $d < 0$ [20].

The algorithm is immediately applicable to integer TVPI problems, but it is not complete. For example, consider $2x + 2y \leq 1, -2x + -2y \leq -1$. This is equivalent to $2x + 2y = 1$ which clearly has no integer solutions. The difficulties arises because these inequalities are equivalent (in the integers) to the tighter constraints $x + y \leq 0$ and $-x + -y \leq -1$.

We extend Shostak's algorithm by adding tightening constraints. The *tightening constraints* of C, denoted $tightening(C)$, are

$$\{a/k\,x + b/k\,y \leq d' \mid \begin{array}{l} ax + by \leq d \in C, gcd(\{|a|, |b|\}) = k, \\ k \neq 1, d' = \lfloor d/k \rfloor, d' < d/k\} \end{array}$$

For example $tightening(\{2x + 2y \leq 1, -2x + -2y \leq -1\})$ is $\{x + y \leq 0, -x - y \leq -1\}$. The tightening constraints give more information, so that we are more likely to find unsatisfiability.

Once we have determined tightening constraints, they need to be added and their transitive consequences found as above. By interleaving tightening and transitive closure we eventually obtain a transitively closed, tightened set of constraints, given the procedure terminates. In general the procedure will not terminate [5]. However, in the case of unit TVPI constraints it is easy to show that it does terminate.

Even when we restrict attention to cases where it terminates, the extended Shostak procedure is incomplete. The following system provides an example. It describes a unit cube with several edges cut off, so that no corner remains. It has no integer solution, but each real projection onto two variables has an integer solution.

$$0 \leq x, y, z \leq 1$$
$$4x + 3y \leq 6$$
$$-3x - 4y \leq -1$$
$$4x - 3z \leq 3$$
$$-3x + 4z \leq 3$$
$$4y - 3z \leq 3$$
$$-3y + 4z \leq 3$$

However, the algorithm is clearly "more complete" than bounds propagation which, in the TVPI case, is simply the application of transitivity to one TVPI constraint and one SVPI constraint (possibly with tightening).

Clearly the above procedure is naive in a number of ways. First, corresponding to tightening we also wish to divide the coefficients and constants of each constraint $ax + by \leq d$ so that $gcd(\{a, b\})$ is 1. Second, we can eliminate redundant constraints that are generated by the method. Detecting all redundant constraints is just as hard as the satisfaction problem, in general, but some kinds of redundancy are easy to detect. A constraint $exp \leq d$ is *quasi-syntactic redundant* [8] with respect to constraints C if a constraint of the form $exp \leq d'$ appears in C where $d' \leq d$. Quasi-syntactic redundancy is particularly easy to detect. More generally, we can remove any TVPI constraints involving x and y that are redundant (in the reals) with respect to the other x, y constraints. Deleting quasi-syntactic redundancy is not sufficient to ensure termination of the above procedure. We conjecture that, for integer TVPI with full real redundancy elimination with respect to each pair of variables, this procedure terminates.

3.2 The Unit TVPI Solver

When dealing with unit TVPI constraints, the transitive closure algorithm above produces new unit TVPI constraints, except in one case. Consider $C = \{x + y \leq 1, x + z \leq 2\}$ and the addition of $-y + -z \leq 0$. One of the consequences is $2x \leq 3$ which is not of the correct form. But we can always simplify such constraints to have unit coefficients, in this case $x \leq 1$. Moreover this is the only way in which tightening is possible.

For each pair of variables x, y there are at most four possible non quasi-syntactic redundant constraints: $\{x + y \leq d_1, x - y \leq d_2, -x + y \leq d_3, -x - y \leq d_4\}$. Hence the maximum number of (non-redundant) constraints that can be produced by closure under transitivity and tightening for a system including n variables is $2n^2$. Quasi-syntactic redundancy elimination is very simple, it just requires maintaining the minimal d for each of the above constraint forms. This, together with the fact that no tightened constraints can create further tightened constraints, gives a polynomial time bound on the algorithm.

Given a new constraint $ax + by \leq d$ and a tightened, transitively closed set of constraints C, there are at most $2n$ constraints in C involving $-ax$ and $2n$ constraints involving $-by$. Thus the cost of transitive closure is $O(n^2)$. Tightening will introduce at most $2n$ constraints, all of which are bounds. Further transitive closure will produce only more bounds, and at most $2n$ of them for each initial bound. Thus tightening and further closure also has cost $O(n^2)$. Hence the cost of producing a new tightened and transitively closed set of constraints is $O(n^2)$. It follows that the cost of testing the satisfiability of N unit TVPI constraints with our algorithm is $O(N^3)$ in time and $O(N^2)$ in space.

The key result relating unit TVPI constraints to transitive closure and tightening is as follows:

Theorem 1. *Let C be a set of unit TVPI constraints that is closed under transitivity and tightening. Let $C|_{-x}$ denote the conjunction of constraints in C that do not contain x. Then $\exists x\ C \leftrightarrow C|_{-x}$* $\square$.

The proof follows the proof of the corresponding result for (arbitrary) inequalities over the reals, with only minor modifications. It extends to general TVPI constraints only to the extent that all occurrences of the eliminated variable have only unit coefficients.

Given the above result it is easy to show that:

Theorem 2. *Let C be a set of unit TVPI constraints that is closed under transitivity and tightening. Then C is satisfiable iff it does not contain a constraint of the form $0 \leq d$ where $d < 0$.* $\square$.

This demonstrates the completeness of our algorithm. Note that propagation-based methods are not complete for unit TVPI constraints, even for finite domain problems. Consider the following example:

$$x - y \leq 2$$
$$x + y \leq 1$$
$$-x + z \leq -2$$
$$-x - z \leq -1$$
$$-20 \leq x, y, z \leq 20$$

Bounds propagation simply determines that the variables lie in the following ranges $-17 \leq x \leq 20$, $-19 \leq y, z \leq 18$. In fact there is no solution: the first two constraints imply $2x \leq 3$ and hence $x \leq 1$; the second two constraints imply $2x \geq 3$ and hence $x \geq 2$. Our approach discovers the unsatisfiability essentially by following the above argument.

We can expect to improve the efficiency of the approach by treating equations, for example $x + y = 3$, directly rather than as two inequalities $x + y \leq 3$, $-x - y \leq -3$. Any unit TVPI equation can be used as a substitution to eliminate one of its variable, for example $x + y = 3$ can be used to replace each occurrence of x by $-y + 3$. Note that applying such a substitution to a unit TVPI constraint either maintains the unit TVPI form or creates a constraint of the form $2y \leq k$ which can be simplified to a unit TVPI constraint (possibly with tightening).

To maintain the transitive closure the approach above is modified to treat an equation $x = t$ as follows: add both the inequalities, $x \leq t, x \geq t$, and close under transitivity and tightening, then remove inequalities involving x. The equations are maintained separately in Gauss-Jordan normal form and they are applied as substitutions to constraints that are added later. Note that we need to fail if we detect equations (after substitution) of the form $2x = k$, where k is odd, and to simplify if we detect equations of the form $2x = k$, where k is even.

Given we are keeping the equations in a separate tableau, it seems worthwhile to extract implicit equations from the inequalities. When we detect a transitive consequence of the form $0 \leq 0$ this signals that the inequalities which produced it are implicit equations. By marking these and waiting till the closure process terminates we can extract the (marked) implicit equations, place them in the equation tableau and simply remove the inequalities that involve a substituted variable.

It is easy to extend this approach to perform other operations of interest. Let the *active store* denote the current set of TVPI constraints in the computation, closed under transitivity and tightening. Any groundness information that is a consequence of the active store will appear in the equation tableau (perhaps through implicit equations). Constraint entailment can be simply determined because of the following result:

Theorem 3. *Let c be a unit TVPI constraint and let C be a satisfiable set of unit TVPI constraints that is closed under transitivity and tightening. Then $C \to c$ iff either c is a tautology, c is implied by the SVPI constraints of C, or c is quasi-syntactic redundant with respect to a constraint in C* $\square$.

Hence to determine whether a unit TVPI constraint is entailed by the active store we simply check if it is quasi-syntactically redundant or implied by bounds (after substitution). It is straightforward to make this check incremental. Projecting out a variable is straightforward: if the variable appears in an equation this can be rewritten to eliminate the variable, otherwise all inequalities involving the variable can simply be removed (c.f. Theorem 1).

Using Theorem 3 we can determine unit TVPI consequences of the disjunction of two tightened transitively closed unit TVPI constraint sets C_1 and C_2, as follows. For each inequality form $ax + by \leq ...$, let $ax \leq d_i^x \in C_i$, $by \leq d_i^y \in C_i$, and $ax + by \leq d_i \in C_i$, for $i = 1, 2$.[6] Then $ax + by \leq d$ is a consequence of $C_1 \vee C_2$, where $d = max(min(d_1, d_1^x + d_1^y), min(d_2, d_2^x + d_2^y))$ if $a, b \neq 0$ and $d = max(d_1, d_2)$ otherwise. The set of such constraints describes the smallest unit TVPI polyhedra that contains both C_1 and C_2. Extending this procedure to handle separate equations is reasonably straightforward. This procedure can be the basis of constructive disjunction in this constraint domain.

3.3 The Solver in a General Setting

In the context of a CLP system we want to handle a larger class of constraints than just unit TVPI constraints. For non-unit TVPI constraints we can use propagation-based methods to extract SVPI information in exactly the same

---

[6] An inequality that is not present in C_i is represented by taking the appropriate constant (d_i, d_i^x, d_i^y) to be ∞.

way as finite domain solvers. Note that the bounds on variables are available in the unit TVPI inequalities. Applying propagation to unit TVPI constraints is unnecessary as they are completely handled already. We can use the equation tableau to simplify non unit TVPI constraints by substitution. The resulting constraints (possibly after tightening) may be unit TVPI constraints. For example, applying the substitution $y = z + 1$ to $5x + 3y + 2z \leq 7$ results in $5x + 5z \leq 4$ and thus $x + z \leq 0$.

An alternative is to apply the (incomplete) method of section 3.1 to all TVPI constraints. Non-TVPI constraints would be treated by propagation methods, as above. This would provide a more powerful, but more expensive, integer solver. The choice between these alternatives can only be made after experimental evaluation.

The TVPI techniques here can also be used together with a real linear arithmetic solver (for example using the Simplex algorithm). This is useful when there are mixed real and integer constraints or if the real solver is used to extract information about the relaxation of integer constraints to the real numbers. Just as with propagation methods, SVPI and TVPI information can be transferred between integer and real solvers. However if the real solver uses floating point then issues of numerical accuracy may also need to be considered if information from the real solver is to be used in the integer solver.

4   Conclusion

Unit TVPI constraints are sufficiently expressive for many problems: for example in scheduling and temporal reasoning. We give an algorithm for incremental satisfiability of unit TVPI constraints. Not only is this algorithm efficiently implementable, it also supports efficient implementation of entailment detection, including constraints entailed by disjunctive constraints, and projection. Finally, for use in a CLP system, constraints more general than unit TVPI must be handled, though not necessarily in a complete way. Our algorithm naturally extends to (non-unit) TVPI constraints, and it can be augmented with a bounds-propagation technique for constraints more general than TVPI. An implementation of the solver is underway as part of the continuing development of CLP($\mathcal{R}$) [9].

Acknowledgement

We thank Warwick Harvey for correcting an error in our formulation of Shostak's algorithm.

References

1. Apsvall, B., Shiloach, Y.: A polynomial time algorithm for solving systems of linear inequalities with two variables per inequality. *SIAM J. of Computing.* **9** (1980) 827–845.

2. Bledsoe, W.W.: A new method for proving certain Presburger formulas. *Proc. of the 4th Joint Conf. on Artificial Intelligence.* (1975) 15–21.

3. Cohen, E., Megiddo, N.: Improved Algorithms for Linear Inequalities with Two Variables per Inequality. *Proc. of the 23rd Symp. on Theory of Computing.* (1991) 145–155.

4. Dincbas, M., Van Hentenryck, P., Simonis, H., Aggoun, A.: The Constraint Logic Programming Language CHIP. *Proc. of the 2nd Intl. Conf. on Fifth Generation Computer Systems.* (1988) 249–264.

5. Harvey, W.: Personal communication. (1994).

6. Van Hentenryck, P., Deville, Y., Teng, C.: A generic arc-consistency algorithm and its specializations. *Artificial Intelligence.* **57** (1992) 291–321.

7. Van Hentenryck, P., Saraswat, V., Deville,Y.: Constraint Processing in cc(FD). Manuscript (1991).

8. Huynh, T., Lassez, J-L., McAloon,K.: Simplification and elimination of redundant linear arithmetic constraints. *Proc. North American Conf. on Logic Programming.* (1989) 37–51.

9. Jaffar, J., Michaylov, S., Stuckey, P.J., Yap, R.H.C.: The CLP($\mathcal{R}$) Language and System. *ACM Trans. on Programming Languages.* **14**(3) (1992) 339–395.

10. Kapur, D., Nie, X.: Reasoning about Numbers in Tecton. *Eighth Intl. Symp. on methodologies for intelligent systems.* To appear (1994).

11. Lagarias, J.C.: The Computational Complexity of Simultaneous Diophantine Approximation Problems. *SIAM J. of Computing.* **14**(1) (1985) 196–209.

12. Lassez, J-L., Maher, M.J.: On Fourier's Algorithm for Linear Arithmetic Constraints. *J. of Automated Reasoning.* **9** (1992) 373–379.

13. Le Pape, C.: Des Systèmes d'Ordonnancement Flexibles et Opportunistes. Thesis. Université de Paris-Sud. 1988.

14. Mackworth, A.K.: *Constraint Satisfaction.* Wiley. New York. 1987.

15. Pugh, W.: The Omega test: A Fast and Practical Integer Programming Algorithm for Dependence Analysis. *Comm. ACM.* **8** (1992) 102–114.

16. Pugh, W., Wonnacott, D.: Experiences with Constraint-based Array Dependence Analysis. *Proc. Principles and Practice of Constraint Programming.PCP'94.* 1994.

17. Pratt, V.R.: Two easy theories whose combination is hard. Tech. Report. Massachusetts Institute of Technology. Cambridge. Mass. 1977.

18. Revesz, P.Z.: A Closed Form for Datalog Queries with Integer Order. *Proc. Intl. Conf. on Database Theory.* 1990.

19. Rosenkrantz, D.J., Hunt, H.B. III.: Processing Conjunctive Predicates and Queries. *Proc. Conf. on Very Large Data Bases.* (1980) 64–72.

20. Shostak, R.: Deciding Linear Inequalities by Computing Loop Residues. *J. of the ACM.* **28**(4) (1981) 769–779.

21. Shostak, R.: On the SUP-INF Method for Proving Presburger Formulas. *J. of the ACM.* **24**(4) (1977) 529–543.

22. Toman, D., Chomicki, J., Rogers, D.S.: Datalog with Periodicity Constraints. *Proc. Intl. Logic Programming Symp.* To appear (1994).

QUAD-CLP(R) :
Adding the Power of Quadratic Constraints

Gilles Pesant and Michel Boyer

University of Montreal,
Département d'Informatique et de Recherche Opérationnelle,
C.P. 6128 Succ. centre-ville, Montréal, Canada, H3C 3J7
({pesant,boyer}@IRO.UMontreal.CA).

Abstract. We report on a new way of handling non-linear arithmetic constraints and its implementation into the QUAD-CLP(**R**) language. Important properties of the problem at hand are a discretization through geometric equivalence classes and decomposition into convex pieces. A case analysis of those equivalence classes leads to a relaxation (and sometimes recasting) of the original constraints into linear constraints, much easier to handle. Complementing earlier expositions in [18] and [19], the present focus is on applications upholding its worth.

1 Motivation

This paper presents the constraint programming language QUAD-CLP(**R**) which offers a powerful novel solving strategy for non-linear arithmetic constraints under the computing paradigm of logic programming. Emphasis will be given here to the techniques involved in the constraint solver for quadratic constraints over **R** and to applications making use of this added power.

Despite the enormous potential of non-linear arithmetic constraints in several spheres of scientific activity, typical efforts to provide for them amidst constraint languages have brought mostly disappointments as the resulting solvers either lacked effectiveness or scalability.

The delay strategy implemented in languages such as CLP(**R**) [10] and PROLOG III [1] yields an incomplete solver which will be effective only if the problem under attack is such that reasoning about linear constraints ultimately becomes sufficient. Unfortunately, this is seldom the case for interesting problems, even very simple ones. One classic example is the multiplication of complex numbers, which can be expressed as cmult((R1,I1),(R2,I2),(R1*R2-I1*I2,R1*I2+R2*I1)) in predicate calculus. Among interesting queries, "?- cmult((R,I),(R,I),(-1,0))." requires reasoning about non-linear system -R*I = R*I, I*I -1 = R*R.
QUAD-CLP(**R**) can easily handle this, giving the answer:

```
I = 1
R = 0
*** Retry? y
```

```
I = -1
R = 0
*** Retry? y
```

```
*** No
```

On the other hand, languages like CAL [20] and RISC-CLP(Real) [7] bear witness that the price to pay to achieve a complete solver seems to be the use of costly computational algebra techniques which confine their usefulness to very small (albeit interesting) problems.

Our approach, introduced in [18], takes advantage of the ease with which quadratic constraints can be replaced or approximated by linear constraints. It is therefore especially well-suited to problems involving quadratic and linear constraints. There is nevertheless the possibility of handling general arithmetic constraints by breaking them down into quadratic components through the introduction of auxiliary variables (we address this further in §5).

Even a restriction to quadratic constraints still provides a rich and expressive extension to the domain brought about by linear constraints. Many problems and solutions in CAD/CAM, spatial databases, motion planning and graphics are naturally expressed through them [2][11][4][3]. They have also been used in seemingly unrelated domains such as molecular biology [14], automobile transmission design [15] and electrical engineering [5].

The rest of the paper is organized as follows. The next section outlines the steps involved in the quadratic solver of QUAD-CLP(R) . Some features of the language and system are described in §3. A large part of the paper is devoted to applications in Solid Modeling and Combinatorial Search problems, described and analyzed in §4. Some relations to other work are established in §5.

2   The Quadratic Solver

The aim of this section is to acquaint the reader with the steps taken by the quadratic solver of QUAD-CLP(**R**) . Details and proofs of the algorithms involved can be found in [17].

Figure 1 illustrates some of the interactions between the quadratic and linear solvers. The latter should be considered here a black box relying on incremental versions of Gaussian elimination and of phase I of the Two-Phase-Simplex method. Upon encountering a constraint in the course of the computation, we first classify it as either linear or quadratic according to its syntax, by considering the number of bound variables in each monomial [1]. In the former case, it is directly fed to a solver for linear constraints. In the latter, it goes through the process summarized below:

---

[1] For simplicity, we do not discuss here the case of monomials whose degree is ≥ 3. The corresponding constraints could be broken into quadratic pieces, as mentioned previously, or just delayed.

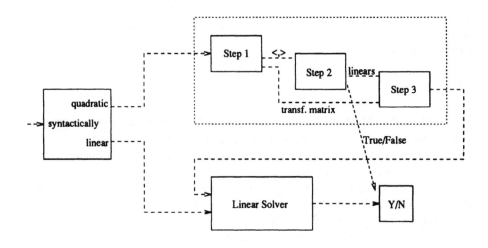

Fig. 1. The constraint solver

Step 1: Discretize

Quadratic arithmetic constraints offer a natural geometric interpretation which leads to a small number of equivalence classes. For example, the constraint $\frac{9}{25}y^2 + \frac{16}{25}x^2 + \frac{24}{25}xy - \frac{4}{5}y + \frac{3}{5}x < -19$ belongs to the class **parabola** whose *canonical representative* is the algebraic equation of the corresponding locus in standard position, $\frac{x^2}{a^2} - by$ (in this case, parameters a and b would both have a value of 1). Those *geometric equivalence classes* allow us to achieve a discretization of the problem. This first step identifies the geometric equivalence class to which the quadratic constraint belongs, producing the canonical representative and a transformation matrix (whose geometric interpretation is the translation and rotations needed to bring the locus to standard position). The computation amounts to the diagonalization of a real symmetric matrix.

Step 2: Simplify

For several of the possible pairs ⟨*canonical representative, relational symbol*⟩, the constraint can be immediately decided or replaced by an equivalent Boolean combination of linear constraints.

Example 1. The geometric equivalence class of $-481x^2 + 216xy - 544y^2 + 3946x + 3272y \geq 37685$ is imaginary ellipse. The pair ⟨ $-\frac{x^2}{a^2} - \frac{y^2}{b^2} - 1$, $\geq (0)$ ⟩ reveals that the constraint is trivially false.

Example 2. Constraint $x^2 - 4xy + 6xz - 8xw + 4y^2 - 12yz + 16yw + 9z^2 - 24zw + 16w^2 - 25 = 0$ is classified as **two points**, leading to the simplification $(x - 2y + 3z - 4w = 5) \vee (x - 2y + 3z - 4w = -5)$. The unexpected feature of this example is that a constraint on four variables falls into a geometric equivalence class seemingly reserved to constraints on one variable. This degenerate case is best viewed through substitution $v = x - 2y + 3z - 4w$, yielding $v^2 - 25 = 0$. In this form, it becomes less surprising that its class should be two points ($v = \pm 5$). Note that step 1 described above does not look for such simplifying substitutions but nevertheless produces equivalent results.

Step 2(bis): Approximate

For each remaining pair ⟨*canonical representative, relational symbol*⟩, a sound approximation made up of linear constraints is computed. The strategy leading to the efficient and accurate production of linear approximations considers a Boolean combination of convex constraints in place of the original constraint (note that it may already be convex). The convex pieces are approximated and the results recombined. That Boolean combination may be equivalent to the initial constraint, in which case it will be termed a *convex expression*, or constitute a relaxation of it and will then be called *convex approximation*. In both cases the resulting combination of linear constraints constitutes an approximation.

Bringing back the example of step 1, the pair ⟨ $x^2 - y$, < ⟩ indicates a constraint which is already convex and for which we can compute a linear approximation such as:

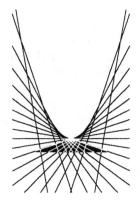

$$0 < y \land$$
$$2.36522x < y + 1.39857 \land$$
$$-1.39857 < y + 2.36522x \land$$
$$0.662911x < y + 0.109863 \land$$
$$-0.109863 < y + 0.662911x \land$$
$$\cdots$$

Step 3: *Realize*

Map the simplification or approximation for the canonical representative to a simplification or approximation for the original constraint. This is achieved by "multiplying" each linear constraint in the Boolean combination by the transformation matrix. The result of step 3 is in turn sent to the linear solver to decide upon the new collection of constraints. If it was an approximation, the original quadratic constraint is also kept (delayed).

The resulting solver is not a complete solver since it partly relies on approximations. It nevertheless exhibits much less incompleteness than one which unilaterally sets aside non-linear constraints. Some of this incompleteness can actually be driven back by choosing an appropriate size for the approximations, as will be seen in the next section. Note that from a logic programming perspective, the nature of the approximations generated ensures the soundness of the inference.

3 Features of the System

QUAD-CLP($\mathbf{R}$) is built on top of the CLP($\mathbf{R}$) system, which allowed us to concentrate on the non-linear component of the solver. It was written in C to facilitate its integration with the host system whose source code is available and also written in C. We discuss some of the additional features provided.

3.1 $\wedge,\vee$-bounds

Recall that in most cases, from a quadratic constraint is extracted a Boolean combination of linear constraints which is sent to the linear solver. It proves convenient to write that Boolean combination in disjunctive normal form:

$$\bigvee_{i=1}^{n} \bigwedge_{j=1}^{m} C_{ij}$$

Each disjunct will give rise to a solver choice point. There are cases where n can be quite large. One may therefore wish to specify an upper bound on n in an effort to control the non-deterministic behavior. QUAD-CLP($\mathbf{R}$) provides the user with a parameter, the $\vee$-*bound*, which has the desired effect. A Boolean combination whose disjunctive normal form exceeds that bound will not be sent to the linear solver. Note that setting it to 1 yields a deterministic solver.

The $\wedge$-*bound* specifies the desired size of an approximation to a convex constraint. Such a name was chosen because it often corresponds to an upper bound on m. A default value of 4 has been found adequate experimentally for a first exploration: refined approximations can always be tried subsequently. For example, the following (unsolvable) system of inequalities,

$$x^2 + y^2 \le 1$$
$$u^2 + v^2 \le 1$$
$$x + y + u + v \ge 3$$

required approximations of size 7 to decide that there was no solution.

3.2 Output

The simplification of the constraint set may be desirable for efficiency reasons, since it reduces its size, but also to ease the understanding of the result by the user, when the answer takes the form of a collection of constraints. Much research has been devoted for example to quantifier elimination in the special case of an existentially quantified conjunction of linear constraints, in an effort to express the output in terms of query variables only [13][8][12][9][7]. We discuss here another aspect of simplification brought about by non-linear constraints.

Seemingly very different answers such as $481x^2 - 216xy + 544y^2 - 3946x - 3272y + 6409 = 0$ and $16x^2 + 25y^2 - 400 = 0$ express a quite similar relationship between the variables (valid pairs (x, y) lie on an ellipse), which is captured by the concept of geometric equivalence classes. An answer like the first one can be complemented by:

```
real ellipse: foci at (7.4,5.8),(2.6,2.2);
              principal axis of length 10.
```

Such information thus allows to deepen the understanding of the relationship between the variables of a solution or may help to determine its solvability if no conclusion was reached.

Redundancy in the solution is also an issue of simplification. Let us mention that the detection of a redundant linear inequality with respect to a quadratic constraint can in some cases be reduced to the efficient computation of a supporting hyperplane. Some heuristics can also be applied for redundancy detection between pairs of quadratic constraints [18].

4 Examples

In this section we describe two applications which demonstrate the expressiveness and efficiency of QUAD-CLP(**R**) .

4.1 Solid Modeling

We consider the Point/Solid Classification and Solid Intersection problems in constructive solid geometry (CSG). In such a representation scheme, a solid is built by combining *primitive solids*, using *regularized Boolean operations* and *rigid motions*(translation and rotations) [6]. These primitive solids are usually chosen among the parallelepiped, triangular prism, sphere, cylinder, cone and torus. The regularized Boolean operations are $\bigcup^*$, $\bigcap^*$ and $-^*$, differing from the set-theoretic operations in that the result is the closure of the operation on the interior of the solids. A solid can be represented as a tree whose leaves are primitive solids and whose internal nodes are the operations on them (an example is given in figure 2).

With the exception of the torus, every primitive solid has an implicit form expressed in terms of quadratic and linear arithmetic inequalities. This makes it particularly attractive to our language. For simplicity, we shall drop the regularization of the Boolean operations: in some applications, this is even desirable. Constraint logic programming allows for an elegant and concise solution to the Point/Solid Classification problem, which consists of deciding if a point lies in-

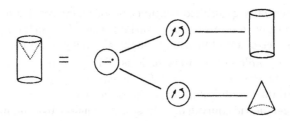

Fig. 2. A solid and its CSG representation

side a solid. The first half of this solution follows:

```
%% inside(Point, Solid): Point lies inside Solid.
inside(Point, solid(and(S1,S2))) :-
    inside(Point, solid(S1)),
    inside(Point, solid(S2)).
inside(Point, solid(or(S1,S2))) :-
    inside(Point, solid(S1));
    inside(Point, solid(S2)).
inside(Point, solid(minus(S1,S2))) :-
    inside(Point, solid(S1)),
    outside(Point, solid(S2)).
```

Our solution also has the advantage of replacing the need to specify rotations and translations to "move" the solid into place by directly giving its position in terms of natural parameters. For example, solid(cylinder((1,1,1),(3,4,2),5)) defines a cylinder of radius 5 whose axis extends from $(1,1,1)$ to $(3,4,2)$. Additional rules must be written for each of the primitives and we give one of them below:

```
%% point (X,Y,Z) lies inside primitive solid "cylinder".
inside((X,Y,Z), solid(cylinder((X0,Y0,Z0),(X1,Y1,Z1),R))) :-
    % orientation of symmetry axis
    Vx = X1-X0, Vy = Y1-Y0, Vz = Z1-Z0,
    % point (Xp,Yp,Zp) is on the axis of symmetry, ...
    Xp = Vx*T + X0,
    Yp = Vy*T + Y0,
    Zp = Vz*T + Z0,
    %... inside the cylinder ...
    T >= 0, T <= 1,
    % ... and on the plane which contains (X,Y,Z) ...
    % ... and is orthogonal to the axis.
    Vx*(X-Xp) + Vy*(Y-Yp) + Vz*(Z-Zp) = 0,
    % constrain the cylinder
    (X-Xp)*(X-Xp) + (Y-Yp)*(Y-Yp) + (Z-Zp)*(Z-Zp) <= R*R.
```

Solid Intersection problems arise not only when we want to avoid overlapping objects but also when we wish to eliminate redundancies in the representation of a solid. A common approach is to verify a criterion for non-intersection obtained by approximating the shape of the solid, usually through "box approximations" (see figure 3). If the approximations do not intersect then certainly neither do the solids. A simple extension to the above provides a solution:

```
%% solids S1 and S2 intersect.
intersect(S1,S2) :-
    inside(Point, S1),
    inside(Point, S2).
```

The above solution, applied to the Point/Solid Classification problem, worked in a satisfactory manner given a suitable linear solver (non-linearities vanished as enough variables were fixed). The present problem on the other hand retains non-linear constraints. Here the strength of QUAD-CLP(**R**) is to provide for free a behavior conceptually similar to "box approximations" but with potentially much closer approximations.

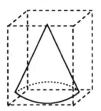

Fig. 3. Box approximation of a cone.

In fact, it generates approximations with "holes" if need be. For example in the following instance, illustrated in figure 4, the conventional approach would have failed to detect the non-intersection, whereas with QUAD-CLP(**R**) :

```
?- Bead = solid(minus(sphere(0,0,0,4),
                    cylinder((-4,-4,-4),(4,4,4),2))),
   Needle = solid(cone((7,6,6),(-6,-5,-5),1)),
   intersect(Needle, Bead).
```

*** No

4.2 Combinatorial Search

We examine next a combinatorial search problem involving Euclidean distances and thus quadratic constraints. Instances of respectable size can be solved in a reasonable amount of time through a simple QUAD-CLP(**R**) program.

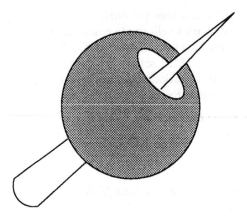

Fig. 4. A Solid Intersection problem.

Graph Geometric Embedding : Given a graph $G(\mathcal{V}, \mathcal{E})$, a label $\ell(e) \in \mathbf{Z}^+$
for each $e \in \mathcal{E}$ and a set P of points in $\mathbf{E}^2$, is there a mapping $f : \mathcal{V} \to \mathbf{E}^2$
such that $P \subseteq \text{codom}(f)$ and $\forall(v, v') \in \mathcal{E}, d(f(v), f(v')) \le \ell((v, v'))$ (where
$d : \mathbf{E}^2 \times \mathbf{E}^2 \to \mathbf{R}$ is the Euclidean metric)?

Intuitively, we are asked to cover certain points in $\mathbf{E}^2$ with vertices of a
labeled graph without "breaking" an edge. When $|\mathcal{V}| = |P|$, a simple generate-
and-test approach will solve the problem, although through considering all $|\mathcal{V}|!$
possible pairings. The test-and-generate paradigm associated with constraint
programming may accelerate our inspection by pruning the search tree. If $|\mathcal{V}| >
|P|$, generating candidate solutions by associating a different vertex with each
point in P will leave some vertices "free". Testing those candidates thus requires
reasoning about quadratic constraints.

The statistics in table 1 were obtained from a straightforward program implementing the test-and-generate algorithm: state all the distance constraints
implicit in the graph, assign vertices to points in P, output candidate solutions.
The tests were run on a SUN SPARCstation 10/42. The problem on 10 vertices
was generated by hand (the 10; 6 instance and its unique solution appear in figure
5). As for the rest, the graphs were randomly generated with an edge-occurrence
probability of about 0.4. Points in P were distributed on a square grid and the
labels ranged from 1 to the length of the diagonal of the grid.

The first three instances were run on both the QUAD-CLP($\mathbf{R}$) and CLP($\mathbf{R}$)
systems, in order to compare the performance of the quadratic solver with that
of the delay strategy implemented by the latter. Important speed-ups were always observed mainly because of the difference in the number of nodes which
were expanded in the search tree, reflecting the amount of pruning that took
place. A notable difference between the results for the 10; 10 and 10; 6 instances
is the number of candidate solutions found by CLP($\mathbf{R}$). These instances share

$P = \{(0,0), (10,0), (4,7), (4,0), (4,4), (7,3)\}$,
$\mathcal{V} = \{v1, v2, v3, v4, v5, v6, v7, v8, v9, v10\}$,
$\ell((v1, v2)) = 3, \ell((v1, v6)) = 5, \ell((v2, v3)) = 1, \ell((v2, v7)) = 5, \ell((v3, v4)) = 3,$
$\ell((v3, v6)) = 3, \ell((v4, v5)) = 3, \ell((v4, v7)) = 3, \ell((v4, v8)) = 5, \ell((v5, v9)) = 5,$
$\ell((v6, v7)) = 3, \ell((v6, v8)) = 1, \ell((v7, v9)) = 1, \ell((v7, v10)) = 5, \ell((v8, v9)) = 3,$
$\ell((v8, v10)) = 3.$

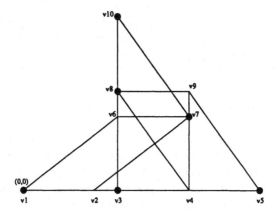

Fig. 5. The $10; 6$ instance.

the graph and six points of P: the first one includes four more points so that $|\mathcal{V}| = |P|$. Consequently in the $10; 10$ instance, a basic pairing procedure guarantees that we will find all and only solutions to the problem, regardless of the strategy used to handle non-linear constraints, since the distance constraints will eventually become ground. However the $10; 6$ instance brings forth the incompleteness of a solver as some of the constraints may never become ground (or even linear) during the search. Thus we obtain a set of 72 possible solutions.

Larger instances (30 and 50 vertices, about 180 and 500 quadratic constraints respectively) were solved on QUAD-CLP($\mathbf{R}$) only as the $20; 8$ instance was already overwhelming for the delay strategy. Despite the surprisingly slight increase in the number of nodes expanded as the problems gain in size, the time taken grows by several orders of magnitude. This should be attributed to the growing system of inequalities that the linear solver has to deal with. For example the largest instance, given a conservative $\wedge$-*bound* of 4 (which is what was used in every instance), spawns a dynamically changing system of around 2000 linear inequalities in 100 variables. As the linear solver relies on a Simplex algorithm, basic feasible solutions must constantly be found at the cost of pivoting operations.

The most accurate rendition of the improvements brought by the approach described in the paper must be found in the pruning of the search tree and the number of candidate solutions offered.

Table 1. Performance statistics for the Graph Geometric Embedding problem.

size ($|\mathcal{V}|$; $|P|$)	language	time (sec)	nodes expanded	# solutions
10;10	QUAD-CLP(**R**)	0.52	38	1
	CLP(**R**)	4.94	1674	1
10;6	QUAD-CLP(**R**)	0.54	36	1
	CLP(**R**)	3.95	1314	72
20;8	QUAD-CLP(**R**)	13.75	35	1
	CLP(**R**)	>14 063.00	>2 411 229	>987 546
30;10	QUAD-CLP(**R**)	276.54	49	0
50;5	QUAD-CLP(**R**)	2 727.41	51	0

5 Related Work

As was noted in §1, computational algebra techniques, currently still very expensive, nevertheless yield a complete solver through a uniform treatment of polynomial constraints. It is not clear how well the approach described in this paper, whose motivation was to solve quadratic constraints, can perform on arbitrary polynomial constraints. The introduction of auxiliary variables fragments the original constraints; separately considering (and most likely approximating) each piece may yield weaker results. Since in general a constraint will admit several possible fragmentations, choosing the best one is an interesting problem in its own right.

As an illustration, consider the following system of non-linear inequalities, borrowed from [7]:

$$s > 0$$
$$s^4 - 0.029901s^3 - 247.971s^2 + 396.01s - 245.03 \geq 0$$
$$s^4 - 2.01005s^3 - 247.246s^2 + 400s - 248.246 \leq 0$$

Use of a computer algebra package reveals that s lies somewhere in $[14.93, 15.98]$. One possible fragmentation,

$$t = s^2$$
$$s > 0$$
$$t^2 - 0.029901st - 247.971s^2 + 396.01s - 245.03 \geq 0$$
$$t^2 - 2.01005st - 247.246s^2 + 400s - 248.246 \leq 0,$$

run on QUAD-CLP(**R**) , constrains s to the slightly larger interval $[4.61, 16.62]$ whereas

$$t_i = s^2, \ i = 1 \dots 8$$
$$s > 0$$
$$t_1 t_2 - 0.029901st_3 - 247.971t_4 + 396.01s - 245.03 \geq 0$$
$$t_5 t_6 - 2.01005st_7 - 247.246t_8 + 400s - 248.246 \leq 0,$$

offers a vastly different result, namely $]0.00, \infty[$.

An even more uniform treatment of constraints is that provided by the language CLP(BNR) [16]. Here relational interval arithmetic is applied to reals, integers and booleans alike. A parallel can be drawn with our approach since interval arithmetic is a form of approximation. Their approach to constraint solving is nevertheless quite different as it is based on the local propagation of bounds on the value of the variables through a constraint network.

We say a few more words on those approximations. In the context of quadratic constraints, they represent a special case of ours. Each bound of an interval can be viewed as a linear inequality. The size of such an approximation for a constraint is consequently determined by the number of variables appearing in it (4 with 2 variables; 6 with 3 variables; ...) and the approximation itself is isothetic (aligned with the coordinate axes). The result is comparable to the "box approximations" of §4.1. It may be sufficient in some cases but is certainly less powerful in general (recall for example figure 4).

6 Conclusion

This report presented a new way of handling non-linear arithmetic constraints and its implementation into the QUAD-CLP(R) language. Important properties of the problem at hand where discretization through geometric equivalence classes and decomposition into convex pieces. A case analysis of those equivalence classes led to a relaxation (and sometimes recasting) of the original constraints into linear constraints, much easier to handle. Applications in Solid Modeling and Combinatorial Search showed both the expressiveness and the efficiency of such a tool within a constraint language.

The latter application revealed a need for more efficient linear solvers when confronted to large systems of inequalities. It proved to be a bottleneck for the speed of the quadratic solver. One must therefore be careful when considering constraints as language primitives: the apparently simple addition or deletion of a constraint may hide a considerable cost in problems involving a large number of constraints.

Acknowledgements

We wish to thank the CLP(R) people whose freely available system greatly facilitated the development of ours. We would also like to thank the anonymous referees whose constructive comments helped to put the present work in perspective. This work was supported by NSERC and FCAR Graduate Scholarships.

References

1. A. Colmerauer. Prolog II Reference Manual and Theoretical Model. Rep. groupe d'intelligence artificielle, Université d'Aix-Marseille II, Luminy, October 1982.

2. S. Donikian and G. Hégron. Constraint Management in a Declarative Design Method for 3D Scene Sketch Modeling. In P. Kanellakis, J.-L. Lassez, C. Lau, V. Saraswat, R. Wachter, and D. Wagner, editors, *PPCP'93*, Newport, RI, April 1993.

3. T. Dubé and C.-K. Yap. The Geometry in Constraint Logic Programs. In P. Kanellakis, J.-L. Lassez, C. Lau, V. Saraswat, R. Wachter, and D. Wagner, editors, *PPCP'93*, Newport, RI, April 1993.

4. M. Gleicher. Practical Issues in Graphical Constraints. In P. Kanellakis, J.-L. Lassez, C. Lau, V. Saraswat, R. Wachter, and D. Wagner, editors, *PPCP'93*, Newport, RI, April 1993.

5. N. Heintze, S. Michaylov, and P. J. Stuckey. CLP($\Re$) and Some Electrical Engineering Problems. In J.-L. Lassez, editor, *Proceedings of the 4th International Conference on Logic Programming*, pages 675–703, Melbourne, May 1987. MIT Press.

6. C.M. Hoffmann. *Geometric and Solid Modeling: An Introduction.* Morgan Kaufmann Publishers, Inc., 1989.

7. H. Hong. Non-linear Constraints Solving over Real Numbers in Constraint Logic Programming (Introducing RISC-CLP). Technical Report 92-16, RISC-Link, January 1992.

8. J.-L. Imbert. *Simplification des systèmes de contraintes numériques linéaires.* PhD thesis, Faculté des Sciences de Luminy, Université Aix-Marseilles II, 1989.

9. J. Jaffar, S. Michaylov, P. J. Stuckey, and R. H. C. Yap. The CLP($\Re$) Language and System. *ACM Transactions on Programming Languages and Systems*, 14(3):339–395, July 1992.

10. J. Jaffar, S. Michaylov, and R. H.C. Yap. A Methodology for Managing Hard Constraints in CLP Systems. *ACM SIGPLAN-PLDI*, 26(6):306–316, 1991.

11. G. Kuper. Aggregation in Constraint Databases. In P. Kanellakis, J.-L. Lassez, C. Lau, V. Saraswat, R. Wachter, and D. Wagner, editors, *PPCP'93*, Newport, RI, April 1993.

12. C. Lassez and J.-L. Lassez. Quantifier Elimination for Conjunctions of Linear Constraints via a Convex Hull Algorithm. IBM Research Report, IBM T.J. Watson Research Center, 1991.

13. J.-L. Lassez, T. Huynh, and K. McAloon. Simplification and Elimination of Redundant Linear Arithmetic Constraints. In *Proceedings of NACLP 89*, pages 37–51. MIT Press, 1989.

14. F. Major, M. Turcotte, D. Gautheret, G. Lapalme, E. Fillion, and R. Cedergren. The combination of symbolic and numerical computation for three-dimensional modeling of RNA. *Science*, 253, September 1991.

15. B. A. Nadel, X. Wu, and D. Kagan. Multiple abstraction levels in automobile transmission design: constraint satisfaction formulations and implementations. *Int. J. Expert Systems: Research and Applications.* (to appear).

16. W. Older and A. Vellino. Constraint Arithmetic on Real Intervals. In F. Benhamou and A. Colmerauer, editors, *Constraint Logic Programming: Selected Research.* MIT Press, 1993.

17. G. Pesant and M. Boyer. Linear Approximations of Quadratic Constraints. (*submitted for publication*).

18. G. Pesant and M. Boyer. A Geometric Approach to Quadratic Constraints in Constraint Logic Programming. In F. Benhamou, A. Colmerauer, and G. Smolka, editors, *Third Workshop on Constraint Logic Programming*, Marseilles, France, March 1993.

19. G. Pesant and M. Boyer. Handling Quadratic Constraints Through Geometry. In D. Miller, editor, *International Logic Programming Symposium*, Vancouver, Canada, October 1993. MIT Press.
20. K. Sakai and A. Aiba. CAL: A Theoretical Background of Constraint Logic Programming and its Applications. *Journal of Symbolic Computation*, 8:589–603, 1989.

Applications in Constraint Logic Programming with Strings

Arcot Rajasekar
Computer Science Department
University of Kentucky, Lexington, KY 40506

Abstract. In this paper, we discuss CLP(S) which combines logic programming with constraint solving over *strings* and show how CLP(S) can be used naturally in several applications ranging from natural language processing, to encoding of genetic operators and DNA grammar rules, to scene analysis in iconic image processing.

1 Introduction

Several applications in artificial intelligence require that one deal with information which is not as precisely encodable as required by logic-based systems. In recent years there has been a number of innovative applications in new fields which makes additional demands on the representational efficiency of logic-based automated reasoning. Some of the most challenging applications have come in diverse fields such as processing textual data [24], processing genome sequences (The Genome Project) [3, 20, 21], representing and reasoning with visual data [8, 4], storing and processing musical compositions, natural language processing [6], etc. These applications have some characteristic commonality - they process strings (or streams) of information, the data may be incomplete and may require approximate reasoning. String-based logic provides a tool for developing such automated reasoning systems.

Strings can be loosely defined as concatenations of variables and constants. String unification is difficult and may not lead to a unique most general unifier and in fact there may be an infinite number of maximally general unifiers. The decidability of the string unification problem (also called as the word problem) was established by Makanin [15] and procedures based on his technique have been developed by other researchers: Abdulrab and Pecuchet [1], Koscielski [14] and Jaffar [10]. But such procedures are not suitable for use in an automated reasoning environment or in a logic programming language because of their generation of multiple (maximally general) unifiers and non-termination when there are infinite number of such unifiers. In [18, 16] (see also [17]) we offer a solution to this dilemma through constraint logic programming [11, 12, 23]. is to apply constraint solving techniques, instead In our approach, we solve the problems of string unification by deferring full unification and performing partial unification at resolution step. By adapting this technique, we generate a set of string equations at each step, which subsumes the sets of (possibly infinite) maximally general unifiers. We define a notion of "partially-solved" form of string equations and develop an algorithm for obtaining such partially-solved forms from any given set of string equations. We discuss, in detail, the theoretical and procedural aspects of CLP(S) in [18] and define a constraint-solver which can be used to provide a sound and complete query answering system for allowed string logic programs.

In this paper we only provide a brief overview of CLP($\mathcal{S}$). We mainly concentrate on describing applications in CLP($\mathcal{S}$).

2 CLP($\mathcal{S}$) - Constraint Logic Programming with Strings

In CLP($\mathcal{S}$), apart from terms (built from constants, function symbols and variables) which can be used as arguments for building predicates, there is a new set of constructs called strings. Strings are built with *string constants* and *string-variable names*. A special symbol ϵ is used to denote an empty string. Each string-variable name has a parameter associated with it called its *size*, which limits the strings that can be bound to the variable to be of the same size. The size can be defined by a positive, integral arithmetic expression, called the *bounds expression* formed using *bounds-constants* and *bounds-variable names*. In essence, one can think of the set of string-variable names to be typed (or sorted) by their size and are limited to acquiring values of the same type (sort). We denote a string variable in the following way: $\overset{t}{W}$, where W is a string-variable name and t is a bounds expression denoting its size.

A *string* is defined recursively as follows: an empty string ϵ is a string; its size is 0. A string-constant is a string; its size is 1. A string-variable $\overset{t}{W}$ is a string; its size is t. If S_1 and S_2 are strings then so is their concatenation, $S_1 S_2$; the size of $S_1 S_2$ is the sum of the sizes of S_1 and S_2. The notions of *ground strings*, *string-atoms* and *string-literals* are defined as in logic programming.

A string equation (or constraint) is of the form $S_1 = S_2$, where S_1 and S_2 are strings and $=$ is a predicate which does not occur in the vocabulary of the logic programming language. An arithmetic equation is of the form $e_1 = e_2$ where e_1 and e_2 are arithmetic expressions. In [17, 18] we provide a string equational theory for $=$.

A CLP($\mathcal{S}$) program is defined as a finite set of rules of the form:

$A \leftarrow C, B_1, \ldots, B_n,$ where $n \geq 0$, $A, B_1, \ldots, B_n$ are string atoms and C is a set of string equations and arithmetic equations. Whenever a string variable occurs in more than once in a rule, we consider it to have the same size at each occurrence. An allowed program rule is a CLP($\mathcal{S}$) program rule in which every variable in A also occurs in $B_1, \ldots, B_n$. A *goal* is of the form:

$\leftarrow C, B_1, \ldots, B_n$ i.e., a rule without a head. Some examples of CLP($\mathcal{S}$) program rules are:

$add(\overset{r}{X}\overset{1}{A}, \overset{m}{Y}\overset{1}{0}, \overset{p}{Z}\overset{1}{A}) \leftarrow add(\overset{r}{X}, \overset{m}{Y}, \overset{p}{Z})$ % addition as a shift operation

$surftolex(n, \overset{n-3}{W}\overset{1}{Nicat}\overset{}{X}, \overset{m}{W}\overset{n-3}{Ny} + \overset{1}{at}\overset{}{X}, 1) \leftarrow nc\_val(\overset{1}{N}).$

% a C-insertion morphological rule (eg. apply + ation = application)

$same\_obj(\overset{r}{X}, \overset{r}{X})$ % two objects are identical (unifiable)

$sim\_obj(\overset{r}{X}, \overset{m}{Y}) \leftarrow \{\overset{r}{X} = \overset{m}{Y}\}$ % two objects are approximately similar; requires using approximate string equality checking.

Jaffar and Lassez [11] show that CLP paradigms can generalize the Horn logic programming semantics based on term structures (operational, algebraic, logical) over to Horn logic programs based on an arbitrary structure which is *solution-compact* and *satisfaction-complete*. The structure $(SU, =)$ ($=$ is equality with associativity) is *solution-compact* and *satisfaction-complete* [11]. The only remaining piece in the puzzle is the definition of constraint-solvers in the string domain for reducing string equations. In [18], we describe such an algorithm, called the reduce algorithm, which reduces a set of string equation into an equivalent set of strings in partially-solved form. The reduce algorithm, used in conjunction with Gaussian elimination (for solving arithmetic equations on string sizes) provides a sound and complete proof procedure for allowed programs, using the constraint logic programming paradigm. These results are shown in [18]. The reduce algorithm is similar to the term rule-based unification algorithm (see eg. [13]). This allows one to easily incorporate approximate string matching techniques during the reduction process. We discuss one such technique later in the paper. We do not provide the definition of the reduce algorithm and the theoretical results due to space constraints!

Prolog III is another example of a string processing constraint language [5]. CLP($\mathcal{S}$) differs from Prolog III in several ways; mainly in the association of an explicit size factor for string variables and in allowing unrestricted concatenation. The integrated structure of string-value and size provides several advantages. First, it provides a notion of 'types' on the string variables and allows one to restrict the domain of values that can be bound for the variable. One can also write equations (both equality and inequalities) on sizes which can ease and speed-up the unification process by allowing one to solve string equations using algebraic equation solvers on size-equations. The size information also allows one to effectively detect inequalities in string equations and fail a derivation earlier than otherwise. Moreover, one can use known string inequalities, such as $aS \neq Sb$ (where S can be taken as a string of arbitrary length), to fail CLP($\mathcal{S}$) derivations. The usage of the reduce algorithm, which is similar to a rule-based unification algorithm and based on the concept of partially-solved forms of string equations, is also unique in our approach and allows unrestricted concatenation and sub-string insertions and deletions. The advantage of this can be seen in the ease with which it can be adapted for approximate reasoning on strings (see [16].) To make the paper more readable, we briefly describe the unify algorithm in the appendix.

3 Applications of CLP($\mathcal{S}$)

We discuss three applications of CLP($\mathcal{S}$): in natural language processing for encoding logic grammar rules and for performing computational morphology; in visual scene processing for picture correspondence and as a picture description language; and, in genetic sequence analysis and for implementing genetic algorithms.

3.1 Natural Language Processing

Natural language sentences are inherently not well-structured. Their processing requires sentences of different types and phraseology to be parsed and analyzed. Even though there are some concrete rules which govern their analyses, for most parts ad hoc analysis needs to be performed. The analysis further deteriorates when one has to deal with spoken and/or colloquial sentences. In such cases, words or even parts of sentences may be missing caused probably by the speaker having a casual locution. Further, in morphological analysis one needs to divide a word into several parts to identify the underlying morphemes; sometimes no division is necessary. For example take the case of the following three transitive verbs, *incite*, *instigate* and *invent*. The first word has to be divided into a prefix *in* and a transitive verb *cite*, whereas the other two need no such division. In the last case, one can actually divide it into a prefix *in* and a transitive verb *vent*, but the recombined meaning of the morphemes *in+vent* is entirely different from the one given by the full word *invent*. In the above analysis, one is neither dealing with a (indivisible) constant nor building a term from constants in the manner of term-based logic. The use of strings as representation would be useful in naturally encoding the different types of grammatical formations and rules used in the lexical and morphological analysis of natural language. The associative property of string concatenation permits one to cut a string into two or more substrings at arbitrary locations.

Another important advantage of using strings as representation of sentences comes from the 'global' view offered by strings as compared to the 'local' view of term-based structures. When one needs to analyze (or process) several parts of the list as the same time, as may be required for extraposition or discontinuity analysis, one has to move (skip) through the list to perform the analyses. Such analysis can be easily done using strings. The use of strings also eases the operations of 'movement', insertions and deletions which are not easily performed with functions or lists. Such insertions and deletions occur quite often in morphological analysis.

To show how logic grammar rules can be encoded as CLP(S) rules, we give an example in Discontinuous grammar [2]. The rules in these grammars are of the form:
$$S, \alpha_0, skip(X_1), \alpha_1, \ldots, skip(X_n), \alpha_n \rightarrow \beta_0, skip(X_1'), \beta_1, \ldots, skip(X_m'), \beta_m$$
where S is a non-terminal and, αs and βs are strings of terminals and non-terminals. (β can also be procedure calls). The Xs denote arbitrary strings which need to be skipped. For example the following rule:

(DG) $Rel\_marker, skip(G), trace \rightarrow Rel\_pronoun, skip(G)$

taken from [2] parses sentences such as "the man that John saw laughed", where it considers the noun phrase "the man that John saw" to be a surface expression of a more explicit statement: "the man [John saw the man]", where the second occurrence of "the man" has been moved to the left and subsumed by the relative pronoun "that". The rule can be translated into a CLP(S) program rule as:

$$sentence(\overset{h}{H}\overset{p}{Y}\overset{r}{Z}\overset{t}{T}) \leftarrow rel\_marker(\overset{n}{X}), trace(\overset{m}{W}), sentence(\overset{h}{H}\overset{n}{X}\overset{r}{Z}\overset{m}{W}\overset{t}{T})$$

The atoms $rel\_marker(\overset{n}{X})$ and $trace(\overset{m}{W})$ are conditions which need to be enforced to make the transformation valid. In [16] we provide transformations for several different types of logic grammars and prove their correctness.

The analysis of word structures using computers is called *computational morphology*. In this section we show, through an example, how one can represent morphological rules using string-based logic. In our discussion on computational morphology we follow the book [19] by Ritchie, Russell, Black and Pulman. A sample rule is given below:

$$+:e <=> \{ < \{c:c \mid s:s\} \ (\ h:h\ )\ >\ \mid z:z \mid x:x \mid y:i \ \} \ \_\_ \ s:s$$

The rule[1] states that the surface character **e** gets deleted and is replaced by a lexical character **+** if and only if it is is preceded by either **ch, sh, z, x** or **i** realized as a lexical **y** and is followed by a **s**. The notation **c:c** denotes that **c** remains unchanged while transforming from surface level to lexical level. The rule can be used to transform the surface form **flies** to lexical form **fly + s**. The equivalent CLP($\mathcal{S}$) program is given by[2]:

$$surftolex(n, \overset{n-3}{X} shes, \overset{n-3}{X} sh+s, 1)$$
$$surftolex(n, \overset{n-3}{X} ches, \overset{n-3}{X} ch+s, 1)$$
$$surftolex(n, \overset{n-2}{X} xes, \overset{n-2}{X} x+s, 1)$$
$$surftolex(n, \overset{n-2}{X} zes, \overset{n-2}{X} z+s, 1)$$

In [16], we provide translations for some of the other morphographemic rules given in [19]. From the rules shown here and in [16] it can be seen that morphological transformation of a surface character into a lexical character requires character strings of variable lengths on either side and also requires insertion and deletion of characters. These operations are well-suited for a string-based representation.

In [16], we also show how one can use CLP($\mathcal{S}$) to perform word segmentation to identify categories and for encoding feature passing conventions. Rules such as generation and analysis of plural nouns, compound nouns, prefixing, etc, are given in [16].

Next, we point out how the CLP($\mathcal{S}$) system can be used for dealing with sentences with simple errors and sentences that are incomplete. In [26] algorithms for several kinds of approximate string matching are provided. They permit mismatches caused by extra characters, missing characters, altered (substituted) characters and interchanged characters. For example, the sentence "The man tat John saw lauhged" has two errors, one caused by a missing character and another by a pair of interchanged characters. Parsing this sentence normally would lead to failure. If we augment string-matching to reason with such errors and build in the mechanism as part of string-constraint solving one can parse the above statement. In [16] we show how one can augment the reduce algorithm to take care of such errors. The case of incomplete sentences, sentences with gaps in them, is easily treated with CLP($\mathcal{S}$), even though computationally it may not

---

[1] $<$ *items* $>$ denotes sequential items and $\{items\}$ denotes choice of items

[2] n and 1 are used as markers and flags used in other clauses. See [16] for details.

be attractive. The following can be given as a goal, when one knows that there are two gaps in the sentences with one of them of bounded size.

$\leftarrow \{n > 3, n < 10\}, sentence(the\ man\ \overset{n}{X}john\ \overset{3}{Y}\ laughed).$

One of the bindings returned may be values "that " and "saw" to X and Y respectively when used with proper rules. The need for parsing such incomplete sentences can be seen in several cases: when parsing old manuscripts with torn or missing segments or when parsing a sentence heard over radio or telephone where one may miss some segments due to noise. Parsing colloquial sentences which may have many missing segments. CLP($\mathcal{S}$) provides a method for parsing such sentences which may not be easily possible with other methods of natural language analysis.

3.2 Image Processing

One of the main areas in image processing deals with picture identification. For example, given a set of pictures one may want to find a picture in which there are two cars or, one may want to check whether another picture is a sub-picture of a picture in the set. A second question may involve approximate reasoning, since the smaller picture may not be a precise sub-picture. One of the ways of representing pictures is to convert them into symbolic forms based on an alphabet of 'icons'. For example, if one wants to represent a map of a region, then one can iconify the objects in the map (such as large lakes (a), mountains (b), forests (c), hills (d),etc.,) and place the icons on a corresponding scaled grid-map. Figure 1 shows such maps. Chang et. al. [4] define a scheme where iconic images are stored as 2-D strings. For example, the 2D-representation of the iconic picture of Figure 1, p is given by $(ad < b < c)(a < bc < d)$.

Note that the symbol $<$ captures the spatial relationship of below and to-the-right-of in the two 2-D string representation. Chang et. al. [4] provide algorithms to translate iconic pictures into 2D-representations and vice versa. In [18] we provide CLP($\mathcal{S}$) programs for performing these translations.

The two-dimensional string representation provides a simple approach to perform subpicture matching. Chang et. al. [4] describe three types of matching with decreasing levels of approximation; the last type (type-2) provides an exact sub-picture of another. In the following $r(a)$ denotes the rank of a non-$<$ symbol in a string and is defined as one plus the number of $<$'s preceding the symbol in s. A string u is a *type-i 1-D subsequence* of a string v if for all a_1s and b_1s, if $a_1 S_1 b_1$ is a substring of u and $a_2 S_2 b_2$ is a substring of v (where S_1 and S_2 are strings) and a_1, b_1 match a_2, b_2 resp., then

(for type-0) $r(b_2) - r(a_2) \geq r(b_1) - r(a_1)$ or $r(b_1) - r(a_1) = 0$

(for type-1) $r(b_2) - r(a_2) \geq r(b_1) - r(a_1) > 0$ or
$\qquad r(b_2) - r(a_2) = r(b_1) - r(a_1) = 0$

(for type-2) $r(b_2) - r(a_2) = r(b_1) - r(a_1)$.

Let (u, v) and (u', v') be 2-D representations of pictures p and p' respectively. Then p' is a *type-i 2-D subpicture* of p if u' is a type-i 1-D subsequence of u, and v' is a type-i 1-D subsequence of v. In Figure 1, p_1, p_2 and p_3 are type-0 subpictures of p; p_1 and p_2 are type-1 subpictures of p; and p_1 is a type-2 subpicture of p.

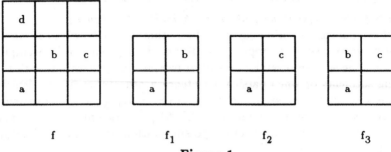

Figure 1

Chang et. al. [4] provide a complicated pseudo code procedure for performing the three matchings. In [18] we use CLP($\mathcal{S}$) programs to encode their definitions of type-i subsequences and to provide matching procedures for picture identification. We do not discuss them due to space constraints.

CLP($\mathcal{S}$) programs can also be used to encode picture description languages (PDLs) [22, 8]. For example, with proper labeling, the string $ababab$ denotes a staircase structure with three stairs. The above description can be captured using string-based logic as follows:

$staircase(ab)$,

$staircase(ab \overset{n}{X}) \leftarrow staircase(\overset{n}{X})$

Similarly, description of compound objects with occlusions can be given succinctly using CLP($\mathcal{S}$):

$occluded\_scene(\overset{n\,m\,p}{WZY}) \leftarrow object(\overset{n\,m\,p}{WXY}), object(\overset{m}{Z})$.

$occluded\_scene(\overset{n\,m}{WZ}) \leftarrow object(\overset{n\,r}{WX}), object(\overset{m}{Z}), m \geq r$.

$occluded\_scene(\overset{m\,n}{ZW}) \leftarrow object(\overset{r\,n}{XW}), object(\overset{m}{Z}), m \geq r$.

The representation can be used to reason about a scene, answering more complicated questions such as 'whether an object is in a scene (probably partially occluded)?' 'whether an object is to the left (or right) of another object?'

3.3 Genetic Operators and DNA Grammar

String-based logic can be used in genetic code processing in two ways. One of the method is to define operators which can be used to *build genetic sequences*. Another method is to use string-based logic to define genetic sequences and use these definitions to *search for sequences* in a given genetic code.

Genetic synthesis can be defined by several operators such as reproduction, crossover, jumping and mutation. These operations can be implemented in CLP($\mathcal{S}$). A somewhat complex cross-overs can easily be defined as follows.

$crossed\_genes(\overset{n\,m\,n}{X_1Y_2Z_1}, \overset{r\,m\,m}{X_2Y_1Z_2}) \leftarrow gene(\overset{n\,m\,n}{X_1Y_1Z_1}), gene(\overset{r\,m\,m}{X_2Y_2Z_2})$.

In [18] we define other operators using CLP($\mathcal{S}$). The new field of Genetic Algorithms is based on these and other operators and [7, 25] shows how Genetic Algorithms can be used to encode and solve several problems including the traveling salesman problem. The advantage gained by encoding the operators using this approach, is that one obtains declarative-procedural duality and a reasoning system based on the logic programming paradigm.

The recent explosion in genetics research, e.g., the *Genome Project*, has lead to the accumulation of a very large database of human (and other species) genetic sequences. Analyzing this massive amount of data would require a vast amount of computation and sophisticated algorithms. As Searls points out in [20, 21] the primary tool currently used to analyze the data is based on linear pattern matching and on viewing the data as a long string [3, 9]. Search for genetic sequences are carried out using regular expressions based on a regular language. In [20, 21] Searls describes a computational linguistic approach where the DNA sequences can be represented using formal grammar, which is better than the linear search techniques.. We translate his DNA grammar rules into $CLP(S)$ rules. He defines complicated genetic structures using simpler structures.

> **gene** $\Rightarrow$ **upstream, xscript, downstream.**
> **upstream** $\Rightarrow$ **catBox,** $40 \dots 50$, **tataBox** , $19 \dots 27$.
> **xscript** $\Rightarrow$ **capSite** , $\dots$, **xlate** , $\dots$, **termination.**

These definitions given above are not regular expressions and require encoding of gaps (both unbound ($\dots$) and variably-bounded ($40 \dots 50$)) in the sequence. These gaps may be unimportant or untranslatable in that particular gene expression. The above rules given above can be directly represented as the following $CLP(S)$ rules:

$$gene(\overset{m\,n\,p}{XYZ}) \leftarrow upstream(\overset{m}{X}), xscript(\overset{n}{Y}), downstream(\overset{p}{Z})$$

$$upstream(\overset{m\,n\,p\,q}{WXYZ}) \leftarrow catbox(\overset{m}{W}), n < 50, n > 40, tatabox(\overset{p}{Y}), q < 27, q > 19$$

$$xscript(\overset{m\,n\,p\,q\,r}{VWXYZ}) \leftarrow capsite(\overset{m}{V}), xlate(\overset{p}{X}), termination(\overset{r}{Z}).$$

Our representation of the DNA grammar rules have the advantage of being straightforward and declarative translations, whereas Searls' transformation into Prolog are interpreter dependent.

There are other genetic features such as a **repeat, inverted repeat, palindromes, tandem repeats, clover-leaf repeat, copia** and so on, which cause the representation of genetic sequences to be beyond the power of context-free languages. In [18] we show how these features can be defined using $CLP(S)$ rules.

Acknowledgement

We wish to express our appreciation to the National Science Foundation for their support of our work under grant number CCR-9110721.

References

1. H. Abdulrab and J-P. Pecuchet. Solving Word Equations. *Jour. Symbolic Computation*, 8:499–521, 1989.

2. H. Abramson and V. Dahl. *Logic Grammars*. Springer-Verlag, 1989.

3. A. Baehr, R. Hagstrom, D. Joerg, and R. Overbeek. Querying Genomic Databases. Technical Report ANL/MCS-TM-155, Argonne National Laboratory, Mathematics and Computer Science Division, 1991.

4. S.K. Chang, Q.Y. Shi, and C.W. Yan. Iconic Indexing by 2-D Strings. *IEEE PAMI*, 9(3):413–428, May 1987.

5. A. Colmeraur. An Introduction to Prolog-III. *Comm. ACM*, pages 70–90, July, 1990.

6. V. Dahl and P. Saint-Dizier. *Natural Language Understanding and Logic Programming*. North Holland, 1988.

7. D.E. Goldberg. *Genetic Algorithms*. Addison Wesley, 1989.

8. R.C. Gonzalez and P. Wintz. *Digital Image Processing*. Addison Wesley, 1987.

9. R. Hagstrom, G.S. Michaels, R. Overbeek, M. Price, R. taylor, K. Yoshida, and D. Zawada. GenoGraphics for Open Windows. Technical Report ANL-92/11, Argonne National Laboratory, Mathematics and Computer Science Division, 1992.

10. J. Jaffar. Minimal and Complete Word Unification. *Jour. ACM*, 37(1):67–85, 1990.

11. J. Jaffar and J.L. Lassez. Constraint Logic Programming. In *Proc. of POPL*, 1987.

12. J. Jaffar and S. Michaylov. Methodology and Implementation of a CLP System. In *Proc. of Logic Programming Conference*, Melbourne, 1987.

13. J-P. Jouannaud and C. Kirchner. Solving Equations in Abstract Algebras: A Rule-based Survey of Unification. In J-L. Lassez and G. Plotkin, editors, *Computational Logic: Essays in honor of Alan Robinson*, pages 257–321. MIT Press, 1991.

14. A. Koscielski. An Analysis of f Makanin's Algorithm Deciding Solvability of Equations in Free Groups. In *Word Equations and Related Topics, LNCS 572*, pages 12–61. Springer-Verlag, 1990.

15. G.S. Makanin. Equations in Free Semigroup. *AMS*, 1979. Also in Math USSR Sbornik, **32,2** (1977).

16. A. Rajasekar. CLP(String) and Computational Linguistics. manuscript.

17. A. Rajasekar. Logic Programming Using Strings. Technical Report 227-93, Department of Computer Science, University of Kentucky, 1993.

18. A. Rajasekar. String-based First Order Logic and Applications, 1993. submitted.

19. G.D. Ritchie, G.J. Russell, A.W. Black, and S.G. Pulman. *Computational Morphology: Practical Mechanisms for the English Lexicon*. MIT Press, Cambridge, Mass., 1992.

20. D.B. Searls. Representing Genetic Information with Formal Grammars. In *Proc. of AAAI*, pages 386–391, 1988.

21. D.B. Searls. Investigating the Linguistics of DNA with Definite Clause Grammars. In *Proc. of NACLP*, pages 189–208, MIT Press, Cambridge, Mass., 1989.

22. A.C. Shaw. Parsing of Graph-Repesentable Pictures. *JACM*, 17(3):453–481, 1970.

23. P. van Hentenryck. *Constraint Satisfaction in Logic Programming*. MIT Press, 1989.

24. E.B. Wendlandt and J.R. Driscoll. Semantic Extensions to Text Retrieval. In *ISMIS 91*, pages 266–275, 1991.

25. P. Winston. *Artificial Intelligence*. Addison Wesley, 1992.

26. Wu and Manber. Fast Text Searching With Errors. Technical report, University of Arizona, Department of Computer Science, 1991.

Appendix

A Unify Algorithm

Definition 1 *A partially-solved form of a set of string equations is a set of string equations $\{R_1 = S_1, \ldots R_n = S_n\}$ such that*

$\forall i, 1 \leq i \leq n$, *either R_i or S_i is of the form $\overset{t}{X_i} Q_i$, where $\overset{t}{X_i}$ is a string-variable with size t and Q_i is a (possibly empty) string, and*

$\forall i, 1 \leq i \leq n$, *either R_i or S_i is of the form $P_i \overset{t}{X_i}$, where $\overset{t}{X_i}$ is a string-variable with size t and P_i is a (possibly empty) string.* □

Definition 2 *A solved form of a set of string equations is a set of string equations $\{\overset{t_1}{X_1} = S_1, \ldots \overset{t_n}{X_n} = S_n\}$ such that $\forall i, 1 \leq i \leq n, \overset{t_i}{X_i}$ is a string-variable, $\forall i, 1 \leq i < j \leq n, X_i \neq X_j$, and $\forall i, 1 \leq i, j \leq n, X_i$ is not in any variable in S_j* □

Every set of equations in solved-form are also in partially-solved form. We next define an algorithm which transforms a set of string equations into a partially-solved form. Proofs of theorems are given in [18].

Algorithm 1 (Reduce Algorithm)
Input *S, a set of string equations*
Output *On SUCCESS returns S', a set of string equations, else returns FAILURE.*
Non-deterministically choose from the set of equation S an equation of a form below and perform the associated action: (in the following i denotes a natural number.)

(A:1) $a = \epsilon$ *halt with FAILURE.*
(A:2) $S_1 S_2 = \epsilon$ *replace by the equations $S_1 = \epsilon, S_2 = \epsilon$.*
(A:3) $aS_1 = aS_2$ *or* $S_1 a = S_2 a$, *replace by the equation $S_1 = S_2$.*
(A:4) $aS_1 = bS_2$ *or* $S_1 a = S_2 b$, *where $a \neq b$, halt with FAILURE.*
(A:5) $S_1 = S_1$ *for any string S_1, delete the equation*
(A:6) $\overset{t}{X} = S_1$ *or* $S_1 = \overset{t}{X}$ *where S_1 is not identical to $\overset{t}{X}$ and $\overset{t}{X}$ has another occurrence in the set of equations.*

   If $\overset{t}{X}$ appears in S_1 then halt with FAILURE.

   Otherwise substitute S_1 wherever $\overset{t}{X}$ appears in every other equation.
(A:7) $S_1 a_1 \ldots a_j S_2 = b_1 \ldots b_k$ *or* $b_1 \ldots b_k = S_1 a_1 \ldots a_j S_2$.
   If $a_1 \ldots a_j$ is not a sub-string of $b_1 \ldots b_k$ then halt with FAILURE;
   else, if $a_1 \ldots a_j$ is a unique substring of $b_1 \ldots b_k$ such that
   $b_1 \ldots b_k = b_1 \ldots b_r a_1 \ldots a_j b_s \ldots b_k$, *replace by equations*
   $S_1 = b_1 \ldots b_r$ *and* $S_2 = b_s \ldots b_k$
(A:8) $\overset{i}{X} S_1 = a_1 \ldots a_j S_2$ *or* $a_1 \ldots a_j S_2 = \overset{i}{X} S_1$
   where S_2 has at least one variable and $S_1 \neq \epsilon$.

If $j > i$, replace by equations $\overset{i}{X} = a_1 \ldots a_i$ and $S_1 = a_{i+1} \ldots a_j S_2$.

If $i \geq j$, replace by equations $\overset{i}{X} = a_1 \ldots a_j \overset{i-j}{W}$ and $S_2 = \overset{i-j}{W} S_1$

(A:8') $S_1 \overset{i}{X} = S_2 a_j \ldots a_1$ or $S_2 a_j \ldots a_1 = S_1 \overset{i}{X}$.

where S_2 has at least one variable and $S_1 \neq \epsilon$

If $j > i$, replace by equations $\overset{i}{X} = a_i \ldots a_1$ and $S_1 = S_2 a_j \ldots a_{i+1}$

If $i \geq j$, replace by equations $\overset{i}{X} = \overset{i-j}{W} a_j \ldots a_1$ and $S_2 = S_1 \overset{i-j}{W}$

(A:9) $\overset{i}{X} S_1 = \overset{j}{Y} S_2$, where S_1 and S_2 are not empty strings.

If $j > i$, replace by equations $\overset{j}{Y} = stackreliX \overset{j-i}{W}$ and $S_1 = \overset{j-i}{W} S_2$

If $i \geq j$, replace by equations $\overset{i}{X} = \overset{j}{Y} \overset{i-j}{W}$ and $S_2 = \overset{i-j}{W} S_1$

(A:9') $S_1 \overset{i}{X} = S_2 \overset{j}{Y}$, where S_1 and S_2 are not empty strings.

If $j > i$, replace by equations $\overset{j}{Y} = \overset{j-i}{W} \overset{i}{X}$ and $S_1 = S_2 \overset{j-i}{W}$

If $i \geq j$, replace by equations $\overset{i}{X} = \overset{i-j}{W} \overset{j}{Y}$ and $S_2 = S_1 \overset{i-j}{W}$

(A:10) $S_1 S_2 = S_3 S_4$ where $|S_1| = |S_3|$ or $|S_2| = |S_4|$,

replace by the equation $S_1 = S_3$ and $S_2 = S_4$

(A:11) If none of the steps (A:1) through (A:10) can be applied,

halt with $SUCCESS$ returning the set of equations. $\square$

Theorem 1 *Let S be a set of string equations which is reduced using the reduce algorithm. Then,*

1. *The algorithm halts in finite steps;*
2. *If S' is the output set of string equations then S is equivalent to S';*
3. *If S' is the output set of string equations then S is in partially-solved form;*
4. *If the algorithm terminates with $FAILURE$ then S is not unifiable.* $\square$

Definition 3 *A string equation is in* size-constant *form if every string-variable occurring in the equation has an integer as its size parameter. A set of string equations is in size-constant form if every equation in the set is in size-constant form. A string is in size-constant form if every string-variable occurring in the string has an integer as its size parameter.* $\square$

Lemma 1 *Let S be a set of string equations in size-constant form. Then the reduce algorithm results in $FAILURE$ if and only if, S has no unifiers, or else results in a solved-form. Moreover, the set of equations in solved form provides the unique (up to renaming) most general unifier for S.* $\square$

Example 1 *Let $S = \{\overset{2}{X}\overset{3}{Y} = \overset{3}{Y}\overset{2}{X}\}$*
The reduce algorithm proceeds as follows:

$S_1 = \{\overset{3}{Y} = \overset{2}{X}\overset{1}{W}, \overset{3}{Y} = \overset{1}{W}\overset{2}{X}\}$ *from* $(A:8)$

$S_2 = \{\overset{3}{Y} = \overset{2}{X}\overset{1}{W}, \overset{2}{X}\overset{1}{W} = \overset{1}{W}\overset{2}{X}\}$ *from* $(A:6)$

$S_3 = \{\overset{3}{Y} = \overset{2}{X}\overset{1}{W}, \overset{2}{X} = \overset{1}{W}\overset{1}{Z}, \overset{2}{X} = \overset{1}{Z}\overset{1}{W}\}$ *from* $(A:8)$

$$S_4 = \{\overset{3}{Y}=\overset{1}{W}\overset{1}{Z}\overset{1}{W}, \overset{2}{X}=\overset{1}{W}\overset{1}{Z}, \overset{1}{W}\overset{1}{Z}=\overset{1}{Z}\overset{1}{W}\} \ \textit{from } (A:6)$$
$$S_5 = \{\overset{3}{Y}=\overset{1}{W}\overset{1}{Z}\overset{1}{W}, \overset{2}{X}=\overset{1}{W}\overset{1}{Z}, \overset{1}{W}=\overset{1}{Z}, \overset{1}{Z}=\overset{1}{W}\} \ \textit{from } (A:8)$$
$$S_6 = \{\overset{3}{Y}=\overset{1}{Z}\overset{1}{Z}\overset{1}{Z}, \overset{2}{X}=\overset{1}{Z}\overset{1}{Z}, \overset{1}{W}=\overset{1}{Z}, \overset{1}{Z}=\overset{1}{Z}\} \ \textit{from } (A:6)$$
$$S_7 = \{\overset{3}{Y}=\overset{1}{Z}\overset{1}{Z}\overset{1}{Z}, \overset{2}{X}=\overset{1}{Z}\overset{1}{Z}, \overset{1}{W}=\overset{1}{Z}\} \ \textit{from } (A:5)$$

Halts with success. □

An advantage of the rule-based reduce algorithm is that one can add failure-rules to it without compromising the soundness or the completeness of the algorithm. Such additions would enable one to fail a reduction process faster than without the rules. For example, it is well known that the following string equations have no unifier: $a \overset{n}{X} = \overset{n}{X} b$ and $\overset{m}{X} a \overset{n}{Y} = \overset{n}{Y} b \overset{m}{X}$. Such rules can be used as additional conditions for failing the unification process of the reduce algorithm.

B CLP($\mathcal{S}$)-Resolution

A CLP($\mathcal{S}$)-derivation is similar to a CLP-derivation [11] but uses algebraic and string constraint solvers.

Definition 4 (SSLD-Derivation)
Let Let $\mathcal{A}$ be an algebraic constraint solver and let $\mathcal{U}$ be a string-constraint solver. Let P be a CLP($\mathcal{S}$) program and let G be a goal. A String SLD-derivation is a sequence of CLP($\mathcal{S}$)-goals $G_0 = G, G_1, \ldots,$ such that $\forall i \geq 0$, G_{i+1} is obtained from $G_i =\leftarrow C_i \cup E_i, A_1, \ldots, A_n$. as follows:
1. *A_m is an atom in G_i and is called the selected atom.*
2. *$A \leftarrow B_1, \ldots B_r$ is a clause in P standardized apart with respect to G_i.*
3. *$C_{i+1} = C_i \cup \{S_1 = S_1', \ldots, S_n = S_n'\}$ and*
   $E_{i+1} = E_i \cup \{|S_1| = |S_1'|, \ldots, |S_n| = |S_n'|\}$
   when A_m and A are of the form $A_m = p(S_1, \ldots, S_n)$ and $A = p(S_1', \ldots, S_n')$.
4. *G_{i+1}' is the goal $\leftarrow C_{i+1} \cup E_{i+1}, A_1, \ldots, A_{m-1}, B_1, \ldots B_r, A_{m+1}, \ldots, A_n$*
5. *θ_i is the string substitution found by applying $\mathcal{A}$ and $\mathcal{U}$ to $C_{i+1} \cup E_{i+1}$.*
6. *G_{i+1} is the goal $\leftarrow (C_{i+1} \cup E_{i+1}, A_1, \ldots, A_{m-1}, B_1, \ldots B_r, A_{m+1}, , \ldots, A_n)\theta_i$*   □

In line 5, θ_i consists only of equations in $C_{i+1} \cup E_{i+1}$ which are in solved form; the rest of the equations in $C_{i+1} \cup E_{i+1}$ may be in partially-solved form.

Definition 5 *Let P be a CLP($\mathcal{S}$) program and let G be a goal. A successful SSLD-derivation is an SSLD-derivation which ends in a goal with only (possibly empty) constraints and no predicate goals.*   □

Definition 6 *Let A be an algebraic constraint solver and let U be a string-constraint solver. Let P be a CLP($\mathcal{S}$) program and let G be a goal. Let $\leftarrow C_n \cup E_n$ be the final goal in a successful SSLD-derivation. Then $E_A \cup E_U$ is a SSLD-computed constraint using A and U for $P \cup \{G\}$ if*
   E_A is a set of integer equations obtained from reducing E_n using A,

and let θ_A be the subset of E_A that are variable substitutions

E_U is a set of string equations obtained from reducing $C_n \theta_A$ using U.
If $E_U \cup E_U$ is a set of string substitutions then the substitutions in $E_A \cup E_U$ restricted to the variables occurring in G is an SSLD-computed answer substitution for $P \cup \{G\}$. $\qquad\qquad\Box$

Note that it is possible that the algebraic constraint solver or the string constraint solver may halt in failure. In such a case the SSLD-resolution is considered to have ended in failure. The soundness and completeness of SSLD-resolution for allowed CLP(S) programs is shown in [18].

The following is an SSLD-derivation for the goal $\leftarrow add(0100, 0101, \overset{s}{P})$ using the program given below: $\quad\{succ(\overset{r}{X}0, \overset{r}{X}1),$

$succ(\overset{r}{X}1, \overset{m}{Y}0) \leftarrow succ(\overset{r}{X}, \overset{m}{Y}),$

$add(\overset{r}{X}, 0, \overset{r}{X}),$

$add(\overset{r}{X}\overset{1}{A}, \overset{m}{Y}0, \overset{p}{Z}\overset{1}{A}) \leftarrow add(\overset{r}{X}, \overset{m}{Y}, \overset{p}{Z}),$

$add(\overset{r}{X}, \overset{m}{Y}1, \overset{p}{Z}\overset{1}{A}) \leftarrow (succ(\overset{r}{X}, \overset{n}{W}\overset{1}{A}) \wedge add(\overset{n}{W}, \overset{m}{Y}, \overset{p}{Z}))\}$

(Instantiations of the variable symbols in the SSLD-derivation is differentiated through subscripts.)

$\leftarrow \{\}, add(0100, 0101, \overset{s}{P})$

$\qquad | \; using \; add(\overset{r}{X}, \overset{m}{Y}1, \overset{p}{Z}\overset{1}{A}) \leftarrow succ(\overset{r}{X}, \overset{n}{W}\overset{1}{A}), add(\overset{n}{W}, \overset{m}{Y}, \overset{p}{Z})$

$\qquad | \; \theta_1 = \{\overset{4}{X} = 0100, \overset{3}{Y} = 010, r = 4, m = 3\}$

$\leftarrow \{\overset{s}{P} = \overset{p}{Z}\overset{1}{A}, s = p + 1\} \cup \theta_1, succ(0100, \overset{n}{W}\overset{1}{A}), add(\overset{n}{W}, 010, \overset{p}{Z})$

$\qquad | \; using \; succ(\overset{r_1}{X_1}0, \overset{r_1}{X_1}1)$

$\qquad | \; \theta_2 = \{\overset{3}{X_1} = 010, \overset{3}{W} = 010, \overset{1}{A} = 1, r_1 = 3, n = 3\}$

$\leftarrow \{\overset{p}{Z}\overset{1}{A} = \overset{s}{P}, s = p + 1\} \cup \theta_1 \cup \theta_2, add(010, 010, \overset{p}{Z})$

$\qquad | \; using \; add(\overset{r_2}{X_2}\overset{1}{A_2}, \overset{m_2}{Y_2}0, \overset{p_1}{Z_1}\overset{1}{A_2}) \leftarrow add(\overset{r_2}{X_2}, \overset{m_2}{Y_2}, \overset{p_1}{Z_1})$

$\qquad | \; \theta_3 = \{\overset{2}{X_2} = 01, \overset{1}{A_2} = 0, \overset{2}{Y_2} = 01, r_2 = 2, m_2 = 2\}$

$\leftarrow \{\overset{s}{P} = \overset{p}{Z}\overset{1}{A}, s = p + 1, \overset{p_1}{Z_1}\overset{1}{A_2} = \overset{p}{Z}, p = p_1 + 1\} \cup \theta_1 \cup \theta_2 \cup \theta_3, add(01, 01, \overset{p_1}{Z_1})$

$\qquad | \; using \; add(\overset{r_3}{X_3}, \overset{m_3}{Y_3}1, \overset{p_2}{Z_2}\overset{1}{A_3}) \leftarrow succ(\overset{r_3}{X_3}, \overset{n_1}{W_1}\overset{1}{A_3}), add(\overset{n_1}{W_1}, \overset{m_3}{Y_3}, \overset{p_2}{Z_2})$

$\qquad | \; \theta_4 = \{\overset{2}{X_3} = 01, \overset{1}{Y_3} = 0, r_3 = 2, m_3 = 1\}$

$\leftarrow \{\overset{s}{P} = \overset{p}{Z}\overset{1}{A}, s = p + 1, \overset{p_1}{Z_1}\overset{1}{A_2} = \overset{p}{Z}, p = p_1 + 1, \overset{p_1}{Z_1} = \overset{p_2}{Z_2}\overset{1}{A_3}, p_1 = p_2 + 1\}$

$\qquad \cup \theta_1 \cup \theta_2 \cup \theta_3 \cup \theta_4, succ(01, \overset{n_1}{W_1}\overset{1}{A_3}), add(\overset{n_1}{W_1}, 0, \overset{p_2}{Z_2})$

$\qquad | \; using \; succ(\overset{r_4}{X_4}1, \overset{m_4}{Y_4}0) \leftarrow succ(\overset{r_4}{X_4}, \overset{m_4}{Y_4})$

$\qquad | \; \theta_5 = \{\overset{1}{X_4} = 0, \overset{1}{Y_4} = \overset{n_1}{W_1}, \overset{1}{A_3} = 0, r_4 = 1, m_4 = 1\}$

$$\leftarrow \{\overset{s}{P}=\overset{p}{Z}\overset{1}{A}, s = p+1, \overset{p_1}{Z_1}\overset{1}{A_2}=\overset{p}{Z}, p = p_1 + 1, \overset{p_1}{Z_1}=\overset{p_2}{Z_2}\overset{1}{A_3}, p_1 = p_2 + 1\}$$

$$\cup\theta_1 \cup \theta_2 \cup \theta_3 \cup \theta_4 \cup \theta_5, succ(0, \overset{n_1}{W_1})add(\overset{n_1}{W_1}, 0, \overset{p_2}{Z_2})$$

$$|\ using\ \ succ(\overset{r_5}{X_5}0, \overset{r_5}{X_5}1)$$

$$|\ \theta_6 = \{\overset{0}{X_5}= \varepsilon, \overset{1}{W_1}= 1, n_1 = 1, r_5 = 0\}$$

$$\leftarrow \{\overset{s}{P}=\overset{p}{Z}\overset{1}{A}, s = p+1, \overset{p_1}{Z_1}\overset{1}{A_2}=\overset{p}{Z}, p = p_1 + 1, \overset{p_1}{Z_1}=\overset{p_2}{Z_2}\overset{1}{A_3}, p_1 = p_2 + 1\}$$

$$\cup\theta_1 \cup \theta_2 \cup \theta_3 \cup \theta_4 \cup \theta_5 \cup \theta_6, add(1, 0, \overset{p_2}{Z_2})$$

$$|\ using\ \ add(\overset{r_6}{X_6}, 0, \overset{r_6}{X_6})$$

$$|\ \theta_7 = \{\overset{1}{X_6}= 1, \overset{1}{Z_2}= 1, p_2 = 1, r_6 = 1\}$$

$$\leftarrow \{\overset{s}{P}=\overset{p}{Z}\overset{1}{A}, s = p+1, \overset{p_1}{Z_1}\overset{1}{A_2}=\overset{p}{Z}, p = p_1 + 1, \overset{p_1}{Z_1}=\overset{p_2}{Z_2}\overset{1}{A_3}, p_1 = p_2 + 1\}$$

$$\cup\theta_1 \cup \theta_2 \cup \theta_3 \cup \theta_4 \cup \theta_5 \cup \theta_6 \cup \theta_7.$$

Applying the Gaussian elimination and the reduce algorithm to the constraint set given by:

$$\{\overset{s}{P}=\overset{p}{Z}\overset{1}{A}, s = p+1, \overset{p_1}{Z_1}\overset{1}{A_2}=\overset{p}{Z}, p = p_1 + 1, \overset{p_1}{Z_1}=\overset{p_2}{Z_2}\overset{1}{A_3}, p_1 = p_2 + 1\} \cup \theta_1 \cup \theta_2 \cup$$
$$\theta_3 \cup \theta_4 \cup \theta_5 \cup \theta_6 \cup \theta_7,$$

we obtain the answer substitution: $\overset{s}{P}= 1001$. $\qquad\qquad\square$

Some Methodological Issues in the Design of CIAO, a Generic, Parallel Concurrent Constraint Logic Programming System

M. Hermenegildo

Facultad de Informática
Universidad Politécnica de Madrid (UPM)
28660-Boadilla del Monte, Madrid, Spain
herme@fi.upm.es

Abstract. We informally discuss several issues related to the parallel execution of logic programming systems and concurrent logic programming systems, and their generalization to constraint programming. We propose a new view of these systems, based on a particular definition of parallelism. We argue that, under this view, a large number of the actual systems and models can be explained through the application, at different levels of granularity, of only a few basic principles: determinism, non-failure, independence (also referred to as stability), granularity, etc. Also, and based on the convergence of concepts that this view brings, we sketch a model for the implementation of several parallel constraint logic programming source languages and models based on a common, generic abstract machine and an intermediate kernel language.

1 Introduction

We present an informal discussion on some methodological aspects regarding the efficient parallel implementation of (concurrent) (constraint) logic programming systems. These efforts represent our first steps towards the development of what we call the CIAO (Concurrent, Independence-based And/Or parallel) system – a platform which we expect will provide efficient implementations of a series of *non-deterministic, concurrent, constraint logic programming languages*, on sequential and multiprocessor machines. Because of broad-view nature of the discussion, in the following a certain familiarity with constraint logic programming and parallel logic programming theory. models, and actual systems such as Muse [1], Aurora [24], &-Prolog [13], GHC [32], PNU-Prolog [26], DDAS [28], Andorra-I [27], AKL [20], and the extended Andorra model [33] is assumed.

2 Separation of issues / Fundamental Principles

We begin our discussion with some very general observations regarding computation rules, concurrency, parallelism, and independence. We believe these observations to be instrumental in understanding our approach and its relationship to others. A motivation for the discussions that follow is the fact that many current proposals for parallel or concurrent logic programming languages and models are actually "bundled packages", in the sense that they offer a combined solution affecting a number of issues such as choice of computation rule, concurrency, exploitation of parallelism, etc. This is understandable since certainly a practical model has to offer solutions for all the problems involved. However, the bundled nature of (the description of) many models often makes it difficult to compare them with each other. It is our view that, in order to be able to perform such comparisons, a "separation analysis" of such models, isolating their fundamental principles in (at least) the coordinates proposed above must be performed. In fact, we also believe that such un-bundling brings the additional benefit of allowing the identification and study of the fundamental principles involved in a system independent manner and the transference of the valuable features of a system to another. In the following we present some ideas on how we believe the separation analysis mentioned above might be approached.

2.1 Separating Control Rules and Parallelism

We start by discussing the separation of parallelism and computation rules in logic programming systems. Of these two concepts, probably the best understood from the formal point of view is that of computation rules. Assuming for example an SLD resolution-based system the "computation rules" amount to a "selection rule" and a "search rule." The objective of such computation rules in general is to minimize work, i.e. to reduce the total amount of resolutions needed to obtain an answer. We believe it is useful, at least from the point of view of analyzing systems, to make a strict distinction between parallelism issues and computation-rule related issues. To this end, we define parallelism as the simultaneous execution of a number of *independent* sequences of resolutions, *taken from those which would have to be performed in any case as determined by the computation rules.* We call each such sequence a *thread* of execution. Note that as soon as there is an *actual* (i.e., run-time) dependency between two sequences, one has to wait for the other and therefore parallelism does not occur for some time. Thus, such sequences contain several threads. Exploiting parallelism means taking a fixed-size computation (determined by the computation rules), splitting it into independent threads related by dependencies (building a dependency graph), and assigning these segments to different agents. Both the partitioning and the agent assignment can be performed statically or dynamically. The objective of parallelism in this definition is simply to *perform the same amount of work in less time.*

We consider as an example a typical or-parallel system. Let us assume a finite tree, with no cuts or side-effects, and that all solutions are required. In a first approximation we could consider that the computation rules in such a system are the same as in Prolog and thus the same tree is explored and the number of resolution steps is the same. Exploiting (or-)parallelism then means taking branches of the resolution tree (which have no dependencies, given the assumptions) and giving them to different agents. The result is a performance gain that is independent of any performance implications of the computation rule. As is well known, however, if only (any) one solution is needed, then such a system can behave quite differently from Prolog: if the leftmost solution (the one Prolog would find) is deep in the tree, and there is another, shallower solution to its right, the or-parallel system may find this other solution first. Furthermore, it may do this after having explored a different portion of the tree which is potentially smaller (although also potentially bigger). The interesting thing to realize from our point of view is that part of the possible performance gain (which sometimes produces "super-linear" speedups) comes in a fundamental way from a change in the computation rule, rather than from parallel execution itself. It is not due to the fact that several agents are operating but to the different way in which the tree is being explored ("more breath-first").[1]

A similar phenomenon appears for example in independent and-parallel systems if they incorporate a certain amount of "intelligent failure": computation may be saved. We would like this to be seen as associated to a smarter computation rule that is taking advantage of the knowledge of the independence of some goals rather than having really anything to do with the parallelism. In contrast, also the possibility of performing additional work arises: unless non-failure can be proved ahead of time, and-parallel systems necessarily need to be speculative to a certain degree in order to obtain speedups. However such speculation can in fact be controlled so that no slow down occurs [14].

Another interesting example to consider is the Andorra-I system. The basic Andorra principle underlying this system states (informally) that deterministic reductions are performed ahead of time and possibly in parallel. This principle would be seen from our point of view as actually two principles, one related to the computation rules and another to parallelism. From the computation rule point of view the bottom line is that deterministic reductions are executed first. This is potentially very useful in practice since it can result in a change (generally a reduction, although the converse may also be true) of the number of resolutions needed to find a solution. Once the computation rule is isolated the remaining part of the rule is related to parallelism and can be seen simply as stating that deterministic reductions can be executed in parallel. Thus, the "parallelism part" of the basic Andorra principle, once isolated from the computation rule part, brings a basic principle to parallelism: that of the general convenience of parallel execution of deterministic threads.

We believe that the separation of computation rule and parallelism issues mentioned above allows enlarging the applicability of the interesting principles brought in by many current models.

---

[1] This can be observed for example by starting a Muse or an Aurora system with several "workers" on a uniprocessor machine. In this experiment it is possible sometimes to obtain a performance gain w.r.t. a sequential Prolog system even though there is no parallelism involved – just a *coroutining* computation rule, in this case implemented by the multitasking operating system.

2.2 Abstracting Away the Granularity Level: Fundamental Principles

Having argued for the separation of parallelism issues from those that are related to computation rules, we now concentrate on the fundamental principles governing parallelism in the different models proposed. We argue that moving a principle from one system to another can often be done quite easily if another such "separation" is performed: isolating the principle itself from the *level of granularity* at which it is applied. This means viewing the parallelizing principle involved as associated to a generic concept of thread, to be particularized for each system, according to the fundamental unit of parallelism used in such system.

As an example, and following these ideas, the fundamental principle of determinism used in the basic Andorra model can be applied to the &-Prolog system. The basic unit of parallelism considered when parallelizing programs in the classical &-Prolog tools is the subtree corresponding to the complete resolution of a given goal in the resolvent. If the basic Andorra principle is applied at this level of granularity its implications are that deterministic subtrees can and should be executed in parallel (even if they are "dependent" in the classical sense). Moving the notions of determinism in the other direction, i.e. towards a finer level of granularity, one can think of applying the principle at the level of bindings, rather than clauses, which yields the concept of "binding determinism" of PNU-Prolog [26].

In fact, the converse can also be done: the underlying principles of &-Prolog w.r.t. parallelism –basically its independence rules– can in fact be applied at the granularity level of the Andorra model. The concept of independence in the context of &-Prolog is defined informally as requiring that a part of the execution "will not be affected" by another. Sufficient conditions –strict and non-strict independence [14]– are then defined which are shown to ensure this property. We argue that applying these concepts at the granularity level of the Andorra model gives some new ways of understanding the model and some new solutions for its parallelization. In order to do this it is quite convenient to look at the basic operations in the light of David Warren's *extended* Andorra model.[2] The extended Andorra model brings in the first place the idea of presenting the execution of logic programs as a series of simple, low level operations on and-or trees. In addition to defining a lower level of granularity, the extended Andorra model incorporates some principles which are related in part to parallelism and in part to computation rule related issues such as the above mentioned basic Andorra principle and the avoidance of re-computation of goals.

On the other hand the extended Andorra model also leaves several other issues relatively more open. One example is that of when nondeterministic reductions may take place in parallel. One answer for this important and relatively open issue was given in the instantiation of the model in the AKL language. In AKL the concept of "stability" is defined as follows: a configuration (partial

---

[2] This is understandable, given that adding independent and-parallelism to the basic Andorra model was one of the objectives in the development of its extended version.

resolvent) is said to be stable if it cannot be affected by other sibling configurations. In that case the operational semantics of AKL allow the non-determinate promotion to proceed. Note that the definition is, not surprisingly, equivalent to that of independence, although applied at a different granularity level. Unfortunately stability/independence is in general an undecidable property. However, applying the work developed in the context of independent and-parallelism at this level of granularity provides sufficient conditions for it. The usefulness of this is underlined by the fact that the current version of AKL incorporates the relatively simple notion of strict independence (i.e. the absence of variable sharing) as its stability rule. However, the presentation above clearly marks the way for incorporating more advanced concepts, such as non-strict independence, as a sufficient condition for the independence/stability rule. As will be mentioned, we are actively working on compile-time detection of non-strict independence, which we believe will be instrumental in this context. Furthermore, and as we will show, when adding constraint support to a system the traditional notions of independence are no longer valid and both new definitions of independence and sufficient conditions for it need to be developed. We believe that the view proposed herein allows the direct application of general results concerning independence in constraint systems to several realms, such as the extended Andorra model and AKL.

Another way of moving the concept of independence to a finer level of granularity is to apply it at the binding level. This yields a rule which states that dependent bindings of variables should wait for their leftmost occurrences to complete (in the same way as subtrees wait for dependent subtrees to their left to complete in the standard independent and-parallelism model), which is essentially the underlying rule of the DDAS model [28]. In fact, one can imagine applying the principle of non-strict independence at the level of bindings, which would yield a "non-strict" version of DDAS which would not require dependent bindings to wait for bindings to their left which are guaranteed to never occur, or for bindings which are guaranteed to be compatible with them.

Recently, new concepts of independence have been proposed for constraint logic programming [6], since the traditional concepts are not valid in this context. It is our belief that these new concepts can also be applied at different granularity levels and thus render "constraint correct" versions of models such as DDAS (and also be used for defining sufficient conditions for stability in the context of constraints other than Herbrand). In order to do this, we have recently proposed a very fine grain, truly concurrent semantics for both CC-type languages with atomic tell and CLP-type languages [2]. Applications of this semantics are illustrated in [25].

With this view in mind we argue that, once thy are abstracted out from the control rules, and from the granularity level at which they are applied, there exist several common, fundamental principles which govern exploitation of parallelism. Our discussion has revolved around:

- *independence*, which allows parallelism among non-deterministic threads, provided they do not "affect" each other,

– *determinacy*, which allows parallelism among dependent threads.

We believe there are other such fundamental principles, among which we would like to mention *non-failure*, which allows avoiding speculativeness, and *granularity*, or thread size, which allows guaranteeing speedup in the presence of overheads. Space limitations prevent us from elaborating on these.

2.3 Parallelism vs. Concurrency

Similarly to the separations mentioned above (parallelism vs. computation rule and principles vs. granularity level of their application) we also believe in a separation of "concurrency" from both parallelism and computation rules. We believe that concurrency is most useful when explicitly controlled by the user and in that sense it should in some ways also be separate from the implicit computation rules, although this is more of a source language semantics choice. This is in contrast with parallelism, which ideally should be transparent to the user, and with smart computation rules of which the user should be aware, in the sense of being able to derive an upper bound on the amount of computation involved in running a program for a given query using that rule. Space limitations prevent us from elaborating more on this topic or that of the separation between concurrency and parallelism. However, an example of an application of the latter can be seen in *schedule analysis*, where the maximal essential components of concurrency are isolated and sequenced to allow the most efficient possible execution of the concurrent program by one agent [21]. Schedule analysis is, after all, an application of the concept of dependence (or, conversely, independence) at a certain level of granularity in order to "unparallelize" a program, and is thus based on the same principles as automatic parallelization.

Furthermore, we believe that there are actually at least two forms of concurrency based on whether or not there is a notion of a "computing agent" attached to the concurrent task. In other words, whether there is a notion of "computational gas" or "fairness" attached to each such task. The first form of concurrency is traditionally referred to as "coroutining". This is the concurrency obtained explicitly with Prolog's "freeze" (and, also, through &-Prolog's "&"), and implicitly in Gödel [15] or in Andorra-I [27] through the basic Andorra principle. The second one is associated with the explicit creation of an actual process and is generally not present in concurrent logic programming systems. The differences between these two forms of concurrency can easily been seen through an example: imagine a procedure "cube(X)" that opens a window in a display and shows a cube which rotates X times. Assume "&" to be the concurrent operator. Now consider the concurrent conjunction "cube(5) & cube(5)". Note that the two tasks are independent and thus need no synchronization. Thus, in the case of a coroutining interpretation of "&" one possible execution would be to execute the two calls sequentially. But it may be that what the programmer actually means is that two windows should be opened (more or less) at the same time and the cubes should rotate (more or less) simultaneously, in which case the second type of concurrency is meant. In any case, the two interpretations

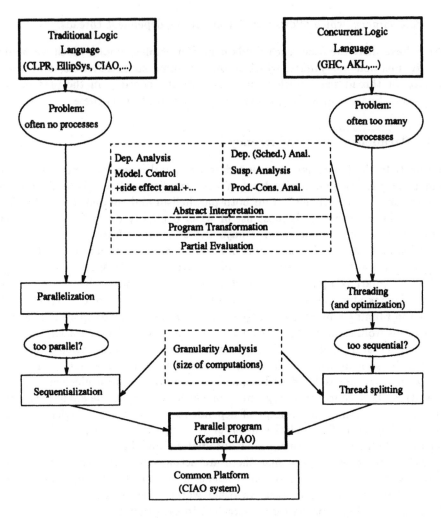

Fig. 1. Common Problems in Compilation

are clearly different. In the CIAO system we propose to support both forms of concurrency through different user-level primitives ("&" and "&&" – for more details, please see [12]).

3   Towards General-Purpose Implementations

We believe that the points regarding the separation of issues and fundamental principles sketched in the previous sections at the same time explain and are supported by the recent trend towards convergence in the analysis and implementation techniques of systems that are in principle very different, such as the various parallel implementations of Prolog on one hand (see, for example, [13, 24, 27]) and the implementations of the various committed choice languages on the other (see, for example, [5, 10, 18, 31, 32]). The former are based on schemes for parallelizing a sequential language; they tend to be stack-based, in the sense that (virtual) processors allocate environments on a stack and execute computations "locally" as far as possible until there is no more work to do, at which point they "steal" work from a busy processor. The latter, by contrast, are based on concurrent languages with dataflow synchronization; they tend to be heap-based, in the sense that environments are generally allocated on a heap, and there is (at least conceptually) a shared queue of active tasks.

The aforementioned convergence can be observed in that, on one hand, driven by the demonstrated utility of delay primitives in sequential Prolog systems (e.g., the **freeze** and **block** declarations of Sicstus Prolog [4], **when** declarations of NU-Prolog [29], etc.), parallel Prolog systems have been incorporating capabilities to deal with user-defined suspension and coroutining behaviors— for example, &-Prolog allows programmer-supplied *wait*-declarations, which can be used to express arbitrary control dependencies. In sequential Prolog systems with delay primitives, delayed goals are typically represented via heap-allocated "suspension records," and such goals are awakened when the variables they are suspended on get bindings [3]. Parallel Prolog systems inherit this architecture, leading to implementations where individual tasks are stack-oriented, together with support for heap-allocated suspensions and dataflow synchronization. On the other hand, driven by a growing consensus that some form of "sequentialization" is necessary to reduce the overhead of managing fine-grained parallel tasks on stock hardware (see, for example, [9, 30, 22, 11]), implementors of committed choice languages are investigating the use of compile-time analyses to coalesce fine-grained tasks into coarser-grained sequential threads that can be implemented more efficiently. This, again, leads to implementations where individual sequential threads execute in a stack-oriented manner, but where sets of such threads are represented via heap-allocated activation records that employ dataflow synchronization. Interestingly, and conversely, in the context of parallel Prolog systems, there is also a growing body of work trying to address the problem of automatic parallelizing compilers often "parallelizing too much" which appears if the target architecture is not capable of supporting fine grain parallelism. Figure 1 illustrates this.

This convergence of trends both at the compiler and the run-time system levels is exciting: it suggests that we are beginning to understand the essential implementation issues for these languages, and that from an implementor's perspective these languages are not as fundamentally different as was originally believed. It also opens up the possibility of having a general purpose kernel language and abstract machine to serve as a compilation target for a variety of user-level languages. As mentioned before this is precisely one of the objectives of the CIAO system. Encouraging initial results in this direction have been demonstrated in the sequential context by the QD-Janus system [8] of S. Debray and his group. QD-Janus, which compiles down to Sicstus Prolog and uses the delay primitives of the Prolog system to implement dataflow synchronization, turns out to be more than three times faster, on the average, than Kliger's customized implementation of FCP(:) [23] and requires two orders of magnitude less heap memory [7]. We believe that this point will also extend to parallel systems: as noted above, the &-Prolog system already supports stack-oriented parallel execution together with arbitrary control dependencies, suspension, and dataflow synchronization via user-supplied *wait*-declarations, all characteristics that CIAO inherits. This suggests that, with some enhancements, the dependence graphs and *wait*-declarations of &-Prolog/CIAO, can serve as a common intermediate language, and its runtime system can act as an appropriate common low-level implementation, for a variety of parallel logic programming implementations.

Along these lines, in [12] we have recently proposed a method for providing user-level access to such a generic implementation, based on the use of attributed variables [19, 3]. Incorporating the possibility of attaching attributes to variables in a logic programming system has been shown to allow the addition of general constraint solving capabilities to it [16, 17]. This approach is very attractive in that by adding a few primitives any logic programming system can be turned into a generic constraint logic programming system in which constraint solving can be user defined, and at source level – an extreme example of the "glass box" approach. In [12] we propose applying the concept of attributed variables to provide the same "glass box" flavor in a generic parallel/concurrent (constraint) logic programming system. We argue that a system which implements attributed variables and a few additional primitives (such as those present in &-Prolog/CIAO) can be easily customized at source level to implement many of the languages and execution models of parallelism and concurrency currently proposed, in both shared memory and distributed systems. We do not mean to suggest that the performance of such a system will be *optimal* for all possible logic programming languages: our claim is rather that it will provide a way to researchers in the community implement their languages with considerably less effort than has been possible to date, and yet attain reasonably good performance. We are currently exploring these points in collaboration with S. Debray, F. Rossi, and U. Montanari, by using the CIAO system as a generic implementation platform.

4 Acknowledgements

The work presented in this paper is funded in part by ESPRIT contracts 6707 "PARFORCE" and 7195 "ACCLAIM", and CICYT contract TIC93-TIC93-0737. This work is part of the joint effort of the CLIP (Computational Logic, Implementation, and Parallelism) group at UPM which includes Francisco Bueno, Daniel Cabeza, Manuel Carro, María José García de la Banda, Pedro López García, Germán de la Puebla, and Manuel Hermenegildo.

References

1. K.A.M. Ali and R. Karlsson. The Muse Or-Parallel Prolog Model and its Performance. In *1990 North American Conference on Logic Programming*. MIT Press, October 1990.

2. F. Bueno, M. Hermenegildo, U. Montanari, and F. Rossi. From Eventual to Atomic and Locally Atomic CC Programs: A Concurrent Semantics. In *Fourth International Conference on Algebraic and Logic Programming*. Springer LNCS, September 1994. To appear.

3. M. Carlsson. Freeze, Indexing, and Other Implementation Issues in the Wam. In *Fourth International Conference on Logic Programming*, pages 40–58. University of Melbourne, MIT Press, May 1987.

4. M. Carlsson. *Sicstus Prolog User's Manual*. Po Box 1263, S-16313 Spanga, Sweden, February 1988.

5. Jim Crammond. Scheduling and Variable Assignment in the Parallel Parlog Implementation. In *1990 North American Conference on Logic Programming*. MIT Press, 1990.

6. M. García de la Banda, M. Hermenegildo, and K. Marriott. Independence in Constraint Logic Programs. In *1993 International Logic Programming Symposium*, pages 130–146. MIT Press, Cambridge, MA, October 1993.

7. S. K. Debray. Implementing logic programming systems: The quiche-eating approach. In *ICLP '93 Workshop on Practical Implementations and Systems Experience in Logic Programming*, Budapest, Hungary, June 1993.

8. S. K. Debray. QD-Janus : A Sequential Implementation of Janus in Prolog. *Software—Practice and Experience*, 23(12):1337–1360, December 1993.

9. S. K. Debray, N.-W. Lin, and M. Hermenegildo. Task Granularity Analysis in Logic Programs. In *Proc. of the 1990 ACM Conf. on Programming Language Design and Implementation*, pages 174–188. ACM Press, June 1990.

10. I. Foster and S. Taylor. *Strand* : A practical parallel programming tool. In *1989 North American Conference on Logic Programming*, pages 497–512. MIT Press, October 1989.

11. P. López García, M. Hermenegildo, and S.K. Debray. Towards Granularity Based Control of Parallelism in Logic Programs. In *Proc. of PASCO'94*. World Scientific Publishing Company, September 1994.

12. M. Hermenegildo, D. Cabeza, and M. Carro. On The Uses of Attributed Variables in Parallel and Concurrent Logic Programming Systems. Technical report clip 5/94.0, School of Computer Science, Technical University of Madrid (UPM), Facultad Informatica UPM, 28660-Boadilla del Monte, Madrid-Spain, June 1994. Presented at the ILPS'94 Post Conference Workshop on Design and Implementation of Parallel Logic Programming Systems.

13. M. Hermenegildo and K. Greene. The &-prolog System: Exploiting Independent And-Parallelism. *New Generation Computing*, 9(3,4):233–257, 1991.

14. M. Hermenegildo and F. Rossi. Strict and Non-Strict Independent And-Parallelism in Logic Programs: Correctness, Efficiency, and Compile-Time Conditions. *Journal of Logic Programming*, 1994. To appear.

15. P. Hill and J. Lloyd. *The Goedel Programming Language*. MIT Press, Cambridge MA, 1994.

16. C. Holzbaur. *Specification of Constraint Based Inference Mechanisms through Extended Unification*. PhD thesis, University of Vienna, 1990.

17. C. Holzbaur. Metastructures vs. Attributed Variables in the Context of Extensible Unification. In *1992 International Symposium on Programming Language Implementation and Logic Programming*, pages 260–268. LNCS631, Springer Verlag, August 1992.

18. A. Houri and E. Shapiro. A sequential abstract machine for flat concurrent prolog. Technical Report CS86-20, Dept. of Computer Science, The Weizmann Institute of Science, Rehovot 76100, Israel, July 1986.

19. Serge Le Huitouze. A New Data Structure for Implementing Extensions to Prolog. In P. Deransart and J. Małuszyński, editors, *Proceedings of Programming Language Implementation and Logic Programming*, number 456 in Lecture Notes in Computer Science, pages 136–150. Springer, August 1990.

20. S. Janson and S. Haridi. Programming Paradigms of the Andorra Kernel Language. In *1991 International Logic Programming Symposium*, pages 167–183. MIT Press, 1991.

21. A. King and P. Soper. Reducing scheduling overheads for concurrent logic programs. In *International Workshop on Processing Declarative Knowledge*, Kaiserslautern, Germany, (1991). Springer-Verlag.

22. Andy King and Paul Soper. Schedule Analysis of Concurrent Logic Programs. In Krzysztof Apt, editor, *Proceedings of the Joint International Conference and Symposium on Logic Programming*, pages 478–492, Washington, USA, 1992. The MIT Press.

23. S. Kliger. *Compiling Concurrent Logic Programming Languages*. PhD thesis, The Weizmann Institute of Science, Rehovot, Israel, October 1992.

24. E. Lusk et. al. The Aurora Or-Parallel Prolog System. *New Generation Computing*, 7(2,3), 1990.

25. U. Montanari, F. Rossi, F. Bueno, M. García de la Banda, and M. Hermenegildo. Towards a Concurrent Semantics based Analysis of CC and CLP. In *Principles and Practice of Constraint Programming*, LNCS. Springer-Verlag, May 1994.

26. L. Naish. Parallelizing NU-Prolog. In *Fifth International Conference and Symposium on Logic Programming*, pages 1546–1564. University of Washington, MIT Press, August 1988.

27. V. Santos-Costa, D.H.D. Warren, and R. Yang. Andorra-I: A Parallel Prolog System that Transparently Exploits both And- and Or-parallelism. In *Proceedings of the 3rd. ACM SIGPLAN Symposium on Principles and Practice of Parallel Programming*. ACM, April 1990.

28. K. Shen. Exploiting Dependent And-Parallelism in Prolog: The Dynamic, Dependent And-Parallel Scheme. In *Proc. Joint Int'l. Conf. and Symp. on Logic Prog.* MIT Press, 1992.

29. J. Thom and J. Zobel. *NU-Prolog Reference Manual*. Dept. of Computer Science, U. of Melbourne, May 1987.

30. E. Tick. Compile-Time Granularity Analysis of Parallel Logic Programming Languages. In *International Conference on Fifth Generation Computer Systems*. Tokyo, November 1988.

31. E. Tick and C. Bannerjee. Performance evaluation of monaco compiler and runtime kernel. In *1993 International Conference on Logic Programming*, pages 757–773. MIT Press, June 1993.

32. K. Ueda. Guarded Horn Clauses. In E.Y. Shapiro, editor, *Concurrent Prolog: Collected Papers*, pages 140–156. MIT Press, Cambridge MA, 1987.

33. D.H.D. Warren. The Extended Andorra Model with Implicit Control. In Sverker Jansson, editor, *Parallel Logic Programming Workshop*, Box 1263, S-163 13 Spanga, SWEDEN, June 1990. SICS.

Encapsulated Search and Constraint Programming in Oz

Christian Schulte, Gert Smolka, and Jörg Würtz

German Research Center for Artificial Intelligence (DFKI)
Stuhlsatzenhausweg 3, D–66123 Saarbrücken, Germany
{schulte,smolka,wuertz}@dfki.uni-sb.de

Abstract. Oz is an attempt to create a high-level concurrent programming language providing the problem solving capabilities of logic programming (i.e., constraints and search). Its computation model can be seen as a rather radical extension of the concurrent constraint model providing for higher-order programming, deep guards, state, and encapsulated search. This paper focuses on the most recent extension, a higher-order combinator providing for encapsulated search. The search combinator spawns a local computation space and resolves remaining choices by returning the alternatives as first-class citizens. The search combinator allows to program different search strategies, including depth-first, indeterministic one solution, demand-driven multiple solution, all solutions, and best solution (branch and bound) search. The paper also discusses the semantics of integer and finite domain constraints in a deep guard computation model.

1 Introduction

Oz [9, 2, 3, 7, 1] is an attempt to create a high-level concurrent programming language providing the problem solving capabilities of logic programming (i.e., constraints and search). Its computation model can be seen as a rather radical extension of the concurrent constraint model [6] providing for higher-order programming, deep guards, state, and encapsulated search. This paper focuses on the most recent extension, a higher-order combinator providing for encapsulated search. The search combinator spawns a local computation space and resolves remaining choices by returning the alternatives as first-class citizens. The search combinator allows to program different search strategies, including depth-first, indeterministic one solution, demand-driven multiple solution, all solutions, and best solution (branch and bound) search. The paper also discusses the semantics of integer and finite domain constraints in a deep guard computation model, which is an interesting issue since these constraints cannot be realized with their declarative semantics (due to intractability and even undecidability of satisfiability and entailment).

The idea behind our search combinator is simple and new. It exploits the fact that Oz is a higher-order language. The search combinator is given an expression E and a variable x (i.e., a predicate x/E) with the idea that E (which declaratively reads as a logic formula) is to be solved for x. The combinator spawns a local computation space for E, which evolves until it fails or becomes stable (a property known from AKL). If the local computation space evolves to a stable expression $(A \vee B) \wedge C$, the two alternatives are returned as predicates:

$$x/(A \vee B) \wedge C \quad \rightarrow \quad x/A \wedge C, \ x/B \wedge C .$$

If the local computation space evolves to a stable expression C not containing a distributable disjunction, it is considered solved and the predicate x/C is returned.

We now relate Oz to AKL and cc(FD), two first-order concurrent constraint programming languages having important aspects in common with Oz.

AKL [4] is a deep guard language aiming like Oz at the integration of concurrent and logic programming. AKL can encapsulate search. AKL admits distribution of a nondeterminate choice in a local computation space spawned by the guard of a clause when the space has become stable (a crucial control condition we have also adopted in Oz). In AKL, search alternatives are not available as first-class citizens. All solutions search is provided through an extra primitive. Best solution and demand-driven multiple solution search are not expressible.

cc(FD) [10] is a constraint programming language specialized for finite domain constraints. It employs a Prolog-style search strategy and three concurrent constraint combinators called cardinality, constructive disjunction, and blocking implication. It is a compromise between a flat and a deep guard language in that combinators can be nested into combinators, but procedure calls (and hence nondeterminate choice) cannot. Encapsulated best solution search is provided as a primitive, but its control (e.g., stability) is left unspecified.

The paper is organized as follows. Section 2 gives an informal presentation of Oz's computation model, and Sect. 3 relates Oz to logic programming by means of examples. Section 4 shows how encapsulated and demand-driven search can be integrated into a reactive language. Section 5 presents the search combinator, and Sect. 6 shows how the search strategies mentioned above can be programmed with it. Section 7 discusses how integer and finite domain constraints are accommodated in Oz. Section 8 puts everything together by showing how the N-Queens problem can be solved in Oz.

2 Computation Spaces, Actors, and Blackboards

The computation model underlying Oz generalizes the concurrent constraint model (CC) [6] by providing for higher-order programming, deep guard combinators, and state. Deep guard combinators introduce local computation spaces, as in the concurrent constraint language AKL [4]. Recall that there is only one computation space in CC.

In [8] we give a formal model of computation in Oz, consisting of a calculus rewriting expressions modulo a structural congruence relation, similar to the setup of the π-calculus [5]. For the purposes of this paper, an informal presentation of Oz's computation model, ignoring state, will suffice.

A computation space consists of a number of actors[1] connected to a blackboard.

Blackboard

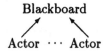

Actor $\cdots$ Actor

The actors read the blackboard and reduce once the blackboard contains sufficient information. The information on the blackboard increases monotonically. When an actor reduces, it may put new information on the blackboard and create new actors. As long as an actor does not reduce, it does not have an outside effect. The actors of a computation space are short-lived: once they reduce they disappear. Actors may spawn local computation spaces.

The blackboard stores a constraint (constraints are closed under conjunction, hence one constraint suffices) and a number of named abstractions (to be explained later). Constraints are formulas of first-order predicate logic with equality that are interpreted in a fixed first-order structure called the Oz Universe. For the purposes of this paper it suffices to know that the Oz Universe provides rational trees (as in Prolog II) and integers. The constraint on the blackboard is always satisfiable in the Oz Universe. We say that a blackboard entails a constraint ψ if the implication $\phi \to \psi$ is valid in the Oz Universe, where ϕ is the constraint stored on the blackboard. We say that a blackboard is consistent with a constraint ψ if the conjunction $\phi \wedge \psi$ is satisfiable in the Oz Universe, where ϕ is the constraint stored on the blackboard. Since the constraint on the blackboard can only be observed through entailment and consistency testing, it suffices to represent it modulo logical equivalence.

There are several kinds of actors. This section will introduce elaborators, conditionals, and disjunctions.

An elaborator is an actor executing an expression. The expressions we will consider in this section are defined as follows:

$$E ::= \phi \quad | \quad E_1 \, E_2 \quad | \quad \textbf{local } x \textbf{ in } E \textbf{ end}$$
$$| \quad \textbf{proc } \{x \, y_1 \ldots y_n\} \, E \textbf{ end} \quad | \quad \{x \, y_1 \ldots y_n\}$$
$$| \quad \textbf{if } C_1 \, [] \, \ldots \, [] \, C_n \textbf{ else } E \textbf{ fi} \quad | \quad \textbf{or } C_1 \, [] \, \ldots \, [] \, C_n \textbf{ ro}$$
$$C ::= E_1 \textbf{ then } E_2 \quad | \quad x_1 \ldots x_n \textbf{ in } E_1 \textbf{ then } E_2$$

Elaboration of a constraint ϕ checks whether ϕ is consistent with the blackboard. If this is the case, ϕ is conjoined to the constraint on the blackboard; otherwise, the computation space is marked failed and all its actors are cancelled. Elaboration of a constraint corresponds to the eventual tell operation of CC.

Elaboration of a concurrent composition $E_1 \, E_2$ creates two separate elaborators for E_1 and E_2.

---

[1] Oz's actors are different from Hewitt's actors. We reserve the term agent for longer-lived computational activities enjoying persistent and first-class identity.

Elaboration of a variable declaration **local** x **in** E **end** creates a new variable (local to the computation space) and an elaborator for the expression E. Within the expression E the new variable is referred to by x. Every computation space maintains a finite set of local variables.

Elaboration of a procedure definition **proc** $\{x\ y_1 \ldots y_n\}$ E **end** chooses a fresh name a, writes the named abstraction $a : y_1 \ldots y_n / E$ on the blackboard, and creates an elaborator for the constraint $x = a$. Names are constants denoting pairwise distinct elements of the Oz Universe; there are infinitely many. Since abstractions are associated with fresh names when they are written on the blackboard, a name cannot refer to more than one abstraction.

Elaboration of a procedure application $\{x\ y_1 \ldots y_n\}$ waits until the blackboard entails $x = a$ and contains a named abstraction $a : x_1 \ldots x_n / E$, for some name a. When this is the case, an elaborator for the expression $E[y_1/x_1 \ldots y_n/x_n]$ is created ($E[y_1/x_1 \ldots y_n/x_n]$ is obtained from E by replacing the formal arguments $x_1, \ldots, x_n$ with the actual arguments $y_1, \ldots, y_n$).

This simple treatment of procedures provides for all higher-order programming techniques. By making variables denote names rather than higher-order values, we obtain a smooth combination of first-order constraints with higher-order programming.

The elaboration of conditional expressions is more involved. We first consider the special case of a one clause conditional with flat guard.

Elaboration of **if** ϕ **then** E_1 **else** E_2 **fi** creates a conditional actor, which waits until the blackboard entails either ϕ or $\neg\phi$. If the blackboard entails ϕ $[\neg\phi]$, the conditional actor reduces to an elaborator for E_1 $[E_2]$. In CC, such a conditional can be expressed as a parallel composition $(\mathbf{ask}\,\phi \to E_1) \,\|\, (\mathbf{ask}\,\neg\phi \to E_2)$ of two ask clauses.

Elaboration of a conditional expression **if** C_1 $[\!]\ldots[\!]$ C_n **else** E **fi** creates a conditional actor spawning a local computation space for each clause C_i. A clause takes the form

$$x_1 \ldots x_k \text{ in } E \text{ then } D$$

where the local variables $x_1, \ldots, x_k$ range over both the guard E and the body D of the clause. We speak of a deep guard if E is not a constraint. In Oz, any expression can be used as a guard. This is similar to AKL and in contrast to CC, where guards are restricted to constraints. The local computation space for a clause

$$x \text{ in } E \text{ then } D$$

(clauses with no or several local variables are dealt with similarly) is created with an empty blackboard and an elaborator for the expression **local** x **in** E **end**.

Constraints from the global blackboard (the blackboard of the computation space the conditional actor belongs to) are automatically propagated to local spaces by elaborating them in the local spaces (propagation of global constraints can fail local spaces). Moreover, named abstractions from global blackboards are copied to local blackboards (conflicts cannot occur).

We say that a clause of a conditional actor is entailed if its associated computation space S is not failed, S has no actors left, and the global board entails

$\exists \bar{y}\, \phi$, where $\bar{y}$ are the local variables of S and ϕ is the constraint of the blackboard of S. Entailment of a local space is a stable property, (i.e., remains to hold when computation proceeds).

A conditional actor must wait until either one of its clauses is entailed or all its clauses (i.e., their associated local spaces) are failed.

If all clauses of a conditional actor **if** $C_1 \ \mathbb{0} \ \ldots \ \mathbb{0} \ C_n$ **else** E **fi** are failed, the conditional actor reduces to an elaborator for the expression E (the else constituent of the conditional).

If a clause x_i **in** E_i **then** D_i of a conditional actor is entailed, the other clauses and their associated spaces are discarded, the space associated with the entailed clause is merged with the global space (conflicts cannot occur), and the conditional actor reduces to an elaborator for D_i (the body of the clause).

Elaboration of a disjunctive expression **or** $C_1 \ \mathbb{0} \ \ldots \ \mathbb{0} \ C_n$ **ro** creates a disjunctive actor spawning a local computation space for every clause $C_1, \ldots, C_n$. The local spaces are created in the same way as for conditionals. As with conditional clauses, constraints and named abstractions from the global blackboard are automatically propagated to local blackboards.

A disjunctive actor must wait until all but possibly one of its clauses are failed, or until a clause whose body is the trivial constraint **true** is entailed. In the latter case, the disjunctive actor just disappears (justified by the equivalence $A \wedge (A \vee B) \equiv A$). If all clauses of a disjunctive actor are failed, the space of the disjunctive actor is failed (i.e., all its actors are cancelled). If all but one clause of a disjunctive actor are failed, it reduces with the unfailed clause. This is done in two steps. First, the space associated with the unfailed clause is merged with the global space, and then an elaborator for the body of the clause is created. The merge of the local with the global space may fail because the local constraint may be inconsistent with the global constraint. In this case the global space will be failed.

3 Example: Length of Lists

This section clarifies how Oz relates to logic programming and Prolog.

The Horn clauses

length (nil,0)
length (X|Xr, s(M)) $\leftarrow$ length (Xr,M)

define a predicate length(Xs,N) that holds if Xs is a list of length N. Numbers are represented as trees 0, $s(0)$, $s(s(0))$, $\ldots$, and lists as trees $t_1|t_2|\ldots|t_n|\text{nil}$. The intended semantics of the clauses is captured by the equivalence

$$\text{length}(Xs, N) \leftrightarrow Xs = \text{nil} \wedge N = 0$$
$$\vee\; \exists X, Xr, M\; (Xs = X|Xr \wedge N = s(M) \wedge \text{length}(Xr, M))\; ,$$

which is obtained from the Horn clauses by Clark's completion. The equivalence exhibits the relevant primitives and combinators of logic programming: constraints (i.e., Xs=nil), conjunction, existential quantification, disjunction, and definition by equivalence. Given the equivalence, it is easy to define the length predicate in Oz:

```
proc {Length Xs N}
    or Xs=nil N=0 then true
    [] X Xr M in Xs=X|Xr N=s(M) then {Length Xr M}
    ro
end
```

There are two things that need explanation. First, the predicate is now referred to by a variable Length, as to be expected in a higher-order language. Second, the two disjunctive clauses have been divided into guards and bodies. The procedure application {Length Xr M} is put into the body to obtain a terminating operational semantics.

To illustrate the operational semantics of Length, assume that the procedure definition has been elaborated. Now we enter the expression

declare Xs N in {Length Xs N}

whose elaboration declares two new variables Xs and N and reduces the procedure application {Length Xs N} to a disjunctive actor. The declare expression is a variant of the local expression whose scope extends to expressions the programmer enters later. The disjunctive actor cannot reduce since there is no information about the variables Xs and N on the global blackboard. It now becomes clear why we did not write the recursive procedure application {Length Xr M} into the guard: this would have caused divergence.

Now we enter the constraint ('_' is a variable occurring only once)

$$N = s(s(\_))$$

Since $N = s(s(\_))$ is inconsistent with the constraint N=0 on the local blackboard, the first clause of the suspended disjunctive actor can now be failed and the disjunctive actor can reduce with its second clause. This will elaborate the recursive application {Length Xr M} and create a new disjunctive actor whose first clause fails immediately. This will create once more a new disjunctive actor, which this time cannot reduce. The global blackboard now entails $Xs = \_|\_|\_$ and $N = s(s(\_))$.

Next we enter the constraint

Xs = 1|2|nil

whose elaboration fails the second clause of the suspended disjunctive actor (since $x = $ nil is inconsistent with $x = y|z$). Hence the suspended actor reduces with its first clause, no new disjunctive actor is created, and the blackboard finally entails $Xs = 1|2|nil$ and $N = s(s(0))$.

The example illustrates important differences between Oz and Prolog: if there are alternatives (specified by the clauses of disjunctions or conditionals), Oz explores the guards of the alternatives concurrently. Only once it is safe to commit to an alternative (e.g., because all other alternatives are failed or because the guard of a conditional clause is entailed), Oz will commit to it. In contrast, Prolog will eagerly commit to the first alternative if a choice is to be made, and backtrack if necessary.

A sublanguage of Oz enjoys a declarative semantics such that computation amounts to equivalence transformation [8]. The declarative semantics of a conditional

$$\text{if } x \text{ in } E_1 \text{ then } E_2 \text{ else } E_3 \text{ fi}$$

with only one clause is $\exists x(E_1 \wedge E_2) \vee (\neg \exists x E_1 \wedge E_3)$. Hence Oz can express negation $\neg E$ as **if** E **then false else true fi**.

The length predicate can also be defined in a functional manner using a conditional:

```
proc {Length Xs N}
   if Xs=nil then N=0
   ▯ X Xr M in Xs=X|Xr then N=s(M) {Length Xr M}
   else false fi
end
```

While the functional version has the same declarative reading as the disjunctive formulation, its operational semantics is different in that it will wait until information about its first argument is available. Thus

```
declare Xs N in N=s(s(0)) {Length Xs N}
```

will create a suspending conditional actor and not write anything on the global blackboard. On the other hand,

```
declare Xs N in Xs=_|_|nil {Length Xs N}
```

will write N=s(s(0)) on the global blackboard (although there is only partial information about Xs).

Oz supports functional syntax: the functional version of the length predicate can equivalently be written as:

```
fun {Length Xs}
   case Xs of nil then 0 ▯ X|Xr then s({Length Xr}) end
end
```

4 Encapsulated and Demand-driven Search

Given the length predicate of the previous section, Prolog allows to enumerate all pairs Xs, N such that length(Xs,N) is satisfied. This service can be obtained in Oz in a more flexible form. Oz provides search agents that can be given queries and be prompted for answers. These search agents take the form of objects, the basic concurrency abstraction of Oz.

An object is a procedure O taking a message M as argument. It encapsulates a reference to a data structure acting as the state of the object. A procedure application {O M} (the object is applied to the message) first competes for exclusive access to the object's state (necessary in a concurrent setting) and then applies the method requested by the message:

$$\text{method: state} \times \text{message} \rightarrow \text{state} .$$

This yields a new state which is released. The message indicates the method to be applied by a name that is mapped to the actual method by the object itself (so-called late binding).

Objects can be expressed in the computation model outlined in Sect. 2 if one further primitive, called cells, is added. Oz's higher-order programming facilities make it straightforward to obtain multiple inheritance of methods. For more information about objects in Oz we refer the reader to [2, 3, 1].

Now suppose Search is a search object as outlined above (any number of search objects can be created by inheritance from a predefined search object). First, we present it a query using the method query:

```
local Q in
    proc {Q A} local Xs N in A=Xs#N {Length Xs N} end end
    {Search query(Q)}
end
```

The query is specified by a unary predicate, so that solutions can be computed uniformly for one variable. Since we have existential quantification and pairing, this is no loss of generality. Using functional notation, we can write the above expression more conveniently as

```
{Search query(proc {A} local Xs N in A=Xs#N {Length Xs N} end end)}
```

Now we can request computation of the first solution by sending the message

```
{Search next}
```

which will produce the pair nil#0. Sending next (i.e., elaborating {Search next}) once more will produce (_|nil)#s(0), and so on. What happens when an solution is found can be specified by sending Search the message action(P), where P is a unary procedure to be applied to every solution found. The procedure P may, for instance, display solutions in a window or send them to other objects.

We remark that Prolog provides demand-driven search at the user interface, but not at the programming level. Aggregation in Prolog (i.e., bagof) is eager and will diverge if there are infinitely many solutions. In Oz, we can have any number of search objects at the same time and request solutions as required.

5   Solvers

We now introduce solvers, which are higher-order actors providing for encapsulated search. Many different search strategies can be programmed with solvers, ranging from demand-driven depth-first (as exemplified by the search object in the previous section) to best solution (branch and bound) strategies. In contrast to this rather informal introduction, in [7] one may find a calculus defining the presented ideas formally.

The key idea behind search in Oz is to exploit the distributivity law and proceed from $(A \lor B) \land C$ to $A \land C$ and $B \land C$. While Prolog commits to $A \land C$ first and considers $B \land C$ only upon backtracking, Oz makes both alternatives available as first-class citizens. To do this, the variable being solved for must be made explicit and abstracted from in the alternatives. For instance, if **or** $x = 1$ **□** $x = 2$ **ro** is being solved for x, distribution will produce the abstractions **proc** $\{x\}$ $x = 1$ **end** and **proc** $\{x\}$ $x = 2$ **end**.

Solvers are created by elaboration of solve expressions

$$\mathsf{solve}[x \colon E; \ u]$$

where x (the variable being solved for) is a local variable taking the expression E as scope. The variable u provides for output. The solver created by elaboration of the above expression spawns a local computation space for the expression

$$\mathsf{local} \ x \ \mathsf{in} \ E \ \mathsf{end}$$

As with other local computation spaces, constraints and named abstractions are propagated from global blackboards to the local blackboards of solvers.

A solver can reduce if its local computation space is either failed or stable. A local computation space is called stable if it is blocked and remains blocked for every consistent extension of the global blackboard. A computation space is called blocked if it is not failed and none of its actors can reduce. Stability is known from AKL [4], where it is used to control nondeterministic promotion. Note that a local computation space is entailed if and only if it is stable and has no actor left.

If the local computation space of a solver has failed, the solver reduces to an elaborator for the constraint (u is the output variable)

$$u = \mathsf{failed} \ .$$

If the local computation space of a solver is stable and does not contain a disjunctive actor, the solver reduces to an elaborator for

$$u = \mathsf{solved}(\mathsf{proc} \ \{x\} \ F \ \mathsf{end})$$

where F is an expression representing the stable local computation space (the nested procedure definition has been explained in the previous section).[2] Abstracting the solution with respect to x is advantageous in case F does not fully

---

[2] The reader might be surprised by the fact that local computation spaces can be represented as expressions. This is however an obvious consequence of the fact that Oz's formal model [8] models computation states as expressions.

determine x; for instance, if F is **local** z **in** $x = f(z)$ **end**, different applications will enjoy different local variables z. A less general way to return the solution would be to reduce to an elaborator for $u =$ **solved**(x) F.

If the local computation space of a solver is stable and contains a disjunctive actor **or** $C_1 \, \Box \ldots \Box \, C_n$ **ro**, the solver reduces to an elaborator for

$$u = \text{distributed}(\textbf{proc } \{x\} \textbf{ or } C_1 \textbf{ ro } F \textbf{ end} \quad \textbf{proc } \{x\} \textbf{ or } C_2 \, \Box \ldots \Box \, C_n \textbf{ ro } F \textbf{ end})$$

where F is an expression representing the stable local computation space after deletion of the disjunctive actor. Requiring stability ensures that distribution is postponed until no other reductions are possible. This is important since repeated distribution may result in combinatorial explosion.

For combinatorial search problems it is often important to distribute the right disjunction and try the right clause first. Oz makes the following commitments about order: clauses are distributed according to their static order; solvers distribute the most recently created disjunctive actor; and elaboration proceeds from left to right, where suspended actors that become reducible are given priority (similar to Prologs with freeze). Taking the most recently created disjunctive actor for distribution seems to be more expressive than taking the least recently created one (see the first failure labeling procedure in Sect. 8).

Solvers cannot express breadth-first search if disjunctions with more than two clauses are used. This can be remedied by also returning the number of remaining clauses when a disjunctive actor is distributed.

Solve expressions are made available through a predefined procedure

$$\textbf{proc } \{\text{Solve P U}\} \, \textbf{solve}[X \colon \{P \, X\}; \, U] \textbf{ end}$$

6   Search Strategies

We start with a function taking a query (i.e., a unary procedure) as argument and trying to solve it following a depth-first strategy:

```
fun {Depth Q}
   local S = {Solve Q} in
      case S of distributed (L R) then
         case {Depth L} of solved (_)=T then T else {Depth R} end
      else S end
   end
end
```

If no solution is found (but search terminates), failed is returned. If a solution is found, solved(A) is returned, where A is the abstracted solution. A procedure solving a query with Depth and displaying the result can be written as follows:

```
fun {One Q}
   local S = {Solve Q} in
      case S of distributed(L R) then
         if T in {One L}=solved(_)=T then T
         [] T in {One R}=solved(_)=T then T
         else failed fi
      else S end
   end
end
```

Fig. 1. Parallel one solution search.

```
proc {SolveAndBrowse Q}
   case {Depth Q} of failed then {Browse 'no solution found'}
   [] solved(A) then {Browse {A}}
   end
end
```

The search performed by Depth is sequential. Figure 1 shows an indeterministic search function One that explores alternatives in parallel guards.[3] The use of deep parallel guards provides a high potential for parallel execution.

Combinatorial optimization problems (e.g., scheduling) often require best solution search. Following a branch and bound strategy, this can be done as follows: once a solution is found, only solutions that are better with respect to a total order are searched for. With every better solution found, the constraints on further solutions can be strengthened, thus pruning the search space.

Figure 2 shows a function Best searching the best solution of a query Q with respect to a total order R (a binary procedure). The local function BAB takes two stacks Fs and Bs of alternatives and the best solution found so far as arguments (if no solution has been found so far, failed is taken as last argument) and returns the best solution. Alternatives which are already constrained to produce a better solution than S reside on the foreground stack Fs, and the remaining alternatives reside on the background stack Bs. If the foreground stack is empty, an alternative B from the background stack is taken. The query A obtained from constraining B to solutions better than S (the best solution so far) is expressed as follows:

$$A = \text{proc } \{X\} \ \{R \ \{S\} \ X\} \ \{B \ X\} \ \text{end}$$

If a new and better solution is obtained, all nodes from the foreground stack are moved to the background stack so that they will be correctly constrained before they are explored.

The program in Fig. 3 defines an object Search realizing the functionality described in Sect. 4. The object must be initialized with messages query(Q)

---

[3] This search function was suggested to us by Sverker Janson.

```
fun {Best Q R}
   local
      fun {BAB Fs Bs S}
         case Fs of nil then
            case Bs of nil then S
            ▯ B|Br then {BAB (proc {X} {R {S} X} {B X} end)|nil Br S}
            end
         ▯ F|Fr then
            case {Solve F} of failed then {BAB Fr Bs S}
            ▯ solved(T) then {BAB nil {Append Fr Bs} T}
            ▯ distributed(L R) then {BAB L|R|Fr Bs S}
            end
         end
      end
   in {BAB Q|nil nil failed} end
end
```

Fig. 2. Best solution search.

and **action**(A) fixing the query to be solved and the action to be taken when a solution is found, respectively. The attribute **stack** stores the unexplored alternatives. If a solution is requested with the method **next**, the alternatives on the stack are explored following a depth-first strategy. If no alternatives are left on the stack, the specified action is applied to the atom **failed**.

The search object illustrates object-oriented constraint programming in Oz. More sophisticated search strategies, for instance iterated depth-first search, can be obtained by refining Search using inheritance.

```
create Search from UrObject
   meth action(A)  action←A end
   meth query(Q)  stack←Q|nil end
   meth next
      case @stack of nil then {@action failed}
      ▯ N|Nr then
         case {Solve N} of failed then stack←Nr ⟪next⟫
         ▯ solved(S) then stack←Nr {@action solved(S)}
         ▯ distributed(L R) then stack←L|R|Nr ⟪next⟫
         end
      end
   end
end
```

Fig. 3. Demand driven depth-first search.

7 Integers and Finite Domains

An implementation of the presented computation model must come with efficient and incremental algorithms for deciding satisfiability and entailment of constraints. This means that a programming language must drastically restrict the constraints a programmer can actually use. For instance, addition and multiplication of integers cannot be made available as purely declarative constraints since satisfiability of conjunctions of such constraints is undecidable (Hilbert's tenth problem).

The usual way to deal with this problem is to base the implementation on incomplete algorithms for satisfiability and entailment (e.g., delay nonlinear arithmetic constraints until they are linear). Consequently, constraints are not anymore fully characterized by their declarative semantics, and the programmer must understand their operational semantics.

In Oz, we make a distinction between basic and virtual constraints. Basic constraints are what has been called constraints so far. Their semantics is given purely declaratively by the Oz Universe. Oz is designed such that the programmer can only write basic constraints whose declarative semantics can be faithfully realized by the implementation (i.e., sound and complete algorithms for satisfiability and entailment). Virtual constraints are procedures whose operational semantics is sound but incomplete with respect to the declarative semantics of the corresponding logic constraint. A typical example of a virtual constraint is the length predicate for lists defined in Sect. 3.

Most constraints expressible over the Oz Universe are only available through predefined virtual constraints (i.e., with incomplete operational semantics). A typical example is addition of integers, whose definition is as follows:

```
proc {`+` X Y Z}
    if int(X) int(Y) isdet[X] isdet[Y] then plus(X,Y,Z) else false fi
end
```

Here plus(X,Y,Z) is the basic constraint expressing integer addition (partial functions are avoided by using relations), int(X) is the basic constraint expressing that X is an integer, and isdet[X] creates an actor that disappears as soon as there is a constant a in the signature of the Oz Universe such that X=a is entailed by the blackboard. Clearly, there is no difficulty in implementing the virtual constraint {`+` X Y Z}. Moreover, its semantics is fully defined in terms of the computation model outlined in Sect. 2 (extended with the isdet[X] actor, of course).

The virtual constraint

```
proc {IsInt X}
    if int(X) isdet[X] then true else false fi
end
```

will fail if the blackboard entails that X is no integer, and disappear (important for deep guards) if there is an integer n such that the blackboard entails X=n.

A further example is the predefined virtual constraint

```
proc {`≤` X Y}
    if {IsInt X} {IsInt Y} then le(X,Y) else false fi
end
```

where and le(X,Y) is the basic constraint expressing the canonical order on integers.

The predefined virtual constraint

```
proc {FdIn X L U}
    if {IsInt L} {IsInt U} then le(L,X) le(X,U) le(Inf,L) le(U,Sup) else false fi
end
```

makes it possible to constrain a variable X to a finite domain L..U (i.e., the value of X must be an integer between L and U). There variables Inf and Sup are predefined by the implementation and fix the maximal size of finite domains (i.e., there are only finitely many finite domains).

Another important predefined virtual constraint is

```
proc {FdNec X C}
    if {FdIn X Inf Sup} {IsInt C} then X ≠ C else false fi
end
```

whose declarative reading says that X is a finite domain variable different from C (X ≠ C is a basic constraint).

Figure 4 shows the definition of a virtual constraint $X \leq' Y$ enforcing domain consistency for finite domain variables (the infix operators $\leq$, $+$, and $-$ expand to applications of the corresponding virtual constraints). For instance, elaboration of the expression

```
local X Y in
    {FdIn X 3 7} {FdIn Y 7 24}
    if X ≤' Y then {Browse yes} else {Browse no} fi
end
```

will reduce the conditional actor to {Browse yes}, and elaboration of

```
{FdIn X 3 7} {FdIn Y 7 24} Y ≤' X
```

will constrain X and Y to 7.

With the outlined techniques we can formally define all finite domain constraints as virtual constraints such that a faithful and efficient implementation is possible. To our knowledge, this is the first formal semantics for finite domain constraints in a deep guard computation model.

To define heuristics such as first failure labeling (see next section), we need a reflective primitive. The actor

$$\text{reflect}[x; y]$$

```
proc {`≤`` X Y}
    if {FdIn X Inf Sup} {FdIn Y Inf Sup} then
    local
        proc {LE Xl Xu Yl Yu}
            if X=Y then true
            [] Xu≤Yl then true
            [] {FdIn X Xl+1 Sup} then {FdIn Y Xl+1 Sup} {LE Xl+1 Xu Yl Yu}
            [] {FdIn X Inf Xu−1} then {LE Xl Xu−1 Yl Yu}
            [] {FdIn Y Yl+1 Sup} then {LE Xl Xu Yl+1 Yu}
            [] {FdIn Y Inf Yu−1} then {FdIn X Inf Yu−1} {LE Xl Xu Yl Yu−1}
            fi
        end
    in {LE Inf Sup Inf Sup} end
    else false fi
end
```

Fig. 4. The virtual constraint $X \leq' Y$.

can reduce as soon as the blackboard constrains the variable x to a finite domain. It will then reduce to an elaborator for the constraint $y = n_1|\ldots|n_k|$nil, where $n_1|\ldots|n_k|$nil is the shortest list in ascending order such that the blackboard entails the constraint $x = n_1 \lor \ldots \lor x = n_k$. Note that the reflection actor is different from all other actors in that its reduction may have different effect if it is postponed.

8 Example: N-queens

Figure 5 shows an Oz program solving the n-queens problem (place n queens on an $n \times n$ chessboard such that no queen is attacked by another queen). The predicate {Queens N Xs} is satisfied iff the list Xs represents a solution to the n-queens problem. The list Xs has length N, where every element is an integer between 1 and N. The ith element of Xs specifies in which row the queen in the ith column is placed. The solutions to the 100-queens problem, say, can be obtained by providing the search object of Sect. 6 with the query

{Search query(proc {Xs} {Queens 100 Xs} end)}

The procedure {Consistent Xs Ys} iterates through the columns of the board, where Ys are the columns already constrained and Xs are the columns still to be constrained. Since a queen only imposes its constraints once it is determined (i.e., {IsInt X} can reduce), there are at most N actors spawned before a distribution.

The procedure {Label Xs} labels the elements of Xs. Different labeling strategies are possible. Figure 6 shows a labeling procedure realizing the first-fail heuristic (label variables with fewest remaining values first). The procedure FdSize yields the number of values still possible for a finite domain variable,

```
local
  proc {NoAttack Xs Y I}
    case Xs of nil then true
    ☐ X|Xr then
       {FdNec X Y} {FdNec X Y + I} {FdNec X Y − I} {NoAttack Xr Y I + 1}
    end
  end
  proc {Consistent Xs Ys}
    case Xs of nil then true
    ☐ X|Xr then
       if {IsInt X} then {NoAttack Xr X 1} {NoAttack Ys X 1} fi
       {Consistent Xr X|Ys}
    end
  end
  proc {Board I N Xs}
    if I=0 then Xs=nil
    else local X Xr in Xs=X|Xr {FdIn X 1 N} {Board I − 1 N Xr} end fi
  end
in
  proc {Queens N Xs} {Board N N Xs} {Consistent Xs nil} {Label Xs} end
end
```

Fig. 5. The n-queens problem.

```
proc {Label Xs}
  case {Sort {Filter Xs proc {X} {FdSize X} > 1 end}
            proc {X Y} {FdSize X} < {FdSize Y} end} of nil then true
  ☐ X|Xr then local M={FdMin X} in
              or X=M then {Label Xr} ☐ {FdNec X M} then {Label X|Xr} ro
          end
  end
end
```

Fig. 6. First-failure labeling.

and FdMin yields the minimal value still possible. Both procedures can be expressed with the reflection actor of Sect. 7.

After all determined elements of Xs have been dropped with the higher-order procedure Filter, the remaining elements are sorted according to the current size of their domain. If X is the variable with the smallest domain, the disjunction **or** X=M **then** {Label Xr} ☐ {FdNec X M} **then** {Label X|Xr} **ro** is created, where M is the minimal possible value for X, and Xr are the remaining variables to be labeled.

Because of the use of the reflective procedures FdSize and FdMin, it is important that the labeling procedure is elaborated only after all constraints have been propagated. This is ensured by the fact that suspended actors are given priority once they become reducible, and that the application of Label appears last. Since the most recently created disjunctive actor is distributed, the latter ensures that the disjunctive actor created by the labeling procedure is distributed even if there are further disjunctive actors (which is not the case in our example).

Acknowledgements

We thank Michael Mehl, Tobias Müller, Konstantin Popov, and Ralf Scheidhauer for discussions and implementing Oz. We also thank Sverker Janson for discussions of search issues.

The research reported in this paper has been supported by the Bundesminister für Forschung und Technologie (FTZ-ITW-9105), the Esprit Project ACCLAIM (PE 7195), and the Esprit Working Group CCL (EP 6028).

The Oz System and its documentation are available through anonymous ftp ps-ftp.dfki.uni-sb.de or through www http://ps-www.dfki.uni-sb.de/.

References

1. M. Henz, M. Mehl, M. Müller, T. Müller, J. Niehren, R. Scheidhauer, C. Schulte, G. Smolka, R. Treinen, and J. Würtz. The Oz Handbook. Research Report RR-94-09, DFKI, 1994. Available through anonymous ftp from duck.dfki.uni-sb.de.
2. M. Henz, G. Smolka, and J. Würtz. Oz—a programming language for multi-agent systems. In *13th International Joint Conference on Artificial Intelligence*, volume 1, pages 404–409, Chambéry, France, 1993. Morgan Kaufmann Publishers. Revised version will appear as [3].
3. M. Henz, G. Smolka, and J. Würtz. Object-oriented concurrent constraint programming in Oz. In P. van Hentenryck and V. Saraswat, editors, *Principles and Practice of Constraint Programming*. The MIT Press, 1994. To appear.
4. S. Janson and S. Haridi. Programming paradigms of the Andorra kernel language. In *Logic Programming, Proceedings of the 1991 International Symposium*, pages 167–186. The MIT Press, 1991.
5. R. Milner. Functions as processes. *Journal of Mathematical Structures in Computer Science*, 2(2):119–141, 1992.
6. V. A. Saraswat and M. Rinard. Concurrent constraint programming. In *Proceedings of the 7th Annual ACM Symposium on Principles of Programming Languages*, pages 232–245, Jan. 1990.
7. C. Schulte and G. Smolka. Encapsulated search in higher-order concurrent constraint programming. In *Logic Programming: Proceedings of the 1994 International Symposium*, Ithaca, New York, USA, Nov. 1994. MIT-Press. To appear.
8. G. Smolka. A calculus for higher-order concurrent constraint programming with deep guards. Research Report RR-94-03, DFKI, Feb. 1994.
9. G. Smolka. A foundation for higher-order concurrent constraint programming. Research Report RR-94-16, DFKI, June 1994. Also in *1st International Conference on Constraints in Computational Logics*, München, Germany, 7–9 September 1994.
10. P. Van Hentenryck, V. Saraswat, and Y. Deville. Design, implementation and evaluation of the constraint language cc(FD). Report CS-93-02, Brown University, Jan. 1993.

Towards a Concurrent Semantics based Analysis of CC and CLP

U. Montanari* F. Rossi*

F. Bueno** M. García de la Banda** M. Hermenegildo**

*{ugo,rossi}@di.unipi.it
Universitá di Pisa
**{bueno,maria,herme}@fi.upm.es
Universidad Politécnica de Madrid (UPM)

1 Introduction

We present in an informal way some preliminary results on the investigation of efficient compile-time techniques for Constraint Logic [JL87] and Concurrent Constraint [Sar89] Programming. These techniques are viewed as source-to-source program transformations between the two programming paradigms and are based on a concurrent semantics of CC programs [MR91].

Previous work [BH92] showed that it is possible to perform program transformations from Prolog to AKL[1] [JH91], allowing the latter to fully exploit the Independent And-Parallelism (IAP) [HR93] present in Prolog programs. However, when extending the transformation techniques to the CLP paradigm [JL87, Col90, VanH89], some issues have to be initially solved. First, the notion of independence has to be extended [GHM93]. Second, compile-time tools based on the extended notions have to be developed in order to capture the independence of goals, allowing such transformation. For this purpose an analysis of the programs turns out to be needed.

Our analysis will be based on a semantics [MR91] which, although originally intended for CC programming, can be also applied to CLP, if suitably extended [BGHMR94]. Such semantics allows us to capture the dependencies present in a CLP program at a finer level of granularity than ever proposed to date in the literature. This provides the knowledge for performing a transformation of the program which will force an execution-time scheduling of processes which preserves those dependencies. When the transformed program is run in a concurrent environment, parallel execution of concurrent processes will be exploited, except for the cases where an explicit ordering has been annotated at compile-time based on the dependencies identified.

The same semantics can also be used to identify dependencies in CC programs. Based on such dependencies, an analysis of parallel and sequential threads in the concurrent computation can be performed, establishing the basis for a transformation of CC programs into parallel CLP programs (with explicit dynamic scheduling). A similar approach (although not based on program trans-

---

[1] AKL is a CC language based on the Extended Andorra Model, which is able to exploit the determinate-goals-first principle as well as various kinds of parallelism.

formation) has recently been proposed in [KS92], in which a static analysis of concurrent languages is proposed based on an algebraic construction of execution trees from which dependencies are identified.

The needed extension of the semantics (for dealing with CLP instead of CC programs) is non-trivial [BGHMR94]. In fact, it consists in capturing the *atomic* (instead of the *eventual*) interpretation of the tell operation: constraints are added only if they are consistent with the current store. This implies the need of having the possibility of knowing immediately if a set of constraints is consistent or not. Thus it may seem that the semantics construction would have to go back to the usual notion of a constraint system as a black box which can answer yes/no questions in one step (which is what is most generally used in all the semantics other than [MR91]). However, this is not really true. In fact, the semantic structure still shows all the atomic entailment steps of the underlying constraint system, thus allowing to derive the correct dependencies among agents.

The paper is organized as follows. Section 2 hints at the new problems arising when trying to understand the concept of goal independence in CLP programs. Then, Section 3 describes the concurrent semantics for CC, both in its eventual and in its atomic version, while Section 4 hints at its modification in order to apply it to the CLP parallelization. Section 5 then describes a meta-interpreter which creates the semantic structure for each CC program, and visualizes it, Section 6 describes how to transform a CLP program into its parallel version, and Section 7 describes the opposite transformation (from CC programs to CLP programs). For reasons of space we assume the reader to be familiar with the syntax and the semantics of both CLP [JL87] and CC [Sar89] programs.

2 Independence in CLP

The general, intuitive notion of independence between goals is that the goals' executions do not interfere with each other, and do not change in any "observable" way. Observables include the solutions and/or the time that it takes to compute them.

Previous work in the context of traditional Logic Programming languages [Con83, DeG84, HR93] has concentrated on defining independence in terms of preservation of search space, and such preservation has then been achieved by ensuring that either the goals do not share variables (*strict independence*) or if they share variables, that they do not "compete" for their bindings (*non-strict independence*).

Recently, the concept of independence has been extended to CLP [GHM93]. It has been shown that search space preservation is no longer sufficient for ensuring the efficiency of several optimizations when arbitrary CLP languages are taken into account. The reason is that while the number of reduction steps will certainly be constant if the search space is preserved, the cost of each step will not: modifying the order in which a sequence of primitive constraints is added to the store may have a critical influence on the time spent by the constraint solver algorithm in obtaining the answer, even if the resulting constraint is consistent (in fact, this issue is the core of the reordering application described in [MS92]). This implies that optimizations which vary the intended execution order established by the user, such as parallel or concurrent execution, must also consider an orthogonal issue – *independence of constraint solving* – which characterizes the properties of the constraint solver behavior when changing the order in which primitive constraints are considered.

3 A Concurrent Semantics for CC and CLP

Usually the semantics of CC programs [Sar89] is given operationally, following the SOS-style operational semantics, and thus suffering from the typical pathologies of an interleaving semantics. On the other hand, the concurrent semantics approach introduced in [MR91] presents a non-monolithic model of the shared store and of its communication with the agents, in which the behavior of the store and that of the agents can be uniformly expressed by context-dependent rewrite rules (i.e. rules which have a left hand side, a right hand side and a context), each of them being applicable if both its left hand side and its context are present in the current state of the computation. An application removes the left hand side and adds the right hand side. In particular, the context is crucial in faithfully representing asked constraints, which are checked for presence but not affected by the computation.

From such rules a semantics structure is then obtained. Such structure is called a contextual net [MR93] and it is constructed by starting from the initial agent and applying all rules in all possible ways. A contextual net is just an acyclic Petri net where the presence of context conditions, besides pre- and post-conditions, is allowed. In a net obtained from a CC program, transitions are labelled by the rule applied for them.

Three relations can be defined on the items (conditions and events) of the obtained net: two items are *concurrent* if they represent objects which may appear together in a computation state, they are *mutually exclusive* if they represent objects which can not appear in the same computation, and they are *dependent* if they represent objects which may appear in the same computation but in different computation steps.

For each computation of the CC program, the net provides a partial order expressing the dependency pattern among the events of the computation. As a result, all such computations are represented in a unique structure, where it is possible to see the maximal degree of both concurrency (via the concurrency relation) and indeterminism (via the mutual exclusion relation) available both at the program level and at the underlying constraint system.

Nevertheless, such semantics is not able to handle failure, in the sense of detecting inconsistencies generated by tell operations, since constraints are added without any consistency check (i.e., the "eventual" interpretation of the tell operation is modelled). We extended such semantics to include the case of failure [BGHMR94]. We showed that the new semantics can be obtained from the old one either by pruning some parts of the semantic structure, or by not generating them at all. On one hand, the semantic structure can be built up by first generating the net as before, and then propagating the failure information through the net by introducing a notion of *mutual inconsistency* between items. The inconsistent items are then pruned out. On the other hand, the net can be generated from scratch with a new computation rule for the semantics which takes mutual inconsistency into account.

The mutual inconsistency relation extends the mutual exclusion relation, in the sense of capturing more objects which are not allowed to be present in the same computation. In fact, in the original semantics, if two objects were mutually exclusive, they could not be present in the same deterministic computation, even at different computation steps, because they belonged to two different non-deterministic (in the sense of "don't-care" nondeterminism, or indeterministic) branches of the program execution. Now, two items exclude one another also when they are mutually inconsistent, that is, when they represent (or generate) objects which are inconsistent.

When introducing an explicit representation for failure in the original semantics, what is achieved in fact is a faithful model for capturing backtracking. In other words, failing branches in a computation are also captured, allowing us to exchange nondeterminism for indeterminism. In the extended semantics, two different branches will be mutually inconsistent if they (together) lead to failure, otherwise, if they are mutually exclusive they will represent two different deterministic computations yielding distinct solutions, i.e. a nondeterministic choice: now mutual exclusion no longer represents commitment, but backtracking.

Thus the new semantics, although originally intended for CC programs, can be used also for describing the behavior of (pure) CLP programs. The only difference is the interpretation of the mutual exclusion relation, which expresses indeterminism when applied to CC programs, and nondeterminism when applied to CLP programs.

4 Local Independence and CLP Parallelization

The semantics obtained above, while being maximally parallel, could be very inefficient if implemented directly as an operational model for CLP. One reason for this is that branches of the search tree may be explored which would have been previously pruned by another goal in the sequential execution. The general problem of finding a rule to avoid the exploration of such branches is directly related to the concept of independence and has been previously addressed in Section 2. In order to avoid such efficiency problems we propose to apply those independence rules, but at the finest possible level of granularity (as proposed in [BGH93]). This is now possible because we have a structure in which all intermediate atomic steps in the execution of a goal and their dependencies are clearly identifiable.

Capturing independence is achieved by identifying dependencies which occur due to subcomputations which affect each other, in the sense of the constraint independence notions above. In our nets, these notions are applied not only at the level of whole computations of different goals, but also at the finer level of subcomputations of those goals, i.e. the actual subcomputations which can affect each other. This new notion of independence (*local independence*) is, to our knowledge, the most general proposed so far (in the sense that it allows the greatest amount of parallelism) which, at the same time, preserves the efficiency of the sequential execution.

A drawback of local independence is that it requires an oracle, since mutual inconsistency of branches is not known a priori, and thus suitable scheduling strategies for AND-OR parallelism must be devised which make sure that the added dependency links are respected (i.e. the strategy is *consistent*), while still taking advantage of the remaining parallelism (i.e. the strategy is, more or less, *efficient*). Such an oracle can be devised at compile-time by means of abstract interpretation based analysis, and a scheduling strategy can be obtained for instance by a suitable program transformation (as that presented in Section 6).

5   A Meta-interpreter of the Concrete Semantics

A meta-interpreter has been implemented which takes as input a CC program and a concrete query, and builds up the associated contextual net as defined by the true concurrency semantics of [MR91], presented in Section 3. The computation of the concrete model is performed in several steps:

1. A program is read in and transformed into a suitable set of context-dependent rules.
2. Starting from the initial (concrete) agent – the query – rules are applied one at a time, until no rule application is possible.
3. Relations of mutual exclusion, causal dependency and concurrency are constructed from the structure given by the previous step.
4. The contextual net giving the program semantics can be visualized in a windows environment, as well as the resulting relations.

Although the method based on rule application to construct the structure is completely deterministic, a fixpoint computation based on memoization is performed in order to ensure termination (whenever the semantics model is finite).

Once the computation is finished, the structure giving the model of the program resembles an event structure [Ros93]. An event structure is a set of events (together with *conflict* and *dependency* relations), where each event represents a single computation step, i.e. a rule application, and contains all the history of the subcomputation leading to the particular step represented. The events represent either program agents, which will be consumed by applying the program rules, or constraint tokens which will be asked for in such rule applications. The former are represented by usual conditions in the net, the latter by *context* conditions.

For simplicity, the current implementation only implements the Herbrand constraint system, leaving to the underlying Prolog machinery much of the entailment relation.

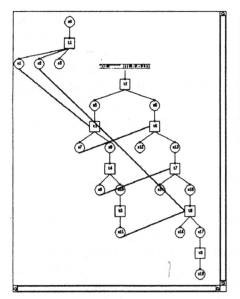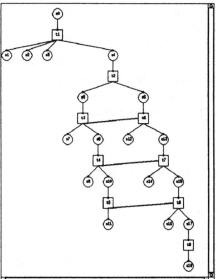

Fig. 1. Contextual Net of the `append3/4` example.

As an example, consider the following definition of **append/3**, which appends two lists into another one, and then splits it into another two. It can be run either first appending and then splitting or "backward" (first splitting and then appending).

```
:- tell(X=[1,2]), tell(Y=[3]), tell(Z=[4]), append3(X,Y,Z,W).

append3(A, B, D, E) :- app(A, B, C), app(C, D, E).

app(X, Y, Z) :- ask(X = []),     tell(Y = Z).
app(X, Y, Z) :- ask(X = [A|B]), tell(Z = [A|D]), app(B, Y, D).
app(X, Y, Z) :- ask(Z = []),     tell(X = []),    tell(Y = Z).
app(X, Y, Z) :- ask(Z = [_|_]), tell(X = []),    tell(Y = Z).
app(X, Y, Z) :- ask(Z = [A|D]), tell(X = [A|B]), app(B, Y, D).
```

A query has been included which performs the "forward" computation, where the second **app/3** goal in the body of the **append3/4** clause has to wait on the first goal to proceed at each step while the resulting list C is being constructed to consume it. The semantic structure resulting for the computation with this query can be seen in Figure 1.

Circles in the figure correspond to agents (either program agents or tokens) and squares correspond to steps. Thin lines correspond to dependency links, and thick lines to context links. Each element (either a circle or a square) is internally represented as a term with his "history", that is, the set of other elements it depends on. Such term can be explicitly seen by clicking on the element itself (like it can be seen for element s_4 in Figure 1 (left picture)).

The partial order derivable from the net corresponds to the causal dependency relation, plus additional dependencies due to the "use" of contexts. Such order appears in Figure 1 (left picture).

In this way, the causal dependency relation captures an optimal scheduling of processes based on producer/consumer relations on the tokens added to the store. This can be augmented with the local independence relation (as explained in Section 4) to capture and-parallel scheduling based on mutually inconsistent computations.

6 Parallelization of CLP via Program Transformation

One possible application of our semantics can be achieved by program transformation from CLP to CC. The purpose of the transformation will be to allow CLP programs to run under CC machinery with an optimal scheduling of processes which ensures no-slowdown and allows for maximal parallelism. In doing this, the target language should allow for the features of CC, including synchronization and indeterminism (although this latter is not needed for our purposes), and also for additional nondeterminism (in the sense of backtracking - which is indeed needed to embed CLP). Examples of such languages are AKL[2] and concurrent (constraint) Prologs (i.e. Prologs with explicit delay) such as PNU-Prolog [Nai88] and CIAO-Prolog [Her94].

The transformation will proceed as follows. First, the CLP program is rewritten into a CC program. This first step will embed a CLP program into CC syntax, by (possibly) normalizing goals and head unifications, and make all constraint operations explicit as tell agents. Second, inconsistency dependencies are identified within the (abstract) semantics via program analysis, and then the program is augmented with sequentialization arguments where required, and suitable ask and tell operations for this are incorporated to the program clauses.

Consider for example the following CLP program (where tell operations are explicitly specified), with the query :- p1,p2.

```
p1 :- tell(c1).
p1 :- tell(c2).
p2 :- tell(c3).
p2 :- tell(c4).
```

and assume that $\{c2, c3\}$ is an inconsistent set of constraints. Then the transformed program, containing the required sequentialization, is:

```
p1 :- tell(c1), tell(c).
p1 :- tell(c2).
p2 :- ask(c) -> tell(c3)
p2 :- tell(c4).
```

---

[2] However, in AKL computations are encapsulated in the so called *deep* guards, an issue that our semantics does not capture yet.

In such a new program, the first alternative (assuming a top-down choice of the clauses) of p2 is allowed to be executed only if p1 chooses its first alternative. In this way any of the alternatives for both p1 and p2 can be executed in parallel without interaction. In other words, the only interaction needed among such alternatives is explicitely specified by the added ask-tell operations over dummy new constraints (c in this case).

The transformed program will allow for or-parallelism (which is captured in the semantics by the mutual exclusion relation) and *locally independent* and-parallelism (which is captured by means of relations derived from the mutual inconsistency relation). An efficient strategy for parallel execution is thus achieved.

7 Static Scheduling in CC via Program Transformation

Another complementary application of the independence detection based on our semantics is schedule analysis. We propose to perform the linearization associated to schedule analysis by means of program transformation from CC to CLP, achieving in addition an efficient parallelization of concurrent goals. In order to do this the intended target language should allow "delay" features able to support concurrency.

Such features allow dynamic scheduling of processes *a la* concurrent logic programming in (otherwise) sequential languages. One such feature is the **when** declaration [Nai88]. This declaration delays execution of a goal until some conditions are met. Usually conditions relate to meta-logical features of the language and are formed of: **nonvar/1** (true if argument is not a variable), **var/1** (true if it is), **ground/1** (true if argument is ground), etc.

The basic idea of our tranformation is related to the approach of [BGH93] and QD-Janus [Deb93]. However, we propose to perform a more "intelligent" transformation (see also [BGH93]), which is based on the results of the analysis performed over the CC program.

Let us illustrate our approach with the **append3/4** example of Section 5. Assume the following query:

```
:- tell(W=[1]), append3(X,Y,Z,W).
```

The resulting contextual net given by our meta-interpreter is that of Figure 2, where the context dependencies links are shown, and the information corresponding to each rule application $(t_1, t_2, \ldots)$ appears explicitly at the top. In the net, it can be seen that only the "backward" version of the predicate **app/3** is used: while the second **app/3** goal in the body of the **append3/4** clause (corresponding to agent s_4) can proceed without suspending, as no context other than the told constraints in the query is needed, the first goal and the goals occurring in its subcomputation always suspend until the third argument becomes instantiated. An identical behavior will occur in all queries in which the three first arguments of **append3/4** are free and the forth is instantiated to a non-incomplete list. With this knowledge the following transformed CLP program can be obtained:

159

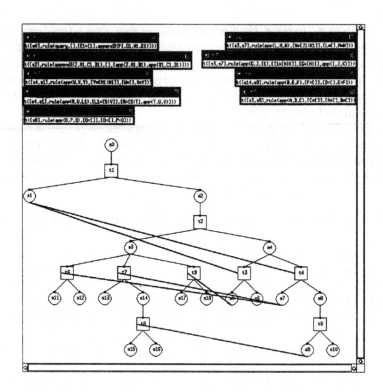

Fig. 2. Contextual net for append3/4 running backward.

```
append3(A, B, D, E) :- when(nonvar(C),app(A, B, C)), app(C, D, E).

app(X, Y, Z) :- X = [],     Y = Z.
app(X, Y, Z) :- Z = [A|D], X = [A|B], when(nonvar(D), app(B, Y, D)).
```

In the schedule analysis of [KS92], a dependency relation among literals of
the program is used to find optimal sequences of the program clause bodies
where the efficient compilation techniques of sequential implementations can
be applied. Each such sequence is a *thread*. Threads should not compromise
the termination properties of the program. Therefore, where dependencies do
not allow to figure out a total ordering of the literals, different single threads
must be allocated. Threads will then be dynamically scheduled, while in each
single thread, one would like to statically schedule the producer(s) before the
corresponding consumer(s), so that the consumers do not need to be suspended
and then woken up later. In the specific case of CC programs, the producers are
the tell operations and the consumers are the ask operations, so this desirable
property of each thread here means that some ask operations could be deleted,
if we can be sure that when they will be scheduled the asked constraint has
already been told.

By using our semantic structures it is easy to see how this can be done. The order between two goals in the body of a clause can be easily decided by looking at the contextual net describing the behaviour of the original CC program: if the subnets rooted at these two goals are linked by dependencies which all go in the same direction (from one subnet to the other one), then this direction is the order to be taken for the scheduling; if instead the dependencies go in both directions, then the two goals must belong to two different threads; otherwise (that is, if there are no dependency links between the two subnets), we can order them in any way. Once the order has been chosen, each ask operation which is scheduled later than all the items of the net on which it depends on can safely be deleted. Following our example, we reorder **app/3** goals in the **append3/4** clause, obtaining:

```
append3(A, B, D, E) :- app(C, D, E), app(A, B, C).

app(X, Y, Z) :- X = [],    Y = Z.
app(X, Y, Z) :- Z = [A|D], X = [A|B], app(B, Y, D).
```

Our aim is to develop an analysis able to infer such invariants based on the semantics. Such analyzer will guarantee that the transformations applied to a CC program in the spirit above are correct.

Acknowledgments

This research has been partially funded by the ACCLAIM Basic Research Esprit project n.7195 and by the COMPUGRAPH Esprit working group n. 7183.

References

[BGH93]   F. Bueno, M. García Banda, and M. Hermenegildo. Compile-time Opti-
            mizations and Analysis Requirements for CC Programs. Technical Report
            CLIP6/93.0, T.U. of Madrid (UPM), July 1993.

[BGHMR94] F. Bueno, M. García Banda, M. Hermenegildo, U. Montanari, and
            F. Rossi. From Eventual to Atomic and Locally Atomic CC Programs:
            A Concurrent Semantics. In *Fourth International Conference on Alge-
            braic and Logic Programming*, Springer–Verlag LNCS, September, 1994.
            To appear.

[BH92]   F. Bueno and M. Hermenegildo. An Automatic Translation Scheme from
            Prolog to the Andorra Kernel Language. In *International Conference on
            Fifth Generation Computer Systems*, pages 759–769. Institute for New
            Generation Computer Technology (ICOT), June 1992.

[Col90]   A. Colmerauer. An Introduction to Prolog III. *CACM*, 28(4):412–418,
            1990.

[Con83]   J. S. Conery. *The And/Or Process Model for Parallel Interpretation of
            Logic Programs*. PhD thesis, The University of California At Irvine, 1983.
            Technical Report 204.

[Deb93]   S.K. Debray. QD-Janus: A Sequential Implementation of Janus in Prolog.
            Technical Report, University of Arizona, 1993.

[GHM93]   M.García de la Banda, M. Hermenegildo, and K. Marriott. Independence in Constraint Logic Programs. In *International Logic Programming Symposium*. MIT Press, Boston, MA, October 1993.

[DeG84]   D. DeGroot. Restricted AND-Parallelism. In *International Conference on Fifth Generation Computer Systems*, pages 471–478. Tokyo, November 1984.

[Her94]   M. Hermenegildo. Towards CIAO-Prolog - A Parallel Concurrent Constraint System. In *Workshop on the Principles and Practice of Constraint Programming*, LNCS, Springer-Verlag, 1994.

[HR93]   M. Hermenegildo and F. Rossi. Strict and Non-Strict Independent And-Parallelism in Logic Programs: Correctness, Efficiency, and Compile-Time Conditions. *Journal of Logic Programming*, 1993. To appear.

[JL87]   J. Jaffar and J.-L. Lassez. Constraint Logic Programming. In *ACM Symp. Principles of Programming Languages*, pages 111–119. ACM, 1987.

[JH91]   S. Janson and S. Haridi. Programming Paradigms of the Andorra Kernel Language. In *International Logic Programming Symposium*, pages 167–183. MIT Press, 1991.

[KS92]   Andy King and Paul Soper. Schedule Analysis of Concurrent Logic Programs. In *Joint International Conference and Symposium on Logic Programming*, pages 478–492, Washington, USA, 1992. The MIT Press.

[MS92]   K. Marriott and P. Stuckey. The 3 R's of Optimizing Constraint Logic Programs: Refinement, Removal, and Reordering. In *19th. Annual ACM Conf. on Principles of Programming Languages*. ACM, 1992.

[MR91]   U. Montanari and F. Rossi. True-concurrency in Concurrent Constraint Programming. In *International Symposium on Logic Programming*, pages 694–716, San Diego, USA, 1991. The MIT Press.

[MR93]   U. Montanari and F. Rossi. Contextual Occurence Nets and Concurrent Constraint Programming. Technical report, U. of Pisa, Computer Science Department, Corso Italia 40, 56100 Pisa, Italy, May 1993.

[Nai88]   L. Naish. Parallelizing NU-Prolog. In *International Conference and Symposium on Logic Programming*, pages 1546–1564, August, 1988. The MIT Press.

[Ros93]   Francesca Rossi. *Constraints and Concurrency*. PhD thesis, Università di Pisa, April 1993.

[Sar89]   V. Saraswat. *Concurrent Constraint Programming Languages*. PhD thesis, Carnegie Mellon, Pittsburgh, 1989. School of Computer Science.

[Sha87]   E.Y. Shapiro, editor. *Concurrent Prolog: Collected Papers*. MIT Press, Cambridge MA, 1987.

[VanH89] P. Van Hentenryck. *Constraint Satisfaction in Logic Programming*. MIT Press, 1989.

CC Programs with both In- and Non-determinism: A Concurrent Semantics

Ugo Montanari* Francesca Rossi* Vijay Saraswat**

* University of Pisa
Computer Science Department
Corso Italia 40, 56100 Pisa, Italy.
E-mail: {ugo,rossi}@di.unipi.it.

** Xerox PARC
3333 Coyote Hill Road, Palo Alto, CA 94304.
E-mail: saraswat@parc.xerox.com.

Abstract. We present a concurrent semantics for concurrent constraint (CC) programs with both ("committed choice") indeterminism and ("backtracking") nondeterminism. The semantics extends the previous semantics for Indeterminate CC by (1) allowing each state to contain different or-parallel components and (2) splitting the concurrency relation into two to distinguish between and- and or-concurrency. Thereby, the construction produces a single representation (an *And-or contextual net*) that captures all the significant relations between events in program runs: concurrency, causal dependency, indeterminism and nondeterminism.
We believe this is a first step towards the formal analysis of the concurrent semantics of practical CC languages containing both in- and non-determinism, such as AKL [HJ90].

1 Introduction

The paper proposes a simple concurrent semantics for concurrent constraint (CC) programs [Sar93] which may contain *both* indeterminism ("don't care" or "committed-choice" nondeterminism) and nondeterminism ("don't know" or "search" non-determinism). Prolog-style nondeterminism is obviously of considerable value in allowing simple, perspicuous representations of search-spaces. Indeterminism arises naturally in reactive distributed contexts, where the relative speeds of processors and relative communication delays across the network are unpredictable. Thus, the combination of indeterminism and nondeterminism we discuss in this paper arises naturally when one seeks to implement simple representations for search problems that are to be solved in a distributed, reactive context. Moreover, it also appears whenever, for any reason, one decides to make some of the choices backtrackable (that is, nondeterministic, or collective), and others committed (that is, indeterministic). Examples of CC programs containing both indeterminism and nondeterminism can be found in [Sar93].

To define the operational behaviour of CC programs, we represent each computation state as a collection of sets of agent and constraint occurrences, where different sets in a collection represent situations which are reached by making different nondeterministic choices. Then, each state is rewritten via rewriting rules, which specify (1) conditions under which they can be executed, and (2) the new configuration (collection of sets) that results on execution of the rule. More precisely, each rule has a left-hand side, a context, and a right-hand side. A rule can be applied if its left-hand side and context are present. Upon application, the left-hand side is cancelled, and the right-hand side is added. The operational semantics then associates with each agent the sequence of configurations that arise as a result of the applications of the rewrite rules generated from the program and the underlying constraint system.

The *concurrent* semantics we develop is derived from the operational semantics by internalizing the history of the computation in the states. The resulting objects in the semantic domain (called *contextual nets* [MR93a]) contain information about concurrency, causal dependency and mutual exclusion. Contextual nets generalize Petri net [Rei85] by allowing each event to have context conditions, in addition to the usual pre- and post-conditions: for the event to occur the context conditions must be present. Causal dependency describes the necessary sequentialization in the program (as introduced by ask conditions). The concurrency relation describes possible parallelism between events. The mutual exclusion relation describes conflict, that is, the impossibility of the related events being in the same computation [MR93b].

To model nondeterminism, we split the concurrency relation into two: *and-concurrency* and *or-concurrency*, obtaining a new kind of net that we call an *and-or contextual net*. Such a refinement of the model is unavoidable if one wants to distinguish among four notions: in-determinism, non-determinism, concurrency and dependency.

The and-or contextual net is derived from a CC program by using just one inference rule, which states that whenever the left hand side and the context of the rule are already represented in the net, then we can add new items to represent its application and its right hand side, and link them suitably to the other elements of the net via the four relations. The applications of such inference rule are Church-Rosser, in the sense that the resulting net does not depend on the order in which they occur. Moreover, it is easy to see that such application is very similar to that of the rules in the operational semantics. In fact, as noted above, the only real difference between the operational and the concurrent semantics (that is, the contextual net) is that the latter generates an object which contains both the final state and the history of the computation, with the appropriate dependencies among the computations steps. This allows to reason more profoundly about several properties of CC programs.

Given the obtained net, it is possible to recover all and only the computations as defined by the operational semantics. Moreover, much more information, about concurrency of the steps involved in each computation, is contained in the net. In fact, both causal and functional dependencies between the items involved in a computation are explicitely expressed in the net.

The net representing the concurrent semantics of a given CC program contains many events and conditions which are uninteresting, like those related to the expansion of a declaration. Therefore an abstraction phase, which removes all such items, is needed if one wants to use in practice such nets to analyse CC programs.

The paper is organized as follows. Section 2 gives the syntax of the CC language framework we consider in this paper. Then, Section 3 provides such framework with an operational semantics, while Section 4 describes and-or contextual nets and Section 5 gives the concurrent semantics based on such nets. Finally, Section 6 relates the concurrent and the operational semantics, and Section 7 discusses a possible abstraction of the concurrent semantics.

The paper is very informal and considers a propositional language only for reasons of space. More formal treatments of some parts of this papers can be found in [MR93a] (about contextual nets) and in [RM94, MR93b] (about the operational and the concurrent semantics). However, none of those papers deals with the coexistence of in-and non-determinism in CC programs.

2 Syntax

In the CC paradigm, we consider the usual description of the chosen constraint system as a *system of partial information* [SRP91] $\langle D, \vdash \rangle$ where D is a set of *tokens* (or primitive constraints) and $\vdash \subseteq \wp(D) \times D$ is the entailment relation which states which tokens are entailed by which sets of other tokens. The language (here we consider a propositional language just for simplicity of the technical developments) is concretely described by the following grammar, where P ranges over programs, F over sequences of procedure declarations, A over agents, and c over constraints:

$$
\begin{array}{lll}
\text{(Programs)} & P ::= F.A & \\
\text{(Declarations)} & F ::= p :: A \mid F.F & \\
\text{(Agents)} & A ::= success & \\
& \mid failure & \\
& \mid c & \text{(Tell)} \\
& \mid c \rightarrow A & \text{(Ask)} \\
& \mid A + A & \text{(Indeterminism)} \\
& \mid A \parallel A & \text{(Parallel composition)} \\
& \mid A \vee A & \text{(Non-determinism)} \\
& \mid p & \text{(Procedure Call)}
\end{array}
$$

3 Operational Semantics

Each state of a CC computation consists of a collection of sets $\langle M_1, \ldots, M_n \rangle$, where each set M_i is called an *or-state* and contains occurrences of agents and constraints. Intuitively, each set M_i represents the (intermediate) result of one nondeterministic branch of a computation. Therefore a state represents the (intermediate) result of all nondeterministic branches occurring in a computation.

Then, each computation step models either the evolution of a single agent, or the entailment of a new token through the $\vdash$ relation. Such a change in the state of the computation will be performed via the application of a rewrite rule

$$r : L(r) \overset{c(r)}{\leadsto} R_1(r); \dots; R_k(r)$$

where $L(r)$ is an agent, $c(r)$ is a constraint, and each $R_i(r)$ is a set of agent and constraint occurrences. The intuitive meaning of a rule is that $L(r)$, called the left hand side of the rule, is deleted from one of the or-states of the current state, say M_j, and k copies of the so obtained or-state are produced. Then, in each of such copies, say copy i, $R_i(r)$ (called a right hand side of the rule) is added. All this is done only if $c(r)$ is present in M_j.

We have as many rewrite rules as the number of agents and declarations in a program (which is finite), plus the number of pairs of the entailment relation (which can be infinite):

$$(c \to A) \overset{c}{\leadsto} A$$
$$A_1 \parallel A_2 \leadsto A_1, A_2$$
$$A_1 + A_2 \leadsto A_1$$
$$A_1 + A_2 \leadsto A_2$$
$$A_1 \vee A_2 \leadsto A_1; A_2$$

In addition, there is a rule

$$p \leadsto A$$

for every program clause $p :: A$ and a rule

$$\overset{S}{\leadsto} t$$

for every entailment pair $S \vdash t$ in the underlying constraint system.

Formally, rule application works as follows. A rule $r : L(r) \overset{c(r)}{\leadsto} R_1(r); \dots; R_k(r)$ is said to be applicable in a state $S_1 = \langle M_1, \dots, M_n \rangle$ if there exists M_i such that $(L(r) \cup c(r)) \subseteq M_i$. In such a case, applying r to S_1 yields the state $S_2 = \langle M_1, \dots, M_{i-1}, (M_i \setminus L(r)) \cup R_1(r), \dots, (M_i \setminus L(r)) \cup R_k(r), M_{i+1}, \dots, M_n \rangle$.

The operational semantics of a given CC program P consists of all the computations for P, i.e., the sequences of computations steps which apply rules representing agents and constraints of P. We will also need the concept of *nonredundant* computations, which are those computations where no entailment rule is ever applied more than once on the same constraint occurrence.

Note that this mechanism of making copies of the current world whenever a nondeterministic choice is accomplished is the usual way to give an operational semantics to languages with nondeterminism. In this way, a computation may contain nondeterminism, and different computations are instead originated by different indeterministic choices.

Let us now consider an example of a simple CC program with both nondeterminism and indeterminism in order to see how these two choice mechanisms interact. Suppose to have the parallel composition

$$(c_1 + c_2) \parallel (c_3 \lor c_4).$$

Although it could seem at first sight that the two choices are independent, and that c_1 and c_2 cannot appear in the same computation, in reality they can, and this depends on the order in which the two choices are made. In fact, if the indeterministic choice is made first, then we have two computations, one with final state $\langle \{c_1, c_3\}, \{c_1, c_4\} \rangle$ and one with final state $\langle \{c_2, c_3\}, \{c_2, c_4\} \rangle$. If instead the nondeterministic choice is made first, then we have other four computations: two of them produce the results written above, and the other two have final state $\langle \{c_1, c_3\}, \{c_2, c_4\} \rangle$ and $\langle \{c_2, c_3\}, \{c_1, c_4\} \rangle$ respectively. Thus in this second case c_1 and c_2 belong to the same computation. In fact, once the state has been divided into two or-states, the computation may proceed in different ways in the two or-states and thus in particular it may choose to evolve to c_1 in one or-state and to c_2 in the other or-state.

We will consider this example again later on in the paper. In fact, although being very simple, it is enough to understand the relationship between nondeterminism and indeterminism from the concurrency point of view and to check whether usual partial order structures may be enough to represent concurrency in CC programs with both kinds of choices.

4   And-Or Contextual Nets

Contextual nets [MR93a] extend standard Petri nets (actually, C/E systems) with the possibility, for each event, of having context-conditions besides pre- and post-conditions. While pre-conditions are deleted by the event occurrence, and post-conditions are created, context conditions are needed for such an occurrence but are left unchanged. Contextual nets are able to specify three relations among their elements: causal dependency, concurrency, and mutual exclusion, which in terms of CC programming can be interpreted as necessary sequentialization, possible concurrency, and indeterminism, respectively.

In order to be able to model CC programs with nondeterminsm as well, we have to extend the semantic structure so that it can express also nondeterminism. To this end we introduce the notion of and-or contextual nets, which add to contextual nets the possibility of stating when some items of the net are "or-concurrent", that is, they belong to different nondeterministic branches.

We will write such nets as $\langle B, E; F_1, F_2, F_3 \rangle$, where B is the set of conditions, E the set of events, F_1 gives the direct causal dependencies, F_2 states the context conditions for each event, and F_3 contains pairs of postconditions of the same event (which have to be considered as or-concurrent). In terms of CC programming, conditions are agents and/or tokens, while events are computation steps.

Each and-or contextual net induces four relations on its elements: causal dependency, mutual exclusion, or-concurrency, and and-concurrency. Causal dependency ($\leq$) is derived from F_1 and F_2, mutual exclusion ($\#$) originates from events sharing a precondition and it is propagated via the $\leq$ relation, or-concurrency (or-co) originates from the F_3 relation and it is propagated via $\leq$, and and-concurrency (and-co) is what is left from the other relations: two items are and-concurrent if they are not in any of the other relations. Two elements which are not concurrent may be in more than one of the other relations. For our semantics we will consider only occurrence nets, i.e., nets where the $\leq$ relation does not have cycles.

And-or context-dependent nets will be graphically represented in the same way as classical and contextual nets. Thus, conditions are circles, events are boxes, and the flow relation F_1 is represented by directed arcs from circles to boxes or viceversa. We choose to represent the context relation F_2 by undirected arcs (since the direction of such relation is unambiguous, i.e. from elements of B to elements of E) and the or-concurrency relation F_3 by undirected labelled arcs (whose label is or). An and-or contextual net can be seen in Figure 1. In this net, for example, events e_1 and e_2 are mutually exclusive, while e_2 and e_4 are and-concurrent. Also, a and b and or-concurrent, and c is a context for both e_2 and e_4.

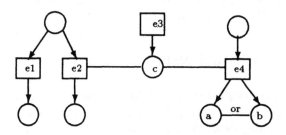

Fig. 1. An and-or contextual net.

5   Concurrent Semantics

In order to give a concurrent semantics to CC programs with both in- and nondeterminism, we follow the same idea used for indeterministic CC programs, that is, to associate a net to each program. However, while the nets used for indeterministic CC programs are contextual nets, here we need and-or nets. Nevertheless, the generating mechanism is very similar: we take the rewrite rules associated to a given CC program and by using them we incrementally construct an and-or contextual net plus a mapping which relates the items of the net to the agents, constraints, and rules of the program. Such incremental construction is achieved via the use of one inference rule (plus another one to start). Each time the inference rule is applied, a rewrite rule is chosen whose left hand side and context are already present in the partially built net. Such elements have to be and-concurrent (which means that they can appear together in the same or-state). Then, a new element representing the rule application is added (as an event), as well as new elements representing the right hand sides of the rule (as conditions).

The elements of the net are structured in such a way that elements generated by using different sequences of rules are indeed different. That is, each element contains its "history". The way this is achieved consists in defining an element as a pair, of which the first element is the *type* of the term, and represents the rule or agent or constraint that the term corresponds to, and the second element is its *history*.

More precisely, assuming the net to be obtained is $\langle B, E, F_1, F_2, F_3 \rangle$, the starting inference rule is:

$$\frac{P = F.A}{\langle A, \emptyset \rangle \in B}$$

which means that we start with one element, which is a condition corresponding to agent A and with empty history. Instead, the main inference rule is:

$$\frac{\begin{array}{c} \{s_0, \ldots, s_{n-1}\} \subseteq B \\ s_i \text{ and-co } s_j \quad (i, j < n) \\ s_i = \langle a_i, e_i \rangle \quad (i < n) \\ a_i \neq a_j \quad (i, j < n) \\ \exists r \in RR(P) \text{ such that } L(r) = \{a_0, \ldots, a_{m-1}\} \text{ and } c(r) = \{a_m, \ldots, a_{n-1}\} \end{array}}{\begin{array}{c} e = \langle r, \{s_0, \ldots, s_{n-1}\} \rangle \in E \\ s_i F_1 e \quad (i < m) \\ s_i F_2 e \quad (m \leq i < n) \\ \forall i = 1, \ldots, k, a \in R_i(r) \text{ implies } \langle a, e \rangle \in B \text{ and } e F_1 \langle a, e \rangle \\ a \in R_i(r) \text{ and } b \in R_j(r) \text{ and } i \neq j \text{ implies } \langle a, b \rangle \in F_3 \end{array}}$$

That is, if we find items of the net which correspond to the left hand side and the context of a rule and which are and-concurrent, then we add a new event corresponding to the rule application, and new conditions corresponding to the elements of all right hand sides of the rule. Then we also suitably link such new objects among them via the F_1 (dependency), F_2 (context), and F_3 (or-concurrency) relations. In particular, the F_3 relation is set to hold among any pair of items representing elements belonging to different right hand sides of the rule. For example, the concurrent semantics of the program described at the end of Section 3 is the and-or contextual net in Figure 2.

Note that the above inference rule is a simplified version of what is actually needed to correctly generate the and-or net corresponding to a given CC program. In fact, we assume here that no rule has the same agent more then once in

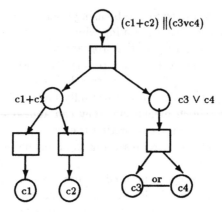

Fig. 2. The and-or contextual net giving the concurrent semantics of a CC program.

its right hand sides. However, if this should happen, a straightforward extension of the term coding, written as triple instead of pairs (where the added element is a natural number used to distinguish the different occurrences of an agent) would be enough (see [MR93b]).

6 Concurrent vs. Operational Semantics

It is important now to understand the relationship between the operational semantics defined in Section 3 and the concurrent semantics defined in Section 5. In particular, it is important to be able to show that from the concurrent semantics it is possible to recover all and only the computations of the operational semantics.

In previous studies concerning the concurrent semantics of indeterministic CC programs via contextual nets [MR93b] such relationship is very simple: any linearization (that is, a total order of the events which is compatible with the partial order) of each (maximal and left-closed) subnet of the semantics structure which does not contain any pair of mutual exclusive elements represents one (non-redundant) computation; and viceversa, each (non-redundant) computation is represented by one linearization of one of such subnets.

When however nondeterminism and indeterminism coexist, the representation of computations via subnets is not possible any more. Consider again the simple CC program whose computations are described at the end of Section 3 and whose semantics structure is depicted in Figure 2. Then, it is easy to see that there is no collection of subnets which may represent all its computations. In fact, if we consider all its subnets which do not contain any pair of mutually exclusive elements (which can be seen in Figure 3), then we are able to represent only those computations where the same branch of the indeterministic choice has been taken in both or-branches (either because the indeterministic choice was done before the or-choice, or because the choices in the two or-branches coincide). But we are not able to represent those computations where the or-choice has been made first, and where each or-branch evolved via a different indeterministic branch (one chose c_1 and the other one c_2).

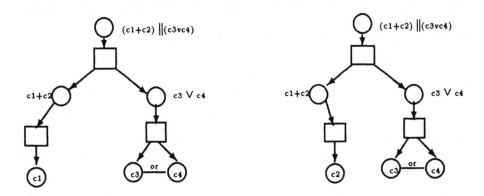

Fig. 3. The non-mutually-exclusive subnets of the and-or contextual net in Figure 2.

A possible solution would be to consider subnets that do not contain pairs of mutually exclusive elements. However, to allow two in-branches to appear in the same computation, we would have to specify that or-choices must occur before in-choices.

Unfortunately, recent approaches to the semantics of some extensions of Petri nets have shown that in presence of some specific features it is not possible to represents concurrency via partial orders, instead pairs of partial orders are required. In the present case, the first partial order would give a subnet, and the second would specify the order of choices. However, this would still not distinguish between a computation in which the first in-choice (c_1) is taken in the first or-state (c_3), and the second (c_2) with the second or-state (c_4) and one in which c_1 is taken with c_4 and c_2 with c_3.

Therefore the usual method of relating semantic nets to programs (using subnet selection), does not seem applicable in the current setting. So we look for alternative ways in which the semantic structure may still represent all and only the computations of the operational semantics of CC programs. To this end we introduce the concept of *net execution*.

Informally, a net execution is a sequence of steps which starts with the entire net and at each intermediate stage reaches a collection of subnets of the original net. Each step *executes* one of the events of the net, among those whose pre- and context-conditions are in the current collection of nets (and are minimals), and the result is that the events and its preconditions are cancelled, together with every item which is mutually exclusive with that event. Moreover, if the event is an or-choice, a replication of the net containing the executed event is made, in the same manner as for the operational semantics.

More precisely, consider an and-or contextual net N. Then let us call $min(N)$ the set of all items of N which are minimal w.r.t. the causal dependency relation. Also, for any event e in N, let us call $pre(e)$ (resp., $con(e)$, $post(e)$) the set of preconditions (resp., context conditions, postconditions) of e. Moreover, given any condition s in a net, let us call $or\text{-}rest(s)$ the set S of all conditions which are siblings of s and or-concurrent with it, plus the set S' which contains all elements (conditions and/or events) which depend on some element of S as well as all events which have some element of S as a context. Finally, given a net N and a set of items S in N, let us call $ex(N, S)$ the net which is obtained from N by deleting all the items which are mutually exclusive with any element in S.

Consider now a CC program P and the corresponding concurrent semantics N, and assume to have a collection of subnets of N, say $\langle N_1, \ldots, N_n \rangle$ (at the beginning we just have $\langle N \rangle$). Then an execution step is accomplished by choosing an event $e \in N_i$ such that $pre(e) \cup con(e) \in min(N_i)$. There are now two cases that can occur :

- there are no $s_1, s_2 \in post(e)$ such that s_1 and s_2 are or-concurrent; then the new collection of nets is

$$\langle N_1, \ldots, N_{i-1}, ex(N_i - (pre(e) \cup e), e), N_{i+1}, \ldots, N_n \rangle$$

- the other case, where there are instead pairs of or-concurrent postconditions of e, is simplified by the fact that this can arise only from the application of the nondeterminism rule, which only generates two postconditions; in this case, assuming $post(e) = \{s_1, s_2\}$, the new collection of nets is
$\langle N_1, \ldots, N_{i-1}, ex(N_i - (pre(e) \cup e), e) - or\text{-}rest(s_1), ex(N_i - (pre(e) \cup e), e) - or\text{-}rest(s_2), N_{i+1}, \ldots, N_n \rangle$

Consider now the set OS all the (non-redundant) computations of a CC program P and the set CS of all the executions of the corresponding and-or contextual net N. Then there is a bijection between OS and CS.

This means that it is possible to recover all computations from the and-or net representing the concurrent semantics of P. Thus the concurrent semantics does not loose any information w.r.t. the operational semantics. Indeed, it adds much information, since the possible concurrency of execution steps, as well as the causal and the functional dependencies, are explicitly represented.

7 Abstraction

The contextual net corresponding to a given CC program can be used to analyse CC programs in terms of concurrency, agent's dependency, choice points, parallelism level, and many others. However, the net as defined in the previous section has many events and conditions which are uninteresting for any reasonable analysis. Therefore one could think of abstracting from the information given by such items, and obtain a net, or a similar structure, where only the relevant information is contained.

A choice that has been adopted also in many other operational semantic approaches for CC programs is to say that only ask and tell agents are important. Therefore, in our terms, it would mean that we only want to keep those events which represent the evolution of ask agents or tell agents.

To do that, consider an and-or net $\langle B, E, F_1, F_2, F_3 \rangle$, plus the mapping to the CC program rules, and the corresponding relations $\leq$, $\#$, or-co, and and-co. Now, consider the set of events $E' \subseteq E$ such that $E' = \{e \in E \mid e = \langle e_1, e_2 \rangle, e_1$ is an ask or a tell rule[1]$\}$. Then the structure $\langle E', \leq_{|_{E'}}, \text{or-co}_{|_{E'}} \rangle$ relates the interesting events via the same relations as above, but projected over E'. This structure is obviously not an and-or contextual net, because it does not contain any conditions. However, it is nevertheless able to provide causality, indeterminism, and-concurrency, and or-concurrency information among the selected events.

Note also that the abstract structure so obtained is able to represent the computations and the dependencies present in many programs, possibly very different among them. Therefore reasoning on the net instead of on the program allows one to focus on the crucial issues regarding causality and functionality, while being independent of the particular recursive set of agent definitions which have been chosen to represent such causality information.

Acknowledgements

This research has been partially supported by the ACCLAIM Basic Research Esprit Project n.7195.

References

[HJ90]   S. Haridi and S. Janson. Kernel andorra prolog and its computational model. In *Proc. ICLP90*. MIT Press, 1990.

[MR93a] U. Montanari and F. Rossi. Contextual nets. Technical Report TR-4/93, CS Department, University of Pisa, Italy, 1993.

[MR93b] U. Montanari and F. Rossi. Contextual occurrence nets and concurrent constraint programming. In *Proc. Dagstuhl Seminar on Graph Transformations in Computer Science*. Springer-Verlag, LNCS, 1993.

[Rei85] W. Reisig. *Petri Nets: An Introduction*. EATCS Monographs on Theoretical Computer Science. Springer Verlag, 1985.

[RM94]   F. Rossi and U. Montanari. Concurrent semantics for concurrent constraint programming. In *Constraint Programming*. NATO ASI Series, B. Mayoh, E. Tyugu, J. Penjam eds., 1994.

[Sar93] V.A. Saraswat. *Concurrent Constraint Programming*. MIT Press, 1993.

[SRP91] V. A. Saraswat, M. Rinard, and P. Panangaden. Semantic foundations of concurrent constraint programming. In *Proc. POPL*. ACM, 1991.

Efficient and Complete Tests for Database Integrity Constraint Checking*

Ashish Gupta
Yehoshua Sagiv[†]
Jeffrey D. Ullman
Jennifer Widom

Department of Computer Science
Stanford University
Stanford, CA 94305-2140
{agupta,sagiv,ullman,widom}@cs.stanford.edu

1 Introduction

An important feature of modern database management systems is the automatic checking of *integrity constraints*. An integrity constraint is a predicate or query such that if the predicate holds on a state of the data, or equivalently if the query produces an empty answer, then the database is considered *valid*. When an integrity constraint is *violated*, i.e., when the predicate does not hold or the query produces a non-empty answer, then the update creating the undesirable database state must be rejected or some other compensating action must be taken.

We are interested in efficient methods for checking integrity constraints (hereafter called constraints) as a database is updated. Here, general efficiency is measured both in the amount of data that needs to be accessed in order to check a constraint, and in whether the check can be performed by submitting a query to the database system (rather than running an algorithm directly on the data). In terms of complexity, we are not interested in methods that are exponential in the size of the data or in the number of constraints, but we are willing to accept methods that are exponential in the size of the constraints themselves since, in databases, constraints tend to be short.

*Research sponsored by NSF grants IRI–91–16646 and IRI–92–23405, by ARO grant DAAL03–91–G–0177, by ARPA contract F33615–93–1–1339, and by a grant of Mitsubishi Electric Corp.

[†]Permanent address: Department of Computer Science, Hebrew University, Jerusalem, Israel.

Suppose that we have a constraint C, and a database update occurs. We need to ensure that C still holds after the update. Assume that we have available at least the update itself and the definition of C. In addition to this information, there are three levels in the amount of data we might use to check the constraint: *none*, *some*, or *all*. Using none of the data corresponds to the *query independent of update* problem, which has been studied in its generality in [BT88, Elk90, LS93] and with respect to constraints by us in [GSUW94]. Using all of the data amounts to efficient evaluation of predicates or queries over the database [BC79, GMS93, HD92, Nic82, QW91, UO92]. We study the case where *some* of the data is used to check the constraint. This scenario arises whenever certain data involved in the constraint is very expensive or impossible to access, such as in distributed database systems or collaborative design [TH93, GT93]. Hereafter we refer to the portion of the data used to check a constraint as *accessible* data, and we refer to the portion of the data involved in a constraint but not used to check the constraint as *inaccessible* data.

Note that, unless all of the relevant data is accessible, our constraint checking methods will be conservative. That is, by looking at only some of the data, we may be able to determine that the constraint still holds, or we may determine that it is necessary to look at all of the data to check the constraint. A check is *correct* if, whenever it determines that a constraint still holds, then indeed the constraint holds. We also want our checks to be *complete*, but completeness is with respect to the accessible data. A check is complete in this sense if, whenever we determine that a constraint may not hold, there is some configuration of the inaccessible data for which the constraint indeed does not hold.

In the remainder of this short paper we outline the languages we have been considering for database constraints and we solidify the notion of using *some* of the data to check a constraint. We then give several examples that illustrate when and how our constraint checking methods apply. (Due to space limitations, complete technical results are not included.) The examples serve to bring out a number of problems we have not yet solved, which are enumerated at the end of the paper.

2 Problem Definition

We consider relational databases where relations are modeled as predicates and queries are expressed as logical rules that derive a *result* predicate, as in, e.g., *Datalog* [Ull88]. Examples are given below. A *constraint* is expressed as a query whose result is a special 0-ary predicate that we call panic. If the query produces $\emptyset$ on a given database D, then the constraint holds for D. If the query produces panic then the constraint is violated. The difficulty of checking constraints depends on the language that we use to express constraint queries. Examples of interesting languages for expressing constraint queries are:

1. Conjunctive queries [CM77].

2. Nonrecursive Datalog, or unions of conjunctive queries [SY80].

3. Conjunctive queries with arithmetic comparisons [Klu88].

4. Datalog with negation [Ull88].

5. Recursive Datalog, possibly with arithmetic comparisons and/or negation and/or arithmetic operators [Ull88].

For some combinations of a language above and an amount of information used (*none*, *some*, or *all*), the constraint checking problem can be reduced to other problems that have been studied in the literature; see [GSUW94] for a discussion. For instance, conjunctive query containment results can be used to check constraints when only updates and constraint definitions are used [LS93].

In this paper we focus our discussion on constraints expressed as conjunctive queries with arithmetic comparisons, we suppose the only accessible relation is the updated relation, and we consider updates that are insertions of a single tuple. The general form of a conjunctive query constraint is:

panic :– l & r_1 & ... & r_n & c_1 & ... & c_k.

Here, l is the predicate for which the corresponding relation L is accessible, the relation R_i for each of the r_i's is inaccessible, and each c_i is an arithmetic comparison involving one of $<, \leq, >, \geq, =$.[1]

Let tuple t be inserted into relation L and assume constraint C holds before the insertion. We want to use L, C, and t to infer that C is not violated after the insertion. We derive a condition that relation L needs to satisfy in order for t not to violate C. We refer to this condition as the *test* condition. If the test condition is satisfiable, then relations $R_1, \ldots, R_n$ do not need to be accessed. The test condition is obtained by reducing the problem outlined above to the problem of checking if a conjunctive query is contained in a union of conjunctive queries; details are in [GSUW94].

---

[1] The use of L and R refers to the fact that, in distributed databases, the "Local" data is accessible and the "Remote" data is inaccessible.

3 Examples

EXAMPLE 1. Consider an employee-department relational database with two relations:

emp(E, D, S) *% employee number E in department D has salary S*
dept(D, MS) *% some manager in department D has salary MS*

Let the constraint assert that every employee earns less than every manager in the same department. This constraint is expressed as a conjunctive query C such that if C produces panic then the constraint is violated:

C: panic :– emp(E, D, S) & dept(D, MS) & $S \geq MS$.

Let relation EMP for predicate emp be accessible and relation DEPT be inaccessible. Suppose tuple emp($e, d1, 50$) is inserted into relation EMP. Constraint C will be violated if department $d1$ has a manager whose salary is ≤ 50. However, suppose department $d1$ already has an employee whose salary is 100. Since constraint C is not violated before the insertion, we can infer that no manager in $d1$ earns as little as 100, and therefore emp($e, d1, 50$) does not violate constraint C.

The above inference procedure can be formalized by specifying a test condition on the relation EMP and the inserted tuple, such that if EMP satisfies the test condition, then the inserted tuple does not violate the constraint. For constraint C, the test condition is the following Datalog query that derives insertion_ok if and only if the inserted tuple does not violate C, independent of the value of relation DEPT.

insertion_ok :– inserted(E, D, S) & emp(X, D, Y) & $Y \geq S$.

Relation INSERTED contains only the inserted tuple and EMP does not contain the inserted tuple. This test is complete with respect to the accessible data, as defined in Section 1. □

Note, the test condition in Example 1 is a single Datalog rule and was derived without using the actual value of the inserted tuple. We now give two examples that illustrate the complexity that simple arithmetic comparison operators $<, >$, $\leq, \geq$ introduce. Example 2 shows that the complete test could be a recursive Datalog program. The constraint in Example 3 also has a complete test in the form of a recursive Datalog program, but illustrates the computational complexity of evaluating the test.

EXAMPLE 2. We shall refer to this example as *forbidden intervals*.

C: panic :– $1(X, Y)$ & $r(Z)$ & $X \leq Z \leq Y$.

Each pair in the accessible relation L can be thought of as the ends of an interval that no Z in the inaccessible relation R may occupy.

Suppose relation L has the tuples $(3, 6)$ and $(5, 10)$. The tuples of relation R that violate the constraint given tuple $1(3, 6)$ lie in the interval $[3, 6]$ and similarly, the tuples of relation R that violate the constraint given tuple $1(5, 10)$ lie in the interval $[5, 10]$. If the constraint is not violated then we can infer that the tuples of the inaccessible relation lie outside the *forbidden intervals* $[3, 6]$ and $[5, 10]$ and therefore outside the combined forbidden interval $[3, 10]$.

Let tuple (a, b) be inserted into relation L. If $a \geq 3$ and $b \leq 10$, then the forbidden interval for $1(a, b)$ is contained in the union of the forbidden intervals of one or more existing tuples, and relation R need not be accessed in order to infer that constraint C is not violated. Note, the complete test may need to access multiple existing tuples in order to make the above inference. An incomplete, but sufficient, test would be to check that the forbidden interval for some single existing tuple contains the forbidden interval for the inserted tuple. That corresponds to using a single tuple in the accessible relation as opposed to using an arbitrary number of tuples, and was the approach taken in our initial work [GW93]. The sufficient test is linear in the number of tuples in L whereas the complete test could be exponential, if implemented naively. With some preprocessing, the complete test can also be evaluated in linear time [GSUW94].

The complete test for this example is the following recursive Datalog program that derives `insertion_ok` if and only if the inserted tuple does not violate C, assuming that C was not violated before the insertion.

```
insertion_ok :- inserted(A, B) & forbidden_int(C, D) &
                A ≥ C & B ≤ D.
forbidden_int(C, D) :- l(C, D).

forbidden_int(C, D) :- forbidden_int(C, X) &
                       forbidden_int(Y, D) & X ≥ Y.
```

□

EXAMPLE 3.   Consider a constraint C that involves two variables in the inaccessible relation:

$$C: \quad \mathsf{panic} :- 1(U, V, W, Z) \ \& \ r(X, Y) \ \& \ U \leq X \leq V \ \& \ W \leq Y \leq Z.$$

Intuitively, the above constraint is the *forbidden interval* constraint in two dimensions. A tuple in relation R defines a point in a two dimensional space and a tuple in relation L defines a rectangular region in this 2-D space. Constraint

C requires that all the points defined by the inaccessible relation R lie outside every rectangular region defined by the accessible tuples. Therefore, an inserted tuple $1(a, b, c, d)$, does not violate C if the rectangle defined by $1(a, b, c, d)$ is contained in the union of the rectangles defined by the existing tuples in L. The test for determining when a rectangle is contained in a set of other rectangles can still be represented as a recursive Datalog program. However, building the program is not as straightforward as in Example 2. In addition, the complexity of the test is high even with preprocessing. Without preprocessing the test is exponential in the number of tuples in L. □

4 Discussion

In [GSUW94] we identify some subclasses of conjunctive query constraints with arithmetic comparisons for which the complete test is a (recursive) Datalog program. We also identify some subclasses where the complete test does not need to consider multiple tuples from the accessible relation, but can consider tuples one at a time (i.e., there is no need to consider combinations of tuples, as in Example 2). The test condition for conjunctive query constraints, including the subclasses, is NP-complete. However, in at least some cases, the exponential behavior is only in the size of the constraint specifications, which we believe will be relatively small. In other cases the tests may be exponential in the size of the database or the number of constraints in the system. In such cases sufficient tests, instead of complete tests, may be preferable.

For conjunctive query constraints that use function symbols like $+$, $-$ (instead of only arithmetic comparisons), the complete test is an implication condition where both sides of the implication use disjunction and the function symbols. Even though the implication condition can be derived in time exponential in the size of the constraint, evaluating the implication may be undecidable or have very high complexity. However, for some subclasses the ideas outlined in this paper can be extended to derive sufficient decidable tests.

5 Future Research Directions

Many interesting avenues remain unexplored in making constraint checking efficient following the framework we outlined above. We plan to:

- Consider more expressive constraint languages. Aggregate functions like $MAX, SUM, AVG, etc.$ make the constraints more general. For instance, we might want a constraint requiring the average gradepoint of a graduating student to be at least 3.

- Use different amounts and type of information. For instance, constraint C_1 might be checked using constraints C_2 and C_3, possibly together with some functional dependency information. In distributed database systems, such algorithms can be used to increase the amount of constraint checking that can be done locally, without accessing remote data.

- Devise algorithms to efficiently perform local tests. As the examples in this paper illustrate, the test conditions often have high complexity. Techniques from constraint logic programming, operations research, and other areas provide ways of evaluating the tests efficiently. For instance, in Examples 2 and 3, algorithms from computational geometry are useful for efficient evaluation.

- For constraints where the complexity of local checking is inherently very high, it is useful to look for sufficient tests that are efficient to implement even though they may not be complete.

References

[BT88]   Jose A. Blakeley and F. W. Tompa. Maintaining materialized views without accessing base data. *Information Systems*, 13(4):393–406, 1988.

[BC79]   Peter O. Buneman and Eric K. Clemons. *Efficiently Monitoring Relational Databases*. In *ACM Transactions on Database Systems*, Vol 4, No. 3, 1979, 368-382.

[CM77]   Ashok K. Chandra and P.M. Merlin. Optimal Implementation on Conjunctive Queries in Relational Databases. In *9th ACM Symposium on Theory of Computing*, pages 77–90, ACM, 1977.

[Elk90]   C. Elkan. Independence of logic database queries and updates. In *Proceedings of the Ninth ACM SIGACT-SIGMOD-SIGART Symposium on Principles of Database Systems*, pages 154–160, 1990.

[GMS93] Ashish Gupta, Inderpal Singh Mumick, and V. S. Subrahmanian. Maintaining Views Incrementally. In *SIGMOD 1993*, pages 157–167.

[GSUW94] Ashish Gupta, Shuky Sagiv, Jeffrey D. Ullman, and Jennifer Widom. Constraint Checking with Partial Information. In PODS 1994.

[GT93]   Ashish Gupta and Sanjai Tiwari. Distributed Constraint Management for Collaborative Engineering Databases. In *Proceedings of the Second International Conference on Information and Knowledge Management (CIKM)*, Washington DC, November 1993.

[GW93]   Ashish Gupta and Jennifer Widom. Local Checking of Global Integrity Constraints . In *Proceedings of ACM SIGMOD 1993 International Conference on Management of Data*, pages 49–59.

[HD92]   John V. Harrison and Suzanne Dietrich. Maintenance of Materialized Views in a Deductive Database: An Update Propagation Approach. In *Workshop on Deductive Databases, JICLSP 1992*, pages 56–65, 1992.

[Klu88]   A. Klug. On Conjunctive Queries Containing Inequalities. *Journal of the ACM*, 1(35):146–160, 1988.

[LS93]   A.Y. Levy and Y. Sagiv. Queries independent of updates. In *Proceedings of the Nineteenth International Conference on Very Large Data Bases*, pages 171–181, Dublin, Ireland, August 1993.

[Nic82]   J. M. Nicolas. Logic for Improving Integrity Checking in Relational Data Bases. *Acta Informatica*, 18(3):227–253, 1982.

[TH93]   Sanjai Tiwari and H. C. Howard. Constraint Management on Distributed AEC Databases. In *Fifth International Conference on Computing in Civil and Building Engineering*, ASCE, 1993.

[QW91]   Xiaolei Qian and Gio Wiederhold. *Incremental Recomputation of Active Relational Expressions*. In *TKDE*, 1991.

[SY80]   Yehoshua Sagiv and Mihalis Yannakakis. Equivalences Among Relational Expressions with the Union and Difference Operators. *Journal of the ACM*, 4(27):633–655, 1980.

[Ull88]   J. D. Ullman. *Principles of Database and Knowledge-Base Systems*, Volumes 1 and 2. Computer Science Press, New York, 1989.

[UO92]   Toni Urpi and Antoni Olive. A method for change computation in deductive databases. In *Proceedings of the Eighteenth International Conference on Very Large Databases (VLDB)*, pages 225–237, Vancouver, British Columbia, 1992.

Linear vs. Polynomial Constraints
in Database Query Languages

Foto Afrati[1] and Stavros S. Cosmadakis[2] and Stéphane Grumbach[3] and
Gabriel M. Kuper[4]

[1] National Technical University of Athens, Computer Science Division, Heroon
Politechniou 9, 157 73 Zographou, Athens, Greece; afrati@theseas.ntua.gr.
[2] New York University,
[3] I.N.R.I.A., Rocquencourt BP 105, 78153 Le Chesnay, France
Stephane.Grumbach@inria.fr.
[4] ECRC, Arabellastr. 17, D-81925 München, Germany

Abstract. We prove positive and negative results on the expressive power
of the relational calculus augmented with linear constraints. We show the
non-expressibility of some properties expressed by polynomial constraints.
We consider in particular some queries involving the existence of lines. We
study mainly constraints over real numbers, but we also present some results
in the case of the natural numbers.

1 Introduction

An active area of recent research is concerned with integrating constraints into logical formalisms for programming languages [DG,JL87,Ma87,Sa] and database query
languages [KKR90,Re90,Kup93,BJM93,KG94]. Constraints are incorporated in logic
programming systems such as CLP, Prolog III and CHIP. The class of *linear* constraints is of particular interest, because of its applicability and the potential for
efficient implementation [HJLL90,JL87,La90].

Kanellakis et al. [KKR90] describe a methodology to combine constraint programming with database query languages. They propose several generalizations of
the traditional relational database calculus (first-order logic). One of the more powerful languages described in [KKR90] is the relational calculus augmented with polynomial constraints, *FO(poly)*. This language is powerful enough to express many
geometric problems, and has NC data complexity; however, the complexity of quantifier elimination (over real closed fields) makes it impractical for most purposes. A
natural question therefore is to ask what happens if constraints are restricted to be
linear.

In this paper we study the expressive power of the relational calculus augmented
with linear constraints, *FO(linear)*. We first give some negative results, showing that
there exist properties in *FO(poly)* which are not expressible in *FO(linear)*. We use
the well-known technique of *Ehrenfeucht-Fraïssé* games [Eh61,Fr54]. We show that,
when constraints are introduced to first-order logic, games can be appropriately
adapted to prove non-definability; by contrast, techniques such as the compactness
theorem (from first-order logic) or locality and 0/1 laws (from finite model theory)
fail with constraints [GS94].

A natural subset of *FO(poly)* singled out in [KKR90] is *FO(lines)*; it extends *FO(linear)* with (second order) variables ranging over lines. We show that *FO(lines)* has the same expressive power as *FO(poly)*. Nevertheless, some queries can be expressed more naturally with higher dimension variables. We also show that some natural queries in *FO(lines)* can be expressed in *FO(linear)* when the output of the query has a simple geometrical relation to the input.

Maybe the most basic query expressed by line variables is "*compute the set of lines contained in the database*". We do not know if it is expressible in *FO(linear)*. We show, however, that it is *linear*, i.e., if the input is defined by linear constraints, the output is defined by linear constraints as well. Linearity is a desirable property of query languages with linear constraints, because it makes it possible to cascade queries. It can be shown that queries expressed in *FO(linear)* are linear. Also, queries expressed in a fragment of *FO(poly)* described in [HJLL90, La90] (the *parametric* queries) are linear. It is an interesting open problem to find the most general fragment of *FO(poly)* which expresses only linear queries.

We also compare the expressiveness of linear vs. polynomial constraints in a different context, namely in the presence of a discrete order. We show that including addition in first-order logic increases its expressive power. Adding multiplication increases the expressive power further. Neither is the case for Datalog, because of the availability of recursion. Results in a similar perspective are presented in [NS93], where it is shown that no formula of first-order logic using linear ordering and the logical relation $y = 2x$ can define the property that the size of a finite model is divisible by 3.

2 Background

2.1 The General Framework

A CDB (Constraint Database) scheme is defined in relation to a class of constraints Φ (to be described below).

Definition 1. [KKR90] Let Φ be a class of constraints.

1. A *generalized k-tuple* (over variables $x_1, \ldots, x_k$) is a finite conjunction $\varphi_1 \wedge \cdots \wedge \varphi_N$, where each $\varphi_i, 1 \leq i \leq N$, is a constraint in Φ. Furthermore, the variables in each φ_i are all free and among $x_1, \ldots, x_k$.
2. A *generalized relation of arity k* is a finite set $r = \{\psi_1, \ldots, \psi_M\}$, where each $\psi_i, 1 \leq i \leq M$ is a generalized k-tuple over the same variables $x_1, \ldots, x_k$.
3. The *formula corresponding to a generalized relation r* is the disjunction $\psi_1 \vee \cdots \vee \psi_M$. We use ϕ_r to denote the quantifier-free formula corresponding to relation r.
4. A *generalized database* is a finite set of generalized relations.□

Definition 2. Let Φ be a class of constraints interpreted over domain D, r a generalized relation of arity k with constraints in Φ, and $\phi_r = \phi_r(x_1, \ldots, x_k)$ the formula corresponding to r with free variables $x_1, \ldots, x_k$. The generalized relation r represents the unrestricted k-ary relation which consists of all $(a_1, \ldots, a_k)$ in D^k such that $\phi_r(a_1, \ldots, a_k)$ is true. A generalized database represents the finite set of unrestricted relations that are represented by its generalized relations. □

Intuitively, an unrestricted relation of arity k is a finite or infinite set of points in a k-dimensional space. A tuple is a finite representation of a set of such points. We can think of a generalized relation as an instance of a relation scheme, and of the corresponding unrestricted relation as the semantics of such a generalized relation.

Definition 3. Let Φ be a class of constraints. Let $R_1, \ldots, R_i, \ldots$ be predicate symbols, each with a fixed arity. A relational calculus $+ \Phi$ query program is a formula of the first-order predicate calculus with equality, such that its atomic formulas are (1) of the form $R_i(x_1, \ldots, x_j)$, where j is the arity of predicate symbol R_i, or (2) formulas from the class Φ of constraints.$\Box$

These programs are the queries in our database language. The semantics of such a query is the mapping of unrestricted relations to unrestricted relations defined by the formula. For the query to be well defined, a corresponding mapping between generalized relations has to exists (the *closure* property). For the classes of constraints that we discuss in this paper, such a mapping does indeed exist.

2.2 Polynomial Constraints

FO(poly) is the language corresponding to the case where Φ is the set of polynomial constraints. This means that *FO(poly)* is the set of first-order formulas (with equality) over atomic formulas as follows:

(i) $S(x_1, \ldots, x_k)$, meaning the point $(x_1, \ldots, x_k)$ is in the relation S.
(ii) *Polynomial constraints* of the form

$$f(x_1, \ldots, x_k) \, \theta \, 0$$

where f is a k-variable polynomial (with real coefficients) and $\theta \in \{>, =\}$.

Note that $\geq, \neq$ are expressed as Boolean combinations of $>, =$. Also, when writing *FO(poly)* formulas we will use abbreviations such as $x < e$ (instead of $-x + e > 0$) and $S(x + 1, y)$ (instead of $\exists z.\{z = x + 1 \land S(z, y)\}$).

Formulas of *FO(poly)* with free variables define queries. If the input to a *FO(poly)* query is a generalized relation over *FO(poly)* the output is also such a generalized relation [KKR90].

2.3 Linear Constraints

FO(linear) is the subset of *FO(poly)* obtained be restricting constraints to be linear.

A *linear* database is a subset of $\mathcal{R}^k$ defined by a Boolean combination of linear constraints. A *linear* query is a function from linear databases to linear databases.

To show that the query language is closed, we have to show that formulas of *FO(linear)* with free variables define linear queries. To see this, consider the formula obtained by substituting the definition of the input (by linear constraints) into the query formula. Now the quantifiers can be eliminated, as follows: if C is a set of linear constraints

$$x > f_i$$
$$x < f_j$$
$$x = f_k$$
$$x = f_l$$

(where x does not occur in the f's), then the formula $\exists x. \bigwedge C$ is equivalent to the formula $\bigwedge C'$, where C' is the set of linear constraints

$$f_i < f_k = f_l < f_j.$$

Note that formulas of *FO(poly)* do not in general define linear queries, as can be seen by standard geometric arguments (consider, for instance, the set of pairs (x, y) satisfying $x^2 + y^2 = 1$). The class of *parametric* queries, however [La90,HJLL90], is a class of formulas of *FO(poly)* which define linear queries (by the *Subsumption Theorem* and variable elimination [La90]).

2.4 Higher-Dimension Variables

FO(lines) is an extension of *FO(linear)* in which variables can range over points and lines in $\mathcal{R}^d$. For a given dimension d, we shall use $x^{[k,d]}$ for a variable of dimension k (where $k \leq d$). For example, a variable $x^{[0,d]}$ ranges over points in $\mathcal{R}^d$; $x^{[1,d]}$ ranges over lines, etc. As an alternative notation, we shall use p for variables of dimension $k = 0$, l for dimension $k = 1$, omitting d when clear from the context.

FO(linear) is extended by allowing atomic formulas of the form

1. $R(x^{[k,d]})$, where R is a relational symbol of arity k, and
2. $x^{[k,d]} \subset y^{[k+1,d]}$.

Note: $x^{[k,d]} \subset y^{[k+1,d]}$ means that the value of x (point, line, etc., interpreted as a set of points), is contained in the value of y (line, plane, etc.). When $k = 0$, we shall write $p \in l$, instead of $p \subset l$, as this is more intuitive.

It has be shown in [KKR90] that *FO(lines)* $\subseteq$ *FO(poly)*, and that extending *FO(poly)* in the same way does not increase its expressive power. Despite this, even in the case of *FO(poly)*, many queries can be expressed much more naturally using higher-dimension variables (see Section 5 for some examples). In this paper, we shall show that, in fact, *FO(lines)* = *FO(poly)*.

3 Games and Constraints

In this section we state the results of the known Ehrenfeucht-Fraïssé games as they apply in the presence of constraints. Constraints are assumed to be any built-in efficiently computable function.

Definition 4. The n-round *Ehrenfeucht-Fraïssé* game is played between two players on two databases $\mathcal{D}, \mathcal{D}' \subseteq \mathcal{R}^k$. At round r player I picks a point $p_r \in \mathcal{R}$ and associates it to either $\mathcal{D}$ or $\mathcal{D}'$; player II responds by picking $q_r \in \mathcal{R}$ and associating it to the other database.

For each r let t_r, t'_r be the points associated with $\mathcal{D}, \mathcal{D}'$ respectively; $\{t_r, t'_r\} = \{p_r, q_r\}$. Player II *wins* the game iff

(i) $t_i = t_j$ iff $t'_i = t'_j$ and
(ii) $(t_{i_1}, \ldots, t_{i_k}) \in \mathcal{D}$ iff $(t'_{i_1}, \ldots, t'_{i_k}) \in \mathcal{D}'$.

The above condition is extended, given a set $\mathcal{C}$ of constraints over n variables, by the clause

(iii) $c(t_{i_1}, \ldots, t_{i_n})$ iff $c(t'_{i_1}, \ldots, t'_{i_n})$, for every constraint c in $\mathcal{C}$.

The well-known theory of Ehrenfeucht-Fraïssé games [Eh61,Fr54] gives the following results:

Theorem 5. *Let Q be a property of databases. For each n and each finite set of constraints $\mathcal{C}$ (over n variables), the following are equivalent:*

(a) Q is not expressible in first-order logic with quantifier depth at most n and constraints from $\mathcal{C}$.
(b) There exist databases $\mathcal{D}_{n,\mathcal{C}}, \mathcal{D}'_{n,\mathcal{C}}$ which differ with respect to Q such that player II has a winning strategy for the n-round game on $\mathcal{D}_{n,\mathcal{C}}, \mathcal{D}'_{n,\mathcal{C}}$.

Corollary 6. *Let Q be a property of databases and let Φ be a set of constraints. The following are equivalent:*

(a) Q is not expressible in first-order logic with constraints from Φ.
(b) For each n and each finite set of constraints $\mathcal{C} \subseteq \Phi$ (over n variables), there exist databases $\mathcal{D}_{n,\mathcal{C}}, \mathcal{D}'_{n,\mathcal{C}}$ which differ with respect to Q such that player II has a winning strategy for the n-round game on $\mathcal{D}_{n,\mathcal{C}}, \mathcal{D}'_{n,\mathcal{C}}$.

Thus, the corollary above defines, as special cases, Ehrenfeucht-Fraïssé games for *FO(poly)*, *FO(linear)*, and the language FO($\leq$, +); i.e., first-order logic with two kinds of constraints, inequality $x \leq y$ and addition $x + y = z$. The latter is the subset of *FO(linear)* where coefficients of linear constraints are restricted to be rational.

4 Linear vs. Polynomial Constraints

Consider databases consisting of a subset U of the real line. We will use Corollary 6 to show:

Theorem 7. *The set of databases satisfying*

$$\exists x. \exists y. \{U(x) \wedge U(y) \wedge x^2 + y^2 = 1\}$$

is not expressible in FO(linear).

Note that the above query is Boolean; contrary to the general case, geometric arguments do not apply straightforwardly to show non-expressibility in *FO(linear)*.

Proof. (Sketch) Given n and C as in Corollary 6, we will find points $\delta, \delta', \epsilon$ such that

$$\delta^2 + \epsilon^2 = 1$$
$$(\delta')^2 + \epsilon^2 \neq 1$$

and player II has a winning strategy for the game played on the databases

$$\mathcal{D} = \{\delta, \epsilon\}$$
$$\mathcal{D}' = \{\delta', \epsilon\}.$$

Let t_r, t_r' be the points associated (at round r) with $\mathcal{D}, \mathcal{D}'$ respectively (Definition 4). For each r, $0 \leq r \leq n$, we define sets of linear constraints C_r, C_r' on the points $\{t_1, \ldots, t_r, \delta, \epsilon\}$ and $\{t_1', \ldots, t_r', \delta', \epsilon\}$ respectively. A constraint $c(t_1, \ldots, t_r, \delta, \epsilon)$ is in C_r iff the *corresponding* constraint $c(t_1', \ldots, t_r', \delta', \epsilon)$ is in C_r'. We proceed by induction on r:

$$r = n : C_n = \{t_i = t_j; i, j = 1, \ldots, n\} \cup$$
$$\{t_i = \delta : i = 1, \ldots, n\} \cup$$
$$\{t_i = \epsilon : i = 1, \ldots, n\} \cup$$
$$\{c(t_{i_1}, \ldots, t_{i_n}) : \text{where } c \in C, 1 \leq i_j \leq n\}.$$

$$0 \leq r < n : C_r = \{t_i = t_j, i, j = 1, \ldots, r\} \cup$$
$$\{t_i = \delta : i = 1, \ldots, r\} \cup$$
$$\{t_i = \epsilon : i = 1, \ldots, r\} \cup$$
$$\{c(t_{i_1}, \ldots, t_{i_n}) : \text{where } c \in C, 1 \leq i_j \leq r\} \cup$$
$$\Delta,$$

where Δ is the set of constraints obtained by eliminating t_{r+1} from the set C_{r+1}.

We say that C_r, C_r' are *equisatisfied* iff a constraint in C_r is true just in case the corresponding constraint in C_r' is true.

Claim: If C_r, C_r' are equisatisfied, then for any choice of t_{r+1} (resp. t_{r+1}') there is a choice of t_{r+1}' (resp. t_{r+1}) such that C_{r+1}, C_{r+1}' are equisatisfied.

This is a consequence of elimination. For instance, suppose t_{r+1} satisfies $t_{r+1} < f$, $t_{r+1} > g$, where f, g do not mention t_{r+1}. Then the constraint $g < f$ is satisfied in C_r, and thus the corresponding constraint $g' < f'$ in C_r' is also satisfied. Therefore, there exists t_{r+1}' satisfying the corresponding constraints $t_{r+1}' < f'$, $t_{r+1}' > g'$.

It follows that, if C_0, C_0' are equisatisfied, player II can play so that C_n, C_n' are equisatisfied. I.e., by the definition of C_n, C_n' player II can win the n-round game, since

$$x \in \mathcal{D} \text{ iff } x = \delta \vee x = \epsilon$$

(resp. $x \in \mathcal{D}'$ iff $x = \delta' \vee x = \epsilon$).

We now show how to pick $\delta, \delta', \epsilon$ so that C_0, C_0' are equisatisfied. Write the constraints in C_0 in the form $\delta \; \theta \; f_m(\epsilon)$, where $\theta \in \{>, <, =\}$. Pick ϵ so that $f_m(\epsilon)^2 + \epsilon^2 \neq 1$ for every m. Pick δ so that $\delta^2 + \epsilon^2 = 1$. Now $\delta \neq f_m(\epsilon)$ for every m, and by choosing δ' close enough to δ we can make sure that C_0, C_0' are equisatisfied. $\qquad\square$

5 Linear Queries and Lines

We consider databases consisting of a binary relation S. We consider the following queries:

Definition 8. .

1. The query *exists-line*: Does the relation contain a line?
2. The query *in-line*: Is the relation contained in a line?
3. The query *lines*: Compute the set of all lines in the relation For this query, we have to specify the form of the output. We define *lines* as the query that returns the set of tuples (u, v, w), each specifying the set of points (x, y) satisfying $ux + vy + w = 0$.
4. The *line-intersection* query: Compute all the intersections of the lines in the relation.

It is easy to see that *exists-line*, *in-line* and *line-intersection* can all be expressed in *FO(lines)*. *exists-line* can be expressed by the query

$$\exists l.S(l).$$

in-line by the query

$$\exists l.\forall p.\{S(p) \to p \in l\}.$$

and *line-intersection* by

$$\exists l_1.\exists l_2.\{S(l_1) \wedge S(l_2) \wedge l_1 \neq l_2 \wedge p \in l_1 \wedge p \in l_2\}.$$

Since $FO(lines) \subseteq FO(poly)$, it follows immediately that these queries are also expressible in $FO(poly)$. The remaining query, *lines*, can also be be expressed in $FO(poly)$, by the formula

$$\forall x.\forall y.\{ux + vy + w = 0 \to S(x, y)\}.$$

The remaining, and much more difficult case, concerns membership in *FO(linear)*. We show several partial results towards resolving these questions:

1. *exists-line*. We conjecture that this query is not in *FO(linear)*. In order to illustrate how difficult it is to resolve this problem, we show that a natural counterexample, the class of *two-slope* databases, that one would expect to be indistinguishable by *FO(linear)* queries, can in fact can be distinguished by such a query.
2. *in-line*. In this case we can show that *in-line* is not expressible in *FO(linear)*. The proof in fact shows more than this: By showing how to simulate multiplication by *in-line*, we show that *FO(lines)* is actually equal to *FO(poly)*.
3. *lines*. Since the result of this query is potentially infinite, the question whether the query is in *FO(linear)* is not meaningful, unless the result of the query is also definable using the same constraint language. We show that for linear constraints this is indeed the case.
4. *line-intersection*. Once more, we conjecture that the query cannot be expressed in *FO(linear)*. On the other hand, we suspect that, if we are given a finite bound on the number of lines in the relation, the *line-intersection* query can be expressed in *FO(linear)*, and we illustrate this for the case of 2 lines.

5.1 The query *exists-line*

Definition 9. A *two-slope* database $S(x, y)$ has the form

$$
\begin{aligned}
& (x \geq \beta_1 \quad \wedge y \leq \alpha_1 x + s_1) \\
\vee \, & (\beta_2 < x < \beta_1 \wedge \quad y \leq \gamma) \\
\vee \, & (x \leq \beta_2 \quad \wedge y \leq \alpha_2 x + s_2)
\end{aligned}
$$

It is clear that a two-slope database contains a line iff $\alpha_1 \geq \alpha_2$.

Theorem 10. *The* exists-line *query can be expressed in* FO(linear) *for two-slope databases.*

Proof. Let φ be the formula

$$
\exists z. \exists w. \{\neg S(x, z) \wedge \neg S(-x, w) \wedge z + w \leq y \wedge x > b_1 \wedge -x < b_2\}.
$$

Suppose that S is a two-slope database with parameters $\beta_1, \beta_2, \alpha_1, \alpha_2, s_1, s_2, \gamma$ as in Definition 9. For $b_1 > \beta_1$, $b_2 < \beta_2$, the formula φ is equivalent to

$$
y > (\alpha_1 - \alpha_2)x + s_1 + s_2 \wedge x > b_1 \wedge x > -b_2
$$

It follows that, for $b_1 > \beta_1$, $b_2 < \beta_2$, the formula $\forall y. \exists x. \varphi$ is true iff $\alpha_1 - \alpha_2 < 0$ (since $b_2 < b_1$ implies $x > 0$).

Therefore the formula

$$
\exists \beta_1. \exists \beta_2. \forall b_1. \forall b_2. \{(b_1 > \beta_1 \wedge b_2 < \beta_2) \rightarrow (\forall y. \exists x. \varphi)\}
$$

is true iff $\alpha_1 - \alpha_2 < 0$, i.e., iff S does not contain a line. □

The next result follows easily.

Corollary 11. FO(lines) = FO(poly).

5.2 The query *in-line*

Theorem 12. *The* in-line *query is not expressible in* FO(linear).

Proof. We show that, if the *in-line* query is expressible in *FO(linear)*, then the set of tuples (x, y, z) satisfying $z = xy$ is definable in *FO(linear)*, which is false.

Given x, y, z, let S be a binary relation containing three tuples:

$$
S = \{[1, x], [0, 0], [y, z]\}.
$$

It is easy to verify that the three points are on a line if and only if $z = xy$. □

5.3 The query *lines*

Theorem 13. *The* lines *query is linear.*

Proof. Write $S(x, y)$ in conjunctive normal form: $\bigwedge_i \bigvee_j C_{ij}(x, y)$, where C_{ij} is a linear constraint. Write the formula

$$\forall x. \forall y. \{ux + vy + w = 0 \to S(x, y)\}$$

in the form

$$\forall x. \{\bigwedge_i \bigvee_j C_{ij}(x, -\frac{ux + w}{v})\},$$

equivalently

$$\bigwedge_i \{\neg \exists x. (\bigwedge_j \neg C_{ij}(x, -\frac{ux + w}{v}))\}$$

(that is to say, assuming that $v \neq 0$, or, symmetrically, $u \neq 0$; in the remaining case $v = u = 0$ the formula is equivalent to

$$w \neq 0 \lor \{\forall x. \forall y. S(x, y)\}$$

which is linear in w).

Now consider eliminating x from the set of linear constraints $\bigwedge_j \neg C_{ij}(x, -\frac{ux+w}{v})$. Eliminating x from

$$d_1 x + d_2(-\frac{ux + w}{v}) + d_3 \,\theta_1\, 0$$
$$d_1' x + d_2'(-\frac{ux + w}{v}) + d_3' \,\theta_2\, 0$$

gives, after simplification and cancellation of a common factor v, a constraint

$$(d_2 d_3' - d_2' d_3)u + (d_3 d_1' - d_3' d_1)v + (d_1 d_2' - d_1' d_2)w \,\theta\, 0$$

which is linear in the free variables of the query, u, v, w. □

5.4 The query *line-intersection*

Theorem 14. *The* line-intersection *query is expressible in* FO(linear) *for databases consisting of at most two lines.*

Proof. Suppose S consists of exactly two lines, neither parallel to the x-axis, intersecting at (a, b) The database

$$S'(x, y) \stackrel{\text{def}}{=} S(x, y) \land S(x + 1, y)$$

consists of two points $(x_1, y_1), (x_2, y_2)$. By a simple geometrical argument,

$$x_1 + x_2 = 2a - 1$$
$$y_1 + y_2 = 2b.$$

Therefore, the formula

$$\exists x_1.\exists y_1.\exists x_2.\exists y_2. \{S'(x_1, y_1) \wedge S'(x_2, y_2) \wedge (x_1 \neq x_2 \vee y_1 \neq y_2)$$
$$\wedge u = \tfrac{x_1 + x_2 + 1}{2} \wedge v = \tfrac{y_1 + y_2}{2}\}$$

is true iff $(u, v) = (a, b)$.

If one line is parallel to the x axis, we proceed as follows. If neither line is parallel to the y-axis, define S' using $S(x, y + 1)$ instead of $S(x + 1, y)$ and modify the final step accordingly. If one line is parallel to the x-axis, and the other to the y-axis, then define S' using $S(x + 1, y + 1)$.

Finally, the lines might be parallel. In such a case, $S'(x, y)$ will either be empty, or infinite. In the former case, the query will produce an empty result, as desired. We can detect the second case by testing whether the result contains at least two distinct points, and, in such a case returning the empty set. $\square$

6 Miscellaneous

In this section we consider first-order logic on finite structures with a discrete (linear) order. We denote by FO (FO($\leq$), FO($\leq$,+), FO($\leq$, +, $\times$)) first-order logic with equality (and order, and addition, and multiplication). Although, in the presence of a discrete order, addition and multiplication can be expressed using recursion, we shall argue here that this is not the case when we are considering first-order logic.

First observe that recursion expresses addition and multiplication as follows: Consider the paradigm of Datalog with negation. It is known that order increases the expressive power of pure Datalog. In order to express addition in Datalog with order, first observe that we can use $\leq$ and negation to define (with a first-order sentence) a successor relation $succ$. Addition can then be defined as a ternary predicate, **PLUS**, as follows:

> **PLUS**$(0, x, x) \leftarrow$,
> **PLUS**$(x', y, z') \leftarrow succ(x, x') \wedge succ(z, z') \wedge$ **PLUS**(x, y, z).

Multiplication can be, also, defined as a ternary predicate, **MULT**, using $+$ as follows:

> **MULT**$(0, x, 0) \leftarrow$,
> **MULT**$(x', y, z') \leftarrow succ(x, x') \wedge z' = z + y \wedge$ **MULT**(x, y, z).

Therefore, in the presence of a discrete order, recursion can be used to show that addition and multiplication do not add expressive power to Datalog. We next see that this is not the case in first-order logic.

Y. Gurevich observed that there is an order independent query expressible in FO($\leq$), but not in FO. We next exhibit a query expressible in FO($\leq$, +), but not in FO($\leq$).

Example 1. Consider the schema $\sigma = (R)$, where R is a binary relation. The universe is the set of natural numbers. The query answers true if and only if (i) the cardinality of the projection of R on the first attribute, R_1, is even, and (ii) the second projection of R, R_2, contains the order of x in R_1 (i.e. $R(x,y)$ iff x is the yth element of R_1).

It is easy to express the query in FO($\leq$,+).

$$\left(\forall x_1 \; x_2 \; y_1 \; y_2 \; \left(\neg\exists x \; ((x_1 < x < x_2) \wedge R_1(x)\right)\right.$$
$$\left.\wedge R_1(x_1) \wedge R_1(x_2) \wedge R(x_1, y_1) \wedge R(x_2, y_2)\right) \rightarrow (y_2 = y_1 + 1)\right)$$
$$\wedge min_{R_2}(1) \wedge \exists n \; (max_{R_2}(n) \wedge \exists m \; (n = m + m)).$$

Here $min_{R_2}(1)$ expresses the fact that the smallest element in the second column of R is 1 and $max_{R_2}(n)$ the fact that the largest element in the second column of R is n. The proof that it cannot be expressed in FO($\leq$) is based on Ehrenfeucht-Fraïssé games.

The following remark relates the expressiveness of FO on finite structures to the power of FO to express subsets of the natural numbers: Consider a finite structure without any relation, just linear order (resp. linear order and addition). A FO formula H is true in a structure of cardinality n iff a corresponding formula $H'(x)$ in the language of integers with order (resp. with order and addition) is true for $x = n$; formula $H'(x)$ is obtained from formula H by including an upper bound $u \leq x$ to each variable u of H, where variable x does not occur in H.

The query "is the cardinality of the domain an even number" is expressible in FO($\leq$, +) but not in FO($\leq$). The fact that it is not expressible in FO($\leq$), is a straightforward consequence of the previous remark and the following known lemma [En72]: A subset of the natural numbers is expressible in FO($\leq$) iff it is either finite or has finite complement. It is easy to express it in FO($\leq$, +).

The query "is the cardinality of the domain a prime number" is expressible in FO($\leq$, +, $\times$) but not in FO($\leq$, +). The fact that it is not expressible in FO($\leq$, +), is, also, a straightforward consequence of the remark above and the following known lemma [En72]: A subset of the natural numbers is expressible in FO($\leq$, +) iff it is eventually periodic (i.e., there exist positive numbers M and p such that for all n greater than M, n belongs to the set iff $n + p$ belongs to the set). It is easy to express it in FO($\leq$, +, $\times$).

We can therefore conclude with the following result.

Theorem 15.

$$FO \subset FO(\leq) \subset FO(\leq, +) \subset FO(\leq, +, \times).$$

Conclusion

We studied the expressive power of various constraint languages. There are still numerous open questions relative to their expressive power. We conjecture in particular that the query *exists-line* is not expressible in *FO(linear)*. Our main motivation is to understand the trade-off between the expressive power and the efficiency of the evaluation of queries. We proved that *FO(poly)* and *FO(lines)* have the same expressive power. Nevertheless, it is unclear if queries can be evaluated as efficiently in both paradigms.

Acknowledgments

We wish to thank Serge Abiteboul, Alex Brodsky, Christophe Tollu and Victor Vianu for helpful discussions, and Paris Kanellakis for providing some of the initial motivation.

References

[BJM93]   A. Brodsky, J. Jaffar and M.J. Maher. Toward Practical Constraint Databases. *Proc. 19th International Conference on Very Large Data Bases*, Dublin, Ireland, 1993.

[DG]   J. Darlington and Y-K. Guo. Constraint Functional Programming. Tech. Report, Dept. of Computing, Imperial College, to appear.

[Eh61]   A. Ehrenfeucht. An Application of Games to the Completeness Problem for Formalized Theories. *Fund. Math.*, 49:129–141, 1961.

[En72]   H. B. Enderton. *A Mathematical Introduction to Logic.* Academic Press 1972.

[Fr54]   R. Fraïssé. Sur quelques classifications des systèmes de relations. *Publications Scientifiques de l'Université d'Alger, Séries A*, 1:35–182, 1954.

[GS94]   S. Grumbach and J. Su. Finitely representable databases. In *Proc. 13th ACM PODS*, 1994.

[HJLL90]   T. Huynh, L. Joskowicz, C. Lassez and J-L. Lassez. Reasoning About Linear Constraints Using Parametric Queries. *Foundations of Software Technology and Theoretical Computer Science*. Lecture Notes in Computer Science, Springer-Verlag vol. 472, 1990.

[JL87]   J. Jaffar and J.L. Lassez. Constraint Logic Programming. *Proc. 14th ACM POPL*, 111–119, 1987.

[KG94]   P. C. Kanellakis and D. Q. Goldin. Constraint programming and database query languages. In *Proc. 2nd Conference on Theoretical Aspects of Computer Software (TACS)*, April 1994. (To appear in LNCS Spring-Verlag volume).

[KKR90]   P. Kanellakis, G. Kuper and P. Revesz. Constraint Query Languages. *Proc. 9th ACM PODS*, pp. 299–313, 1990. To appear in JCSS.

[Kup93]   G.M. Kuper. Aggregation in constraint databases. In *Proc. First Workshop on Principles and Practice of Constraint Programming*, 1993.

[La90]   J.L. Lassez. Querying Constraints. *Proc. 9th ACM PODS*, 1990.

[Ma87]   M. Maher. A Logic Semantics for a class of Committed Choice Languages. *Proc. ICLP4*, MIT Press 1987.

[NS93]   D. Niwinski and A. Stolboushkin. y=2x vs. y=3x. In *Proc. IEEE Symp. of Logic in Computer Science*, pages 172–178, Montreal, June 1993.

[Re90]   P.Z. Revesz. A Closed Form for Datalog Queries with Integer Order. *Proc. 3rd International Conference on Database Theory*, 1990. To appear in TCS.

[Sa]   V. Saraswat. Concurrent Constraint Logic Programming. MIT Press, to appear.

Foundations of Aggregation Constraints

Kenneth A. Ross[1], Divesh Srivastava[2], Peter J. Stuckey[3], S. Sudarshan[2]

[1] Columbia University, New York, NY 10027, USA
[2] AT&T Bell Laboratories, Murray Hill, NJ 07974, USA
[3] University of Melbourne, Parkville, 3052, Australia

Abstract. We introduce a new constraint domain, *aggregation constraints*, which is useful in database query languages, and in constraint logic programming languages that incorporate aggregate functions. We study the fundamental problem of checking if a conjunction of aggregation constraints is *solvable*, and present undecidability results for many different classes of aggregation constraints. We describe a complete and minimal axiomatization of the class of aggregation constraints over finite multisets of reals, which permits a natural reduction from the class of aggregation constraints to the class of mixed integer/real, non-linear arithmetic constraints. We then present a polynomial-time algorithm that directly checks for solvability of a useful class of aggregation constraints, where the reduction-based approach does not lead to efficient checks for solvability.

1 Introduction

Database query languages, such as SQL, allow the use of the grouping construct in conjunction with aggregate functions (such as $min, max, sum, count$ and *average*) to obtain summary information from the database. These database query languages also allow constraints to be specified on values, e.g., the results of aggregate functions, to restrict the answers to a query.

Example 1 (Aggregation and Constraints). Consider the following program and query pair (using the notation of [3]):

$$q\_depts(Dept, M1, M2, C, S) :- groupby(employee(Emp, Dept, Sal),$$
$$[Dept], [M1 = min\langle Sal\rangle, M2 = max\langle Sal\rangle, C = count\langle Sal\rangle,$$
$$S = sum\langle Sal\rangle]), C \leq 10, M1 > 0, M2 \leq 10000.$$
Query: ?-$q\_depts(D, M1, M2, C, S)$.

A bottom-up evaluation of the above program examines all the tuples in the *employee* relation (the first argument of the *groupby*), and for each department (the variable within [ ] in the second argument of the *groupby*), computes the $min, max, count$ and sum of the salaries of all the employees in that department. Tuples corresponding to departments where the minimum salary is > 0, where the maximum salary is ≤ 10000 and where the number of employees is ≤ 10 are answers to the query ? $q\_depts(D, M1, M2, C, S)$. □

The electronic mail addresses of the authors are kar@cs.columbia.edu, divesh@research.att.com, pjs@cs.mu.oz.au and sudarsha@research.att.com.

A fundamental operation on any constraint domain is checking if a conjunction of constraints is *solvable*. Consider the program in the above example, and the query $? q\_depts(D, M1, M2, C, S), S > 100000$. To determine (at compile-time) that there are no answers to this query, we need to determine that the conjunction of *aggregation constraints*: $min(MS_D) > 0 \land count(MS_D) \leq 10 \land max(MS_D) \leq 10000 \land sum(MS_D) > 100000$ is unsolvable, where MS_D is the finite multiset of salaries of employees in department D, which can be of unbounded cardinality. This can be determined by observing that the results of different aggregate functions on a multiset MS_D are not independent of each other. For example, the results of the $sum, count$ and max aggregate functions are related as follows:

$$sum(MS_D) \leq count(MS_D) * max(MS_D).$$

This inequality can be used to infer the unsolvability of the previous conjunction of aggregation constraints, and hence determine that the query $? q\_depts(D, M1, M2, C, S), S > 100000$ has no answers. The techniques described in this paper can be used to efficiently check for solvability of such aggregation constraints.

Checking solvability of aggregation constraints can be used much like checking solvability of ordinary arithmetic constraints in a constraint logic programming system like $CLP(\mathcal{R})$. Aggregate functions are typically applied only after multisets have been constructed. However, checking solvability of aggregation constraints even before the multisets have been constructed can be used to restrict the search space by not generating subgoals that are guaranteed to fail, as illustrated by the above program and query, $? q\_depts(D, M1, M2, C, S), S > 100000$.

Our contributions in this paper are as follows:

1. We introduce a new constraint domain, *aggregation constraints*, which is useful in database query languages, and in constraint logic programming languages that incorporate aggregate functions [2] (Section 2).
2. We show undecidability results for checking for the *solvability* of conjunctions of certain simple kinds of aggregation constraints. We also discuss the factors that determine the complexity of checking for the solvability of special classes of aggregation constraints (Section 3).
3. We present a reduction from the domain of aggregation constraints over finite multisets of reals to the domain of mixed integer/real, non-linear arithmetic constraints (Section 4).

   This reduction enables us to use existing techniques to check solvability of aggregation constraints. Checking solvability of mixed integer/real non-linear arithmetic constraints is undecidable in general. However, we point out interesting special cases of aggregation constraints where the reduction-based approach does, in fact, allow for tractable checks for solvability.
4. We describe a polynomial-time algorithm that checks for solvability of a useful class of aggregation constraints (Section 5). Our algorithm operates directly on the aggregation constraints, rather than on the reduced form; it

is not clear how to operate directly on the reduced form to attain the same complexity.

Our work provides the *foundations* of the area of aggregation constraints. We believe there is a lot of interesting research to be done in the further study of aggregation constraints, as well as in applications of aggregation constraints. The following example illustrates a possible avenue for use of aggregation constraints in query optimization.

Example 2 (Aggregation Constraints as Filters). Consider the program of Example 1, and the query ? $q\_depts(D, \_, M2, \_, \_), M2 \geq 5000$, i.e., the user is interested only in departments where the maximum salary is ≥ 5000. This constraint can be used as a *filter* on the tuples of the underlying *employee* relation; *employee* tuples that do not satisfy this criterion need not be considered for the *groupby* operation.

This fact has been noted by Sudarshan and Ramakrishnan [6] and by Levy et al. [1], who look at some simple cases of query optimization in the presence of aggregate functions. Using more general aggregation constraints in such situations remains to be studied. □

2 Aggregation Constraints

The *primitive terms* of this constraint domain are integer constants, real constants and *aggregation terms*, which are formed using aggregate functions on multiset variables that range over finite multisets. Thus, $7, 3.142$ and $max(S)$ are primitive terms, where S is a multiset variable that ranges over finite multisets. For simplicity, we do not consider integer and real-valued variables as primitive terms in our treatment. *Complex terms* are constructed using primitive terms and arithmetic functions such as $+, -, *$ and $/$. Thus, $min(S_1) + max(S_2) - 3.142 * count(S_2)$ is a complex term.

A *primitive aggregation constraint* is constructed using complex terms and arithmetic predicates such as $\leq, <, =, \neq, >$ and $\geq$. Thus, $sum(S_1) \leq min(S_1) + max(S_2) + 3$ is a primitive aggregation constraint. Complex aggregation constraints can be constructed using conjunction, disjunction and complementation, in the usual manner. However, in this paper, we shall only deal with conjunctions of primitive aggregation constraints. In the sequel, we often use "aggregation constraints" to loosely refer to primitive aggregation constraints.

The fundamental problem that we are interested in is the following problem:

Solvability: Given a conjunction $\mathcal{C}$ of primitive aggregation constraints, does there exist an assignment σ of finite multisets to the multiset variables in $\mathcal{C}$, such that $\mathcal{C}\sigma$ is satisfied?

Checking for solvability of more complex aggregation constraints can be reduced to this fundamental problem. The other important problems of checking *implication* (or entailment) and *equivalence* of pairs of conjunctions of aggregation constraints can be reduced to checking solvability of (collections of other) conjunctions of aggregation constraints, in polynomial-time.

3 Complexity of Solvability

3.1 Undecidability Results

We show undecidability by a linear-time, linear-space reduction from quadratic arithmetic constraints over the non-negative integers to *linear* aggregation constraints, where, (1) the multiset elements are drawn from the reals, and (2) the aggregate functions $sum, count$ and $average$ are used. The reduction makes essential use of the relationship $sum(S) = count(S) * average(S)$ between the results of these three aggregate functions.

Consider a conjunction C of quadratic primitive arithmetic constraints over the non-negative integers. Replace each quadratic term $X_j * X_k$ (where X_j and X_k are not necessarily distinct variables) in C by a "new" non-negative integer variable X_i, and conjoin a quadratic equation of the form $X_i = X_j * X_k$ to C. The resulting conjunction of constraints C_1 is equivalent to C (on the variables of C). Further, C_1 contains only linear arithmetic constraints and quadratic equations of the form $X_i = X_j * X_k$ over the non-negative integers.

For each variable X_i in C_1, the reduction algorithm creates a new multiset variable S_i, and replaces each occurrence of X_i in the linear arithmetic constraints of C_1 by the aggregation term $count(S_i)$. For each quadratic equation of the form $X_i = X_j * X_k$ in C_1, the reduction algorithm creates a new multiset variable S_{ijk}, and replaces the above quadratic equation by the following three linear aggregation equations:

$$count(S_i) = sum(S_{ijk})$$
$$count(S_j) = count(S_{ijk})$$
$$count(S_k) = average(S_{ijk})$$

The resulting conjunction of linear aggregation constraints C_2 is solvable over finite multisets of reals if and only if the original conjunction of quadratic constraints C is solvable over the non-negative integers.

There is a similar reduction using the aggregate functions sum, min, max and $count$, where the quadratic arithmetic equation $X_i = X_j * X_k$ is replaced by the following four linear aggregation equations: $count(S_i) = sum(S_{ijk}), count(S_j) = count(S_{ijk}), count(S_k) = min(S_{ijk})$ and $count(S_k) = max(S_{ijk})$. Again, the resulting conjunction of linear aggregation constraints is solvable over finite multisets of reals if and only if the original conjunction of quadratic constraints is solvable over the non-negative integers.

The undecidability of the solvability of quadratic arithmetic constraints over the non-negative integers (e.g., Diophantine equations) leads to the following results:

Theorem 1. *Checking solvability of a conjunction C of linear aggregation constraints over finite multisets of reals is undecidable if:*

1. C involves the sum, count and average aggregate functions, or
2. C involves the sum, min, max and count aggregate functions. □

The second part of the above theorem also holds for linear aggregation constraints over finite multisets of integers.

For integer linear arithmetic constraints, there is a reduction to linear aggregation constraints, where integer variable X_i is replaced by any of the aggregation terms, $count(S_i), min(S_i), max(S_i)$ or $sum(S_i)$, where S_i is a new multiset variable ranging over finite multisets of integers. Checking for solvability of linear arithmetic constraints over the non-negative integers is NP-complete [4]. Hence, we have the following results:

Theorem 2. *Checking solvability of a conjunction of linear aggregation constraints, over finite multisets of values drawn from any domain, involving just the count aggregate function is NP-hard.*

Checking solvability of a conjunction of linear aggregation constraints, over finite multisets of integers, involving just min, max or sum is NP-hard. □

3.2 Special Cases: A Taxonomy

Although checking for solvability of aggregation constraints is undecidable in general, there are many special cases that are tractable. We present below several factors that affect the complexity of checking for solvability, and in later sections present tractable special cases defined on the basis of these factors.

Domain of multiset elements : This determines the feasible assignments to the multiset variables in checking for solvability. Possibilities include integers and reals; correspondingly, the multiset variables range over finite multisets of integers or finite multisets of reals. In general, restricting the domain of the multiset elements to integers increases the difficulty of the problem.

Aggregate functions : This determines the possible aggregation terms that are allowed. Possibilities include $min, max, sum, count, average$, etc. In general, the complexity of checking for solvability increases if more aggregate functions are allowed.

Class of constraints : This determines the form of the primitive aggregation constraints considered. There are at least two factors that are relevant:

1. **Linear vs. Non-linear** constraints: Checking for solvability of linear constraints is, in general, easier than for non-linear constraints. By restricting the form even further, such that each primitive aggregation constraint has at most one or two aggregation terms, the problem can become even simpler.

2. **Constraint predicates** allowed: The complexity of checking for solvability also depends on which types of the constraint predicates are allowed. We can choose to allow only equational constraints ($=$) or add inequalities ($<, \leq$) or possibly even disequalities ($\neq$). In general, the difficulty of the solvability problem increases with each new type.

Separability : This also determines the form of the primitive aggregation constraints considered. The two possible dimensions in this case are:

1. **Multiset variables**: A conjunction of primitive aggregation constraints is *multiset-variable-separable* if each primitive aggregation constraint involves only one multiset variable. For example, the conjunction of primitive aggregation constraints $min(S_1) + max(S_1) \leq 5 \wedge sum(S_2) \geq 10$ is multiset-variable-separable, while $min(S_1) + min(S_2) \leq 10$ is not. In general, multiset-variable-separability makes the solvability problem easier since one can check solvability of the aggregation constraints separately for each multiset variable.

2. **Aggregate functions**: A conjunction of primitive aggregation constraints is *aggregate-function-separable* if each primitive aggregation constraint involves only one aggregate function. For example, the conjunction $min(S_1) \leq min(S_2) \wedge sum(S_1) \geq sum(S_2) + 2$ is aggregate-function-separable, although it is not multiset-variable-separable.

4 A Reduction-based Approach To Solvability

Our first approach to checking for the solvability of a conjunction of aggregation constraints is to try and reduce aggregation constraints to an *existing* constraint domain. The advantage of this approach is that, if successful, solvability checking techniques from previously known constraint domains can be used to check for solvability in our new constraint domain. In this section, we present some results in this direction.

4.1 An Axiomatization

The key idea behind our reduction algorithm is to add to the conjunction of aggregation constraints a *complete* and *minimal* set of relationships between the aggregate functions on a *single* multiset. The intuition here is that the constraint domain of "aggregation constraints" only allows primitive aggregate functions on individual multisets. Interactions between different multisets is possible only via arithmetic constraints between the results of the aggregate functions on individual multisets. Consequently, relationships between the results of aggregate functions on different multisets can be inferred using techniques from the domain of ordinary arithmetic constraints (see [4], for example).

Theorem 3. *The following relationships provide a* correct, complete *and* minimal *axiomatization of the relationships between aggregate functions* min, max, sum, count *and* average *on a finite multiset S of reals.*

(1) count(S) is an integer ≥ 0.
(2) if (count(S) = 0) then min(S) and max(S) are undefined.[4]
(3) if (count(S) > 0) then min(S) $\leq$ max(S).
(4) if (count(S) = 0) then sum(S) = 0.
(5) if (count(S) > 0) then (count(S) − 1) * min(S) + max(S) $\leq$ sum(S).
(6) if (count(S) > 0) then sum(S) $\leq$ min(S) + (count(S) − 1) * max(S).
(7) if (count(S) = 0) then average(S) is undefined.
(8) if (count(S) > 0) then sum(S) = average(S) * count(S).

Proof. We first prove correctness and completeness of the relationships (1)–(8).

The finite multiset S of reals clearly has 0 or more elements. If S has 0 elements, relationships (2), (4) and (7) are obviously correct and complete. If S has 1 element, then S can be represented as $\{X_1\}$. In this case, we have the constraints: $min(S) = X_1 \wedge max(S) = X_1 \wedge sum(S) = X_1 \wedge average(S) = X_1$. Projecting out the variable X_1 (using, e.g., Fourier elimination), we have:

$$min(S) = max(S) \wedge min(S) = sum(S) \wedge min(S) = average(S).$$

It is easy to verify that the conjunction of relationships (3), (5), (6) and (8) are equivalent to the above conjunction, when $count(S) = 1$.

If S has 2 elements, then S can be represented as $\{X_1, X_2\}$, where $X_1 \leq X_2$. In this case, we have the constraints: $X_1 \leq X_2 \wedge min(S) = X_1 \wedge max(S) = X_2 \wedge sum(S) = X_1 + X_2 \wedge average(S) = (X_1 + X_2)/2$. Projecting out the variables X_1 and X_2, we have:

$$min(S) \leq max(S) \wedge sum(S) = min(S) + max(S) \wedge \\ average(S) = sum(S)/2.$$

It is easy to verify that the conjunction of relationships (3), (5), (6) and (8) are equivalent to the above conjunction, when $count(S) = 2$.

If S has 3 elements, then S can be represented as $\{X_1, X_2, X_3\}$, where $X_1 \leq X_2$ and $X_2 \leq X_3$. In this case, we have the constraints: $X_1 \leq X_2 \wedge X_2 \leq X_3 \wedge min(S) = X_1 \wedge max(S) = X_3 \wedge sum(S) = X_1 + X_2 + X_3 \wedge average(S) = (X_1 + X_2 + X_3)/3$. Projecting out the variables X_1, X_2 and X_3, we have:

$$min(S) \leq max(S) \wedge sum(S) \geq 2 * min(S) + max(S) \wedge \\ sum(S) \leq min(S) + 2 * max(S) \wedge average(S) = sum(S)/3.$$

It is easy to verify that the conjunction of relationships (3), (5), (6) and (8) are equivalent to the above conjunction, when $count(S) = 3$.

If S has $n \geq 4$ elements, then S can be represented as $\{X_1, X_2, \ldots, X_n\}$, where $X_1 \leq X_2 \leq \ldots \leq X_n$. In this case, we have $min(S) = X_1 \wedge max(S) = X_n \wedge sum(S) = X_1 + X_2 + \ldots + X_n \wedge average(S) = sum(S)/n$. Aggregation constraints involving $min, max, sum, count$ or $average$ do not allow direct reference to any of the values $X_2, \ldots, X_{n-1}, n \geq 4$.[5] Without loss of generality, we can assume that all the $n - 2$ values $X_2, \ldots, X_{n-1}$ are identical (say $= X_2$), where $X_1 \leq X_2 \leq X_n$. Consequently, we can simplify the above relationships as follows:

$$min(S) = X_1 \wedge max(S) = X_n \wedge average(S) = sum(S)/n \wedge \\ sum(S) = X_1 + (n - 2) * X_2 + X_n \wedge X_1 \leq X_2 \wedge X_2 \leq X_n.$$

---

[4] An alternative is to take $min(\emptyset) = \infty$ and $max(\emptyset) = -\infty$. While this is useful in an inductive characterization of the min and max aggregate functions, it violates our intuition that $min(S)$ should be $\leq max(S)$.

[5] For $n = 3$, it is possible to directly reference X_2 using $sum(S) - min(S) - max(S)$. Hence, the proof requires a separate case for a three element multiset. We would like to thank Gilles Pesant for pointing this out.

We can now replace the variables X_1 and X_n by $min(S)$ and $max(S)$. Since X_2 cannot be directly referenced in the aggregation constraints, and the only other constraints known about X_2 are its bounds, we can project it out to obtain:

$$sum(S) = average(S) * n \land sum(S) \leq min(S) + (n-1) * max(S) \land$$
$$sum(S) \geq (n-1) * min(S) + max(S) \land min(S) \leq max(S).$$

It is easy to verify that the conjunction of relationships (3), (5), (6) and (8) are equivalent to the above conjunction, when $count(S) = n$. This completes the proof of correctness and completeness. Minimality follows from the fact that none of the relationships is entailed by the others. □

The above reduction results in non-linear, mixed integer/real constraints, even when applied to linear aggregation constraints.

Note that since $min(S)$ is undefined when $count(S) = 0$, the aggregation constraint $min(S) = min(S)$ is not a tautology; it implies that $min(S)$ is defined, which implies that $count(S) > 0$. Other relationships between the results of aggregate functions can be inferred using these basic relationships. For example, we can infer that $count(S) = 1$ implies that $min(S) = max(S)$. Similarly, we can infer that the constraint $max(S) < average(S)$ is unsolvable.

Consider the linear aggregation constraint $min(S) = max(S)$, where S ranges over finite multisets of reals. For this aggregation constraint to be solvable, $min(S)$ and $max(S)$ must be defined. Hence, this implies the additional constraint $(count(S) > 0) \land (sum(S) = count(S) * max(S))$. Since the values of $min(S)$ and $max(S)$ are not constrained any further, this is not equivalent to any finite collection of linear constraints. The following theorem formalizes this idea.

Theorem 4. *There is no finite collection of linear arithmetic constraints over the reals and integers that correctly and completely axiomatizes the relationships between the aggregate functions min, max, sum and count.* □

4.2 Efficient Special Cases

In general, checking for solvability of aggregation constraints, even after the reduction, is undecidable. In this section, we briefly describe two cases where the reduction-based approach leads to polynomial-time algorithms for checking solvability. The intuition is that in each of the two cases the axiomatization of the relationships between the results of the various aggregate functions can be simplified to a conjunction of linear arithmetic constraints.

The first case is when the conjunction of constraints involves only min and max. If we want such constraints to be solvable, we must make the assumption that $min(S)$ and $max(S)$ are defined, and hence $count(S) > 0$. Hence, in this case, only the relationship $min(S) \leq max(S)$ (which assumes $count(S) > 0$) needs to be added. If the original conjunction of aggregation constraints is linear and the multiset elements are drawn from the reals, the transformed conjunction of arithmetic constraints is also linear over the reals; solvability can now be checked in time polynomial in the size of the aggregation constraints, using any of the standard techniques (see [4], for example) for solving linear arithmetic constraints over the reals.

The second case is when the conjunction of linear aggregation constraints explicitly specifies the cardinality of each multiset, i.e., for each multiset variable S_i, we know that $count(S_i) = k_i$, where k_i is a constant. In this case, each of the non-linear constraints in our axiomatization can be simplified to linear constraints; checking for solvability again takes time polynomial in the size of the aggregation constraints if the multiset elements are drawn from the reals.

5 Linear Separable Aggregation Constraints

In this section, we examine a very useful class of aggregation constraints, and present a polynomial-time algorithm to check for solvability of constraints in the class. Our technique operates directly on the aggregation constraints, rather than on their reduction to arithmetic constraints. The reduced form of this class includes mixed integer/real constraints, and is non-linear; it is not clear how to operate directly on the reduced form and attain the same complexity as our algorithm.

We specify the class of constraints in terms of the factors, described in Section 3, that affect the complexity of checking for solvability. We require that: (1) the domain of multiset elements is the *reals*, (2) the only aggregate functions present are $min, max, sum, average$ and $count$, (3) the constraints are linear and specified using $\leq, <, =, >$ and $\geq$, and (4) the constraints are aggregate-function-separable and multiset-variable-separable. Intuitively, the above four restrictions ensure that we can simplify the given conjunction of aggregation constraints to range constraints on each aggregate function on each multiset variable. In addition, we require that: (5) for each multiset variable S_i, the ranges for $min(S_i)$ and $max(S_i)$ are identical, and (6) for each multiset variable S_i, the range for $average(S_i)$ contains the range for $min(S_i)$ (equivalently, $max(S_i)$). These two conditions ensure that the multisets can contain *any* finite collection of elements from the given range for $min(S_i)$ (equivalently $max(S_i)$). We refer to this class of aggregation constraints as $\mathcal{LS}$-aggregation-constraints.

Most aggregation constraints occurring in database queries are multiset-variable-separable since typically a single grouping literal appears in each rule. Only when we consider constraint propagation or fold/unfold transformations are we likely to obtain non-multiset-variable-separable aggregation constraints. The further restrictions for $\mathcal{LS}$-aggregation-constraints are not onerous; the example aggregation constraint in the introduction is such a constraint, once we add the implied constraints $M1 \leq 10000 \wedge M2 > 0$.

5.1 Multiset Ranges

The heart of our algorithm is a function Multiset_Ranges that takes three ranges, two real ranges $\langle m_l, m_h \rangle$ and $\langle v_l, v_h \rangle$, and an integer range $\langle k_l, k_h \rangle$, along with information about whether each side of each range is open or closed, and answers the following question:

> Do there exist $k \geq 0$ numbers, k between k_l and k_h, each number between m_l and m_h, such that the sum of the k numbers is between v_l and v_h?

For simplicity of exposition, we present a special case of the algorithm below, where each range is assumed to be finite (i.e., no value is infinite), closed on both sides, and feasible. The general case does not add to the intuition, but makes the description of the algorithm more verbose.

```
function Multiset_Ranges (m_l, m_h, v_l, v_h, k_l, k_h) {
    /* we assume finite numbers: k_l ≥ 0, k_l ≤ k_h, m_l ≤ m_h and v_l ≤ v_h,
        and closed ranges. */
    (1) if (m_l ≤ 0 and m_h ≥ 0) then    /* Case 1: [m_l, m_h] includes 0. */
        (a) if (v_h < m_l * k_h or v_l > m_h * k_h) then
            return 0.    /* sum is too low or too high. */
        (b) else return 1.
    /* Case 2: m_l and m_h are both < 0. switch everything. */
    (2) if (m_h < 0) then
        (a) temp = −m_l; m_l = −m_h; m_h = temp.
            /* both m_l and m_h become positive and m_l ≤ m_h. */
        (b) temp = −v_l; v_l = −v_h; v_h = temp.
    /* Case 3: m_l and m_h are both > 0. */
    (3) if (v_h < k_l * m_l or v_l > k_h * m_h) then
        return 0.    /* sum is too low or too high. */
    (4) define k_1 and k_2 by v_l = k_1 * m_h − k_2, 0 ≤ k_2 < m_h.
            /* k_1 is the smallest number of possible values from [m_l, m_h],
                whose sum is ≥ v_l. */
    (5) define k_3 and k_4 by v_h = k_3 * m_l + k_4, 0 ≤ k_4 < m_l.
            /* k_3 is the largest number of possible values from [m_l, m_h],
                whose sum is ≤ v_h. */
    /* check if the [k_l, k_h] range overlaps with the [k_1, k_3] range. */
    (6) if (k_1 ≤ k_3 and k_1 ≤ k_h and k_l ≤ k_3) then
        return 1.    /* the intersection gives a possible value for k */
    (7) else return 0.
}
```

Theorem 5. *Function Multiset_Ranges returns 1 iff there exist $k \geq 0$ real numbers, $k_l \leq k \leq k_h$, each number is greater than or equal to m_l and less than or equal to m_h, such that the sum of the k numbers is greater than or equal to v_l and less than or equal to v_h.*

Proof. The algorithm has three cases, based on the location of the $[m_l, m_h]$ range with respect to zero. The first case is when this range includes zero; in this case the sum can take any value in the continuous range $[k_h * m_l, k_h * m_h]$. The second case is when the $[m_l, m_h]$ range includes only negative numbers, and the third case is when this range includes only positive numbers. These two cases are symmetric, and we transform the second case into the third case, and consider only the third case in detail.

In the third case, the sum lies within the range $[k_l * m_l, k_h * m_h]$, but it *cannot* take all values within this range; it can take values only from the union of the ranges $[k_l * m_l, k_l * m_h], [(k_l + 1) * m_l, (k_l + 1) * m_h], \ldots, [k_h * m_l, k_h * m_h]$. This union of ranges need not be convex; there may be gaps. The conjunction of constraints is unsolvable iff the $[v_l, v_h]$ range lies outside the $[k_l * m_l, k_h * m_h]$ range, or entirely within one of the gaps. This concludes the proof. □

5.2 Checking for Solvability

The conjunction of $\mathcal{LS}$-aggregation constraints is multiset-variable-separable. Hence, the primitive aggregation constraints can be partitioned based on the multiset variable, and the conjunction of aggregation constraints in each partition can be solved separately. The overall conjunction is solvable iff the conjunction in each partition is separately solvable.

By definition, we can simplify a conjunction of $\mathcal{LS}$-aggregation-constraints on a single multiset variable S_i to range constraints on each aggregation term. We can then check whether each range is feasible, whether the ranges for $min(S_i)$ and $max(S_i)$ are identical, and whether the range for $average(S_i)$ contains the range for $min(S_i)$ (equivalently $max(S_i)$). If so, the algorithm Check_LS_Solvability that checks for solvability first takes into account the special case of $count(S_i) = 0$. It then calls function Multiset_Ranges with the range for $min(S_i)$ (equivalently $max(S_i)$), the range for $sum(S_i)$ and the range for $count(S_i)$.

If, for each multiset variable S_i, function Multiset_Ranges returns 1, then algorithm Check_LS_Solvability returns SOLVABLE.

Theorem 6. *Given a conjunction of $\mathcal{LS}$-aggregation-constraints, Check_LS_Solvability returns SOLVABLE, in time polynomial in the size of the conjunction of $\mathcal{LS}$-aggregation-constraints, iff the conjunction is solvable.* □

Though $\mathcal{LS}$-aggregation-constraints are restricted, they are strong enough to infer useful new aggregate constraint information. They can be used to infer some information about an *arbitrary* aggregation constraint C by determining an $\mathcal{LS}$-aggregation-constraint H that is implied by C; any aggregation constraints implied by H are then also implied by C.

6 Conclusions and Future Work

We presented a new and extremely useful class of constraints, *aggregation constraints*, and studied the problem of checking for solvability of conjunctions of aggregation constraints. There are many interesting directions to pursue. An important direction of active research is to significantly extend the class of aggregation constraints for which solvability can be efficiently checked. We believe that our algorithm works on a larger class of aggregation constraints than presented here—for instance, we believe that our algorithm will work correctly even if we relax the conditions to not require *min* and *max* to be separated; characterizing this class will be very useful.

Combining aggregation constraints with multiset constraints that give additional information about the multisets (using functions and predicates such as $\cup, \in, \subseteq$, etc.) will be very important practically.

Another important direction is to examine how this research can be used to improve query optimization and integrity constraint verification in database query languages such as SQL. Sudarshan and Ramakrishnan [6] and Levy et al. [1] consider how to use simple aggregate conditions for query optimization; it would be interesting to see how their work can be generalized. It would also be interesting to see how to use aggregation constraints in conjunction with Stuckey and Sudarshan's technique [5] for compilation of query constraints.

We believe that we have identified an important area of research, namely aggregation constraints, in this paper and have laid the foundations for further research in the area.

Acknowledgements

The research of Kenneth A. Ross was supported by NSF grant IRI-9209029, by a grant from the AT&T Foundation, by a David and Lucile Packard Foundation Fellowship in Science and Engineering, and by a Sloan Foundation Fellowship. The research of Peter J. Stuckey was partially supported by the Centre for Intelligent Decision Systems and ARC Grant A49130842.

References

1. A. Y. Levy, I. S. Mumick, and Y. Sagiv. Query optimization by predicate move-around. In *Proceedings of the International Conference on Very Large Databases*, Santiago, Chile, Sept. 1994.
2. K. Marriott and P. J. Stuckey. Semantics of constraint logic programs with optimization. *Letters on Programming Languages and Systems*, 1994.
3. I. S. Mumick, H. Pirahesh, and R. Ramakrishnan. Duplicates and aggregates in deductive databases. In *Proceedings of the Sixteenth International Conference on Very Large Databases*, Aug. 1990.
4. A. Schrijver. *Theory of Linear and Integer Programming*. Discrete Mathematics and Optimization. Wiley-Interscience, 1986.
5. P. J. Stuckey and S. Sudarshan. Compiling query constraints. In *Proceedings of the ACM Symposium on Principles of Database Systems*, May 1994.
6. S. Sudarshan and R. Ramakrishnan. Aggregation and relevance in deductive databases. In *Proceedings of the Seventeenth International Conference on Very Large Databases*, Sept. 1991.

Constraint-Generating Dependencies *

Marianne Baudinet,[1] Jan Chomicki,[2] and Pierre Wolper[3]

[1] Université Libre de Bruxelles, Informatique,
50 Avenue F.D. Roosevelt, C.P. 165, 1050 Brussels, Belgium
Email: mb@cs.ulb.ac.be
[2] Kansas State University, Dept of Computing and Information Sciences,
234 Nichols Hall, Manhattan, KS 66506-2302, U.S.A.
Email: chomicki@cis.ksu.edu
[3] Université de Liège, Institut Montefiore, B28
4000 Liège Sart-Tilman, Belgium
Email: pw@montefiore.ulg.ac.be

Abstract. Traditionally, dependency theory has been developed for uninterpreted data. Specifically, the only assumption that is made about
the data domains is that data values can be compared for equality. However, data is often interpreted and there can be advantages in considering
it as such, for instance obtaining more compact representations as done
in constraint databases. This paper considers dependency theory in the
context of interpreted data. Specifically, it studies *constraint-generating
dependencies*. These are a generalization of equality-generating dependencies where equality requirements are replaced by constraints on an
interpreted domain. The main technical results in the paper are decision
procedures for the implication and consistency problems for constraint-
generating dependencies. These decision procedures proceed by reducing
the dependency problem to a decision problem for the constraint theory
of interest, and are applicable as soon as the underlying constraint theory is decidable. Furthermore, complexity results for specific constraint
domains can be transferred quite directly to the dependency problem.

1 Introduction

Relational database theory is largely built upon the assumption of uninterpreted
data. While this has advantages, mostly generality, it foregoes the possibility
of exploiting the structure of specific data domains. The introduction of constraint databases [19] was a break with this uninterpreted-data trend. Rather
than defining the extension of relations by an explicit enumeration of tuples, a
constraint database uses constraint expressions to implicitly specify sets of tuples. Of course, for this to be possible in a meaningful way, one needs to consider
interpreted data, that is, data from a specific domain on which a basic set of
predicates and functions is defined. A typical example of constraint expressions

---

* This work was supported by NATO Collaborative Research Grant CRG 940110 and
by NSF Grant IRI-9110581.

and domain are linear inequalities interpreted on the reals. The potential gains from this approach are in the compactness of the representation (a single constraint expression can represent many, even an infinite number of, explicit tuples) and in the efficiency of query evaluation (computing with constraint expressions amounts to manipulating many tuples simultaneously).

Related developments have concurrently been taking place in temporal databases. Indeed, time values are intrinsically interpreted and this can be exploited for finitely representing potentially infinite temporal extensions. For instance, in [18] infinite temporal extensions are represented with the help of periodicity and inequality constraints, whereas in [9, 10] and [2] deductive rules over the integers are used for the same purpose. Constraints have also been used recently for representing incomplete temporal information [30, 22].

If one surveys the existing work on databases with interpreted data and implicit representations, one finds contributions on the expressiveness of the various representation formalisms [1, 4, 3], on the complexity of query evaluation [8, 11, 24, 30], and on data structures and algorithms to be used in the representation of constraint expressions and in query evaluation [27, 6, 7, 20]. However, much less has been done on extending other parts of traditional database theory, for instance schema design and dependency theory. It should be clear that dependency theory is of interest in this context. For instance, in [17], one finds a taxonomy of dependencies that are useful for temporal databases. Moreover, many *integrity constraints* over interpreted data can be represented as generalized dependencies. For instance, the integrity constraints over databases with ordered domains studied in [16, 31] can be represented as generalized dependencies. Also, some versions of the constraint checking problem studied in [15] can be viewed as generalized dependency implication problems.

One might think that the study of dependency theory has been close to exhaustive. While this is largely so for dependencies over uninterpreted data (that is, the context in which data values can only be compared for equality) [28], the situation is quite different for dependencies over data domains with a richer structure. The subject of this paper is the theory of these interpreted dependencies.

Specifically, we study the class of *constraint-generating dependencies*. These are the generalization of equality-generating dependencies [5], allowing arbitrary constraints on the data domain to appear wherever the latter only allow equalities. For instance, a constraint-generating dependency over an ordered domain can specify that if the value of an attribute A in a tuple t_1 is less than the value of the same attribute in a tuple t_2, then an identical relation holds for the values of an attribute B. This type of dependency can express a wide variety of constraints on the data. For instance, most of the temporal dependencies appearing in the taxonomy of [17] are constraint-generating dependencies.

Our technical contributions address the implication and the consistency[4] problems for constraint-generating dependencies. The natural approach to these

---

[4] Though consistency is always satisfied for equality-generating dependencies, more general constraints turn it into a nontrivial problem.

problems is to write the dependencies as logical formulas. Unfortunately, the resulting formulas are not just formulas in the theory of the data domain. Indeed, they also contain uninterpreted predicate symbols representing the relations and thus are not a priori decidable, even if the data domain theory is decidable.

To obtain decision procedures, we show that the predicate symbols can be eliminated. Since the predicate symbols are implicitly universally quantified, this can be viewed as a form of second-order quantifier elimination. It is based on the fact that it is sufficient to consider relations with a small finite number of tuples. This then allows quantifier elimination by explicit representation of the possible tuples. The fact that one only needs to consider a small finite number of tuples is analogous to the fact that the implication problem for functional dependencies can be decided over 2-tuple relations [23]. Furthermore, for pure functional dependencies, our quantifier elimination procedures yields exactly the usual reduction to propositional logic. For more general constraint dependencies, it yields a formula in the theory of the data domain. Thus, if this theory is decidable, the implication and the consistency problems for constraint-dependencies are also decidable. Our approach is based on simple general logical arguments and provides a clear and straightforward justification for the type of procedure based on containment mappings used for instance in [15].

The complexity of the decision procedure depends on the specific data domain being considered and on the exact form of the constraint dependencies. We consider three typical constraint languages: equalities/inequalities, ordering constraints, and linear arithmetic constraints. We give a detailed picture of the complexity of the implication problem for dependencies over these theories and show the impact of the form of the dependencies on tractability.

2 Constraint-Generating Dependencies

Consider a relational database where some attributes take their values in specific domains, such as the integers or the reals, on which a set of predicates and functions are defined. We call such attributes *interpreted*. For the simplicity of the presentation, let us assume that the database only contains one (universal) relation r and let us ignore the noninterpreted attributes. In this context, it is natural to generalize the notion of equality-generating dependency [5]. Rather than specifying the propagation of equality constraints, we write similar statements involving arbitrary constraints (i.e., arbitrary formulas in the theory of the data domain). Specifically, we define *constraint-generating k-dependencies* as follows (the constant k specifies the number of tuples the dependency refers to).

Definition 1. Given a relation r, a *constraint-generating k-dependency* over r (with $k \geq 1$) is a first-order formula of the form

$$(\forall t_1) \cdots (\forall t_k) \left[\left[r(t_1) \wedge \cdots \wedge r(t_k) \wedge C[t_1, \ldots, t_k] \right] \Rightarrow C'[t_1, \ldots, t_k] \right]$$

where $C[t_1, \ldots, t_k]$ and $C'[t_1, \ldots, t_k]$ denote arbitrary constraint formulas relating the values of various attributes in the tuples $t_1, \ldots, t_k$. There are no restrictions on these formulas, they can include all constructs of the constraint theory under consideration, including quantification on the constraint domain. For instance, a constraint $C[t_1, t_2]$ could be $\exists z(t_1[A] < z \wedge z < t_2[A])$.

Note that we have defined constraint-generating dependencies in the context of a single relation, but the generalization to several relations is immediate.

Constraint-generating 1-dependencies as well as constraint-generating 2-dependencies are the most common. Notice that functional dependencies are a special form of constraint-generating 2-dependencies. Constraint-generating dependencies can naturally express a variety of arithmetic integrity constraints. The following examples illustrate their definition and show some of their potential applications.

Example 1. In [17], an exhaustive taxonomy of dependencies that can be imposed on a temporal relation is given. Of the more than 30 types of dependencies that are defined there, all but 4 can be written as constraint-generating dependencies. These last 4 require a generalization of tuple-generating dependencies [5] (see Section 5).

For instance, let us consider a relation $r(tt, vt)$ with two temporal attributes: transaction time (tt) and valid time (vt). The property of r being "strongly retroactively bounded" with bound $c \geq 0$ is expressed as the constraint-generating 1-dependency

$$(\forall t_1)\Big[r(t_1) \Rightarrow [(t_1[tt] \leq t_1[vt] + c) \wedge (t_1[vt] \leq t_1[tt])]\Big].$$

The property of r being "globally nondecreasing" is expressed as the constraint generating 2-dependency

$$(\forall t_1)(\forall t_2)\Big[[r(t_1) \wedge r(t_2) \wedge (t_1[tt] < t_2[tt])] \Rightarrow (t_1[vt] \leq t_2[vt])\Big].$$

Example 2. Let us consider a relation $emp(name, boss, salary)$. Then the fact that an employee cannot make more than her boss is expressed as

$$(\forall t_1)(\forall t_2)\Big[[emp(t_1) \wedge emp(t_2) \wedge (t_1[boss] = t_2[name])] \Rightarrow (t_1[salary] \leq t_2[salary])\Big].$$

3 Decision Problems for Constraint-Generating Dependencies

The basic decision problems for constraint-generating dependencies are:

- *implication:* does a finite set of dependencies D imply a dependency d_0?
- *consistency:* does a finite set of dependencies D have a non-trivial model, that is, is D true in a nonempty relation?

The first problem is a classical problem of database theory. Its practical motivation comes from the need to detect *redundant* dependencies, that is, those that are implied by a given set of dependencies. The second problem has a trivial answer for uninterpreted dependencies: every set of equality- and tuple-generating dependencies has a 1-element model. However, even a single constraint-generating dependency may be inconsistent, as illustrated by

$$(\forall t)[r(t) \Rightarrow t[1] < t[1]].$$

We only study the *implication* problem since the consistency problem is its dual: a set of dependencies D is inconsistent if and only if D implies a dependency of the form:

$$(\forall t)[r(t) \Rightarrow C]$$

where C is any unsatisfiable constraint (we assume the existence of at least one such unsatisfiable constraint formula).

The result we prove in this section is that the implication problem for constraint-generating dependencies reduces to the validity problem for a formula in the underlying constraint theory. Specific dependencies and theories will be considered in Section 4, and the corresponding complexity results provided. The reduction proceeds in three steps. First, we prove that the implication problem is equivalent to the implication problem restricted to finite relations of bounded size. Second, we eliminate from the implication to be decided the second-order quantification (over relations). Third, we eliminate the first-order quantification (over tuples) from the dependencies themselves and replace it by quantification over the domain – a process that we call *symmetrization*. This gives us the desired result.

3.1 Statement of the Problem and Notation

Let r denote a relation with n interpreted attributes. Let $d_0, d_1, \ldots, d_m$ denote constraint-generating k-dependencies over the attributes of r. The value of k need not be the same for all d_i's. We denote by k_0 the value of k for d_0.

The *dependency implication problem* consists in deciding whether d_0 is implied by the set of dependencies $D = \{d_1, \ldots, d_m\}$. In other words, it consists in deciding whether d_0 is satisfied by every interpretation that satisfies D, which can be formulated as

$$(\forall r)\Big[r \models D \Rightarrow r \models d_0\Big], \tag{1}$$

where D stands for $d_1 \wedge \cdots \wedge d_m$. We equivalently write (1) as

$$(\forall r)\Big[D(r) \Rightarrow d_0(r)\Big]$$

when we wish to emphasize the fact that the dependencies apply to the tuples of r.

3.2 Towards a Decision Procedure

We first prove that, when dealing with constraint-generating k-dependencies, it is sufficient to consider relations of size[5] k.

Lemma 2. *Let d denote any constraint-generating k-dependency. If a relation r does not satisfy d, then there is a relation r' of size k that does not satisfy d. Furthermore, r' is obtained from r by removing and/or duplicating tuples.*

Proof. Straightforward.

Lemma 3. *If a relation r satisfies a set of constraint-generating k-dependencies $D = \{d_1, \ldots d_m\}$ and does not satisfy a constraint-generating k_0-dependency d_0, then there is a relation r' of size k_0 that satisfies D but does not satisfy d_0.*

Proof. Straightforward from Lemma 2.

From Lemma 3, one then directly obtains the following.

Lemma 4. *Consider an instance (D, d_0) of the dependency implication problem where d_0 is a constraint-generating k_0-dependency. The dependency d_0 is implied by D over all relations if and only if it is implied by D over relations of size k_0; i.e., $(\forall r)\left[r \models D \Rightarrow r \models d_0\right]$ iff $(\forall r')\left[|r'| = k_0 \Rightarrow \left[r' \models D \Rightarrow r' \models d_0\right]\right]$.*

By Lemma 4, in order to decide the implication problem, we just need to be able to decide this problem over relations of size k for a given k. Deciding the implication (1) thus reduces to deciding

$$(\forall r')\left[[|r'| = k \wedge D(r')] \Rightarrow d_0(r')\right]. \tag{2}$$

Let $r' = \{t_{x_1}, \ldots, t_{x_k}\}$ denote an arbitrary relation of size k where $t_{x_1}, \ldots, t_{x_k}$ are arbitrary tuples. We can eliminate the (second-order) quantification over relations from the implication (2) and replace it with a quantification over tuples (that is, over vectors of elements of the domain). We get

$$(\forall t_{x_1}) \cdots (\forall t_{x_k})\left[D(\{t_{x_1}, \ldots, t_{x_k}\}) \Rightarrow d_0(\{t_{x_1}, \ldots, t_{x_k}\})\right]. \tag{3}$$

Next, we simplify the formula (3), whose validity is equivalent to the constraint dependency implication problem, by eliminating the quantification over tuples that appears in the dependencies. We refer to this quantifier elimination procedure for dependencies as *symmetrization*. For the sake of clarity, we present the details of the symmetrization process for the case where $k = 2$. The process can be generalized directly to the more general case.

For the case where $k = 2$, the formula (3) to be decided is the following.

$$(\forall t_x)(\forall t_y)\left[D(\{t_x, t_y\}) \Rightarrow d_0(\{t_x, t_y\})\right].$$

---

[5] In what follows, we consider relations as multisets rather than sets. This has no impact on the implication problem, but simplifies our procedure.

We can simplify this formula further by eliminating the quantification over tuples that appears in the dependencies $d(\{t_x, t_y\})$ in $D \cup \{d_0\}$. Every such dependency $d(\{t_x, t_y\})$ can indeed be rewritten as a constraint formula $cf(d)$ in the following manner.

1. Let d be a 1-dependency, that is, d is of the form $(\forall t)\Big[[r'(t) \wedge C[t]] \Rightarrow C'[t]\Big]$.

   This dependency considered over $r' = \{t_x, t_y\}$ is equivalent to the constraint formula
   $$cf(d) : \Big[C[t_x] \Rightarrow C'[t_x]\Big] \wedge \Big[C[t_y] \Rightarrow C'[t_y]\Big],$$

   which is a conjunction of $k = 2$ constraint implications. Notice that the t_x and t_y appearing in this formula are just tuples of variables ranging over the domain of the constraint theory of interest.

2. Let d be a 2-dependency, that is, d is of the form
   $$(\forall t_1)(\forall t_2)\Big[[r'(t_1) \wedge r'(t_2) \wedge C[t_1, t_2]] \Rightarrow C'[t_1, t_2]\Big].$$

   This dependency considered over $r' = \{t_x, t_y\}$ is equivalent to the constraint formula
   $$cf(d) : \Big[C[t_x, t_y] \Rightarrow C'[t_x, t_y]\Big] \wedge \Big[C[t_y, t_x] \Rightarrow C'[t_y, t_x]\Big] \wedge$$
   $$\Big[C[t_x, t_x] \Rightarrow C'[t_x, t_x]\Big] \wedge \Big[C[t_y, t_y] \Rightarrow C'[t_y, t_y]\Big],$$

   which is a conjunction of $k^k = 4$ constraint implications.

The rewriting of d as $cf(d)$ is what we call the *symmetrization* of d, for rather obvious reasons. It extends directly to any value of k. Notice that for a given k, any j-dependency d is rewritten as a constraint formula $cf(d)$, which is a conjunction of k^j constraint implications. Interestingly, in the case of functional dependencies, symmetrization is not needed. This is due to the fact that the underlying constraints are equalities, which are ... symmetric. Hence, in that special case, symmetrization would produce several instances of the same constraint formulas.

Applying the symmetrization process to all the dependencies appearing in the formula (3), we get

$$(\forall t_{x_1}) \cdots (\forall t_{x_k})\Big[cf(d_1) \wedge \cdots \wedge cf(d_m) \Rightarrow cf(d_0)\Big]. \tag{4}$$

Notice that in formula (4), each tuple variable can be replaced by n domain variables, and thus the quantification over tuples can be replaced by a quantification over elements of the domain. For the sake of clarity, we simply denote by $(\forall *)$ the adequate quantification over elements of the domain (the *universal closure*). Formula (4) thus becomes

$$(\forall *)\Big[cf(d_1) \wedge \cdots \wedge cf(d_m) \Rightarrow cf(d_0)\Big], \tag{5}$$

where each $cf(d)$ is a conjunction of k^j constraint implications if d is a j-dependency and d_0 is a k-dependency. Thus, we have proved the following theorem.

Theorem 5. *For constraint-generating k-dependencies, with bounded k, the implication problem is linearly reduced to the validity of a universally quantified formula of the constraint theory.*

Example 3. Let us consider the following constraint-generating 2-dependencies over a relation r with a single attribute.

$$d_1 : (\forall x)(\forall y)\Big[r(x) \wedge r(y) \Rightarrow x \leq y\Big]$$
$$d_2 : (\forall x)(\forall y)\Big[r(x) \wedge r(y) \Rightarrow x = y\Big]$$

Symmetrizing them produces the following constraint formulas.

$$cf(d_1) : x \leq y \wedge y \leq x \wedge x \leq x \wedge y \leq y$$
$$cf(d_2) : x = y \wedge y = x \wedge x = x \wedge y = y$$

It is clear that these two constraint formulas are equivalent, as they should be.

4 Complexity Results

4.1 Clausal dependencies

In this section, we study the complexity of the implication problem for some classes of constraint-generating dependencies occurring in practice, in particular dependencies with equality, order, and arithmetic constraints. We restrict our attention to atomic constraints and clausal dependencies defined below.

Definition 6. An *atomic constraint* is a formula consisting of an interpreted predicate symbol applied to terms. A *clausal* constraint-generating dependency is a constraint-generating dependency such that the constraint in the antecedent is a conjunction of atomic constraints and the constraint in the consequent is an atomic constraint.

Notice that a constraint-generating dependency such that the constraint in the antecedent and the constraint in the consequent are both conjunctions of atomic constraints can be rewritten as a set of clausal constraint-generating dependencies (by decomposing the conjunction in the consequent). Essentially all the dependencies mentioned in [17] can be written in clausal form.

Moreover, we assume that the constraint language is *closed under negation*.[6] This is again satisfied by many examples of interest, the most notable exception being the class of functional dependencies.

Finally, we study classes of k-dependencies for fixed values of k (mainly $k = 2$). This makes it possible to contrast our results with the results about functional dependencies which are 2-dependencies and for which the implication problem can be solved in $O(n)$.

---

[6] Note that in this context, the distinction between positive and negative atomic constraints is meaningless.

Simple transformations demonstrate that for clausal dependencies and constraint languages closed under negation, the implication problem can be expressed as the unsatisfiability of a formula of the following form:

$$\Psi = (\exists*)\left[\bigwedge_i\left(\bigvee_j(c_{ij})\right)\right].$$

where each c_{ij} is an atomic constraint. When $|D| = m$ and d_0 is a k-dependency, the number of clauses in the formula Ψ above is at most equal to $m \cdot k^k$ plus the number of constraints in d_0. Thus deciding the validity of the implication problem for k-dependencies (k fixed) can be done by checking the unsatisfiability of a conjunction of clauses of length that is linear in the size of $D \cup \{d_0\}$. We can replace the variables in the constraint formulas by the corresponding Skolem constants and view Ψ as a ground formula.

The opposite LOGSPACE reduction, from unsatisfiability to implication, also exists and only requires 1-dependencies.

4.2   Equality and order constraints

We consider here atomic constraints of the form $x\theta y$ where $\theta \in \{=, \neq, <, \leq\}$ over integers, rationals, or reals.[7] This constraint language has two sublanguages closed under negation: $\{=, \neq\}$-constraints and $\{<, \leq\}$-constraints. We study the dependencies over such restricted constraint languages as well. We make the additional assumption that *no domain constants appear in the dependencies*. (If this assumption is not satisfied, the complexity usually shifts up. For example, in Theorem 7 the first case becomes co-NP-complete for the integers by the results of [25].)

Theorem 7. *The implication problem for clausal constraint-generating k-dependencies is:*

- *in PTIME for dependencies with one atomic $\{=, \neq, <, \leq\}$-constraint (no constraints in the antecedent),*
- *co-NP-complete for dependencies with two or more atomic $\{=, \neq\}$-constraints,*
- *co-NP-complete for dependencies with two or more atomic $\{<, \leq\}$-constraints.*

The above results are rather negative. To obtain more tractable classes, we propose to further restrict the syntax of dependencies by typing.

Definition 8. A clausal dependency is *typed* if each atomic constraint involves only the values of one given attribute in different tuples.

The second dependency in Example 1 is typed, while the first one and the one in Example 2 are not. Functional dependencies are typed as well.

Theorem 9. *The implication problem for typed clausal constraint-generating 2-dependencies is:*

---

[7] In fact, our lower bounds hold for any infinite linearly-ordered set.

- in PTIME $(O(n^2))$ for dependencies with at most two atomic $\{=,\neq,<,\leq\}$-constraints,
- co-NP-complete for dependencies with three or more atomic $\{=,\neq\}$-constraints,
- co-NP-complete for dependencies with three or more atomic $\{<,\leq\}$-constraints.

The first result in the above theorem yields a new class of dependencies with a tractable implication problem. Note that the first result is different from the well-known result about linear-time implication for functional dependencies. Functional dependencies viewed as constraint-generating dependencies allow only equality constraints which are not closed under negation. Moreover, constraint-generating dependencies with two constraints in the body correspond to *unary* functional dependencies.

Together, Theorems 7 and 9 give a *complete classification* of tractable and intractable classes of untyped and typed 2-dependencies with $\{=,\neq,<,\leq\}$-constraints.

4.3 Linear arithmetic constraints

We consider now *linear arithmetic constraints*, i.e., atomic constraints of the form $a_1 x_1 + \cdots + a_k x_k \leq a$ (domain constants are allowed here). We can use here directly the results about the complexity of linear programming [26].

Theorem 10. *For linear arithmetic constraints, the implication problem for clausal constraint-generating k-dependencies with one atomic constraint per dependency is in PTIME for the reals, and co-NP-complete for the integers.*

The case of more than one linear arithmetic constraint per dependency remains to be investigated.

5 Conclusions and Related Work

A brief summary of this paper is that constraint-generating dependencies are an interesting concept, and that deciding implication of such dependencies is basically no harder than deciding the underlying constraint theory, which, a priori, was not obvious. Apart from the constraint languages considered in this paper, other languages may be relevant as well, for instance *congruence constraints* that appear in [17]. Also, the impact that the presence of domain constants in equality and order constraints has on the complexity of implication should be fully studied.

Other forms of constraint dependencies can also be of interest. An obvious candidate is the concept of *tuple-generating* constraint dependency. Unfortunately, the implication problem for these dependencies is harder to decide and more closely linked to the underlying theory. Indeed, tuple-generating constraint dependencies can, for example, specify a dense domain. The obvious applications of constraint-generating dependencies are constraint database design theory and consistency checking.

As far as related work, we should first mention that Jensen and Snodgrass [17] induced us to think about constraint dependencies. We should note that the integrity constraints over temporal databases postulated there involve both typed and untyped constraint-generating dependencies, as well as tuple-generating ones.

Two recent papers on *implication constraints* by Ishakbeyoğlu, Ozsoyoğlu and Zhang [16, 31], as well as a paper on efficient integrity checking by Gupta, Sagiv, Ullman, and Widom [15] contain work fairly close to ours. However, there are several important differences. Foremost, all three papers discuss a fixed language of constraint formulas, namely equality ($=$), inequality ($\neq$), and order ($<, \leq$) constraints, while our results are applicable to any decidable constraint theory thanks to our general reduction strategy. In particular, the papers [31, 15], which were written independently of the first version of this paper, both present results equivalent to our Theorem 5, but formulated in the context of a fixed constraint language. Also, the proof techniques in those papers, based on the theory of conjunctive queries, are quite different from ours. Moreover, the complexity results of [31] are obtained in a slightly different model. Both the number of database literals and the arity of relations in a dependency are considered as parts of the input, while we consider only the latter. We think that our model is more intuitive because it is difficult to come up with a meaningful dependency that references more than a few tuples in a relation. Our intractability results are stronger than those of [31] while our positive characterizations of polynomial-time decidable problems do not necessarily carry over to the framework of [31]. Also, in [16, 31], the tractable classes of dependencies are not defined syntactically but rather by the presence or absence of certain types of refutations.

A clausal constraint-generating dependency (quantifiers omitted)

$$r(t_1) \wedge \cdots \wedge r(t_k) \wedge C_1 \wedge \cdots \wedge C_n \Rightarrow C_0$$

can be viewed as an integrity constraint (in the notation of [15])

$$\textbf{panic} \; : - \; r(t_1) \,\&\, \cdots \,\&\, r(t_k) \,\&\, C_1 \,\&\, \cdots \,\&\, C_n \,\&\, \neg C_0.$$

Thus the implication of a dependency by a set of dependencies is equivalent to the subsumption of an integrity constraint by a set of integrity constraints. Therefore the results about the complexity of implication from Section 4 transfer directly to the context of constraint subsumption. The paper [15] applies the results about constraint subsumption to develop techniques for efficient integrity checking. Unfortunately, this application requires introducing constants into constraints, so our complexity results, developed under the assumption that constants do not appear in dependencies, are not applicable here, though our general reduction is.

Order dependencies, proposed by Ginsburg and Hull [13, 14], are typed clausal 2-dependencies over the theory of equality and order (without $\neq$). The order is not required to be total. Ginsburg and Hull provided an axiomatization of such dependencies and proved that the implication problem is co-NP-complete for dependencies with at least three constraints. This result corresponds to the fifth case of our Theorem 9. This does not subsume any of our results. They also supplied a number of tractable dependency classes which are, again, different from ours and involve mainly partial orders.

References

1. M. Baudinet. On the expressiveness of temporal logic programming. To appear in *Information and Computation*.
2. M. Baudinet. Temporal logic programming is complete and expressive. In *Sixteenth ACM Symp. on Principles of Programming Languages*, pp. 267–280, Austin, TX, Jan. 1989.
3. M. Baudinet, J. Chomicki, and P. Wolper. Temporal deductive databases. In A. Tansel, J. Clifford, S. Gadia, S. Jajodia, A. Segev, and R. Snodgrass, eds., *Temporal Databases. Theory, Design, and Implementation*, chapter 13, pp. 294–320. Benjamin/Cummings, 1993.
4. M. Baudinet, M. Niézette, and P. Wolper. On the representation of infinite temporal data and queries. In *Tenth ACM Symp. on Principles of Database Systems*, pp. 280–290, Denver, CO, May 1991.
5. C. Beeri and M. Vardi. A proof procedure for data dependencies. *J. ACM*, 31(4):718–741, Oct. 1984.
6. A. Brodsky, J. Jaffar, and M. J. Maher. Toward practical constraint databases. In *19th Intl. Conf. on Very Large Data Bases*, Dublin, Ireland, Aug. 1993.
7. A. Brodsky, C. Lassez, and J.-L. Lassez. Separability of polyhedra and a new approach to spatial storage. In *Proc. of the First Workhop on Principles and Practice of Constraint Programming*, Newport, Rhode Island, Apr. 1993.
8. J. Chomicki. Polynomial time query processing in temporal deductive databases. In *Ninth ACM Symp. on Principles of Database Systems*, pp. 379–391, Nashville, TN, Apr. 1990.
9. J. Chomicki and T. Imieliński. Temporal deductive databases and infinite objects. In *Seventh ACM Symp. on Principles of Database Systems*, pp. 61–73, Austin, TX, Mar. 1988.
10. J. Chomicki and T. Imieliński. Finite Representation of Infinite Query Answers. *ACM Transactions on Database Systems*, 18(2):181–223, June 1993.
11. J. Cox and K. McAloon. Decision procedures for constraint based extensions of Datalog. In F. Benhamou and A. Colmerauer, eds., *Constraint Logic Programming: Selected Research*. MIT Press, 1993.
12. M. R. Garey and D. S. Johnson. *Computers and Intractability: A Guide to the Theory of NP-Completeness*. W.H. Freeman and Company, New York, 1979.
13. S. Ginsburg and R. Hull. Order dependency in the relational model. *Theoretical Computer Science*, 26:149–195, 1983.
14. S. Ginsburg and R. Hull. Sort sets in the relational model. *J. ACM*, 33(3):465–488, July 1986.
15. A. Gupta, Y. Sagiv, J. D. Ullman, and J. Widom. Constraint checking with partial information. In *Thirteenth ACM Symp. on Principles of Database Systems*, pp. 45–55, Minneapolis, MN, May 1994.
16. N. S. Ishakbeyoğlu and Z. M. Ozsoyoğlu. On the maintenance of implication integrity constraints. In *Fourth Intl. Conf. on Database and Expert Systems Applications*, pp. 221–232, Prague, Sept. 1993. LNCS 720, Springer-Verlag.

17. C. Jensen and R. Snodgrass. Temporal specialization. In *Eighth Intl. Conf. on Data Enfineering*, pp. 594–603, Tempe, AZ, Feb. 1992. IEEE.

18. F. Kabanza, J.-M. Stévenne, and P. Wolper. Handling infinite temporal data. In *Ninth ACM Symp. on Principles of Database Systems*, pp. 392–403, Nashville, TN, Apr. 1990.

19. P. C. Kanellakis, G. M. Kuper, and P. Revesz. Constraint query languages. In *Ninth ACM Symp. on Principles of Database Systems*, pp. 299–313, Nashville, TN, Apr. 1990.

20. P. C. Kanellakis, S. Ramaswamy, D. E. Vengroff, and J. S. Vitter. Indexing for data models with constraints and classes. In *Twelfth ACM Symp. on Principles of Database Systems*, pp. 233–243, Washington, DC, May 1993.

21. M. Koubarakis. Dense time and temporal constraints with $\neq$. In *Proc. of the Third Intl. Conf. On Principles of Knowledge Representation and Reasoning*, pp. 24–35, Oct. 1992.

22. M. Koubarakis. Representation and querying in temporal databases : the power of temporal constraints. In *Ninth Intl. Conf. on Data Engineering*, Vienna, Apr. 1993.

23. D. Maier. *The Theory of Relational Databases*. Computer Science Press, 1983.

24. P. Revesz. A closed form for Datalog queries with integer order. In S. Abiteboul and P. Kanellakis, eds., *ICDT '90, Proc. of the Third Intl. Conf. on Database Theory*, pp. 187–201, Paris, Dec. 1990. LNCS 470, Springer-Verlag.

25. D. Rosenkrantz and H. B. I. Hunt. Processing conjunctive predicates and queries. In *Intl. Conf. on Very Large Data Bases*, pp. 64–72, 1980.

26. A. Schrijver. *Theory of Linear and Integer Programming*. John Wiley & Sons, 1986.

27. D. Srivastava. Subsumption in constraint query languages with linear arithmetic constraints. In *Second Intl. Symp. on Artificial Intelligence and Mathematics*, Fort Lauderdale, FL, Jan. 1992.

28. B. Thalheim. *Dependencies in Relational Databases*. Teubner-Texte zur Mathematik, Band 126. B.G. Teubner Verlagsgesellschaft, Stuttgart, 1991.

29. J. D. Ullman. *Principles of Database and Knowledge-Base Systems – Volume II: The New Technologies*. Computer Science Press, 1989.

30. R. van der Meyden. The complexity of querying indefinite data about linearly ordered domains. In *Eleventh ACM Symp. on Principles of Database Systems*, pp. 331–345, San Diego, CA, June 1992.

31. X. Zhang and Z. M. Ozsoyoğlu. On efficient reasoning with implication constraints. In *Third Intl. Conf. on Deductive and Object-Oriented Databases*, Phoenix, AZ, Dec. 1993.

Constraint Objects

Divesh Srivastava[1], Raghu Ramakrishnan[2], Peter Z. Revesz[3]

[1] AT&T Bell Laboratories, Murray Hill, NJ 07974, USA
[2] University of Wisconsin, Madison, WI 53706, USA
[3] University of Nebraska, Lincoln, NE 68588, USA

Abstract. We describe the Constraint Object Data Model (CODM), which enhances an object-based data model with existential constraints to naturally represent partially specified information. We present the Constraint Object Query Language (COQL), a declarative, rule-based, language that can be used to infer relationships about and monotonically refine information represented in the CODM. COQL has a model-theoretic and a fixpoint semantics based on the notions of constraint entailment and "proofs in all possible worlds". We also provide a novel polynomial-time algorithm for quantifier elimination for set-order constraints, a restricted class of set constraints that uses $\in$ and $\subseteq$.

1 Introduction

Object-oriented database (OODB) systems will, most probably, have a significant role to play in the next generation of commercial database systems. While OODB systems have a sophisticated collection of features for data modeling, current-day OODB systems provide little or no support for representing and manipulating partially specified values.

For example, suppose that an OODB is used to represent knowledge about plays and playwrights. If Shakespeare's year of birth were known to be 1564, this could be represented easily in the database. However, historians do not have complete information about playwrights such as Shakespeare; they only have estimates of his date of birth and when he wrote his various plays. Partial information about Shakespeare's year of birth can be naturally represented as a conjunction of *constraints*, Shakespeare.Year_of_birth $\geq$ 1560 $\wedge$ Shakespeare.Year_of_birth $\leq$ 1570.

Occasionally these estimates are refined reflecting the results of new research. For example, suppose research determined that Shakespeare could have been born no later than 1565. Then the information about Shakespeare's year of birth can be refined by conjoining the constraint, Shakespeare.Year_of_birth $\leq$ 1565, to the previous conjunction of constraints.

Combining constraints with the notion of objects with unique identifiers offers a powerful mechanism for constraint specification and refinement. Our technical contributions in this paper are as follows:

The electronic mail addresses of the authors are divesh@research.att.com, raghu@cs.wisc.edu and revesz@cse.unl.edu.

1. We describe how an object-based data model can be enhanced with (existential) constraints to naturally represent partially specified information (Section 2). We refer to this as the Constraint Object Data Model (CODM).
2. We present a declarative, rule-based language that can be used to manipulate information represented in the CODM. We refer to this as the Constraint Object Query Language (COQL) (Section 3). COQL has a model-theoretic and a fixpoint semantics, based on the notions of constraint entailment and "proofs in all possible worlds". One of the novel features of COQL is the notion of *monotonic refinement* of partial information in object-based databases.
3. We present a novel polynomial-time algorithm for quantifier elimination for a restricted class of set constraints that uses $\in$ and $\subseteq$ (Section 4). We refer to this class as *set-order* constraints. The quantifier elimination algorithm can be used to check entailment of conjunctions of set-order constraints in polynomial time.

Both the constraint object data model and the constraint object query language are easily extended to compactly represent sets of fully specified values using universal constraints, and manipulate such values using a declarative, rule-based language, following the approach of [5, 7]. Indeed, it appears that both existential and universal constraints are instances of a more general paradigm—in essence, an underlying set of values is defined intensionally, and a number of different interpretations arise by considering various operations on this set. For reasons of space, we do not pursue this further in the paper.

Integration of constraints with objects has also been considered in [2, 3]. Their work differs from ours, since their languages, Kaleidoscope'90 and Kaleidoscope'91, are imperative languages. We are interested in the incorporation of constraints into objects in a more declarative setting.

This paper is based on work in progress, and the various ideas are motivated primarily through examples.

2 Constraint Object Data Model

The Constraint Object Data Model (CODM) allows facts (tuples) as well as objects, which are essentially facts with unique identifiers [1]. The novel feature is that certain attribute values can be "don't know" nulls whose possible values are specified using constraints. We refer to attributes that can take on such values as *E-attributes*. Relations and classes are collections of facts and objects, respectively.[4]

Conceptually, all the constraints on E-attributes are maintained globally. This allows for specification of, e.g., inter-object constraints, which are very useful in many situations. However, in many of the examples discussed in the paper it suffices to associate constraints with the objects whose E-attributes

---

[4] Classes can be organized into an inheritance hierarchy; however, this is orthogonal to our discussion, and we do not deal with inheritance in this paper.

they constrain; when possible, we depict the constraints in this fashion for ease of understanding.

Example 1 (Playwrights and Plays). There are two classes of objects in the database: *playwrights* and *plays*. Partial information is represented about the year of composition of the plays, the writers of the plays, and the year of birth of the playwrights.

playwrights			
Oid	Name	Year_of_birth	Constraints
oid1	Shakespeare	$Y1$	$Y1 \leq 1570 \wedge Y1 \geq 1560$
oid2	Fletcher	$Y2$	
oid3	Kalidasa	$Y3$	$Y3 \leq 1000$

The constraints are *existential* constraints in that the value of the E-attribute is some unique value from the domain satisfying these constraints. Note that there is no information on Fletcher's year of birth, which is equivalent to stating that Fletcher could have been born in any year.

plays				
Oid	Name	Writers	Year_of composition	Constraints
oid10	Othello	{ oid1 }	$Y10$	$(Y10 \leq 1605 \wedge Y10 \geq 1601) \vee$ $(Y10 \leq 1598 \wedge Y10 \geq 1595)$
oid11	Macbeth	{ oid1 }	$Y11$	$Y11 \leq 1608 \wedge Y11 \geq 1604$
oid12	Henry VIII	$S1$	$Y12$	$Y12 \leq 1613 \wedge Y12 \geq 1608 \wedge$ $oid2 \in S1 \wedge S1 \subseteq \{ oid1, oid2 \}$
oid13	Meghdoot	{ oid3 }	$Y13$	$Y13 \leq 1050$

The form of the constraints allowed depends on the types of the E-attributes. The Year_of_birth and the Year_of_composition E-attributes are of type integer, and hence they are constrained using arithmetic constraints over integers. Similarly, the Writers E-attribute of *plays* is of type set of playwrights and it is constrained using set constraints $\supseteq, \subseteq, \in$. For example, the constraint on the Writers attribute of oid12 indicates that either Fletcher is the sole writer of Henry VIII, or Fletcher and Shakespeare are joint writers of that play; this represents partial information on the set of playwrights. □

We note that the Constraint Object Data Model only allows *first-order* constraints, i.e., the names and types of the attributes are fixed for each fact and object, and cannot be partially specified using constraints; only the values of these attributes can be partially specified using constraints.

3 Constraint Object Query Language

We present the declarative Constraint Object Query Language (COQL) that can be used to reason with facts and objects in the CODM. A COQL program is a collection of rules similar to Horn rules, where each rule has a body and a head. The body of a rule is a conjunction of literals and constraints, and the head of the rule can be either a positive literal or a constraint. COQL allows arbitrary constraints, not just conjunctions of primitive constraints, to occur in the bodies and heads of program rules.

3.1 COQL: Inferring New Relationships

A COQL program can be used to infer new relationships, as facts, between existing objects and facts. For simplicity, we assume that COQL rules do not create new objects; this condition can be checked syntactically by having a safety requirement, that any object identifier appearing in the head of a COQL rule also appears in a body literal of that rule. Our results are orthogonal to proposals that permit the creation of new objects using rules (e.g., [6]), and can be combined with them in a clean fashion. We now present some example queries to motivate the inference of new relationships using COQL rules.

Example 2 (Selection). Consider the database of plays and playwrights from Example 1. Suppose we want to know the names of all playwrights born before the year 1700. The following rule expresses this query, using the dot notation for accessing object attributes:

q1 (P.Name) : – playwrights (P), P.Year_of_birth < 1700.

If the years of birth of all the playwrights in the database are completely specified, the meaning of this query is straightforward. In the presence of partial information about the years of birth of the playwrights, there are (at least) three possible semantics that can be used to assign meaning to this query.

1. Proof/Truth in *at least one possible world*.
   Under this semantics, a playwright "satisfies" the query if *at least one* assignment of fully specified values to the Year_of_birth attribute of the playwright, consistent with the object constraints, satisfies the query. All three playwrights, Shakespeare, Fletcher and Kalidasa would be retrieved as answers to the query under this semantics. Shakespeare could have been born in 1564, Fletcher in 1600 and Kalidasa in 975; these values are consistent with the constraints on the object attributes.
   To compute this answer set to the query, we need to check *satisfiability* of the conjunction of constraints present in the object and the constraints present in the query. For example, the conjunction of constraints oid3.Year_of_birth $\leq$ 1000 $\land$ oid3.Year_of_birth < 1700 (where oid3 is the identifier of the object representing Kalidasa) is satisfiable in the domain of integers.

2. Truth in *all possible worlds*.
   Under this semantics, a playwright "satisfies" the query if *every* assignment of a fully specified value to the Year_of_birth attribute of the playwright, consistent with the object constraints, satisfies the query. Only Shakespeare

and Kalidasa would be retrieved as answers to the query under this semantics. Fletcher could have been born in 1800; this value is consistent with the object constraints, while being inconsistent with the query constraints.

3. Proofs in *all possible worlds*.

Under this semantics, a playwright "satisfies" the query if: (1) *every* assignment of a fully specified value to the Year_of_birth attribute of the playwright, consistent with the object constraints, satisfies the query, and (2) the derivation trees corresponding to each of the possible assignments are "similar". (The derivation trees constitute the "proofs".) In this example, the answers to the query under this semantics are the same as under the "truth in all possible worlds" semantics.

To compute this answer set to the query, we need to check that the constraints present in the objects *entail* (i.e., imply) the query constraints. For example, the object constraints oid1.Year_of_birth $\leq$ 1570 $\wedge$ oid1.Year_of_birth $\geq$ 1560 entail the (instantiated) query constraint oid1.Year_of_birth $<$ 1700 (where oid1 is the identifier of the object representing Shakespeare) in the domain of integers. However, the object constraints associated with Fletcher do not entail the (instantiated) query constraint oid2.Year_of_birth $<$ 1700 (where oid2 is the identifier of the object representing Fletcher) in the domain of integers.

The first two semantics are closely related to the semantics of Imielinski et al. [4] for OR-objects; we do not elaborate on these relationships in the paper for lack of space. □

Example 3 (Set Constraints). Suppose we want to know the names of all the plays written by Shakespeare. The following rule expresses the query:

q3 (P.Name) : − plays (P), playwrights (W), W.Name = "Shakespeare",
P.Writers = S, W ∈ S.

Under the "proof/truth in at least one possible world" semantics, the play Henry VIII would be an answer (since Shakespeare could have written it together with Fletcher) as would Othello and Macbeth (since Shakespeare is known to have written these). The first answer can be obtained by checking the *satisfiability* of the conjunction of the object constraints oid2 ∈ oid12.Writers $\wedge$ oid12.Writers ⊆ { oid1, oid2 } with the (instantiated) query constraint oid1 ∈ oid12.Writers.

Under the "truth in all possible worlds" as well as "proofs in all possible worlds" semantics, however, Henry VIII would not be an answer. This is because the object constraints oid2 ∈ oid12.Writers $\wedge$ oid12.Writers ⊆ { oid1, oid2 } do not entail the (instantiated) query constraint oid1 ∈ oid12.Writers. Othello and Macbeth would be the only answers in this case. □

3.2 COQL: Monotonically Refining Objects

COQL programs can also be used to *monotonically refine* objects, in response to additional information available about the objects. For example, suppose research determined that Shakespeare could have been born no later than 1565, then the object **Shakespeare** can be refined by conjoining the constraint **Shakespeare.Year_of_birth** $\leq$ 1565.

The notion of *declarative monotonic refinement* of partially specified objects is one of the novel contributions of this paper. Object refinement can be formalized in terms of a lattice structure describing the possible states of an object, with a given information theoretic ordering. The value $\perp$ corresponds to having no information about the attribute values of the object, and $\top$ corresponds to having inconsistent information about the object. (There are many different complete and consistent values for the object attributes; each of these is just below $\top$ in this information lattice.) Object refinement now can be thought of as moving up this information lattice.

We give an example of declarative, rule-based object attribute refinement next. The body of a refinement rule is similar to the body of a rule used to infer new relationships. The head of a refinement rule, on the other hand, is a constraint (not necessarily a conjunction of primitive constraints).

Example 4 (Refining Attributes of Objects). The following refinement rule expresses the intuition that a playwright cannot write a play before birth:

W.Year_of_birth $\leq$ P.Year_of_composition : $-$ playwrights (W),
plays (P), W $\in$ P.Writers.

The right hand side (body) of the rule is the condition, and the left hand side (head) is the action of the rule. If the body is satisfied, then the instantiated head constraint is conjoined to the (global) constraints on the E-attributes. (This is an example where the instantiated head constraint is an inter-object constraint, and hence cannot be associated with a single object.)

In the presence of partial information, we give a meaning to refinement rules based on the "proofs in all possible worlds" semantics. (In Example 6, we show that the "proof/truth in at least one possible world" is order dependent, and that the "truth in all possible worlds" semantics requires case-based reasoning, which is computationally intractable.) In this case, we would conjoin the constraint Fletcher.Year_of_birth $\leq$ Henry VIII.Year_of_composition to the global collection of constraints. Conflicting refinements could, of course, result in an inconsistent constraint set. $\square$

Rules that refine objects can be combined cleanly with rules that infer relationships between existing objects in COQL programs. For example, the rule in Example 4 can be combined with the rule in Example 2. In the resulting program, Fletcher would also be an answer to the query $q1$ under the "proofs in all possible worlds" semantics.

Rules that refine objects can be used to create new objects as well, in a fashion similar to the proposals that permit the creation of new objects using rules (e.g., [6]). Our technique avoids the problem faced by many object-creating proposals of ensuring that the "same" object is not created multiple times. If an object is created multiple times, possibly with different constraints on the E-attributes, the result is to conjoin all the constraints on the E-attributes.

4 Set-Order Constraints

In the examples discussed in the paper, we used order constraints (i.e., arithmetic constraints involving $<, \leq, =, \geq$ and $>$, but no arithmetic functions such as $+, -$ or $*$) and *set-order* constraints, a restricted form of set constraints involving $\in, \subseteq$ and $\supseteq$, but no set functions such as $\cup$ and $\cap$. Techniques for quantifier elimination, checking satisfaction and entailment for order constraints over various domains are known (see [9], for instance). We now briefly describe a polynomial-time quantifier elimination algorithm for a conjunction of set-order constraints. Satisfaction and entailment of conjunctions of set-order constraints can be solved (in polynomial-time) using our quantifier elimination algorithm.

4.1 Quantifier Elimination for Set-Order Constraints

We will use the symbols $\hat{X}, \hat{Y}, \hat{Z}$ to denote set variables that range over finite sets of elements of type D. A *set-order* constraint is of one of the following types:

$$c \in \hat{X}, \hat{X} \subseteq s, s \subseteq \hat{X}, \hat{X} \subseteq \hat{Y}$$

where c is a constant of type D, and s is a set of constants of type D.

---

procedure Quantifier_Elimination

Input: A conjunction Q of set-order constraints and a set variable $\hat{Y}$ to be eliminated.
Output: A conjunction Q' of set-order constraints, such that $\exists \hat{Y} Q$ and Q' are equivalent.
Algorithm: Do the following steps in order:

1. First rewrite every constraint of the form $c \in \hat{X}$ into $\{c\} \subseteq \hat{X}$.
2. For each set variable $\hat{X}$, take the union of all sets s, such that $s \subseteq \hat{X}$ is in the conjunction. Let the union be the set L_X. Delete all constraints of the form $s \subseteq \hat{X}$ from the conjunction, and add the constraint $L_X \subseteq \hat{X}$ to the conjunction.
3. For each set variable $\hat{X}$ take the intersection of all sets s, such that $\hat{X} \subseteq s$ is in the conjunction. Let the intersection be the set U_X. Delete all constraints of the form $\hat{X} \subseteq s$ from the conjunction and add the constraint $\hat{X} \subseteq U_X$.
4. For each pair of constraints of the form $N \subseteq \hat{Y}$ and $\hat{Y} \subseteq M$, where $\hat{Y}$ is the set variable to be eliminated, and N and M are either set variables or sets of constants, add the constraint $N \subseteq M$. After this is done for each such pair, delete all constraints in which $\hat{Y}$ occurs. Repeat steps 2 and 3.
5. Check each constraint of the form $s_1 \subseteq s_2$ where s_1 and s_2 are sets of constants from domain D. If they are all satisfied, delete all such constraints from the conjunction and return the conjunction of the remaining constraints. If any one of these constraints is not satisfied, then return FALSE. □

Example 5 (Quantifier elimination). Let Q be the following conjunction of set-order constraints: $3 \in \hat{Z}, \hat{Z} \subseteq \hat{X}, \hat{X} \subseteq \{3,4,8,9\}, \hat{X} \subseteq \hat{Y}, \hat{Y} \subseteq \{2,3,5,7,8\}$. From constraint Q we can eliminate set variable $\hat{Y}$ as follows:

Step 1 : Replace $3 \in \hat{Z}$ by $\{3\} \subseteq \hat{Z}$.
Steps 2-3 : No change.
Step 4 : We get $\{3\} \subseteq \hat{Z}, \hat{Z} \subseteq \hat{X}, \hat{X} \subseteq \{3,4,8,9\}, \hat{X} \subseteq \{2,3,5,7,8\}$.
Step 2 : No change.
Step 3 : We get $\{3\} \subseteq \hat{Z}, \hat{Z} \subseteq \hat{X}, \hat{X} \subseteq \{3,8\}$.
Step 5 : No change. Hence, we return $\{3\} \subseteq \hat{Z}, \hat{Z} \subseteq \hat{X}, \hat{X} \subseteq \{3,8\}$.

Suppose now, that we also want to eliminate set variable $\hat{Z}$. This will be done by quantifier elimination algorithm as follows:

Steps 1–3 : No change.
Step 4 : We get $\{3\} \subseteq \hat{X}, \hat{X} \subseteq \{3,8\}$.
Step 5 : No change. Hence, we return $\{3\} \subseteq \hat{X}, \hat{X} \subseteq \{3,8\}$.   □

Theorem 1. *Let Q be a conjunction of set-order constraints and $\hat{Y}$ be a set variable. The quantifier elimination algorithm on input Q and $\hat{Y}$ will yield in PTIME, in the size of Q, a conjunction of set-order constraints Q' such that $\exists \hat{Y} Q$ and Q' are equivalent.*

Further, if Q' has n set variables, then the number of conjuncts in Q' is at most $n^2 + 2*n$.   □

Checking the entailment of a conjunction of set-order constraints Q_2 by a conjunction of set-order constraints Q_1 can be done by reduction to a number of entailment checks of each set-order constraint in Q_2 by the conjunction Q_1. The following result shows how the quantifier elimination algorithm can be used to check for entailment of a set-order constraint by an arbitrarily large conjunction of set-order constraints.

Theorem 2. *Let Q be a conjunction of set-order constraints over the set variables $\hat{X}_1, \ldots, \hat{X}_m$. Let Q_1 be the result of elimination of variables $\hat{X}_3, \ldots, \hat{X}_m$ from Q. Let Q_2 be the result of elimination of variable $\hat{X}_2$ from Q_1. Then, (1) Q entails $\hat{X}_1 \subseteq \hat{X}_2$ if and only if Q_1 entails $\hat{X}_1 \subseteq \hat{X}_2$, (2) Q entails $\hat{X}_1 \subseteq s$ if and only if Q_2 entails $\hat{X}_1 \subseteq s$, and (3) Q entails $s \subseteq \hat{X}_1$ if and only if Q_2 entails $s \subseteq \hat{X}_1$.*   □

5   COQL: Model Theory and Fixpoint Semantics

COQL has a model-theoretic and a fixpoint semantics, based on the notions of constraint entailment and "proofs in all possible worlds". The semantics of COQL is based on the notion of "proofs in all possible worlds' for several reasons.

First, if we adopted the "proof/truth in at least one possible world" semantics, object refinement becomes order dependent, and the program cannot be assigned a unique meaning. Under the "proofs in all possible worlds" semantics, object refinement is order independent. The following example illustrates this:

Example 6 (Order Dependence). Consider a program with the following two refinement rules:[5]

W.Year_of_birth ≤ 1560 : − playwrights (W), W.Year_of_birth ≤ 1565.
W.Year_of_birth ≥ 1570 : − playwrights (W), W.Year_of_birth ≥ 1566.

In Example 1, Shakespeare's year of birth is known to be between 1560 and 1570. Under the "proof/truth in at least one possible world" semantics, the order in which these two rules are applied could result in Shakespeare's year of birth being refined to either 1560 or 1570. (Once one of the rules is applied, the other rule becomes inapplicable.) Under the "proofs in all possible worlds" semantics, neither of these rules would be applicable, and Shakespeare's year of birth would not be refined. □

Second, if we adopted the "truth in all possible worlds" semantics, answering a query is computationally intractable. The "proofs in all possible worlds" semantics of a program can, however, be computed more efficiently.

Example 7 (Computational Intractability). Consider a program with the following two refinement rules, and the objects from Example 1:

W.Year_of_birth = 1565 : − playwrights (W), W.Year_of_birth ≤ 1566.
W.Year_of_birth = 1565 : − playwrights (W), W.Year_of_birth ≥ 1564.

The constraint Shakespeare.Year_of_birth = 1565 would be conjoined to the object constraints, in each of the possible worlds consistent with the constraints on Shakespeare's age, and hence under the "truth in all possible worlds" semantics. Determining this, however, requires reasoning by cases, which can be computationally intractable. Under the "proofs in all possible worlds" semantics, Shakespeare's year of birth would not be refined, since the different possible worlds have different justifications for the addition of this constraint. □

We briefly describe the model-theoretic and fixpoint semantics here; details are omitted for reasons of space. Consider a COQL program P, and a collection of facts and objects I. We assume that all the variables in each rule body of P have been standardized apart (i.e., no variable occurs more than once in the body literals of a rule), possibly by introducing equality constraints between some of the variables; this is important for checking for entailment.

5.1 Model-theoretic Semantics

An assignment of facts and objects to the body literals of a rule r of program P makes the body of r *true* if the constraints associated with the facts and the objects *entail* the (instantiated) constraints between the variables present in the body of rule r. A relationship inferring rule r is true in I if, for every assignment

---

[5] Although the rules are unintuitive, this example is purely for illustrating a point.

of facts and objects to the body literals of r that makes the body true, the instantiated head fact of rule r is *entailed* by (the constraints associated with) some fact f in I. An object refinement rule r is true in I if, for every assignment of facts and objects to the body literals of r that makes the body true, the instantiated head object o_r occurs in I, and the instantiated head constraint of the rule is *entailed* by the object constraints associated with o_r. The collection I of facts and objects is said to be a *model* of P if each program rule is true in I.

The model-theoretic semantics of COQL is a *least model* semantics, where model M_1 is "lesser than" model M_2, denoted $M_1 \preceq M_2$, if for each fact (or object) f_1 in M_1, there is a fact (or object) f_2 in M_2, such that f_2 entails f_1. The existence of a least model is guaranteed since the "intersection" of COQL program models is also a COQL program model.

5.2 Fixpoint semantics

The fixpoint semantics is defined in terms of an immediate consequence operator, T_P. Given the collection I of facts and objects, we define $T_P(I)$ as follows. Let r be a rule. If there is an assignment of facts and objects from I to literals in the body of r such that the body is true, then the instantiated head fact (or head object) is in $T_P(I)$.

The fixpoint semantics of COQL is based on the least fixpoint of the T_P operator, which can be computed starting from the empty collection of facts and objects, as $T_P(\emptyset) \cup T_P(T_P(\emptyset)) \cup \ldots$. In computing the unions, all the object constraints have to be conjoined together. The existence of the least fixpoint is guaranteed by the monotonicity of the T_P operator.

We conjecture that a result such as the following holds for COQL programs.

Proposition 3. *Consider a COQL program P. It has a least model and a least fixpoint, which coincide.* □

To prove such a result requires that we develop the underlying framework more rigorously than we have done in this abstract. We are currently working on developing such a machinery.

The techniques of [5] can be used to show that if a COQL program and facts/objects use only arithmetic order constraints, the answer to a query can be computed in PTIME data complexity. A similar result can be obtained for the case of COQL programs with only refinement rules and set-order constraints.

6 Conclusions and Future Work

We presented the Constraint Object Data Model, and the Constraint Object Query Language, which we believe go a long way in incorporating the ability to represent and manipulate partially specified information in object-based database systems.

There are many interesting directions to pursue. Determining classes of programs with tractable data complexity is extremely important. Optimizing COQL queries is another important direction of research. Stuckey and Sudarshan [8] present compilation techniques for query constraints in logic programs, essentially extending Magic sets to handle general query constraints, not just equality constraints on queries. It would be interesting to see how these techniques apply to COQL programs. Finally, many of our ideas and techniques seem applicable to temporal database languages. Exploring the interconnections is likely to be an interesting direction of research.

Acknowledgements

The research of Raghu Ramakrishnan was supported by a David and Lucile Packard Foundation Fellowship in Science and Engineering, a Presidential Young Investigator Award with matching grants from DEC, Tandem and Xerox, and NSF grant IRI-9011563. The research of Peter Z. Revesz was supported by an Oliver E. Bird faculty fellowship.

References

1. S. Abiteboul and P. C. Kanellakis. Object identity as a query language primitive. In *Proceedings of the ACM SIGMOD Conference on Management of Data*, pages 159–173, Portland, Oregon, June 1989.
2. B. N. Freeman-Benson and A. Borning. The design and implementation of Kaleidoscope'90: A constraint imperative programming language. In *Proceedings of the International Conference on Computer Languages*, pages 174–180, Apr. 1992.
3. B. N. Freeman-Benson and A. Borning. Integrating constraints with an object-oriented language. In *Proceedings of the European Conference on Object-Oriented Programming*, pages 268–286, June 1992.
4. T. Imielinski, S. Naqvi, and K. Vadaparty. Incomplete objects—a data model for design and planning applications. In *Proceedings of the ACM SIGMOD Conference on Management of Data*, pages 288–297, Denver, CO, May 1991.
5. P. C. Kanellakis, G. M. Kuper, and P. Z. Revesz. Constraint query languages. In *Proceedings of the Ninth ACM Symposium on Principles of Database Systems*, pages 299–313, Nashville, Tennessee, Apr. 1990.
6. M. Kifer, W. Kim, and Y. Sagiv. Querying object-oriented databases. In *Proceedings of the ACM SIGMOD Conference on Management of Data*, pages 393–402, San Diego, California, 1992.
7. R. Ramakrishnan. Magic templates: A spellbinding approach to logic programs. *Journal of Logic Programming*, 11(3):189–216, 1991.
8. P. J. Stuckey and S. Sudarshan. Compiling query constraints. In *Proceedings of the ACM Symposium on Principles of Database Systems*, May 1994.
9. J. D. Ullman. *Principles of Database and Knowledge-Base Systems, Volumes I and II*. Computer Science Press, 1989.

Specification and Verification
of Constraint-Based Dynamic Systems

Ying Zhang and Alan K. Mackworth*

Department of Computer Science
University of British Columbia
Vancouver, B.C.
Canada V6T 1Z4
zhang,mack@cs.ubc.ca

Abstract. Constraint satisfaction can be seen as a dynamic process that approaches the solution set of the given constraints asymptotically [6]. Constraint programming is seen as creating a dynamic system with the required property. We have developed a semantic model for dynamic systems, Constraint Nets, which serves as a useful abstract target machine for constraint programming languages, providing both semantics and pragmatics. Generalizing, here we view a constraint-based dynamic system as a dynamic system which approaches the solution set of the given constraints persistently. Most robotic systems are constraint-based dynamic systems with tasks specified as constraints. In this paper, we further explore the specification and verification of constraint-based dynamic systems. We first develop generalized ∀-automata for the specification and verification of general (hybrid) dynamic systems, then explicate the relationship between constraint-based dynamic systems and their requirements specification.

1 Motivation and Introduction

We have previously proposed viewing constraints as relations and constraint satisfaction as a dynamic process of approaching the solution set of the constraints asymptotically [6]. Under this view, constraint programming is the creation of a dynamic system with the required property. We have developed a semantic model for dynamic systems, Constraint Nets, which serves as a useful abstract target machine for constraint programming languages, providing both semantics and pragmatics. Properties of various discrete and continuous constraint methods for constraint programming have also been examined [6].

Generalizing, here we consider a constraint-based dynamic system as a dynamic system which approaches the solution set of the given constraints persistently. One of the motivations for this view is to design and analyze a robotic system composed of a controller that is coupled to a plant and an environment.

---

* Shell Canada Fellow, Canadian Institute for Advanced Research

The required properties of the controller may be specified as a set of constraints, which, in general, vary with time. Thus, the controller should be synthesized so as to solve the constraints on-line. Consider a tracking system where the target may move from time to time. A well-designed tracking control system has to ensure that the target can be tracked down persistently.

Here we start with general concepts of dynamic systems using abstract notions of time, domains and traces. With this abstraction, hybrid as well as discrete and continuous dynamic systems can be studied in a unitary framework. The behavior of a dynamic system is then defined as the set of possible traces produced by the system.

In order to specify required properties of a dynamic system, we develop a formal specification language, a generalized version of ∀-automata [3]. In order to verify that the behavior of a dynamic system satisfies its requirements specification, we develop a formal model checking method with generalized Liapunov functions.

A constraint-based dynamic system is a special type of dynamic system. We explore the properties of constraint-based dynamic systems and constraint-based requirements specification, then relate behavior verification to control synthesis.

The rest of this paper is organized as follows. Section 2 briefly presents concepts of general dynamic systems and constraint net modeling. Section 3 develops generalized ∀-automata for specifying and verifying required properties of dynamic systems. Section 4 characterizes constraint-based dynamic systems and requirements specification. Section 5 concludes the paper and points out related work.

2 General Dynamic Systems

In this section, we first introduce some basic concepts in general dynamic systems: time, domains and traces, then present a formal model for general dynamic systems.

2.1 Concepts in dynamic systems

In order to model dynamic systems in a unitary framework, we present abstract notions of time, domains and traces. Both time structures and domains are defined on metric spaces.

Let $\mathcal{R}^+$ be the set of nonnegative real numbers. A *metric space* is a pair $\langle X, d \rangle$ where X is a set and $d : X \times X \to \mathcal{R}^+$ is a *metric* defined on X, satisfying the following axioms for all $x, y, z \in X$:

1. $d(x, y) = d(y, x)$.
2. $d(x, y) + d(y, z) \geq d(x, z)$.
3. $d(x, y) = 0$ iff $x = y$.

In a metric space $\langle X, d \rangle$, $d(x, y)$ is called "the distance between x and y." We will use X to denote metric space $\langle X, d \rangle$ if no ambiguity arises.

A *time structure* is a metric space $\langle T, d \rangle$ where T is a linearly ordered set with a least element 0 and d is a metric satisfying that for all $t_0 \leq t_1 \leq t_2, d(t_0, t_2) = d(t_0, t_1) + d(t_1, t_2)$. We will use T to denote time structure $\langle T, d \rangle$ if no ambiguity arises. In this paper, we consider a time structure T with the following properties: (1) T is *infinite*, i.e., $\sup_{t \in T} \{d(0, t)\} = \infty$, and (2) T is *complete*, i.e., if $T \subset T$ has an upper bound, T has a least upper bound. T can be either discrete or continuous. For example, the set of natural numbers defines discrete time and the set of nonnegative real numbers defines continuous time.

Let X be a metric space representing a discrete or continuous *domain*. A *trace* $v : T \to X$ is a function from time to a domain.

2.2 Constraint Nets: a model for dynamic systems

We have developed a semantic model, Constraint Nets, for general (hybrid) dynamic systems [8]. We have used the Constraint Net model as an abstract target machine for constraint programming languages [6], while constraint programming is considered as designing a dynamic system that approaches the solution set of the given constraints asymptotically.

Intuitively, a constraint net consists of a finite set of locations, a finite set of transductions, each with a finite set of input ports and an output port, and a finite set of connections between locations and ports of transductions. A location can be regarded as a wire, a channel, a variable, or a memory cell, whose values may change over time. A transduction is a mapping from input traces to output traces, with the causal restriction, viz., the output value at any time is determined by the input values up to that time. For example, a temporal integration with an initial value is a typical transduction on continuous time and any state automaton with an initial state defines a transduction on discrete time.

A location l is the *output location* of a transduction F iff it connects to the output port of F; l is an *input location* of F iff it connects to an input port of F. Let CN be a constraint net. A location is an *output location* of CN if it is an output location of some transduction in CN; it is otherwise an *input location* of CN. CN is *open* if there are input locations; it is otherwise *closed*.

Semantically, a transduction F denotes an equation $l_0 = F(l_1, \ldots, l_n)$ where l_0 is the output location of F and $\langle l_1, \ldots, l_n \rangle$ is the tuple of input locations of F. A constraint net CN denotes a set of equations, each corresponds to a transduction in CN. The semantics of CN, denoted $[\![CN]\!]$, is a "solution" of the set of equations [8], which is a transduction from input to output traces. The *behavior* of a dynamic system is defined as a set of possible input/output traces produced by the system. We will also use $[\![CN]\!]$ to denote the behavior of a dynamic system modeled by CN if no ambiguity arises.

We have modeled two types of constraint solver, state transition systems and state integration systems, in constraint nets. The former models discrete dynamic processes and the latter models continuous dynamic processes [6]. Hybrid dynamic systems, with both discrete and continuous components, can also be modeled in constraint nets [7, 8].

We illustrate the constraint net modeling with two simple examples. Without loss of generality, let time be the set of nonnegative real numbers $\mathcal{R}^+$ and domains be the set (or product) of real numbers $\mathcal{R}$.

Consider a "standard" example of *Cat and Mouse* modified from [1]. Suppose a cat and a mouse start running from initial positions X_c and X_m respectively, $X_c > X_m > 0$, with constant velocities $V_c < V_m < 0$. Both of them will stop running when the cat catches the mouse, or the mouse runs into the hole in the wall at 0. The behavior of this system is modeled by the following set of equations CM_1:

$$x_c = \int (X_c)(V_c \cdot c), \quad x_m = \int (X_m)(V_m \cdot c), \quad c = (x_c > x_m) \wedge (x_m > 0)$$

where $\int(X)$ is a temporal integration with initial state X. At any time, c is 1 if the running condition $(x_c > x_m) \wedge (x_m > 0)$ is satisfied and 0 otherwise. This is a closed system. If the cat catches the mouse before the mouse runs into the hole in the wall at 0, i.e., $0 \le x_c \le x_m$, the cat wins; if the mouse runs into the hole before the cat, i.e., $x_m \le 0 \le x_c$, the mouse wins.

Consider another *Cat and Mouse* problem, where the controller of the cat is synthesized from its requirements specification, i.e., $x_c = x_m$. Suppose the plant of the cat obeys the dynamics $u = \dot{x}_c$ where u is the control input, i.e., the velocity of the cat is controlled. One possible design for the cat controller uses the gradient descent method [6] on the energy function $(x_m - x_c)^2$ to synthesize the feedback control law $u = k \cdot (x_m - x_c), k > 0$ where the distance between the cat and the mouse $x_m - x_c$ can be sensed by the cat. The cat can be modeled as an open constraint net with the following set of equations CM_2:

$$x_c = \int (X_c)(u), \quad u = k \cdot (x_m - x_c).$$

Will the cat catch the mouse?

3 Generalized $\forall$-Automata

While modeling focuses on the underlying structure of a system — the organization and coordination of components or subsystems — the overall behavior of the modeled system is not explicitly expressed. However, for many situations, it is important to specify some global properties and guarantee that these properties hold in the proposed design.

We advocate a formal approach to specifying required properties and to verifying the relationship between the behavior of a dynamic system and its requirements specification. A trace $v : T \to X$ is a generalization of a sequence. In fact, when T is the set of natural numbers, v is an infinite sequence. A set of sequences defines a conventional formal language. If we take the behavior of a system as a language and a specification as an automaton, then verification is to check the inclusion relation between the language of the system and the language accepted by the automaton.

∀-automata [3] are non-deterministic finite state automata over infinite sequences. These automata were proposed as a formalism for the specification and verification of temporal properties of concurrent programs. In this section, we generalize ∀-automata to specify languages composed of traces on continuous as well as discrete time, and modify the formal verification method [3] by generalizing both Liapunov functions [6] and the method of continuous induction [2].

3.1   Requirements specification

Let an *assertion* be a logical formula defined on a domain X, i.e., an assertion α for a value $x \in X$ will be evaluated to either *true*, denoted $x \models \alpha$, or *false*, denoted $x \not\models \alpha$.

A ∀-*automaton* $\mathcal{A}$ is a quintuple $\langle Q, R, S, e, c \rangle$ where Q is a finite set of *automaton-states*, $R \subseteq Q$ is a set of *recurrent states* and $S \subseteq Q$ is a set of *stable states*. With each $q \in Q$, we associate an assertion $e(q)$, which characterizes the *entry condition* under which the automaton may start its activity in q. With each pair $q, q' \in Q$, we associate an assertion $c(q, q')$, which characterizes the *transition condition* under which the automaton may move from q to q'. R and S are the generalization of *accepting* states to the case of infinite inputs. We denote by $B = Q - (R \cup S)$ the set of *non-accepting (bad)* states.

Let $\mathcal{T}$ be a time structure and $v : \mathcal{T} \to X$ be a trace. A *run* of $\mathcal{A}$ over v is a trace $r : \mathcal{T} \to Q$ satisfying

1. *Initiality*: $v(0) \models e(r(0))$;
2. *Consecution*:
   - inductivity: $\forall t > 0, \exists q \in Q, t' < t, \forall t'', t' \leq t'' < t, r(t'') = q$ and $v(t) \models c(r(t''), r(t))$, and
   - continuity: $\forall t, \exists q \in Q, t' > t, \forall t'', t < t'' < t', r(t'') = q$ and $v(t'') \models c(r(t), r(t''))$.

A trace v is *specifiable* by $\mathcal{A}$ iff there is a run of $\mathcal{A}$ over v. The behavior of a system is *specifiable* by $\mathcal{A}$ iff every trace of the behavior is specifiable.

If r is a run, let $Inf(r)$ be the set of automaton-states appearing "infinitely many times" in r, i.e., $Inf(r) = \{q | \forall t \exists t_0 \geq t, r(t_0) = q\}$. A run r is defined to be *accepting* iff:

1. $Inf(r) \cap R \neq \emptyset$, i.e., *some* of the states appearing infinitely many times in r belong to R, or
2. $Inf(r) \subseteq S$, i.e., *all* the states appearing infinitely many times in r belong to S.

A ∀-automaton $\mathcal{A}$ *accepts* a trace v, written $v \models \mathcal{A}$, iff *all* possible runs of $\mathcal{A}$ over v are accepting; $\mathcal{A}$ *accepts* a behavior $\mathcal{B}$, written $\mathcal{B} \models \mathcal{A}$, iff $\forall v \in \mathcal{B}, v \models \mathcal{A}$.

One of the advantages of using automata as a specification language is its graphical representation. It is useful and illuminating to represent ∀-automata by diagrams. The basic conventions for such representations are the following:

- The automaton-states are depicted by nodes in a directed graph.
- Each initial state is marked by a small arrow, called the *entry arc*, pointing to it.
- Arcs, drawn as arrows, connect some of the states.
- Each recurrent state is depicted by a diamond shape inscribed within a circle.
- Each stable state is depicted by a square inscribed within a circle.

Nodes and arcs are labeled by assertions. A node or an arc that is left unlabeled is considered to be labeled with *true*. The labels define the entry conditions and the transition conditions of the associated automaton as follows:

- Let $q \in Q$ be a node in the diagram. If q is labeled by ψ and the entry arc is labeled by φ, the entry condition $e(q)$ is given by $e(q) = \varphi \wedge \psi$. If there is no entry arc, $e(q) = false$.
- Let q, q' be two nodes in the diagram. If q' is labeled by ϕ, and arcs from q to q' are labeled by $\varphi_i, i = 1 \cdots n$, the transition condition $c(q, q')$ is given by $c(q, q') = (\varphi_1 \vee \cdots \vee \varphi_n) \wedge \psi$. If there is no arc from q to q', $c(q, q') = false$.

This type of automaton is powerful enough to specify various qualitative properties. Some typical required properties are shown in Fig. 1: (a) accepts a trace which satisfies $\neg G$ only in finite time, (b) accepts a trace which never satisfies B, and (c) accepts a trace which will satisfy S in the finite future whenever it satisfies R.

(a)   (b)   (c)

Fig. 1. ∀-automata: (a) reachability (b) safety (c) bounded response

For the *Cat and Mouse* examples, we can have the formal requirements specifications shown in Fig. 2.

3.2 Behavior verification

Given a constraint net model of a discrete- or continuous-time dynamic system, the behavior of the system is obtained from a "solution" of the set of equations denoted by the model. Given a behavior and a ∀-automata specification of requirements, a formal method is developed here for verifying that the behavior satisfies its requirements specification.

For any trace $v : T \to X$, let $\{\varphi\}v\{\psi\}$ denote the validity of the following two consecutive conditions:

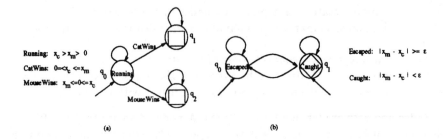

Fig. 2. (a) Either the cat or the mouse wins (b) The cat catches the mouse persistently

- $\{\varphi\}v^-\{\psi\}$: for all $t > 0$, $\exists t' < t, \forall t'', t' \le t'' < t, v(t'') \models \varphi$ implies $v(t) \models \psi$.
- $\{\varphi\}v^+\{\psi\}$: for all t, $v(t) \models \varphi$ implies $\exists t' > t, \forall t'', t < t'' < t', v(t'') \models \psi$.

Let $\mathcal{B}$ be a behavior with time T and domain X, $\Theta = \{v(0)|v \in \mathcal{B}\}$ be the set of initial values of $\mathcal{B}$, and $\mathcal{A} = \langle Q, R, S, e, c \rangle$ be a $\forall$-automaton. A set of assertions $\{\alpha_q\}_{q \in Q}$ is called a set of *invariants* for $\mathcal{B}$ and $\mathcal{A}$ iff

- *Initiality:* $\forall q \in Q, \Theta \wedge e(q) \to \alpha_q$.
- *Consecution:* $\forall v \in \mathcal{B}, \forall q, q' \in Q, \{\alpha_q\}v\{c(q, q') \to \alpha_{q'}\}$.

Without loss of generality, we assume that time is encoded in domain X by $t_c : X \to T$. Given that $\{\alpha_q\}_{q \in Q}$ is a set of invariants for $\mathcal{B}$ and $\mathcal{A}$, a set of partial functions $\{\rho_q\}_{q \in Q} : X \to \mathcal{R}^+$ is called a set of *Liapunov functions* for $\mathcal{B}$ and $\mathcal{A}$ iff the following conditions are satisfied:

- *Definedness:* $\forall q \in Q, \ \alpha_q \to \exists w, \rho_q = w$.
- *Non-increase:* $\forall v \in \mathcal{B}, \forall q \in S, q' \in Q$,

$$\{\alpha_q \wedge \rho_q = w\}v^-\{c(q, q') \to \rho_{q'} \le w\}$$

and $\forall q \in Q, q' \in S$,

$$\{\alpha_q \wedge \rho_q = w\}v^+\{c(q, q') \to \rho_{q'} \le w\}.$$

- *Decrease:* $\forall v \in \mathcal{B}, \exists \epsilon > 0, \forall q \in B, q' \in Q$,

$$\{\alpha_q \wedge \rho_q = w \wedge t_c = t\}v^-\{c(q, q') \to \frac{\rho_{q'} - w}{d(t, t_c)} \le -\epsilon\}$$

and $\forall q \in Q, q' \in B$,

$$\{\alpha_q \wedge \rho_q = w \wedge t_c = t\}v^+\{c(q, q') \to \frac{\rho_{q'} - w}{d(t, t_c)} \le -\epsilon\}.$$

We conclude that if the behavior of a system $\mathcal{B}$ is specifiable by a $\forall$-automaton $\mathcal{A}$ and the following requirements are satisfied, the validity of $\mathcal{A}$ over $\mathcal{B}$ is proved:

(I) Associate with each automaton-state $q \in Q$ an assertion α_q, such that $\{\alpha_q\}_{q \in Q}$ is a set of invariants for $\mathcal{B}$ and $\mathcal{A}$.

(L) Associate with each automaton-state $q \in Q$ a partial function $\rho_q : X \rightarrow \mathcal{R}^+$, such that $\{\rho_q\}_{q \in Q}$ is a set of Liapunov functions for $\mathcal{B}$ and $\mathcal{A}$.

Theorem 1 *If $\mathcal{B}$ is specifiable by $\mathcal{A}$, and both (I) and (L) are satisfied, $\mathcal{B} \models \mathcal{A}$.*

Proof: (Sketch, details in appendix) Use the method of continuous induction to show that $\forall v \in \mathcal{B}$ and a run r of $\mathcal{A}$ over v, $v(t) \models \alpha_{r(t)}$, $\forall t \in \mathcal{T}$. $\square$

We illustrate this verification method by the *Cat and Mouse* examples.

Consider the first *Cat and Mouse* example adopted from [1]. We show that the constraint net model CM_1 in section 2 satisfies the requirements specification in Fig. 2(a).

Associate with q_0, q_1 and q_2 assertions $Running, CatWins$ and $MouseWins$, respectively. Therefore, the set of assertions is a set of invariants.

Associate with q_0, q_1 and q_2 the same function $\rho : \mathcal{R} \times \mathcal{R} \times \{0, 1\} \rightarrow \mathcal{R}^+$, such that $\rho(x_c, x_m, 0) = 0$ and $\rho(x_c, x_m, 1) = -(\frac{x_m}{V_m} + \frac{x_c}{V_c})$. Clearly, ρ is decreasing at q_0 with rate 2. Therefore, it is a Liapunov function.

The behavior of CM_1 is specifiable by the automaton in Fig. 2(a) since x_c and x_m are continuous. Therefore, CM_1 satisfies the required property.

If we remove the square $\square$ from node q_2 in Fig. 2(a), i.e., $q_2 \in B$, the modified requirements specification declares that "the cat always wins." Not every trace of the behavior of CM_1 satisfies this specification. However, if the initial value $\langle X_c, X_m \rangle$ satisfies $\frac{X_c}{V_c} > \frac{X_m}{V_m}$, in addition to $X_c > X_m > 0$, we can prove that "the cat always wins." To see this, let $\Delta = \frac{X_c}{V_c} - \frac{X_m}{V_m}$ and let Inv denote $\frac{x_c}{V_c} - \frac{x_m}{V_m} = \Delta$.

Associate with q_0, q_1 and q_2 assertions $Running \wedge Inv$, $CatWins$ and $false$, respectively. Note that for all $v \in [\![CM_1]\!]$,

$$\{Running \wedge Inv\} v \{Running \rightarrow Running \wedge Inv\}$$

since the derivative of $\frac{x_c}{V_c} - \frac{x_m}{V_m}$ is 0 given that $Running$ is satisfied, and

$$\{Running \wedge Inv\} v \{MouseWin \rightarrow false\}$$

since x_c and x_m are continuous. Therefore, the set of assertions is a set of invariants.

Associate with q_0, q_1 and q_2 the same function $\rho : \mathcal{R} \times \mathcal{R} \times \{0, 1\} \rightarrow \mathcal{R}^+$, such that $\rho(x_c, x_m, 0) = 0$ and $\rho(x_c, x_m, 1) = -(\frac{x_m}{V_m} + \frac{x_c}{V_c})$. Again, it is a Liapunov function.

Consider the second *Cat and Mouse* example, in which the motion of the mouse is unknown, but the cat tries to catch the mouse anyhow. Clearly, not every trace of the behavior of the constraint net CM_2 satisfies the requirements specification in Fig. 2(b). For example, if $\dot{x}_c = \dot{x}_m$ all the time, the distance between the cat and the mouse will be constant and the cat may never catch the mouse. However, suppose the mouse is short-sighted, i.e., it can only see the cat if their distance $|x_m - x_c| < \delta < \epsilon$, and when it does not see the cat, it will stop running within time τ.

The short-sighted property of the mouse is equivalent to adding the following assumption to CM_2: for all $v \in [\![CM_2]\!]$,

$$\{|x_m - x_c| \geq \delta \wedge \dot{x}_m = 0\}v\{|x_m - x_c| \geq \delta \rightarrow \dot{x}_m = 0\}$$

i.e., the mouse will not run if it does not see the cat. The maximum running time property of the mouse is equivalent to adding the following assumption to CM_2: let l_t be the time left for the mouse to run when it does not see the cat, for all $v \in [\![CM_2]\!]$,

$$\{|x_m - x_c| < \delta\}v\{|x_m - x_c| \geq \delta \wedge \dot{x}_m \neq 0 \rightarrow l_t \leq \tau\}$$

and

$$\{|x_m - x_c| \geq \delta \wedge \dot{x}_m \neq 0 \wedge l_t = l \wedge t_c = t\}v\{|x_m - x_c| \geq \delta \wedge \dot{x}_m \neq 0 \rightarrow l_t \leq l - d(t_c, t)\}.$$

We show that no matter how fast the mouse may run, the cat tracks down the mouse persistently (including the case in which the mouse is caught permanently).

In order to prove this claim, we decompose the automaton-state q_0 in Fig. 2(b) into two automaton-states q_{00} and q_{01} as shown in Fig. 3.

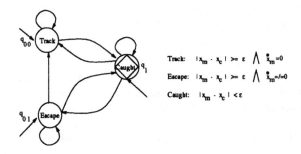

Fig. 3. A refinement of the cat-mouse specification

Associate with automaton-states q_{00}, q_{01} and q_1 assertions *Track*, *Escape* and *Caught*, respectively. Note that $\forall v \in [\![CM_2]\!]$, $\{Track\}v\{Escape \rightarrow false\}$. Therefore, $[\![CM_2]\!]$ is specifiable and the set of assertions is a set of invariants.

Let $V_m \in \mathcal{R}^+$ be the maximum speed of the mouse and $D_m = V_m \tau + \delta$. Associate with automaton-states q_{00}, q_{01} and q_1 functions $\rho_{q_{00}}, \rho_{q_{01}}$ and ρ_{q_1}, respectively, where

$$\rho_{q_{00}} = (x_m - x_c)^2, \quad \rho_{q_{01}} = D_m^2 + l_t, \quad \rho_{q_1} = 0.$$

The feedback control law of the cat guarantees that $\rho_{q_{00}}$ decreases at q_{00} at a rate no less than $2k\epsilon^2$. The maximum running time property of the mouse guarantees that $\rho_{q_{01}}$ decrease at q_{01} at a rate no less than 1. Therefore, ρ decreases at q_0 with minimum rate $\min(2k\epsilon^2, 1)$. We can check that the set of functions is a set of Liapunov functions.

4 Constraint-Based Dynamic Systems

In this section, we first explore the relationship between a constraint solver and its requirements specification, then define constraint-based dynamic systems as a generalization of constraint solvers.

4.1 Constraint solver

Constraint satisfaction can be seen as a dynamic process that approaches the solution set of the given constraints asymptotically, and a constraint solver, modeled by a constraint net, satisfies this required property [6]. Here we briefly introduce some related concepts.

Let $\langle X, d \rangle$ be a metric space. Given a point $x \in X$ and a subset $X^* \subset X$, the *distance* between x and X^* is defined as $d(x, X^*) = \inf_{x^* \in X^*}\{d(x, x^*)\}$. For any $\epsilon > 0$, the ϵ-*neighborhood* of X^* is defined as $N^\epsilon(X^*) = \{x | d(x, X^*) < \epsilon\}$; it is *strict* if it is a strict superset of X^*. Let $v : T \to X$ be a trace, v *approaches* X^* iff $\forall \epsilon \exists t_0 \forall t \geq t_0, d(v(t), X^*) < \epsilon$.

Given a dynamic process [6] $p : X \to (T \to X)$ and $X^* \subset X$, let $\phi_p(X^*) = \{p(x)(t) | x \in X^*, t \in T\}$. X^* is an *equilibrium* of p iff $\phi_p(X^*) = X^*$. X^* is a *stable equilibrium* of p iff X^* is an equilibrium and $\forall \epsilon \exists \delta, \phi_p(N^\delta(X^*)) \subseteq N^\epsilon(X^*)$. X^* is an *attractor* of p iff there exists a strict ϵ-neighborhood $N^\epsilon(X^*)$ such that $\forall x \in N^\epsilon(X^*)$, $p(x)$ approaches X^*; X^* is an *attractor in the large* iff $\forall x \in X$, $p(x)$ approaches X^*. If X^* is an attractor (in the large) and X^* is a stable equilibrium, X^* is an *asymptotically* stable equilibrium (in the large).

Let $C = \{C_i\}_{i \in I}$ be a set of constraints, whose solution $sol(C) = \{x | \forall i \in I, C_i(x)\}$ is a subset of domain X. A *constraint solver* for C is a constraint net CS whose semantics is a dynamic process $p : X \to (T \to X)$ with $sol(C)$ as an asymptotically stable equilibrium. *CS solves C globally* iff $sol(C)$ is an asymptotically stable equilibrium in the large.

We have discussed two types of constraint solvers: state transition systems and state integration systems. Various discrete and continuous constraint methods have been presented, and also analyzed using Liapunov functions [6].

4.2 Constraint-based requirements specification

Given a set of constraints C, let C^ϵ denote the assertion which is true on the ϵ-neighborhood of its solution set $N^\epsilon(sol(C))$, and let $\mathcal{A}(C^\epsilon; \Box)$ denote the $\forall$-automaton in Fig. 4(a). Using the asymptotic property of constraint solvers, we can verify that CS solves C iff there exists an initial condition $\Theta \supset sol(C)$ such that $\forall \epsilon, [\![CS(\Theta)]\!] \models \mathcal{A}(C^\epsilon; \Box)$; CS solves C globally when Θ is the domain itself. We call $\mathcal{A}(C^\epsilon; \Box)$ an *open specification* of the set of constraints C. Note that it is important to have open specification, otherwise, if we replace C^ϵ with $sol(C)$, a constraint solver for C may never satisfy the specification, since it may take *infinite* time to approach $sol(C)$.

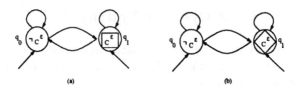

(a)   (b)

Fig. 4. Specification for (a) constraint solver (b) constraint-based dynamic system

However, requiring the integration of a controller with its environment to be a constraint solver is still too stringent for a control problem, with disturbance and uncertainty in its environment. If we consider the solution set of a set of constraints as the "goal" for the controller to achieve, one relaxed requirement for the controller is to make the system "stable" at the goal. In other words, if the system diverges from the goal by some disturbance, the controller should always be able to regulate the system back to its goal. We call a system CB *constraint-based* w.r.t. a set of constraints C iff there exists an initial condition $\Theta \supset sol(C)$ such that $\forall \epsilon, \llbracket CB(\Theta) \rrbracket \models \mathcal{A}(C^\epsilon; \Diamond)$ where $\mathcal{A}(C^\epsilon; \Diamond)$ denotes the $\forall$-automaton in Fig. 4(b). In other words, a dynamic system is constraint-based iff it approaches the solution set of the given constraints persistently.

We may relax this condition further and define constraint-based systems with errors. We call a system CB *constraint-based* w.r.t. a set of constraints C with error δ iff $\forall \epsilon > \delta, \llbracket CB(\Theta) \rrbracket \models \mathcal{A}(C^\epsilon; \Diamond)$; δ is called the *steady-state error* of the system. Normally, steady-state errors are caused by uncertainty and disturbance of the environment. For example, the second cat-mouse system CM_2 is a constraint-based system with steady-state error δ, which is the radius of the mouse sensing range.

If $\mathcal{A}(C^\epsilon; \Box)$ is considered as an open specification of a constraint-based *computation* for a closed system, $\mathcal{A}(C^\epsilon; \Diamond)$ can been seen as an *open specification* of a constraint-based *control* for an open or embedded system.

4.3 Constraint-based control and behavior verification

We have developed a systematic approach to control synthesis from requirements specification [6]. In particular, requirements specification imposes constraints over a system's global behavior and controllers can be synthesized as embedded constraint solvers which solve constraints over time. By exploring a relation between constraint satisfaction and dynamic systems via constraint methods, discrete/continuous constraint solvers or constraint-based controllers are derived.

We have developed here a requirements specification language and a formal verification method for dynamic systems. With this approach, control synthesis and behavior verification are coupled via requirements specification and Liapunov functions. If we consider a Liapunov function for a set of constraints as a measurement of the degree of satisfaction, this function can be used for both control synthesis and behavior verification.

5 Conclusion and Related Work

We have presented a formal language, generalized ∀-automata, for specifying required properties of dynamic systems, and a formal method, based on generalized Liapunov functions, for verifying that the behavior of a dynamic system satisfies its requirements specification. A constraint-based dynamic system can be modeled by a constraint net, whose desired behavior can be specified by a ∀-automaton.

Some related work has also been done. Nerode and Kohn have proposed the notion of open specification for control systems [4]. Saraswat et al. have developed a family of timed concurrent constraint languages for modeling and specification of discrete dynamic systems [5]. Problems on the specification and verification of hybrid dynamic systems have become a new challenge to both the traditional control systems design and the traditional programming methodology [1].

Acknowledgement

We wish to thank Nick Pippenger and Runping Qi for valuable discussions. This research was supported by the Natural Sciences and Engineering Research Council and the Institute for Robotics and Intelligent Systems.

References

1. R. L. Grossman, A. Nerode, A. P. Ravn, and H. Rischel, editors. *Hybrid Systems*. Number 736 in Lecture Notes on Computer Science. Springer-Verlag, 1993.
2. G. F. Khilmi. *Qualitative Methods in the Many Body Problem*. Science Publishers Inc. New York, 1961.
3. Z. Manna and A. Pnueli. Specification and verification of concurrent programs by ∀-automata. In *Proc. 14th Ann. ACM Symp. on Principles of Programming Languages*, pages 1–12, 1987.
4. A. Nerode and W. Kohn. Models for hybrid systems: Automata, topologies, controllability, observability. In R. L. Grossman, A. Nerode, A. P. Ravn, and H. Rischel, editors, *Hybrid Systems*, number 736 in Lecture Notes on Computer Science. Springer-Verlag, 1993.
5. V. Saraswat, R. Jagadeesan, and V. Gupta. Programming in timed concurrent constraint languages. In B. Mayoh, E. Tyugu, and J. Penjam, editors, *Constraint Programming*, NATO Advanced Science Institute Series, Series F: Computer And System Sciences. 1994.
6. Y. Zhang and A. K. Mackworth. Constraint programming in constraint nets. In *First Workshop on Principles and Practice of Constraint Programming*, pages 303–312, 1993. A revised version will appear in a book with the same title in MIT Press, 1995.
7. Y. Zhang and A. K. Mackworth. Design and analysis of embedded real-time systems: An elevator case study. Technical Report 93-4, Department of Computer Science, University of British Columbia, February 1993.
8. Y. Zhang and A. K. Mackworth. Constraint Nets: A semantic model for hybrid dynamic systems, 1994. Accepted for TCS Special Issue on Hybrid Systems.

A Proof of Theorem 1

In order to prove this theorem, we shall introduce a method of continuous induction modified from [2]. A property Γ is *inductive* on a time structure $\mathcal{T}$ iff Γ is satisfied at all $t < t_0 \in \mathcal{T}$ implies that Γ is satisfied at t_0, for all $t_0 \in \mathcal{T}$. Γ is *continuous* iff Γ is satisfied at $t_0 \in \mathcal{T}$ implies that $\exists t_1 > t, \forall t, t_0 < t < t_1$, Γ is satisfied at t. We should notice that when $\mathcal{T}$ is discrete, any property is continuous. The theorem of continuous induction says:

Theorem 2 *If a property Γ is inductive and continuous on a time structure $\mathcal{T}$ and Γ is satisfied at 0, Γ is satisfied at all $t \in \mathcal{T}$.*

Proof: We call a time point $t \in \mathcal{T}$ *regular* iff Γ is satisfied at all t', $0 \le t' \le t$. Let T denote the set of all regular time points. T is not empty since Γ is satisfied at 0. We prove the theorem by contradiction, i.e., assume that Γ is not satisfied at all $t \in \mathcal{T}$. Therefore, $T \subset \mathcal{T}$ is bounded above; let $t_0 = \bigvee T \in \mathcal{T}$ be the least upper bound of T ($\mathcal{T}$ is complete). Since t_0 is the least upper bound, it follows that Γ is satisfied at all t, $0 \le t < t_0$. Since Γ is inductive, it is satisfied at time t_0. Therefore, $t_0 \in T$.

Since $T \subset \mathcal{T}$, t_0 is not the greatest element in $\mathcal{T}$. Let $T' = \{t | t > t_0\}$. There are two cases: (1) if T' has a least element t', since Γ is inductive, $t' \in T$ is a regular time point. (2) otherwise, for any $t' \in T'$, $\{t | t_0 < t < t'\} \ne \emptyset$. Since Γ is also continuous, we can find a $t' \in T'$ such that Γ is satisfied at all $T'' = \{t | t_0 < t < t'\}$. Therefore, t is a regular time point $\forall t \in T''$. Both cases contradict the fact that t_0 is the least upper bound of the set T. $\square$

Using the method of continuous induction, we obtain the following two lemmas.

Lemma 1 *Let $\{\alpha_q\}_{q \in Q}$ be invariants for $\mathcal{B}$ and $\mathcal{A}$. If r is a run of $\mathcal{A}$ over $v \in \mathcal{B}$, $\forall t \in \mathcal{T}, v(t) \models \alpha_{r(t)}$.*

Proof: We prove that the property $v(t) \models \alpha_{r(t)}$ is satisfied at 0 and is both inductive and continuous on any time structure $\mathcal{T}$.

- Initiality: Since $v(0) \models \Theta$ and $v(0) \models e(r(0))$, we have $v(0) \models \Theta \wedge e(r(0))$. According to the *Initiality* condition of invariants, we have $v(0) \models \alpha_{r(0)}$.
- Inductivity: Suppose $v(t) \models \alpha_{r(t)}$ is saisfied at $0 \le t < t_0$. Since r is a run over v, $\exists q \in Q$ and $t'_1 < t_0, \forall t, t'_1 \le t < t_0$, $r(t) = q$ and $v(t_0) \models c(q, r(t_0))$. According to the *Consecution* condition of the invariants, $\exists t'_2 < t_0, \forall t, t'_2 \le t < t_0$, $v(t) \models \alpha_q$ implies $v(t_0) \models c(q, r(t_0)) \rightarrow \alpha_{r(t_0)}$. Therefore, $\forall t, \max(t'_1, t'_2) \le t < t_0$, $r(t) = q$, $v(t) \models \alpha_q$ (assumption), $v(t_0) \models c(q, r(t_0)) \rightarrow \alpha_{r(t_0)}$ and $v(t_0) \models c(q, r(t_0))$. Thus, $v(t_0) \models \alpha_{r(t_0)}$.
- Continuity: Suppose $v(t_0) \models \alpha_{r(t_0)}$. Since r is a run over v, $\exists q \in Q$ and $t'_1 > t_0, \forall t, t_0 < t < t'_1$, $r(t) = q$ and $v(t) \models c(r(t_0), q)$. According to the *Consecution* condition of the invariants, $\exists t'_2 > t_0, \forall t, t_0 < t < t'_2$, $v(t_0) \models \alpha_{r(t_0)}$ implies $v(t) \models c(r(t_0), q) \rightarrow \alpha_q$. Therefore, $\forall t, t_0 < t < \min(t'_1, t'_2)$, $r(t) = q$, $v(t_0) \models \alpha_{r(t_0)}$ (assumption), $v(t) \models c(r(t_0), q) \rightarrow \alpha_q$ and $v(t) \models c(r(t_0), q)$. Thus, $\forall t, t_0 < t < \min(t'_1, t'_2)$, $v(t) \models \alpha_{r(t)}$.

$\square$

Given any interval I of time $\mathcal{T}$, let $\mu(I) = \int_I dt$ be the measurement of the interval. Given a property Γ, let $\mu(I_\Gamma) = \int_I \Gamma(t)dt$ be the measurement of time points at which Γ is satisfied.

Lemma 2 *Let $\{\alpha_q\}_{q\in Q}$ be invariants for $\mathcal{B}$ and $\mathcal{A}$ and r be a run of $\mathcal{A}$ over a trace $v \in \mathcal{B}$. If $\{\rho_q\}_{q\in Q}$ is a set of Liapunov functions for $\mathcal{B}$ and $\mathcal{A}$, then*

- $\rho_{r(t_2)}(v(t_2)) \leq \rho_{r(t_1)}(v(t_1))$ *when* $\forall t_1 \leq t \leq t_2, r(t) \in B \cup S,$
- $\dfrac{\rho_{r(t_2)}(v(t_2)) - \rho_{r(t_1)}(v(t_1))}{d(t_1, t_2)} \leq -\epsilon$ *when* $t_1 < t_2$ *and* $\forall t_1 \leq t \leq t_2, r(t) \in B$, *and*
- *for any interval I with only bad and stable automaton-states, $\mu(I_B)$ is finite.*

Proof: For any run r over v and for any segments $q^* : I \to Q$ of r with only bad and stable states, ρ on q^* is nonincreasing, i.e., for any $t_1 < t_2 \in I$, $\rho_{r(t_1)}(v(t_1)) \geq \rho_{r(t_2)}(v(t_2))$, and the decreasing speed at the bad states is no less than ϵ. Let m be the upper bound of $\{\rho_{r(t)}(v(t)) | t \in I\}$. Since $\rho_q \geq 0$, $\mu(I_B) \leq m/\epsilon < \infty$. $\square$

Proof of Theorem 1: For any trace v of $\mathcal{B}$, there is a run since $\mathcal{B}$ is specifiable by $\mathcal{A}$. For any run r of $\mathcal{A}$ over v, if any automaton-state in R appears infinitely many times in r, r is accepting. Otherwise there is a time point t_0, the sub-sequence r on $I = \{t \in \mathcal{T} | t \geq t_0\}$, denoted q^*, has only bad and stable automaton-states. If there exist a set of invariants and a set of Liapunov functions, $\mu(I_B)$ is finite. Since time is infinite, all the automaton-states appearing infinitely many times in r belong to S; r is accepting too. Therefore, every trace is accepting for the automaton. $\square$

GSAT and Dynamic Backtracking

Matthew L. Ginsberg[1] and David McAllester[2]

[1] CIRL, 1269 University of Oregon, Eugene, OR 97403
[2] MIT Artificial Intelligence Laboratory, 545 Technology Square, Cambridge, MA
02139

Abstract. There has been substantial recent interest in two new families of search techniques. One family consists of nonsystematic methods such as GSAT; the other contains systematic approaches that use a polynomial amount of justification information to prune the search space. This paper introduces a new technique that combines these two approaches. The algorithm allows substantial freedom of movement in the search space but enough information is retained to ensure the systematicity of the resulting analysis. Bounds are given for the size of the justification database and conditions are presented that guarantee that this database will be polynomial in the size of the problem in question.

1 INTRODUCTION

The past few years have seen rapid progress in the development of algorithms for solving constraint-satisfaction problems, or CSPs. CSPs arise naturally in subfields of AI from planning to vision, and examples include propositional theorem proving, map coloring and scheduling problems. The problems are difficult because they involve search; there is never a guarantee that (for example) a successful coloring of a portion of a large map can be extended to a coloring of the map in its entirety.

The algorithms developed recently have been of two types. *Systematic* algorithms determine whether a solution exists by searching the entire space. *Local* algorithms use hill-climbing techniques to find a solution quickly but are *nonsystematic* in that they search the entire space in only a probabilistic sense.

The empirical effectiveness of these nonsystematic algorithms appears to be a result of their ability to follow local gradients in the search space. Traditional systematic procedures explore the space in a fixed order that is independent of local gradients; the fixed order makes following local gradients impossible but is needed to ensure that no node is examined twice and that the search remains systematic.

Dynamic backtracking [Ginsberg,1993] attempts to overcome this problem by retaining specific information about those portions of the search space that have been eliminated and then following local gradients in the remainder. Unlike previous algorithms that recorded such elimination information, such as dependency-directed backtracking [Stallman and Sussman,1977], dynamic backtracking is selective about the information it caches so that only a polynomial amount of memory is required. These earlier techniques cached a new result with every backtrack, using an amount of memory that was linear in the run time and thus exponential in the size of the problem being solved.

Unfortunately, neither dynamic nor dependency-directed backtracking (or any other known similar method) is truly effective at local maneuvering within the search space, since the basic underlying methodology remains simple chronological backtracking. New techniques are included to make the search mc.c̣ ciﬁcient, but an exponential number of nodes in the search space must still be examined before early choices can be retracted. No existing search technique is able to both move freely within the search space and keep track of what has been searched and what hasn't.

The second class of algorithms developed recently presume that freedom of movement is of greater importance than systematicity. Algorithms in this class achieve their freedom of movement by abandoning the conventional description of the search space as a tree of partial solutions, instead thinking of it as a space of total assignments of values to variables. Motion is permitted between any two assignments that differ on a single value, and a hill-climbing procedure is employed to try to minimize the number of constraints violated by the overall assignment. The best-known algorithms in this class are min-conflicts [Minton et al.,1990] and GSAT [Selman et al.,1992].

Min-conflicts has been applied to the scheduling domain specifically and used to schedule tasks on the Hubble space telescope. GSAT is restricted to Boolean satisfiability problems (where every variable is assigned simply true or false), and has led to remarkable progress in the solution of randomly generated problems of this type; its performance is reported [Selman and Kautz,1993, Selman et al.,1992, Selman et al.,1993] as surpassing that of other techniques such as simulated annealing [Kirkpatrick et al.,1982] and systematic techniques based on the Davis-Putnam procedure [Davis and Putnam,1960].

GSAT is not a panacea, however; there are many problems on which it performs fairly poorly. If a problem has no solution, for example, GSAT will never be able to report this with confidence. Even if a solution does exist, there appear to be at least two possible difficulties that GSAT may encounter.

First, the GSAT search space may contain so many local minima that it is not clear how GSAT can move so as to reduce the number of constraints violated by a given assignment. As an example, consider the CSP of generating crossword puzzles by filling words from a fixed dictionary into an empty frame [Ginsberg et al.,1990]. The constraints indicate that there must be no conflict in each of the squares; thus two words that begin on the same square must also begin with the same letter. In this domain, getting "close" is not necessarily any indication that the problem is nearly solved, since correcting a conflict at a single square may involve modifying much of the current solution. Konolige has recently reported that GSAT specifically has difficulty solving problems of this sort [Konolige,1994].

Second, GSAT does no forward propagation. In the crossword domain once again, selecting one word may well force the selection of a variety of subsequent words. In a Boolean satisfiability problem, assigning one variable the value true may cause an immediate cascade of values to be assigned to other variables via a technique known as *unit resolution*. It seems plausible that forward propagation will be more common on realistic problems than on randomly generated ones; the most difficult random problems appear to be tangles of closely related individual variables while naturally occurring problems tend to be tangles of sequences of related variables. Furthermore, it appears that GSAT's performance degrades (relative to systematic approaches) as these sequences of variables arise [Crawford and Baker,1994].

Our aim in this paper is to describe a new search procedure that appears to combine the benefits of both of the earlier approaches; in some very loose sense, it can be thought of as a systematic version of GSAT.

The next three sections summarize the original dynamic backtracking algorithm [Ginsberg,1993], presenting it from the perspective of local search. The termination proof is somewhat subtle [Ginsberg,1993, McAllester,1993] and is not given here. Section 5 present a modification of dynamic backtracking called *partial-order dynamic backtracking*, or PDB. PDB builds on work of McAllester's [McAllester,1993]. Partial-order dynamic backtracking provides greater flexibility in the allowed set of search directions while preserving systematicity and polynomial worst case space usage. Section 6 presents a new variant of dynamic backtracking that is still more flexible in the allowed set of search directions. While this final procedure is still systematic, it can use exponential space in the worst case. Section 7 presents some empirical results comparing PDB with other well known algorithms on a class of "local" randomly generated 3-SAT problems. Concluding remarks are contained in Section 8, and proofs appear in the appendix.

2 CONSTRAINTS AND NOGOODS

We begin with a slightly nonstandard definition of a CSP.

Definition 1. By a *constraint satisfaction problem* (I, V, κ) we will mean a finite set I of variables; for each $x \in I$, there is a finite set V_x of possible values for the variable x. κ is a set of constraints each of the form $\neg[(x_1 = v_1) \wedge \cdots \wedge (x_k = v_k)]$ where each x_j is a variable in I and each v_j is an element of V_{x_j}. A *solution* to the CSP is an assignment P of values to variables that satisfies every constraint. For each variable x we require that $P(x) \in V_x$ and for each constraint $\neg[(x_1 = v_1) \wedge \cdots \wedge (x_k = v_k)]$ we require that $P(x_i) \neq v_i$ for some x_i.

By the *size* of a constraint-satisfaction problem (I, V, κ), we will mean the product of the domain sizes of the various variables, $\prod_x |V_x|$.

The technical convenience of the above definition of a constraint will be clear shortly. For the moment, we merely note that the above description is clearly equivalent to the conventional one; rather than represent the constraints in terms of allowed value combinations for various variables, we write axioms that disallow specific value combinations one at a time. The size of a CSP is the number of possible assignments of values to variables.

Systematic algorithms attempting to find a solution to a CSP typically work with partial solutions that are then discovered to be inextensible or to violate the given constraints; when this happens, a backtrack occurs and the partial solution under consideration is modified. Such a procedure will, of course, need to record information that guarantees that the same partial solution not be considered again as the search proceeds. This information might be recorded in the structure of the search itself; depth-first search with chronological backtracking is an example. More sophisticated methods maintain a database of some form indicating explicitly which choices have been eliminated and which have not. In this paper, we will use a database consisting of a set of *nogoods* [de Kleer,1986].

Definition 2. A *nogood* is an expression of the form

$$(x_1 = v_1) \wedge \cdots \wedge (x_k = v_k) \rightarrow x \neq v \tag{1}$$

A nogood can be used to represent a constraint as an implication; (1) is logically equivalent to the constraint

$$\neg[(x_1 = v_1) \wedge \cdots \wedge (x_k = v_k) \wedge (x = v)]$$

There are clearly many different ways of representing a given constraint as a nogood.

One special nogood is the *empty* nogood, which is tautologically false. We will denote the empty nogood by $\bot$; if $\bot$ can be derived from the given set of constraints, it follows that no solution exists for the problem being attempted.

The typical way in which new nogoods are obtained is by resolving together old ones. As an example, suppose we have derived the following:

$$(x = a) \wedge (y = b) \rightarrow u \neq v_1$$
$$(x = a) \wedge (z = c) \rightarrow u \neq v_2$$
$$(y = b) \rightarrow u \neq v_3$$

where v_1, v_2 and v_3 are the only values in the domain of u. It follows that we can combine these nogoods to conclude that there is no solution with

$$(x = a) \wedge (y = b) \wedge (z = c) \tag{2}$$

Moving z to the conclusion of (2) gives us

$$(x = a) \wedge (y = b) \rightarrow z \neq c$$

In general, suppose we have a collection of nogoods of the form

$$x_{i1} = v_{i1} \wedge \cdots \wedge x_{in_i} = v_{in_i} \rightarrow x \neq v_i$$

as i varies, where the same variable appears in the conclusions of all the nogoods. Suppose further that the antecedents all agree as to the value of the x_i's, so that any time x_i appears in the antecedent of one of the nogoods, it is in a term $x_i = v_i$ for a fixed v_i. If the nogoods collectively eliminate all of the possible values for x, we can conclude that $\bigwedge_j (x_j = v_j)$ is inconsistent; moving one specific x_k to the conclusion gives us

$$\bigwedge_{j \neq k} (x_j = v_j) \rightarrow x_k \neq v_k \qquad (3)$$

As before, note the freedom in our choice of variable appearing in the conclusion of the nogood. Since the next step in our search algorithm will presumably satisfy (3) by changing the value for x_k, the selection of consequent variable corresponds to the choice of variable to "flip" in the terms used by GSAT or other hill-climbing algorithms.

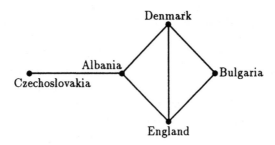

Fig. 1. A small map-coloring problem

As we have remarked, dynamic backtracking accumulates information in a set of nogoods. To see how this is done, consider the map coloring problem in Figure 1, repeated from [Ginsberg,1993]. The map consists of five countries: Albania, Bulgaria, Czechoslovakia, Denmark and England. We assume – wrongly – that the countries border each other as shown in the figure, where countries are denoted by nodes and border one another if and only if there is an arc connecting them.

In coloring the map, we can use the three colors red, green and blue. We will typically abbreviate the colors and country names to single letters in the obvious way. The following table gives a trace of how a conventional dependency-directed backtracking scheme might attack this problem; each row shows a state of the procedure in the middle of a backtrack step, after a new nogood has been identified but before colors are erased to reflect the new conclusion. The coloring that is about to be removed appears in boldface. The "drop" column will be discussed shortly.

A	B	C	D	E	add		drop
r	g	$\mathbf{r}$			$A = r \rightarrow C \neq r$	1	
r	g	b	$\mathbf{r}$		$A = r \rightarrow D \neq r$	2	
r	g	b	$\mathbf{g}$		$B = g \rightarrow D \neq g$	3	
r	g	b	b	$\mathbf{r}$	$A = r \rightarrow E \neq r$	4	
r	g	b	b	$\mathbf{g}$	$B = g \rightarrow E \neq g$	5	
r	g	b	b	$\mathbf{b}$	$D = b \rightarrow E \neq b$	6	
r	g	b	$\mathbf{b}$		$(A = r) \wedge (B = g)$ $\rightarrow D \neq b$	7	6
r	$\mathbf{g}$	b			$A = r \rightarrow B \neq g$	8	$3, 5, 7$

We begin by coloring Albania red and Bulgaria green, and then try to color Czechoslovakia red as well. Since this violates the constraint that Albania and Czechoslovakia be different colors, nogood (1) in the above table is produced.

We change Czechoslovakia's color to blue and then turn to Denmark. Since Denmark cannot be colored red or green, nogoods (2) and (3) appear; the only remaining color for Denmark is blue.

Unfortunately, having colored Denmark blue, we cannot color England. The three nogoods generated are (4), (5) and (6), and we can resolve these together because the three conclusions eliminate all of the possible colors for England. The result is that there is no solution with $(A = r) \wedge (B = g) \wedge (D = b)$, which we rewrite as (7) above. This can in turn be resolved with (2) and (3) to get (8), correctly indicating that the color of red for Albania is inconsistent with the choice of green for Bulgaria. The analysis can continue at this point to gradually determine that Bulgaria has to be red, Denmark can be green or blue, and England must then be the color not chosen for Denmark.

As we mentioned in the introduction, the problem with this approach is that the set Γ of nogoods grows monotonically, with a new nogood being added at every step. The number of nogoods stored therefore grows linearly with the run time and thus (presumably) exponentially with the size of the problem. A related problem is that it may become increasingly difficult to extend the partial solution P without violating one of the nogoods in Γ.

Dynamic backtracking deals with this by discarding nogoods when they become "irrelevant" in the sense that their antecedents no longer match the partial solution in question. In the example above, nogoods can be eliminated as indicated in the final column of the trace. When we derive (7), we remove (6) because Denmark is no longer colored blue. When we derive (8), we remove all of the nogoods with $B = g$ in their antecedents. Thus the only information we retain is that Albania's red color precludes red for Czechoslovakia, Denmark and England (1, 2 and 4) and also green for Bulgaria (8).

3 DYNAMIC BACKTRACKING

Dynamic backtracking uses the set of nogoods to both record information about the portion of the search space that has been eliminated and to record the current partial assignment being considered by the procedure. The current partial assignment is encoded in the antecedents of the current nogood set. More formally:

Definition 3. An *acceptable next assignment* for a nogood set Γ is an assignment P satisfying every nogood in Γ and every antecedent of every such nogood. We will call a set of nogoods Γ *acceptable* if no two nogoods in Γ have the same conclusion and either $\bot \in \Gamma$ or there exists an acceptable next assignment for Γ.

If Γ is acceptable, the antecedents of the nogoods in Γ induce a partial assignment of values to variables; any acceptable next assignment must be an extension of this partial assignment. In the above table, for example, nogoods (1) through (6) encode the partial assignment given by $A = r$, $B = g$, and $D = b$. Nogoods (1) though (7) fail to encode a partial assignment because the seventh nogood is inconsistent with the partial assignment encoded in nogoods (1) through (6). This is why the sixth nogood is removed when the seventh nogood is added.

Procedure 4 (Dynamic backtracking) To solve a CSP:

$P :=$ any complete assignment of values to variables
$\Gamma := \emptyset$
until either P is a solution or $\bot \in \Gamma$:
    $\gamma :=$ any constraint violated by P
    $\Gamma := \text{simp}(\Gamma \cup \gamma)$
    $P :=$ any acceptable next assignment for Γ

To simplify the discussion we assume a fixed total order on the variables. Versions of dynamic backtracking with dynamic rearrangement of the variable order can be found elsewhere [Ginsberg,1993, McAllester,1993]. Whenever a new nogood is added, the fixed variable ordering is used to select the variable that appears in the conclusion of the nogood – the latest variable always appears in the conclusion. The subroutine simp closes the set of nogoods under the resolution inference rule discussed in the previous section and removes all nogoods which have an antecedent $x = v$ such that $x \neq v$ appears in the conclusion of some other nogood. Without giving a detailed analysis, we note that simplification ensures that Γ remains acceptable. To prove termination we introduce the following notation:

Definition 5. For any acceptable Γ and variable x, we define the *live domain of* x to be those values v such that $x \neq v$ does not appear in the conclusion of any nogood in Γ. We will denote the size of the live domain of x by $|x|_\Gamma$, and will denote by $m(\Gamma)$ the tuple $\langle |x_1|_\Gamma, \ldots, |x_n|_\Gamma \rangle$ where $x_1, \ldots, x_n$ are the variables in the CSP in their specified order.

Given an acceptable Γ, we define the *size of* Γ to be

$$\text{size}(\Gamma) = \prod_x |V_x| - \sum_x \left[(|V_x| - |x|_\Gamma) \prod_{x_i > x} |V_{x_i}| \right]$$

Informally, the size of Γ is the size of the remaining search space given the live domains for the variables and assuming that all information about x_i will be lost when we change the value for any variable $x_j < x_i$.

The following result is obvious:

Lemma 6. *Suppose that Γ and Γ' are such that $m(\Gamma)$ is lexicographically less than $m(\Gamma')$. Then $\text{size}(\Gamma) < \text{size}(\Gamma')$.* ∎

The termination proof (which we do not repeat here) is based on the observation that every simplification lexicographically reduces $m(\Gamma)$. Assuming that $\Gamma = \emptyset$ initially, since

$$\text{size}(\emptyset) = \prod_x |V_x|$$

it follows that the running time of dynamic backtracking is bounded by the size of the problem being solved.

Proposition 7. *Any acceptable set of nogoods can be stored in $o(n^2 v)$ space where n is the number of variables and v is the maximum domain size of any single variable.*

It is worth considering the behavior of Procedure 4 when applied to a CSP that is the union of two disjoint CSPs that do not share variables or constraints. If each of the two subproblems is unsatisfiable and the variable ordering interleaves the variables of the two subproblems, a classical backtracking search will take time proportional to the product of the times required to search each assignment space separately.[3] In contrast, Procedure 4 works on the two problems independently, and the time taken to solve the union of problems is therefore the sum of the times needed for the individual subproblems. It follows that Procedure 4 is fundamentally different from classical backtracking or backjumping procedures; Procedure 4 is in fact what has been called a *polynomial space aggressive backtracking procedure* [McAllester,1993].

4   DYNAMIC BACKTRACKING AS LOCAL SEARCH

Before proceeding, let us highlight the obvious similarities between Procedure 4 and Selman's description of GSAT [Selman *et al.*,1992]:

---

[3] This observation remains true even if backjumping techniques are used.

Procedure 8 (GSAT) To solve a CSP:

for $i := 1$ to MAX-TRIES
    $P :=$ a randomly generated truth assignment
    for $j := 1$ to MAX-FLIPS
        if P is a solution, **then** return it
        else flip any variable in P that results in
                the greatest decrease in the number
                of unsatisfied clauses
        end if
    end for
end for
return failure

The inner loop of the above procedure makes a local move in the search space in a direction consistent with the goal of satisfying a maximum number of clauses; we will say that GSAT follows the local gradient of a "maxsat" objective function. But local search can get stuck in local minima; the outer loop provides a partial escape by giving the procedure several independent chances to find a solution.

Like GSAT, dynamic backtracking examines a sequence of total assignments. Initially, dynamic backtracking has considerable freedom in selecting the next assignment; in many cases, it can update the total assignment in a manner identical to GSAT. The nogood set ultimately both constrains the allowed directions of motion and forces the procedure to search systematically. Dynamic backtracking cannot get stuck in local minima.

Both systematicity and the ability to follow local gradients are desirable. The observations of the previous paragraphs, however, indicate that these two properties are in conflict – systematic enumeration of the search space appears incompatible with gradient descent. To better understand the interaction of systematicity and local gradients, we need to examine more closely the structure of the nogoods used in dynamic backtracking.

We have already discussed the fact that a single constraint can be represented as a nogood in a variety of ways. For example, the constraint $\neg(A = r \land B = g)$ can be represented either as $A = r \to B \neq g$ or as $B = g \to A \neq r$. Although these nogoods capture the same information, they behave differently in the dynamic backtracking procedure because they encode different partial truth assignments and represent different choices of variable ordering. In particular, the set of acceptable next assignments for $A = r \to B \neq g$ is quite different from the set of acceptable next assignments for $B = g \to A \neq r$. In the former case an acceptable assignment must satisfy $A = r$; in the latter case, $B = g$ must hold. Intuitively, the former nogood corresponds to changing the value of B while the latter nogood corresponds to changing that of A. The manner in which we represent the constraint $\neg(A = r \land B = g)$ influences the direction in which the search is allowed to proceed. In Procedure 4, the choice of representation is forced by the need to respect the fixed variable ordering and to change the latest variable in the constraint.[4] Similar restrictions exist in the original presentation of dynamic backtracking itself [Ginsberg,1993].

5   PARTIAL-ORDER DYNAMIC BACKTRACKING

Partial-order dynamic backtracking [McAllester,1993] replaces the fixed variable order with a *partial* order that is dynamically modified during the search. When a new nogood is added, this partial ordering need not fix a unique representation – there can be considerable choice in the selection of the variable to appear in the conclusion of the nogood. This leads to freedom in the selection of the variable whose value is to be changed, thereby allowing greater flexibility in the directions that the procedure can take while traversing the search space. The partial order on variables is represented by a set of ordering constraints called *safety conditions*.

Definition 9. A *safety condition* is an assertion of the form $x < y$ where x and y are variables. Given a set S of safety conditions, we will denote by $\leq_S$ the transitive closure of $<$, saying that S is *acyclic* if $\leq_S$ is antisymmetric. We will write $x <_S y$ to mean that $x \leq_S y$ and $y \not\leq_S x$.

In other words, $x \leq y$ if there is some (possibly empty) sequence of safety conditions

$$x < z_1 < \ldots < z_n < y$$

Definition 10. For a nogood γ, we will denote by S_γ the set of all safety conditions $x < y$ such that x is in the antecedent of γ and y is the variable in its conclusion.

Informally, we require variables in the antecedent of nogoods to precede the variables in their conclusions, since the antecedent variables have been used to constrain the live domains of the conclusions.

The state of the partial order dynamic backtracking procedure is represented by a pair $\langle \Gamma, S \rangle$ consisting of a set of nogoods and a set of safety conditions. In many cases, we will be interested in only the ordering information about variables that can precede a fixed variable x. To discard the rest of the ordering information, we discard all of the safety conditions involving any variable y that follows x, and then record only that y does indeed follow x. Somewhat more formally:

Definition 11. For any set S of safety conditions and variable x, we define the *weakening of S at x*, to be denoted $W(S, x)$, to be the set of safety conditions given by removing from S all safety conditions of the form $z < y$ where $x <_S y$ and then adding the safety condition $x < y$ for all such y.

---

[4] Note, however, that there is still considerable freedom in the choice of the constraint itself. A total assignment usually violates many different constraints.

The set $W(S, x)$ is a weakening of S in the sense that every total ordering consistent with S is also consistent with $W(S, x)$. However $W(S, x)$ usually admits more total orderings than S does; for example, if S specifies a total order then $W(S, x)$ allows any order which agrees with S up to and including the variable x. In general, we have the following:

Lemma 12. *For any set S of safety conditions, variable x, and total order $<$ consistent with the safety conditions in $W(S, x)$, there exists a total order consistent with S that agrees with $<$ through x.*

We now state the PDB procedure.

Procedure 13 To solve a CSP:

$P :=$ any complete assignment of values to variables
$\Gamma := \emptyset$
$S := \emptyset$
until either P is a solution or $\bot \in \Gamma$:
    $\gamma :=$ a constraint violated by P
    $\langle \Gamma, S \rangle := \mathbf{simp}(\Gamma, S, \gamma)$
    $P :=$ any acceptable next assignment for Γ

Procedure 14 To compute $\mathbf{simp}(\Gamma, S, \gamma)$:

select the conclusion x of γ so that $S \cup S_\gamma$ is acyclic
$\Gamma := \Gamma \cup \{\gamma\}$
$S := W(S \cup S_\gamma, x)$
remove from Γ each nogood with x in its antecedent
if the conclusions of nogoods in Γ rule out all
      possible values for x **then**
    $\rho :=$ the result of resolving all nogoods in Γ with x
      in their conclusion
    $\langle \Gamma, S \rangle := \mathbf{simp}(\Gamma, S, \rho)$
end if
return $\langle \Gamma, S \rangle$

The above simplification procedure maintains the invariant that Γ be acceptable and S be acyclic; in addition, the time needed for a single call to $\mathbf{simp}$ appears to grow significantly sublinearly with the size of the problem in question (see Section 7).

Theorem 15. *Procedure 13 terminates. The number of calls to $\mathbf{simp}$ is bounded by the size of the problem being solved.*

As an example, suppose that we return to our map-coloring problem. We begin by coloring all of the countries red except Bulgaria, which is green. The following table shows the total assignment that existed at the moment each new nogood was generated.

A	B	C	D	E	add		drop
r	g	r	r	r	$C = r \rightarrow A \neq r$	1	
b	g	r	r	r	$D = r \rightarrow E \neq r$	2	
b	g	r	r	g	$B = g \rightarrow E \neq g$	3	
b	g	r	r	b	$A = b \rightarrow E \neq b$	4	
					$(A = b) \wedge (B = g)$	5	2
					$\rightarrow D \neq r$		
					$D < E$	6	
b	g	r	g	r	$B = g \rightarrow D \neq g$	7	
b	g	r	b	r	$A = b \rightarrow D \neq b$	8	
					$A = b \rightarrow B \neq g$	9	$3, 5, 7$
					$B < E$	10	6
					$B < D$	11	

The initial coloring violates a variety of constraints; suppose that we choose to work on one with Albania in its conclusion because Albania is involved in three violated constraints. We choose $C = r \rightarrow A \neq r$ specifically, and add it as (1) above.

We now modify Albania to be blue. The only constraint violated is that Denmark and England be different colors, so we add (2) to Γ. This suggests that we change the color for England; we try green, but this conflicts with Bulgaria. If we write the new nogood as $E = g \rightarrow B \neq g$, we will change Bulgaria to blue and be done. In the table above, however, we have made the less optimal choice (3), changing the coloring for England again.

We are now forced to color England blue. This conflicts with Albania, and we continue to leave England in the conclusion of the nogood as we add (4). This nogood resolves with (2) and (3) to produce (5), where we have once again made the worst choice and put D in the conclusion. We add this nogood to Γ and remove nogood (2), which is the only nogood with D in its antecedent. In (6) we add a safety condition indicating that D must continue to precede E. (This safety condition has been present since nogood (2) was discovered, but we have not indicated it explicitly until the original nogood was dropped from the database.)

We next change Denmark to green; England is forced to be red once again. But now Bulgaria and Denmark are both green; we have to write this new nogood (7) with Denmark in the conclusion because of the ordering implied by nogood (5) above. Changing Denmark to blue conflicts with Albania (8), which we have to write as $A = b \rightarrow D \neq b$. This new nogood resolves with (5) and (7) to produce (9).

We drop (3), (5) and (7) because they involve $B = g$, and introduce the two safety conditions (10) and (11). Since E follows B, we drop the safety condition

$E < D$. At this point, we are finally forced to change the color for Bulgaria and the search continues.

It is important to note that the added flexibility of PDB over dynamic backtracking arises from the flexibility in the first step of the simplification procedure where the conclusion of the new nogood is selected. This selection corresponds to a selection of a variable whose value is to be changed.

As with the procedure in the previous section, when given a CSP that is a union of disjoint CSPs the above procedure will treat the two subproblems independently. The total running time remains the sum of the times required for the subproblems.

6 ARBITRARY MOVEMENT

Partial-order dynamic backtracking still does not provide total freedom in the choice of direction through the search space. When a new nogood is discovered, the existing partial order constrains how we are to interpret that nogood – roughly speaking, we are forced to change the value of late variables before changing the values of their predecessors. The use of a partial order makes this constraint looser than previously, but it is still present. In this section, we allow cycles in the nogoods and safety conditions, thereby permitting arbitrary choice in the selection of the variable appearing in the conclusion of a new nogood.

The basic idea is the following: Suppose that we have introduced a loop into the variable ordering, perhaps by including the pair of nogoods $x \rightarrow \neg y$ and $y \rightarrow x$. Rather than rewrite one of these nogoods so that the same variable appears in the conclusion of both, we will view the (x, y) combination as a single variable that takes a value in the product set $V_x \times V_y$.

If x and y are variables that have been "combined" in this way, we can rewrite a nogood with (for example) x in its antecedent and y in its conclusion so that both x and y are in the conclusion. As an example, we can rewrite

$$x = v_x \land z = v_z \rightarrow y \neq v_y \tag{4}$$

as

$$z = v_z \rightarrow (x, y) \neq (v_x, v_y) \tag{5}$$

which is logically equivalent. We can view this as eliminating a particular value for the pair of variables (x, y).

Definition 16. Let S be a set of safety conditions (possibly not acyclic). We will write $x \equiv_S y$ if $x \leq_S y$ and $y \leq_S x$. The equivalence class of x under $\equiv$ will be denoted $\langle x \rangle_S$. If γ is a nogood whose conclusion involves the variable x, we will denote by γ_S the result of moving to the conclusion of γ all terms involving members of $\langle x \rangle_S$. If Γ is a set of nogoods, we will denote by Γ_S is the set of nogoods of the form γ_S for $\gamma \in \Gamma$.

It is not difficult to show that for any set S of safety conditions, the relation $\equiv_S$ is an equivalence relation. As an example of rewriting a nogood in the presence of ordering cycles, suppose that γ is the nogood (4) and let S be such that $\langle y \rangle_S = \{x, y\}$; now γ_S is given by (5).

Placing more than one literal in the conclusions of nogoods forces us to reconsider the notion of an acceptable next assignment:

Definition 17. A *cyclically acceptable next assignment* for a nogood set Γ under a set S of safety conditions is a total assignment P of values to variables satisfying every nogood in Γ_S and every antecedent of every such nogood.

We now define a third dynamic backtracking procedure. Note that $W(S, x)$ remains well defined even if S is not acyclic, since $W(S, x)$ drops ordering constraints only on variables y such that $x <_S y$.

Procedure 18 To solve a CSP:

$P := $ any complete assignment of values to variables
$\Gamma := \emptyset$
$S := \emptyset$
until either P is a solution or $\bot \in \Gamma$:
    $\gamma := $ a constraint violated by P
    $\langle \Gamma, S \rangle := \mathbf{simp}(\Gamma, S, \gamma)$
    $P := $ any cyclically acceptable next assignment
        for Γ under S

Procedure 19 To compute $\mathbf{simp}(\Gamma, S, \gamma)$:

select a conclusion x for γ (now unconstrained)
$\Gamma := \Gamma \cup \{\gamma\}$
$S := W(S \cup S_\gamma, x)$
remove from Γ each nogood α with an element of $\langle x \rangle_S$
        in the antecedent of α_S
if the conclusions of nogoods in Γ_S rule out all
        possible values for the variables in $\langle x \rangle_S$ **then**
    $\rho := $ the result of resolving all nogoods in Γ_S whose
        conclusions involve variables in $\langle x \rangle_S$
    $\langle \Gamma, S \rangle := \mathbf{simp}(\Gamma, S, \rho)$
    end if
return $\langle \Gamma, S \rangle$

If the conclusion is selected so that S remains acyclic, the above procedure is identical to the one in the previous section.

Proposition 20. *Suppose that we are working on a problem with n variables, that the size of the largest domain of any variable is v, and that we have constructed Γ and S using repeated applications of* **simp**. *If the largest equivalence class $\langle x \rangle_S$ contains d elements, the space required to store Γ is $o(n^2 v^d)$.*

If we have an equivalence class of d variables each of which has v possible values then the number of possible values of the "combined variable" is v^d. The above procedure can now generate a distinct nogood to eliminate each of the v^d possible values, and the space requirements of the procedure can therefore grow exponentially in the size of the equivalence classes. The time required to find a cyclically allowed next assignment can also grow exponentially in the size of the equivalence classes. We can address these difficulties by selecting in advance a bound for the largest allowed size of any equivalence class. In any event, termination is still guaranteed:

Theorem 21. *Procedure 18 terminates. The number of calls to* **simp** *is bounded by the size of the problem being solved.*

Selecting a variable to place in the conclusion of a new nogood corresponds to choosing the variable whose value is to be changed on the next iteration and is analogous to selecting the variable to flip in GSAT. Since the choice of conclusion is unconstrained in the above procedure, the procedure has tremendous flexibility in the way it traverses the search space. Like the procedures in the previous sections, Procedure 18 continues to solve combinations of independent subproblems in time bounded by the sum of the times needed to solve the subproblems individually.

Here are these ideas in use on a Boolean CSP with the constraints $a \rightarrow b$, $b \rightarrow c$ and $c \rightarrow \neg b$. As before, we present a trace and then explain it:

a	b	c	add to Γ		remove from Γ
t	f	f	$a \rightarrow b$	1	
t	t	f	$b \rightarrow c$	2	
t	t	t	$c \rightarrow \neg b$	3	
			$\neg a$	4	1
			$a < b$	5	

The first three nogoods are simply the three constraints appearing in the problem. Although the orderings of the second and third nogoods conflict, we choose to write them in the given form in any case.

Since this puts b and c into an equivalence class, we do not drop nogood (2) at this point. Instead, we interpret nogood (1) as requiring that the value taken by (b, c) be either (t, t) or (t, f); (2) disallows (t, f) and (3) disallows (t, t). It follows that the three nogoods can be resolved together to obtain the new nogood given simply by $\neg a$. We add this as (4) above, dropping nogood (1) because its antecedent is falsified.

7 EXPERIMENTAL RESULTS

In this section, we present preliminary results regarding the implemented effectiveness of the procedure we have described. The implementation is based on the somewhat restricted Procedure 13 as opposed to the more general Procedure 18. We compared a search engine based on this procedure with two others, TABLEAU [Crawford and Auton,1993] and WSAT, or "walk-sat" [Selman et al.,1993]. TABLEAU is an efficient implementation of the Davis-Putnam algorithm and is systematic; WSAT is a modification to GSAT and is not. WSAT seems more effective than GSAT on a fairly wide range of problem distributions [Selman et al.,1993].

The experimental data was not collected using the random 3-SAT problems that have been the target of much recent investigation, since there is growing evidence that these problems are not representative of the difficulties encountered in practice [Crawford and Baker,1994]. Instead, we generated our problems so that the clauses they contain involve groups of locally connected variables as opposed to variables selected at random.

Somewhat more specifically, we filled an $n \times n$ square grid with variables, and then required that the three variables appearing in any single clause be neighbors in this grid. LISP code generating these examples appears in the appendix. We believe that the qualitative properties of the results reported here hold for a wide class of distributions where variables are given spatial locations and clauses are required to be local.

The experiments were performed at the crossover point where approximately half of the instances generated could be expected to be satisfiable, since this appears to be where the most difficult problems lie [Crawford and Auton,1993]. Note that not all instances at the crossover point are hard; as an example, the local variable interactions in these problems can lead to short resolution proofs that no solution exists in unsatisfiable cases. This is in sharp contrast with random 3-SAT problems (where no short proofs appear to exist in general, and it can even be shown that proof lengths are growing exponentially on average [Chvátal and Szemerédi,1988]). Realistic problems may often have short proof paths: A particular scheduling problem may be unsatisfiable simply because there is no way to schedule a specific resource as opposed to because of global issues involving the problem in its entirety. Satisfiability problems arising in VLSI circuit design can also be expected to have locality properties similar to those we have described.

The problems involved 25, 100, 225, 400 and 625 variables. For each size, we generated 100 satisfiable and 100 unsatisfiable instances and then executed the three procedures to measure their performance. (WSAT was not tested on the unsatisfiable instances.) For WSAT, we measured the number of times specific variable values were flipped. For PDB, we measured the number of top-level calls to Procedure 14. For TABLEAU, we measured the number of choice nodes expanded. WSAT and PDB were limited to 100,000 flips; TABLEAU was limited to a running time of 150 seconds.

The results for the satisfiable problems were as follows. For TABLEAU, we give the node count for successful runs only; we also indicate parenthetically what fraction of the problems were solved given the computational resource limitations. (WSAT and PDB successfully solved all instances.)

Variables	PDB	WSAT	TABLEAU
25	35	89	9 (1.0)
100	210	877	255 (1.0)
225	434	1626	504 (.98)
400	731	2737	856 (.70)
625	816	3121	502 (.68)

For the unsatisfiable instances, the results were:

Variables	PDB	TABLEAU
25	122	8 (1.0)
100	509	1779 (1.0)
225	988	5682 (.38)
400	1090	558 (.11)
625	1204	114 (.06)

The times required for PDB and WSAT appear to be growing comparably, although only PDB is able to solve the unsatisfiable instances. The eventual *decrease* in the average time needed by TABLEAU is because it is only managing to solve the easiest instances in each class. This causes TABLEAU to become almost completely ineffective in the unsatisfiable case and only partially effective in the satisfiable case. Even where it does succeed on large problems, TABLEAU's run time is greater than that of the other two methods.

Finally, we collected data on the time needed for each top-level call to **simp** in partial-order dynamic backtracking. As a function of the number of variables in the problem, this was:

Number of variables	PDB (msec)	WSAT (msec)
25	3.9	0.5
100	5.3	0.3
225	6.7	0.6
400	7.0	0.7
625	8.4	1.4

All times were measured on a Sparc 10/40 running unoptimized Allegro Common Lisp. An efficient C implementation could expect to improve either method by approximately an order of magnitude. As mentioned in Section 5, the time per flip is growing sublinearly with the number of variables in question.

8 CONCLUSION AND FUTURE WORK

Our aim in this paper has been to make a primarily theoretical contribution, describing a new class of constraint-satisfaction algorithms that appear to combine many of the advantages of previous systematic and nonsystematic approaches. Since our focus has been on a description of the algorithms, there is obviously much that remains to be done.

First, of course, the procedures must be tested on a variety of problems, both synthetic and naturally occurring; the results reported in Section 7 only scratch the surface. It is especially important that realistic problems be included in any experimental evaluation of these ideas, since these problems are likely to have performance profiles substantially different from those of randomly generated problems [Crawford and Baker,1994]. The experiments of the previous section need to be extended to include unit resolution, and we need to determine the frequency with which exponential space is needed in practice by the full procedure 18.

Finally, we have left completely untouched the question of how the flexibility of Procedure 18 is to be exploited. Given a group of violated constraints, which should we pick to add to Γ? Which variable should be in the conclusion of the constraint? These choices correspond to choice of backtrack strategy in a more conventional setting, and it will be important to understand them in this setting as well.

A PROOFS

Proposition 7 *Any acceptable set of nogoods can be stored in $o(n^2 v)$ space where n is the number of variables and v is the maximum domain size of any single variable.*

Proof. This can be done by first storing the partial assignment encoded in Γ using $o(n)$ space. The antecedent of each nogood can now be represented as a bit vector specifying the set of variables appearing in the antecedent, allowing the nogood itself to be stored in $o(n)$ space. Since no two nogoods share the same conclusion there are at most nv nogoods. ∎

Lemma 12 *For any set S of safety conditions, variable x and total order $<$ consistent with the safety conditions in $W(S, x)$, there is a total order consistent with S that agrees with $<$ through x.*

Proof. Suppose that the ordering $<$ is given by

$$x_1 < \cdots < x_k = x < y_1 < \cdots < y_m \tag{6}$$

Now let $<'$ be any ordering consistent with S, and suppose that the ordering given by $<'$ on the y_i in (6) is

$$z_1 <' \cdots <' z_m$$

We claim that the ordering given by

$$x_1, \ldots, x_k = x, z_1, \ldots, z_m \tag{7}$$

is consistent with all of S. We will show this by showing that (7) is consistent with any specific safety condition $u < v$ in S.

If both u and v are x_i's, then the safety condition $u < v$ will remain in $W(S, x)$ and is therefore satisfied by (7). If both u and v are z_i's, they are ordered as $u < v$ by $<'$ which is known to satisfy the safety conditions in S. If u is an x_i and v is a z_j, $u < v$ clearly follows from (7).

The remaining case is where $u = z_i$ and $v = x_j$ for some specific z_i and x_j. The safety condition $z_i < x_j$ cannot appear in $W(S, x)$, since it is violated by $<$ in (6). It must therefore be the case that $x_j >_S x$. But now $W(S, x)$ will include the safety condition $x_j > x$, in conflict with the ordering given by (6). This contradiction completes the proof. ∎

Theorem 15 *Procedure 13 terminates. The number of calls to* simp *is bounded by the size of the problem being solved.*

Proof. In fact, we will not prove the theorem using Procedure 14 as stated. Instead, consider the following simplification procedure:

Procedure 22 To compute $\mathrm{simp}'(\Gamma, S, \gamma)$:

select the conclusion x of γ so that $S \cup S_{\{\gamma\}}$ is acyclic
$\Gamma := \Gamma \cup \{\gamma\}$
$S := W(S \cup S_\gamma, x)$
remove from Γ any nogood with conclusion y such
       that $y >_S x$
if the conclusions of nogoods in Γ rule out all
       possible values for x **then**
   $\rho :=$ the result of resolving all nogoods in Γ with x
       in their conclusion
   $\langle \Gamma, S \rangle := \mathrm{simp}(\Gamma, S, \rho)$
end if
return $\langle \Gamma, S \rangle$

The difference between this procedure and Procedure 14 is that where Procedure 14 removed only nogoods with x in their antecedents, Procedure 22 removes all nogoods with conclusion following x in the partial order $<_S$.

We now have the following:

Lemma 23. *Suppose that* Γ *and* S *are chosen so that* $S \supseteq S_\gamma$ *for each* $\gamma \in \Gamma$. *Now if* γ *is a nogood that violates some acceptable next assignment for* Γ *and* $\langle \Gamma', S' \rangle = \mathrm{simp}'(\Gamma, S, \gamma)$, $S' \supseteq S_\gamma$ *for each* $\gamma \in \Gamma'$.

Proof. It is clear that the lemma would hold if we were to take $S := S \cup S_\gamma$, so we must only show that the weakening at x cannot drop the safety condition associated with some nogood in Γ'. But if the weakening drops the safety condition $z < y$, it must be that $y >_{S \cup S_\gamma} x$. Since x is the variable in the conclusion of γ, this implies that we must have $y >_S x$, in which case the underlying nogood with y in its conclusion will have been deleted as well. ∎

It follows from the lemma that if simp removes a nogood γ, simp' will drop it as well, since if y is the variable in the conclusion of γ, we clearly have of

$y >_{S_\gamma} x$ (since **simp** drops only nogoods with x in their antecedents) so that $y >_S x$ by virtue of the lemma and **simp'** drops the nogood as well.

We therefore see that the difference between the two procedures is only in the set of nogoods maintained; Procedure 13 as stated retains a superset of the nogoods retained by a version based on **simp'**. The set S of safety conditions is the same in both cases, and the nogood set is acceptable in both cases. It thus suffices to prove the theorem for **simp'**, since the larger set of nogoods computed using **simp** will simply result in fewer acceptable next assignments for the procedure to consider.

To see that the procedure using **simp'** terminates, we begin with the following definition:

Definition 24. Given a set of safety conditions S and a fixed variable ordering $x_1 < x_2 < \cdots < x_n$ that respects $<_S$, let $m(\Gamma, S, <)$ be the tuple $\langle |x_1|_\Gamma, \ldots, |x_n|_\Gamma \rangle$. We will denote by **size**$(\Gamma, S, <)$ the size of the remaining search space as given in Definition 5, and will denote by **size**(Γ, S) the maximum size as $<$ is allowed to vary.

Proposition 25. *Suppose that Γ is acceptable, S is acyclic, and $S \supseteq S_\gamma$ for each $\gamma \in \Gamma$. Now if γ is a nogood that violates some acceptable next assignment for Γ and $\langle \Gamma', S' \rangle = \text{simp}'(\Gamma, S, \gamma)$, then $\text{size}(\Gamma', S') < \text{size}(\Gamma, S)$.*

Proof. Let x be the variable in the conclusion of γ. The first nontrivial step of the procedure **simp'** is $\Gamma := \Gamma \cup \{\gamma\}$. This reduces $|x|_\Gamma$. The next step is $S := W(S \cup S_\gamma, x)$. This introduces new orderings. Let $<$ be any total ordering consistent with $W(S \cup S_\gamma, x)$. There must now exist a total ordering $<'$ which is consistent with $S \cup S_\gamma$ such that $<$ and $<'$ agree through x. Since $|x|_\Gamma$ has been reduced, the tuple associated with $<$ must be lexicographically smaller then the tuple associated with $<'$ at the time the procedure was called. This implies that all tuples allowed after $S := W(S, x) \cup S_\Gamma$ are lexicographically smaller than some tuple allowed at the beginning of the simplification. Applying Lemma 6, we can conclude that the size of the $\langle \Gamma, S \rangle$ pair has been reduced.

The next step removes from Γ all nogoods with conclusion $y >_S x$. Although this increases the size of the live domain for y, the fact that $y >_S x$ allows us to repeat the lexicographic argument of the preceding paragraph. Finally, if the simplification performs a resolution and executes a recursive call, then that recursion must continue to decrease the size of $\langle \Gamma, S \rangle$. ∎

It follows that a modification of Procedure 13 using **simp'** will in fact terminate in a number of steps bounded by the original value of $\text{size}(\Gamma, S)$, which is the size of the problem being solved. Procedure 13 itself will terminate no less quickly. ∎

Proposition 20 *Suppose that we are working on a problem with n variables, that the size of the largest domain of any variable is v, and that we have constructed Γ and S using repeated applications of **simp**. If the largest equivalence class $\langle x \rangle_S$ contains d elements, the space required to store Γ is $o(n^2 v^d)$.*

Proof. We know that the nogood set will be acyclic if we group together variables that are equivalent under $\leq_\Gamma$. Since this results in at most d variables being grouped together at any point, the maximum domain size in the reduced problem is v^d and the maximum number of nogoods stored is thus bounded by nv^d. As previously, the amount of space needed to store each nogood is $o(n)$. ∎

Theorem 21 *Procedure 18 terminates. The number of calls to* simp *is bounded by the size of the problem being solved.*

Proof. The proof is essentially unchanged from that of Theorem 15; we provide only a sketch here. The only novel features of the proof involve showing that the lexicographic size falls as either variables are merged into an equivalence class or an equivalence class is broken so that the variables it contains are once again handled separately. In order to do this, we extend Definition 24 to handle equivalence classes as follows:

Definition 26. Given a set of safety conditions S and a fixed variable ordering $x_1 < x_2 < \cdots < x_n$ that respects $<_S$, let $||x_i||$ be given by

$$||x_i|| = \begin{cases} 1, & \text{if } x_i \equiv x_{i+1}; \\ \prod_{y \in (x_i)_S} |y|_\Gamma, & \text{otherwise.} \end{cases} \tag{8}$$

Now denote by $\hat{m}(\Gamma, S, <)$ the tuple $\langle ||x_1||, \ldots, ||x_n|| \rangle$. We will denote by $\hat{m}(\Gamma, S)$ that tuple which is lexicographically maximal as $<$ is allowed to vary.

This definition ensures that the lexicographic value decreases whenever we combine variables, since the remaining choices for the combined variable aren't counted until the latest possible point. It remains to show that the removal of nogoods or safety conditions does not split an equivalence class prematurely.

This, however, is clear. If removing a safety condition $y < z$ causes two other variables y_1 and y_2 to become not equivalent, it must be the case that $y_1 \equiv y_2 \equiv z$ before the safety condition was removed. But note that when the safety condition is removed, we must have made progress on a variable $x <_S z$. There is thus no lexicographic harm in splitting z's equivalence class. ∎

B Experimental code

Here is the code used to generate instances of the class of problems on which our ideas were tested. The two arguments to the procedure are the size s of the variable grid and the number c of clauses to be "centered" on any single variable.

For each variable x on the grid we generated either $\lfloor c \rfloor$ or $\lfloor c \rfloor + 1$ clauses at random subject to the constraint that the variables in each clause form a right triangle with horizontal and vertical sides of length 1 and where x is the vertex opposite the hypotenuse. There are four such triangles for a given x. There are eight assignments of values to variable for each triangle giving 32 possible clauses. Our Common Lisp code for generating these 3-SAT problems is given below. Variables at the edge of the grid usually generate fewer than c clauses so the boundary of the grid is relatively unconstrained.

```
(defun make-problem (s c &aux result xx yy)
  (dotimes (x s)
    (dotimes (y s)
      (dotimes (i (+ (floor c)
                     (if (> (random 1.0)
                            (rem c 1.0))
                         0 1)))
        (setq xx (+ x -1 (* 2 (random 2)))
              yy (+ y -1 (* 2 (random 2))))
        (when (and (< -1 xx) (< xx s)
                   (< -1 yy) (< yy s))
          (push (new-clause x y xx yy s)
                result)))))
  result))

(defun new-clause (x y xx yy s)
  (mapcar
   #'(lambda (a b &aux (v (+ 1 (* s a) b)))
       (if (zerop (random 2)) v (- v)))
   (list x xx x) (list y y yy)))
```

Acknowledgement

This work has been supported by the Air Force Office of Scientific Research under contract 92-0693, by ARPA/Rome Labs under contracts numbers F30602-91-C-0036 and F30602-93-C-00031, and by ARPA under contract F33615-91-C-1788. We would like to thank Jimi Crawford, Ari Jónsson, Bart Selman and the members of CIRL for taking the time to discuss these ideas with us. Crawford especially contributed to the development of Procedure 13.

References

[Chvátal and Szemerédi,1988] V. Chvátal and E. Szemerédi. Many hard examples for resolution. *JACM*, 35:759–768, 1988.

[Crawford and Auton,1993] James M. Crawford and Larry D. Auton. Experimental results on the crossover point in satisfiability problems. In *Proceedings of the Eleventh National Conference on Artificial Intelligence*, pages 21–27, 1993.

[Crawford and Baker,1994] James M. Crawford and Andrew B. Baker. Experimental results on the application of satisfiability algorithms to scheduling problems. In *Proceedings of the Twelfth National Conference on Artificial Intelligence*, 1994.

[Davis and Putnam,1960] M. Davis and H. Putnam. A computing procedure for quantification theory. *J. Assoc. Comput. Mach.*, 7:201–215, 1960.

[de Kleer,1986] Johan de Kleer. An assumption-based truth maintenance system. *Artificial Intelligence*, 28:127–162, 1986.

[Ginsberg et al.,1990] Matthew L. Ginsberg, Michael Frank, Michael P. Halpin, and Mark C. Torrance. Search lessons learned from crossword puzzles. In *Proceedings of the Eighth National Conference on Artificial Intelligence*, pages 210–215, 1990.

[Ginsberg,1993] Matthew L. Ginsberg. Dynamic backtracking. *Journal of Artificial Intelligence Research*, 1:25–46, 1993.

[Kirkpatrick et al.,1982] S. Kirkpatrick, C.D. Gelatt, and M.P. Vecchi. Optimization by simulated annealing. *Science*, 220:671–680, 1982.

[Konolige,1994] Kurt Konolige. Easy to be hard: Difficult problems for greedy algorithms. In *Proceedings of the Fourth International Conference on Principles of Knowledge Representation and Reasoning*, Bonn, Germany, 1994.

[McAllester,1993] David A. McAllester. Partial order backtracking. ftp.ai.mit.edu: /pub/dam/dynamic.ps, 1993.

[Minton et al.,1990] Steven Minton, Mark D. Johnston, Andrew B. Philips, and Philip Laird. Solving large-scale constraint satisfaction and scheduling problems using a heuristic repair method. In *Proceedings of the Eighth National Conference on Artificial Intelligence*, pages 17–24, 1990.

[Selman and Kautz,1993] Bart Selman and Henry Kautz. Domain-independent extensions to GSAT: Solving large structured satisfiability problems. In *Proceedings of the Thirteenth International Joint Conference on Artificial Intelligence*, pages 290–295, 1993.

[Selman et al.,1992] Bart Selman, Hector Levesque, and David Mitchell. A new method for solving hard satisfiability problems. In *Proceedings of the Tenth National Conference on Artificial Intelligence*, pages 440–446, 1992.

[Selman et al.,1993] Bart Selman, Henry A. Kautz, and Bram Cohen. Local search strategies for satisfiability testing. In *Proceedings 1993 DIMACS Workshop on Maximum Clique, Graph Coloring, and Satisfiability*, 1993.

[Stallman and Sussman,1977] R. M. Stallman and G. J. Sussman. Forward reasoning and dependency-directed backtracking in a system for computer-aided circuit analysis. *Artificial Intelligence*, 9(2):135–196, 1977.

Foundations of Indefinite Constraint Databases

Manolis Koubarakis*

IC-Parc
Imperial College
London SW7 2AZ
United Kingdom
msk@doc.ic.ac.uk

Abstract. We lay the foundations of a theory of constraint databases with indefinite information based on the relational model. We develop the scheme of indefinite $\mathcal{L}$-constraint databases where $\mathcal{L}$, the parameter, is a first-order constraint language. This scheme extends the proposal of Kanellakis, Kuper and Revesz to include indefinite information in the style of Imielinski and Lipski. We propose declarative and procedural query languages for the new scheme and study the semantics of query evaluation.

1 Introduction

In this paper we lay the foundations of a theory of *indefinite constraint databases* based on the relational model [Mai83]. As a starting point of our investigation, we take the model of constraint databases proposed in [KKR90]. This model is useful for the representation of *unrestricted* (i.e., finite or infinite) *definite* information. However, indefinite information is also important in many applications e.g., planning and scheduling, medical expert systems, geographical information systems and natural language processing systems. Motivated by these practical considerations, we develop the model of *indefinite constraint databases* which allows the representation of *definite, indefinite, finite* and *infinite* information in a single unifying framework.

Our contributions to the theory of constraint databases can be summarized as follows:

- We develop the scheme of *indefinite $\mathcal{L}$-constraint databases* where $\mathcal{L}$, the parameter, is a first-order *constraint language*. This parameterized model extends the scheme of [KKR90] to include indefinite information in the style of [IL84, Gra89] (section 3).
- We propose *modal relational calculus* with $\mathcal{L}$-constraints as a declarative query languages for indefinite $\mathcal{L}$-constraint databases (section 4). We also

---

* Most of this research was carried out while the author was with the Computer Science Division, Dept. of Electrical and Computer Engineering, National Technical University of Athens, Greece.

propose a procedural query language: the *modal $\mathcal{L}$-constraint algebra* (section 5). The introduction of modal operators gives us the ability to ask "possibility" and "certainty" queries - a very useful feature in any indefinite information setting.

– We show that expressions of modal relational calculus with $\mathcal{L}$-constraints can be evaluated *bottom-up in closed form* on indefinite $\mathcal{L}$-constraint databases. This is a direct consequence of the fact that every expression of modal relational calculus with $\mathcal{L}$-constraints has an equivalent expression in modal $\mathcal{L}$-constraint algebra (section 7). This result could be the first step in developing optimization techniques for $\mathcal{L}$-constraint databases and indefinite $\mathcal{L}$-constraint databases. Our analysis is carried out in an abstract setting and therefore subsumes previous work on specific classes of constraints [KKR90, KSW90, Kou93, Kou94c, KG94, PVdBVG94].

This paper is organized as follows. The next section presents some examples of constraint languages and defines the relevant abstract concepts. In section 3 we present the scheme of indefinite $\mathcal{L}$-constraint databases. In sections 4 and 5 we discuss the modal relational calculus with $\mathcal{L}$-constraints and the modal $\mathcal{L}$-constraint algebra. In section 6 we present several results concerning algebraic query evaluation in $\mathcal{L}$-constraint databases and indefinite $\mathcal{L}$-constraint databases. In section 7 we discuss the translation of expressions of modal relational calculus with $\mathcal{L}$-constraints into expressions of modal $\mathcal{L}$-constraint algebra. Finally, section 8 presents related work and future research. All proofs are omitted. The interested reader can consult [Kou94a].

2   Constraint Languages

In this paper we consider many-sorted languages, structures and theories [End72]. Every language $\mathcal{L}$ will be interpreted over a *fixed* structure, called the *intended structure*, which will usually be denoted by $\mathbf{M}_{\mathcal{L}}$. If $\mathbf{M}$ is a structure then $Th(\mathbf{M})$ will denote the theory of $\mathbf{M}$ i.e., the set of sentences which are true in $\mathbf{M}$. For every language $\mathcal{L}$, we will distinguish a class of quantifier free formulas called $\mathcal{L}$-*constraints*. The atomic formulas of $\mathcal{L}$ will be included in the class of $\mathcal{L}$-constraints. There will also be two distinguished $\mathcal{L}$-constraints *true* and *false* with obvious semantics. Similar assumptions have been made in [Mah93] in the contex of the CLP scheme. A set of $\mathcal{L}$-constraints will be the algebraic counterpart of the logical conjunction of its members. Thus we will freely mix the terms "set of $\mathcal{L}$-constraints" and "conjunction of $\mathcal{L}$-constraints". We will assume that the reader is familiar with the notions of *solution, consistency* and *equivalence* of sets of constraints [Mah93].

Let us now give some examples of constraint languages.

Example 1. The language *ECL* (*Equality Constraint Language*) with predicate symbols $=$, $\neq$ and an infinite number of constants has been defined in [KKR90]. The intended structure for this language interprets $=$ as equality, $\neq$ as non-equality and constants as "themselves". An *ECL-constraint* is an ECL formula of the form $x_1 = x_2$ or $x_1 \neq x_2$ where x_1, x_2 are variables or constants. ECL has been used by [KKR90] for the development of an extended relational model based on ECL-constraints.

We now present a language for expressing *temporal constraints*.

Example 2. The language *dePCL* (*dense Point Constraint Language*) allows us to make stamements about points in dense time. dePCL is a first-order language with equality and the following set of non-logical symbols: the set of rational numerals, function symbol $-$ of arity 2 and predicate symbol $<$ of arity 2. The *terms* and *atomic formulas* of dePCL are defined as follows. Constants and variables are terms. If t_1 and t_2 are variables or constants then $t_1 - t_2$ is a term. An *atomic formula* of dePCL is a formula of the form $t \sim c$ or $c \sim t$ where $\sim$ is $<$ or $=$ and t is a term.

The intended structure for dePCL is **Q**. **Q** interprets each rational numeral by its corresponding rational number, function symbol $-$ by the subtraction operation over the rationals and $<$ by the relation "less than". The theory $Th(\mathbf{Q})$ is a subtheory of real addition with order [Rab77].

A *dePCL-constraint* is a dePCL formula of the form $t \sim c$ where t is a term, c is a constant and $\sim$ is $=, <, >, \leq$ or $\geq$. For example, the formulas $p_1 < p_2$, $p_3 - p_4 \geq 15$, $p_3 = 5/4$ are dePCL-constraints.

Example 3. Let us also consider the many-sorted language ECL+dePCL which is the union of ECL and dePCL. The sorts of ECL+dePCL are $\mathcal{D}$ (for the infinite set of constants of ECL) and $\mathcal{Q}$ (for the rational numerals of dePCL). The symbols of ECL+dePCL are interpreted by the many-sorted structure which is the union of the intended structures for ECL and dePCL.

Let us now define the concept of *variable elimination*.[2]

Definition 1. Let $\mathcal{L}$ be a many-sorted first-order language. The class of $\mathcal{L}$-constraints *admits variable elimination* iff for every boolean combination ϕ of $\mathcal{L}$-constraints in variables $\bar{x}$, and every vector of variables $\bar{z} \subseteq \bar{x}$, there exists a disjunction ϕ' of conjunctions of $\mathcal{L}$-constraints in variables $\bar{x} \setminus \bar{z}$ such that

1. If $\bar{x}^0$ is a solution of ϕ then $\bar{x}^0 \setminus \bar{z}^0$ is a solution of ϕ'.
2. If $\bar{x}^0 \setminus \bar{z}^0$ is a solution of ϕ' then this solution can be extended to a solution $\bar{x}^0$ of ϕ.

---

[2] Notation: The vector of symbols $(o_1, \ldots, o_n)$ will be denoted by $\bar{o}$. The natural number n will be called the *size* of $\bar{o}$ and will be denoted by $|\bar{o}|$. This notation will be used for vectors of variables but also for vectors of domain elements. Variables will be denoted by x, y, z, t etc. and vectors of variables by $\bar{x}, \bar{y}, \bar{z}, \bar{t}$ etc. If $\bar{x}$ and $\bar{y}$ are vectors of variables then $\bar{x} \setminus \bar{y}$ will denote the vector obtained from $\bar{x}$ by deleting the variables in $\bar{y}$. If $\bar{x}$ is a vector of variables then $\bar{x}^0$ will be a vector of constants of the same size.

Some people might find the above definition overly strong. But requiring ϕ' to be just a boolean combination of $\mathcal{L}$-constraints would turn out to be unsatisfactory for the database models discussed in section 3. The reason is very simple: when we eliminate variables, we would have to deal with negations of $\mathcal{L}$-constraints. Similar arguments and definitions appear in [Stu91].

The following definition will be useful in the forthcoming sections.

Definition 2. Let $\mathcal{L}$ be a many-sorted first-order language. The class of $\mathcal{L}$-constraints is *weakly closed under negation* if the negation of every $\mathcal{L}$-constraint is equivalent to a disjunction of $\mathcal{L}$-constraints.

In the rest of this paper we will only be interested in constraints which admit variable elimination and are weakly closed under negation. Many interesting classes of constraints fall under this category. The following proposition shows that this is also the case for the constraint classes defined in this section.

Proposition 3. *The classes of ECL-constraints, dePCL-constraints and ECL+dePCL-constraints admit variable elimination and are weakly closed under negation.*

3 Indefinite Constraint Databases

We will now extend the $\mathcal{L}$-constraint database model of [KKR90] to account for indefinite information in the style of [IL84, Gra89]. For the rest of this section, let $\mathcal{L}$ be a many-sorted language and $\mathbf{M}_\mathcal{L}$ be the *intended $\mathcal{L}$-structure*. Let us also assume that the class of $\mathcal{L}$-constraints admits variable elimination and is weakly closed under negation.

For each sort $s \in sorts(\mathcal{L})$, let U_s be a countably infinite set of *attributes* of sort s. The set of all attributes, denoted by $\mathcal{U}$, is $\bigcup_{s \in sorts(\mathcal{L})} U_s$. The sort of attribute A will be denoted by $sort(A)$. With each $A \in \mathcal{U}$ we associate a set of values $dom(A) = dom(s, \mathbf{M}_\mathcal{L})$ called the *domain* of A.[3] A *relation scheme* R is a finite subset of $\mathcal{U}$.

We will first define $\mathbf{M}_\mathcal{L}$-relations which are unrestricted (i.e., finite or infinite) standard relations. $\mathbf{M}_\mathcal{L}$-relations are a theoretical device for giving semantics to indefinite $\mathcal{L}$-constraint relations.

Definition 4. Let R be a relation scheme. An $\mathbf{M}_\mathcal{L}$-*relational tuple* t over scheme R is a mapping from R to $\bigcup_{s \in sorts(\mathcal{L})} dom(s, \mathbf{M}_\mathcal{L})$ such that $t(A) \in dom(sort(A), \mathbf{M}_\mathcal{L})$. An $\mathbf{M}_\mathcal{L}$-*relation* r over scheme R is an *unrestricted* set of $\mathbf{M}_\mathcal{L}$-relational tuples over R.

For every $s \in sorts(\mathcal{L})$, we now assume the existence of two disjoint countably infinite sets of *variables*: the set of u-variables $UVAR_\mathcal{L}^s$ and the set of e-variables $EVAR_\mathcal{L}^s$. Let $UVAR_\mathcal{L}$ and $EVAR_\mathcal{L}$ denote $\bigcup_{s \in sorts(\mathcal{L})} UVAR_\mathcal{L}^s$ and $\bigcup_{s \in sorts(\mathcal{L})} EVAR_\mathcal{L}^s$ respectively. The intersection of the sets $UVAR_\mathcal{L}$ and $EVAR_\mathcal{L}$ with the domains of attributes is empty.

---

[3] If s is a sort and M is a structure then $dom(s, \mathbf{M})$ denotes the domain of s in structure **M**.

Notation 3.1 U-variables will be denoted by letters of the English alphabet, usually x, y, z, t, possibly subscripted. E-variables will be denoted by letters of the Greek alphabet, usually $\omega, \lambda, \zeta, \nu$, possibly subscripted.

Definition 5. Let R be a relation scheme. An *indefinite $\mathcal{L}$-constraint tuple t* over scheme R is a mapping from $R \cup \{CON\}$ to $UVAR_\mathcal{L} \cup WFF(\mathcal{L})$ such that (i) $t(A) \in UVAR_\mathcal{L}^{sort(A)}$ for each $A \in R$, (ii) $t(A_i)$ is different than $t(A_j)$ for all distinct A_i, $A_j \in R$, (iii) $t(CON)$ is a conjunction of $\mathcal{L}$-constraints and (iv) the free variables of $t(CON)$ are included in $\{t(A) : A \in R\} \cup EVAR_\mathcal{L}$. $t(CON)$ is called the *local condition* of the tuple t while $t(R)$ is called the *proper part* of t.

Definition 6. Let R be a relation scheme. An *indefinite $\mathcal{L}$-constraint relation* over scheme R is a *finite* set of indefinite $\mathcal{L}$-constraint tuples over R. Each indefinite $\mathcal{L}$-constraint relation r is associated with a boolean combination of $\mathcal{L}$-constraints $G(r)$, called the *global condition* of r.

Similarly we can define database schemes, $M_\mathcal{L}$-relational databases and indefinite $\mathcal{L}$-constraint databases [Kou94a]. Database schemes and databases will usually be denoted by $\tilde{R}$ and $\tilde{r}$ respectively.

The above definitions extend the model of [KKR90] by introducing *e-variables* which have the semantics of marked nulls of [IL84]. As in [Gra89], the possible values of the e-variables can be constrained by a *global condition*.

Example 4. BOOKED is an indefinite ECL+dePCL-constraint relation giving the times that rooms are booked. The first tuple says that room WP212 is booked from 1:00 to 7:00. For room WP219 the information is indefinite: it is booked from 1:00 until some time between 5:00 and 8:00. This indefinite information is captured by the *e-variable* ω and its global condition $5 \leq \omega \leq 8$. *E-variables* can be understood as being existentially quantified and their scope is the entire database. They represent values that exist but are not known precisely [IL84, Gra89]. All we know about these values is captured by the global condition. *U-variables* (e.g., x_1, x_2, t_1, t_2) can be understood as being universally quantified and their scope is the tuple in which they appear [KKR90].

BOOKED

Room	Time	CON
x_1	t_1	$x_1 = WP212, 1 \leq t_1 < 7$
x_2	t_2	$x_2 = WP219, 1 \leq t_2 < \omega$

$G(BOOKED): 5 \leq \omega \leq 8$

3.1 Semantics

Let us first define two special kinds of valuations. An *e-valuation* in $M_\mathcal{L}$ is a valuation whose domain is restricted to the set $EVAR_\mathcal{L}$. Similarly, a *u-valuation* in $M_\mathcal{L}$ is a valuation whose domain is restricted to the set $UVAR_\mathcal{L}$. The symbols

$Val^e_{\mathbf{M}_\mathcal{L}}$ and $Val^u_{\mathbf{M}_\mathcal{L}}$ will denote the set of e-valuations and u-valuations in $\mathbf{M}_\mathcal{L}$ respectively. The result of applying an e-valuation v to an indefinite $\mathcal{L}$-constraint relation r over R will be denoted by $v(r)$. $v(r)$ is an $\mathcal{L}$-constraint relation over R obtained from r by substituting each e-variable ω of r by the constant symbol whose denotation in structure $\mathbf{M}_\mathcal{L}$ is $v(\omega)$. The result of applying a u-valuation of $\mathbf{M}_\mathcal{L}$ to the proper part of a tuple can be defined as follows. If t is an $\mathcal{L}$-constraint tuple on scheme R and u is a u-valuation in $\mathbf{M}_\mathcal{L}$ then $u(t)$ is an $\mathbf{M}_\mathcal{L}$-tuple over R such that for each $A \in R$, $u(t)(A) = u(t(A))$.

The semantics of an $\mathcal{L}$-constraint relation is given by the function *points* [KKR90]. *points* takes as argument an $\mathcal{L}$-constraint relation r over R and returns the $\mathbf{M}_\mathcal{L}$-relation over R which is finitely represented by r:

$$points(r) = \{u(t) : t \in r, \ u \in Val^u_{\mathbf{M}_\mathcal{L}} \text{ and } \mathbf{M}_\mathcal{L} \models t(CON)[u]\}.$$

The *semantics* of an indefinite $\mathcal{L}$-constraint relation r over scheme R is defined to be the following set of $\mathbf{M}_\mathcal{L}$-relations:

$$sem(r) = \{points(v(r)) : \text{ there exists } v \in Val^e_{\mathbf{M}_\mathcal{L}} \text{ s.t. } \mathbf{M}_\mathcal{L} \models G(r)[v]\}.$$

The function *rep* will also be useful in the rest of this paper. If r is an indefinite $\mathcal{L}$-constraint relation over scheme R then *rep* gives the set of $\mathcal{L}$-constraint relations represented by r:

$$rep(r) = \{v(r) : \text{ there exists } v \in Val^e_{\mathbf{M}_\mathcal{L}} \text{ s.t. } \mathbf{M}_\mathcal{L} \models G(r)[v]\}$$

The functions *points*, *sem* and *rep* can be extended to databases in the obvious way.[4]

4 Declarative Query Languages

[KKR90] proposed *relational calculus with $\mathcal{L}$-constraints* as a declarative query language for $\mathcal{L}$-constraint databases. In this section we propose *modal relational calculus with $\mathcal{L}$-constraints* as a declarative query language for indefinite $\mathcal{L}$-constraint databases. Similar modal query languages have been investigated in [Lip79, Lev84, Rei88].

Definition 7. Let $\tilde{R}$ be a database scheme and $R(C_1, \ldots, C_m)$ be a relation scheme. An expression over $\tilde{R}$ in *modal relational calculus with $\mathcal{L}$-constraints* is $\{R(C_1, \ldots, C_m), x_1/s_1, \ldots, x_m/s_m : OP \ \phi(x_1, \ldots, x_m)\}$ where $s_i \in sorts(\mathcal{L})$ is the sort of C_i, OP is an *optional* modal operator $\Diamond$ or $\Box$, ϕ is a well-formed formula of relational calculus with $\mathcal{L}$-constraints and $x_1, \ldots, x_m$ are the only free variables of ϕ. If an expression does not contain a modal operator then it will be called *pure*, otherwise it will be called *modal*.

---

[4] The above definitions imply that indefinite $\mathcal{L}$-constraint relations are interpreted in a *closed-world* fashion. They are assumed to represent all facts relevant to an application domain. However the exact value of any attribute of these facts may not be known precisely.

We will now define the *value* of expressions in modal relational calculus.

Definition 8. Let f be the pure expression $\{R(C_1,\ldots,C_m),x_1/s_1,\ldots,x_m/s_m :$
$\phi(x_1,\ldots,x_m)\}$ over $\tilde{R}$ in modal relational calculus with $\mathcal{L}$-constraints. If $\tilde{r}$ is an indefinite $\mathcal{L}$-constraint database over $\tilde{R}$ then the *value* of f on the set of $\mathbf{M}_\mathcal{L}$-relational databases $sem(\tilde{r})$, whose finite representation is $\tilde{r}$, is the following set of $\mathbf{M}_\mathcal{L}$-relations:

$$f(sem(\tilde{r})) = \{ \ \{(a_1,\ldots,a_m) \in dom(s_1) \times \cdots \times dom(s_m) :$$
$$(\mathbf{M}_\mathcal{L}, Dom, \tilde{r}') \models \phi(a_1,\ldots,a_m)\} \ : \tilde{r}' \in sem(\tilde{r})\}$$

The question left open by the above definition is whether we can guarantee *closure* as required by the constraint query language principles laid out in [KKR90]. In other words, given a pure expression f of modal relational calculus with $\mathcal{L}$-constraints, and an indefinite $\mathcal{L}$-constraint database $\tilde{r}$, is it possible to find an indefinite $\mathcal{L}$-constraint relation which finitely represents $f(sem(\tilde{r}))$? In section 7, we show that the answer to this question is in the affirmative.

Example 5. The query "Find all rooms that are booked at 6:00" over the database of example 4 can be expressed as $\{BOOKED\_AT\_6(Room),x/\mathcal{D} : BOOKED(x,6)\}$. The answer to this query is given by the following relation:

BOOKED_AT_6

Room	CON
x_1	$x_1 = WP212$
x_2	$x_2 = WP219, \ \omega > 6$

This answer is *conditional*. Room WP212 is booked on time 6. However, room WP219 is booked on time 6 *only under the condition* that ω is greater than 6. In section 7 we will show how to evaluate calculus queries and compute a finite representation of the answer.

Definition 9. Let f be the modal expression $\{R(C_1,\ldots,C_m),x_1/s_1,\ldots,x_m/s_m$
$\Box \ \phi(x_1,\ldots,x_m)\}$ over $\tilde{R}$ in modal relational calculus with $\mathcal{L}$-constraints. If $\tilde{r}$ is an indefinite $\mathcal{L}$-constraint database over $\tilde{R}$ then the *value* of f on the set of $\mathbf{M}_\mathcal{L}$-relational databases $sem(\tilde{r})$, whose finite representation is $\tilde{r}$, is the following *singleton* set of $\mathbf{M}_\mathcal{L}$-relations:

$$f(sem(\tilde{r})) = \{ \ \{(a_1,\ldots,a_m) \in dom(s_1) \times \cdots \times dom(s_m) : \text{for every}$$
$$\mathbf{M}_\mathcal{L}\text{-relational database } \tilde{r}' \in sem(\tilde{r})$$
$$(\mathbf{M}_\mathcal{L}, Dom, \tilde{r}') \models \phi(a_1,\ldots,a_m)\} \ \}$$

The value of a $\Diamond$-expression is defined in the same way but now the quantification over $\mathbf{M}_\mathcal{L}$-relational databases in $sem(\tilde{r})$ is existential. Section 7 demonstrates that expressions of modal relational calculus with $\mathcal{L}$-constraints can also be evaluated in closed form. In summary, for every expression f (pure or modal) in modal relational calculus with $\mathcal{L}$-constraints and indefinite $\mathcal{L}$-constraint database $\tilde{r}$, it is possible to find an indefinite $\mathcal{L}$-constraint relation which finitely represents $f(\tilde{r})$.

Example 6. The query "Find all rooms that are possibly booked at 6:00" over the database of example 4 can be expressed as $\{POSS\_BOOKED\_AT\_6(Room), x/\mathcal{D} : \Diamond BOOKED(x,6)\}$. If this query is evaluated using the method of section 7, the answer will be the following relation:

POSS_BOOKED_AT_6

Room	CON
x_1	$x_1 = WP212$
x_2	$x_2 = WP219$

The above answer is *unconditional.* It is possible that both rooms WP212 and WP219 are booked on time 6.

The next lemma demonstrates an intuitive property of modal relational calculus with $\mathcal{L}$-constraints. If $\mathcal{S}$ is a set of sets then $\bigcap \mathcal{S}$ (resp. $\bigcup \mathcal{S}$) denotes the set $\{\cap_{s \in \mathcal{S}} s\}$ (resp. $\{\cup_{s \in \mathcal{S}} s\}$).

Lemma 10. *Let f be a $\Box$-expression (resp. $\Diamond$-expression) over $\widetilde{R}$ in modal relational calculus with $\mathcal{L}$-constraints. Let f' be the pure expression which corresponds to f. Then for all indefinite $\mathcal{L}$-constraint databases $\widetilde{r}$ over $\widetilde{R}$, $f(sem(\widetilde{r})) = \bigcap f'(sem(\widetilde{r}))$ (resp. $f(sem(\widetilde{r})) = \bigcup f'(sem(\widetilde{r})))$.*

5 Procedural Query Languages

In this section, we briefly sketch three procedural query languages, one for each of the models discussed in section 3: the $\mathbf{M}_{\mathcal{L}}$-*relational algebra*, the $\mathcal{L}$-*constraint algebra* and the *modal $\mathcal{L}$-constraint algebra*. The $\mathbf{M}_{\mathcal{L}}$-relational algebra is a procedural query language for $\mathbf{M}_{\mathcal{L}}$-relational databases. It is interesting only from a theoretical point of view because $\mathbf{M}_{\mathcal{L}}$-relations are unrestricted. The operations of $\mathbf{M}_{\mathcal{L}}$-relational algebra can be defined verbatim as in the case of finite relations [Kan90].

The operations of the $\mathcal{L}$-constraint algebra are extensions of similar operations of standard relational algebra [Kan90]. The $\mathcal{L}$-constraint algebra has not been presented in [KKR90] where the model of $\mathcal{L}$-constraint databases was originally defined. However its definition is straightforward and can be found in [Kou94a] and in the full version of this paper. The algebras of [KSW90, Kou93, Kou94c, KG94, PVdBVG94] are essentially instances of the $\mathcal{L}$-constraint algebra.[5]

The operations of the *modal $\mathcal{L}$-constraint algebra* take as input one (or two) indefinite $\mathcal{L}$-constraint relations associated with a common global condition and return an indefinite $\mathcal{L}$-constraint relation associated with the *same* global

---

[5] The algebra of [KG94] also explores *canonical forms* for databases with dense order constraints. This issue is not discussed in this paper because our model is abstract. One might also add that canonical forms are important *only* in the context of a specific implementation.

condition. The modal $\mathcal{L}$-constraint algebra contains an operation for every $\mathcal{L}$-constraint algebra operation. The definitions of these operations were originally given in [Kou93] for the special case of indefinite dePCL-constraint relations.[6] These operations treat e-variables as uninterpreted parameters thus they are defined exactly as the $\mathcal{L}$-constraint algebra operations. Similar operations were defined in [IL84, Gra89] for the special case of conditional tables.

The modal algebra also includes two additional operations $POSS$ and $CERT$, which take a more active stand towards e-variables. Given an indefinite $\mathcal{L}$-constraint relation r, the expression $POSS(r)$ evaluates to an $\mathcal{L}$-constraint relation which finitely represents the set of all tuples contained in *any* relation of $sem(r)$. The expression $CERT(r)$ evaluates to an $\mathcal{L}$-constraint relation which finitely represents the set of all tuples contained in *every* relation of $sem(r)$.

Possibility. Let r be an indefinite $\mathcal{L}$-constraint relation on scheme R. Then $POSS(r)$ is an *$\mathcal{L}$-constraint relation* defined as follows:

1. $sch(POSS(r)) = sch(r)$
2. $POSS(r) = \{poss(t) : t \in r\}$.

For each tuple t on scheme R, $poss(t)$ is a tuple on scheme R such that $poss(t)(R) = t(R)$ and $poss(t)(CON) = \psi$ where ψ is obtained by eliminating all e-variables from the boolean combination of $\mathcal{L}$-constraints $G(r) \wedge t(CON)$. The expression $poss(t)(CON)$ is well-defined since the class of $\mathcal{L}$-constraints admits variable elimination.

Certainty. Let r be an indefinite $\mathcal{L}$-constraint relation on scheme R. Then $CERT(r)$ is an $\mathcal{L}$-constraint relation defined as follows:

1. $sch(CERT(r)) = sch(r)$
2. $CERT(r) = \{cert(t) : t \in r^{\downarrow}\}^{\uparrow}$.

For each tuple t on scheme R, $cert(t)$ is a tuple on scheme R such that $cert(t)(R) = t(R)$ and $cert(t)(CON) = \neg\psi$ where ψ is obtained by eliminating all e-variables from the boolean combination of $\mathcal{L}$-constraints $G(r) \wedge \neg t(CON)$. The expression $cert(t)(CON)$ is well-defined since the class of $\mathcal{L}$-constraints admits variable elimination.

The operation $r^{\downarrow}$ has the effect of *denormalizing* $\mathcal{L}$-constraint relation r. This is achieved by collecting all tuples $\{t_1, \ldots, t_{|r|}\}$ of r into a single tuple t' on scheme R such that $t'(R) = (x_1, \ldots, x_{|R|})$ and $t'(CON) = t'_1(CON) \vee \cdots \vee t'_{|r|}(CON)$. In the new tuple t' u-variables have been standardized apart: $x_1, \ldots, x_{|R|}$ are brand new u-variables, and for $1 \leq i \leq |r|$, $t'_i(CON)$ is the same as $t_i(CON)$ except that $t(X)$ has been substituted by $t'(X)$ for each $X \in R$.

The operation $r^{\uparrow}$ has the effect of *normalizing* the local conditions of a relation r in order to obtain a true $\mathcal{L}$-constraint relation. This is done by the following three steps:

- Application of De Morgan's laws to transform the negated parts of each local condition of r into a disjunction whose disjuncts are $\mathcal{L}$-constraints.

---

[6] [Kou93] uses the term *temporal tables* for indefinite dePCL-constraint relations.

This operation is well-defined since the class of $\mathcal{L}$-constraints is weakly closed under negation.

- Application of the law of associativity of conjunction with respect to disjunction to transform each local condition of r into a disjunction of conjunctions of $\mathcal{L}$-constraints.
- Splitting of disjuncts into different tuples.

Let us now define modal $\mathcal{L}$-constraint algebra expressions.

Definition 11. A *pure expression* over scheme $\widetilde{R}$ in modal $\mathcal{L}$-constraint algebra is any well-formed expression built from constant $\mathcal{L}$-constraint relations, relation schemes from $\widetilde{R}$ and the above operators excluding $POSS$ and $CERT$. A *modal $\mathcal{L}$-constraint algebra expression* is a pure expression, or an expression of the form $CERT(g)$ or $POSS(g)$ where g is a pure expression. Expressions of the form $CERT(g)$ or $POSS(g)$ are called *CERT-expressions* or *POSS-expressions* respectively.

Modal $\mathcal{L}$-constraint algebra expressions define functions from indefinite $\mathcal{L}$-constraint databases to indefinite $\mathcal{L}$-constraint relations. The result of applying an expression e to an indefinite $\mathcal{L}$-constraint database $\widetilde{r}$ is defined as for the $\mathcal{L}$-constraint algebra. Let us simply stress that $G(e(\widetilde{r})) = G(\widetilde{r})$ for all indefinite $\mathcal{L}$-constraint databases $\widetilde{r}$ and expressions e over $\widetilde{R}$.

The following lemma gives an intuitive property of $POSS$ and $CERT$.

Lemma 12. *Let e be a pure expression over scheme $\widetilde{R}$ in modal $\mathcal{L}$-constraint algebra. Then for all indefinite $\mathcal{L}$-constraint databases $\widetilde{r}$ over $\widetilde{R}$*

$$sem(CERT(e(\widetilde{r}))) = \bigcap sem(e(\widetilde{r})) \text{ and } sem(POSS(e(\widetilde{r}))) = \bigcup sem(e(\widetilde{r})).$$

6 On the Semantics of Algebraic Query Evaluation

Let $\widetilde{r}$ be an $\mathcal{L}$-constraint database, e an $\mathcal{L}$-constraint algebra expression and $e1$ its corresponding $\mathbf{M}_{\mathcal{L}}$-relational algebra expression. Recall that an $\mathcal{L}$-constraint relation $\widetilde{r}$ is a finite representation of the unrestricted set of tuples $points(\widetilde{r})$. The following theorem shows that the operations of $\mathcal{L}$-constraint algebra "behave" according to our intuitions: when we evaluate e on $\widetilde{r}$, we essentially evaluate $e1$ on the unrestricted relation $points(\widetilde{r})$. This theorem generalizes the results of [KG94, Kou94c, PVdBVG94] who consider *specific* constraint languages.

Theorem 13. *Let e be an $\mathcal{L}$-constraint algebra expression over $\widetilde{R}$ and $e1$ be its corresponding $\mathbf{M}_{\mathcal{L}}$-relational algebra expression. If $\widetilde{r}$ is an $\mathcal{L}$-constraint database over scheme $\widetilde{R}$, then $points(e(\widetilde{r})) = e1(points(\widetilde{r}))$.*

Let us now assume that $\widetilde{r}$ is an indefinite $\mathcal{L}$-constraint database, e is a pure expression of modal $\mathcal{L}$-constraint algebra and $e1$ is its corresponding expression in $\mathcal{L}$-constraint algebra. Recall that the semantic function $sem(\widetilde{r})$ returns all the "possible worlds" represented by $\widetilde{r}$. When we evaluate e on indefinite

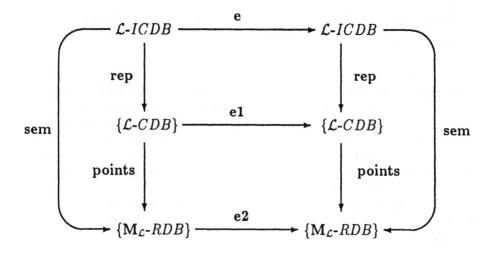

Fig. 1. Relating the three algebras

$\mathcal{L}$-constraint database $\widetilde{r}$ using the operations defined above, we essentially evaluate the corresponding $\mathbf{M}_{\mathcal{L}}$-relational algebra expression on each possible world in $sem(\widetilde{r})$. As discussed in [Imi89], an extension of an $\mathbf{M}_{\mathcal{L}}$-relational algebra expression $e1$ to an expression e for an $\mathcal{L}$-constraint representation of indefinite information can claim to be "faithful to the underlying semantics" if and only if for every indefinite $\mathcal{L}$-constraint database $\widetilde{r}$,

$$sem(e(\widetilde{r})) = e1(sem(\widetilde{r})) = \{e1(r_1) : \ r_1 \in sem(\widetilde{r})\}.$$

Equivalently, one would like to guarantee that there is always an indefinite $\mathcal{L}$-constraint database $\widetilde{r}'$ such that $sem(\widetilde{r}') = e1(sem(\widetilde{r}))$. The following theorem demonstrates that $\mathcal{L}$-constraint databases satisfy this form of algebraic closure. This theorem generalizes a result of [Kou94c] who considers databases with dePCL-constraints.

Theorem 14. *Let e be a pure expression of modal $\mathcal{L}$-constraint algebra over $\widetilde{R}$, $e1$ its corresponding $\mathcal{L}$-constraint algebra expression and $e2$ its corresponding $\mathbf{M}_{\mathcal{L}}$-relational algebra expression. If $\widetilde{r}$ is an indefinite $\mathcal{L}$-constraint database over scheme $\widetilde{R}$ then $rep(e(\widetilde{r}))$ is equivalent to $e1(rep(\widetilde{r}))$ and $sem(e(\widetilde{r})) = e2(sem(\widetilde{r}))$.*

The above theorems are summarized graphically in the commutative diagram of figure 1 where $\mathbf{M}_{\mathcal{L}}$-RDB denotes the set of all $\mathbf{M}_{\mathcal{L}}$-relational databases, $\mathcal{L}$-CDB denotes the set of all $\mathcal{L}$-constraint databases and $\mathcal{L}$-$ICDB$ denotes the set of all indefinite $\mathcal{L}$-constraint databases. Since the above results have been proved in our general framework, specific cases of constraint databases [KKR90, KSW90, Kou93, Kou94c, KG94, PVdBVG94] can simply refer to these theorems to demonstrate the "correctness" of the operations of their algebraic query languages.

7 Translating Calculus Expressions into Algebraic Expressions

In this section we show that expressions of modal relational calculus with $\mathcal{L}$-constraints have equivalent expressions in modal $\mathcal{L}$-constraint algebra. Thus we can evaluate a calculus expression by evaluating an equivalent algebraic expression. As we have seen in section 5, algebraic query evaluation can be done bottom-up and the answer is obtained in closed form. Therefore calculus expressions can also be evaluated bottom-up in closed form on indefinite $\mathcal{L}$-constraint databases. [Kou94a] gives an alternative proof of this result by employing quantifier elimination techniques as suggested in [KKR90].

We start by considering the simpler case of $\mathcal{L}$-constraint databases. The following theorem generalizes the analogous results of [KKR90, Kou94c, PVdBVG94] who consider *specific* constraint languages.

Theorem 15. *For every expression f over $\widetilde{R}$ in relational calculus with $\mathcal{L}$-constraints there exists an $\mathcal{L}$-constraint algebra expression e over $\widetilde{R}$ such that the following property holds. If $\widetilde{r}$ is an $\mathcal{L}$-constraint database over $\widetilde{R}$ then $f(points(\widetilde{r})) = points(e(\widetilde{r}))$.*

Let us note here that the analogous proofs of [KKR90] rely on quantifier elimination methods which achieve good data complexity lower bounds but do not seem to have practical implementations. In contrast, the above theorem (as well as the analogous theorems of [KG94, Kou94c, PVdBVG94]) provides a translation of calculus expressions into algebraic expressions. This translation can be the first step in optimizing the evaluation of expressions in relational calculus with $\mathcal{L}$-constraints.

Let us now turn to modal relational calculus with $\mathcal{L}$-constraints and modal $\mathcal{L}$-constraint algebra.

Lemma 16. *Let e be a pure expression over $\widetilde{R}$ in modal $\mathcal{L}$-constraint algebra and e' be its corresponding $\mathcal{L}$-constraint algebra expression. Then $sem(e(\widetilde{r})) = \{points(e'(\widetilde{r}')) : \widetilde{r}' \in rep(\widetilde{r})\}$ for all indefinite $\mathcal{L}$-constraint databases $\widetilde{r}$ over $\widetilde{R}$.*

The following theorem demonstrates that pure expressions of modal relational calculus with $\mathcal{L}$-constraints over indefinite $\mathcal{L}$-constraint databases can also be evaluated bottom-up in closed form.

Theorem 17. *For every pure expression f over $\widetilde{R}$ in relational calculus with $\mathcal{L}$-constraints there exists a pure expression e over $\widetilde{R}$ in modal $\mathcal{L}$-constraint algebra such that the following property holds. If $\widetilde{r}$ is an indefinite $\mathcal{L}$-constraint database over $\widetilde{R}$ then $f(sem(\widetilde{r})) = sem(e(\widetilde{r}))$.*

Example 7. The algebraic expression equivalent to the calculus expression of example 5 is

$$\pi_{Room}(\sigma_{Time=6}(BOOKED)).$$

Finally we turn to modal expressions.

Theorem 18. *Let f be a $\Box$-expression (resp. $\Diamond$-expression) over $\widetilde{R}$ in modal relational calculus with $\mathcal{L}$-constraints. Then there exists a $CERT$-expression (resp. POSS-expression) e over $\widetilde{R}$ in modal $\mathcal{L}$-constraint algebra such that the following property holds. If $\widetilde{r}$ is an indefinite $\mathcal{L}$-constraint database over $\widetilde{R}$ then $f(sem(\widetilde{r})) = sem(e(\widetilde{r}))$.*

Example 8. The algebraic expression equivalent to the calculus expression of example 6 is

$$POSS(\pi_{Room}(\sigma_{Time=6}(BOOKED))).$$

8   Related Work and Future Research

The results of this study are extended in [Kou94b, Kou94a] where we concentrate on *temporal constraint databases* (with or without indefinite information). In particular, we study the complexity of query evaluation in $\mathcal{L}$-constraint databases and indefinite $\mathcal{L}$-constraint databases where $\mathcal{L}$ ranges over several temporal constraint languages (including dePCL). Our analysis shows that the worst-case data/combined complexity of query evaluation *does not change* when we move from queries in relational calculus over relational databases, to queries in relational calculus with temporal constraints over temporal constraint databases. This fact remains true even if we consider indefinite relational databases vs. indefinite temporal constraint databases. Unfortunately, the presence of indefinite information makes query evaluation intractable in many cases. Our analysis complements the results of [Rev90, CM93] and extends the results of [KKR90, vdM92].

The research reported in [SRR] is closely related to our own. This paper investigates the use of constraints for the representation of infinite and indefinite information in a simple object-oriented model. The authors do not consider the properties of an abstract constraint-object model; instead, they concentrate on a special case which uses order constraints and simple set constraints (e.g., constraints using $\in$, $\subseteq$ but not $\cap$ or $\cup$). The important contribution of this paper is the study of quantifier-elimination for this simple class of set constraints and the development of a Datalog-like query language which incorporates them. This query language is intended for the expression of "certainty" queries only; "possibility" queries are not considered.

In other related work [ACGK, GS94, PVdBVG94] study the expressive power of query languages with linear and polynomial constraints. [GS94] in particular demonstrate that the theory of finitely representable models differs substantially from classical model theory and finite model theory. This suggests a need for developing new tools for considering definability of queries in the constraint database context.

We are currently considering query languages based on first-order constraint languages more expressive than diPCL and dePCL. The interesting question is whether the results of [Kou94a] carry over to the new classes. Another interesting question is the study of tractable cases of indefinite diPCL/dePCL-constraint databases. The work of [vdM92] can serve as the basis for such an effort.

Acknowledgements

I would like to thank Timos Sellis and Barry Richards for their support and encouragement. I would also like to thank Peter Revesz and Paris Kanellakis for promptly answering my questions concerning their work on constraint databases.

References

[ACGK]   F. Afrati, S. Cosmadakis, S. Grumbach, and G. Kuper. Linear vs. Polynomial Constraints in Database Query Languages. In this volume.

[CM93]   J. Cox and K. McAloon. Decision Procedures for Constraint Based Extensions of Datalog. In F. Benhamou and A. Colmerauer, editors, *Constraint Logic Programming: Selected Research*. MIT Press, 1993. Originally appeared as Technical Report No. 90-09, Dept. of Computer and Information Sciences, Brooklyn College of C.U.N.Y.

[End72]   H.B. Enderton. *A Mathematical Introduction to Logic*. Academic Press, 1972.

[Gra89]   Gosta Grahne. The Problem of Incomplete Information in Relational Databases. Technical Report Report A-1989-1, Department of Computer Science, University of Helsinki, Finland, 1989. Also published as Lecture Notes in Computer Science 554, Springer Verlag, 1991.

[GS94]   S. Grumbach and J. Su. Finitely representable databases. In *Proceedings of the 13th ACM SIGACT-SIGMOD-SIGART Symposium on Principles of Database Systems*, pages 289–300, 1994.

[IL84]   T. Imielinski and W. Lipski. Incomplete Information in Relational Databases. *Journal of ACM*, 31(4):761–791, 1984.

[Imi89]   T. Imielinski. Incomplete Information in Logical Databases. *Data Engineering*, 12(2):29–39, 1989.

[Kan90]   Paris Kanellakis. Elements of Relational Database Theory. In J. van Leeuwen, editor, *Handbook of Theoretical Computer Science*, volume B, chapter 17. North-Holland, 1990.

[KG94]   P.C. Kanellakis and D. Goldin. Constraint Programming and Database Query Languages. In *Proceedings of Theoretical Aspects of Computer Software (TACS)*, volume 789 of *Lecture Notes in Computer Science*, pages 96–120. Springer-Verlag, April 1994.

[KKR90]   Paris C. Kanellakis, Gabriel M. Kuper, and Peter Z. Revesz. Constraint Query Languages. In *Proceedings of the 9th ACM SIGACT-SIGMOD-SIGART Symposium on Principles of Database Systems*, pages 299–313, 1990. Long version to appear in Journal of Computer and System Sciences.

[Kou93]   Manolis Koubarakis. Representation and Querying in Temporal Databases: the Power of Temporal Constraints. In *Proceedings of the 9th International Conference on Data Engineering*, pages 327–334, April 1993.

[Kou94a] M. Koubarakis. *Foundations of Temporal Constraint Databases*. PhD thesis, Computer Science Division, Dept. of Electrical and Computer Engineering, National Technical University of Athens, February 1994.

[Kou94b]   Manolis Koubarakis. Complexity Results for First-Order Theories of
            Temporal Constraints. In *Principles of Knowledge Representation and
            Reasoning: Proceedings of the Fourth International Conference (KR'94)*,
            pages 379–390. Morgan Kaufmann, San Francisco, CA, May 1994.

[Kou94c]   Manolis Koubarakis. Database Models for Infinite and Indefinite Tem-
            poral Information. *Information Systems*, 19(2):141–173, March 1994.

[KSW90]   F. Kabanza, J.-M. Stevenne, and P. Wolper. Handling Infinite Temporal
            Data. In *Proceedings of ACM SIGACT-SIGMOD-SIGART Symposium
            on Principles of Database Systems*, pages 392–403, 1990.

[Lev84]   H.J. Levesque. Foundations of a Functional Approach to Knowledge
            Representation. *Artificial Intelligence*, 23:155–212, 1984.

[Lip79]   Witold Jr. Lipski. On Semantic Issues Connected with Incomplete Infor-
            mation Databases. *ACM Transcactions on Database Systems*, 4(3):262–
            296, September 1979.

[Mah93]   M. Maher. A Logic Programming View of CLP. In *Proceedings of the
            10th International Conference on Logic Programming*, pages 737–753,
            1993.

[Mai83]   David Maier. *The theory of relational databases*. Computer Science
            Press, 1983.

[PVdBVG94] J. Paredaens, J. Van den Bussche, and D. Van Gucht. Towards a theory
            of spatial database queries. In *Proceedings of the 13th ACM SIGACT-
            SIGMOD-SIGART Symposium on Principles of Database Systems*, pages
            279–288, 1994.

[Rab77]   M.O. Rabin. Decidable theories. In *Handbook of Mathematical Logic*,
            volume 90 of *Studies in Logic and the Foundations of Mathematics*, pages
            595–629. North-Holland, 1977.

[Rei88]   Ray Reiter. On Integrity Constraints. In *Proceedings of the 2nd Con-
            ference on Theoretical Aspects of Reasoning About Knowledge*, pages 97–
            111, Asilomar, CA, 1988.

[Rev90]   Peter Z. Revesz. A Closed Form for Datalog Queries with Integer Order.
            In *Proceedings of the 3rd International Conference on Database Theory*,
            pages 187–201, 1990. Long version to appear in Theoretical Computer
            Science.

[SRR]   D. Srivastava, R. Ramakrishnan, and P. Revesz. Constraint Objects. In
            this volume.

[Stu91]   P.J. Stuckey. Constructive Negation for Constraint Logic Programming.
            In *Proceedings of Symposium on Logic in Computer Science*, pages 328–
            339, 1991.

[vdM92]   Ron van der Meyden. The Complexity of Querying Indefinite Data
            About Linearly Ordered Domains (Preliminary Version). In *Proceedings
            of the 11th ACM SIGACT-SIGMOD-SIGART Symposium on Principles
            of Database Systems*, pages 331–345, 1992.

Set Constraints and Set-Based Analysis

Nevin Heintze[1] and Joxan Jaffar[2]

[1] School of Computer Science, Carnegie Mellon University, Pittsburgh, PA 15213
[2] IBM T.J. Watson Research Center, PO Box 704, Yorktown Heights, NY 10598

1 Introduction

Set expressions over a signature Σ of function symbols are a natural representation of sets of elements constructed from Σ, and set constraints express basic relationships between these sets. In the literature, set constraints have between used mostly in the context of uninterpreted (or Herbrand) function symbols. Although these applications have used set constraints in quite different ways, a common theme is the use of set constraints to obtain an *approximation* of some aspects of a program.

This paper contains two main parts. The first examines the set constraint calculus, discusses its history, and overviews the current state of known algorithms and related issues. Here we will also survey the uses of set constraints, starting from early work in (imperative) program analysis, to more recent work in logic and functional programming systems.

The second part describes *set-based analysis*. The aim here is a declarative interpretation of what it means to approximate the meaning of a program in just one way: ignore dependencies between variables, and instead, reason about each variable as the set of its possible runtime values. The basic approach starts with some description of the operational semantics, and then systematically replaces descriptions of environments (mappings from program variables to values) by set environments (mappings from program variables to *sets* of values) to obtain an approximate semantics called the *set-based program semantics*. The next step is to transform this semantics into a set constraint problem, and finally, the set constraints are solved.

2 Set Constraints

We present here the general calculus, followed by a brief survey of related work.

2.1 The Calculus

The set constraint calculus is parameterized by an underlying domain of discourse, and a set of functions Σ. For the purposes of most this paper, we choose Σ to be a given collection of uninterpreted function symbols, and the domain of discourse is then the ground terms constructed from Σ. In addition to Σ, we consider a fixed set of set operators consisting of union, intersection, complementation and projections of Σ functions.

A *set expression* is either a set variable (denoted $\mathcal{V}$, $\mathcal{W}$, $\mathcal{X}$, $\mathcal{Y}$, etc.), or of one of the forms $f(se_1, \ldots, se_n)$ or $op(se_1, \ldots, se_n)$, where $f \in \Sigma$, the se_i are set expressions, and op is a set operator. The set operators include union, intersection, complementation and projection (denoted $f_{(i)}^{-1}$ where f is an n-ary function symbol and $1 \leq i \leq n$). As an example of projection, the operator $cons_{(1)}^{-1}$ denotes the first projection with respect to the constructor $cons$, and is the "set" counterpart of car. It is also convenient to include $\top$ and $\bot$ in the definition of set expressions to respectively denote the set of all terms and the empty set (some works use 1 and 0 instead of $\top$ and $\bot$). A *set constraint* is of the form $se \supseteq se'$ where se and se' are set expressions. We write $se = se'$ as an abbreviation for the two constraints $se \supseteq se'$ and $se' \supseteq se$.

A *solution* to a collection C of set constraints is an assignment of sets to set variables that satisfies each constraint. Specifically, let $\mathcal{I}$ be a mapping from set variables into sets of terms. Such a mapping can be extended to map from set expressions into sets of values:

- $\mathcal{I}(f(se_1, \ldots, se_n)) = \{f(v_1, \ldots, v_n) : v_i \in \mathcal{I}(se_i)\}$;
- $\mathcal{I}(se_1 \cup se_2) = \mathcal{I}(se_1) \cup \mathcal{I}(se_2)$;
- $\mathcal{I}(se_1 \cap se_2) = \mathcal{I}(se_1) \cap \mathcal{I}(se_2)$;
- $\mathcal{I}(f_{(i)}^{-1}(se)) = \{v_i : f(v_1, \ldots, v_n) \in \mathcal{I}(se)\}$;
- $\mathcal{I}(\overline{se})) = \{v : v \notin \mathcal{I}(se)\}$;
- $\mathcal{I}(\top) = $ all values, and $\mathcal{I}(\bot) = \{\}$

$\mathcal{I}$ is a *solution* of a collection of constraints C if $\mathcal{I}(se) \supseteq \mathcal{I}(se')$ for each constraint $se \supseteq se'$ in C.

For example, let C denote the single constraint $\mathcal{X} \supseteq c \cup f(f(\mathcal{X}))$, where c is a constant and f is a unary symbol. C has many models, including the mapping that maps all set variables into the set $\{c, f(c), f(f(c)), \ldots\}$. Another solution of C is the mapping $\mathcal{I}$ defined by

$$\mathcal{I}(\mathcal{Y}) = \begin{cases} \{c, f^2(c), f^4(c), \ldots\} & \text{if } \mathcal{Y} \text{ is } \mathcal{X} \\ \{\} & \text{if } \mathcal{Y} \text{ is different from } \mathcal{X} \end{cases}$$

where f^n abbreviates n applications of f. This solution is smaller than the first, and is in fact the smallest solution of C. As another example, the smallest solution of the following constraint collection maps $\mathcal{X}$ into $\{a, f^3(a), f^6(a), \ldots\}$, maps $\mathcal{Y}$ into $\{a, f^2(a), f^4(a), \ldots\}$ and maps $\mathcal{Z}$ into $\{f^5(a), f^{11}(a), f^{17}(a), \ldots\}$.

$$\mathcal{X} \supseteq a \cup f^3(\mathcal{X})$$
$$\mathcal{Y} \supseteq a \cup f^2(\mathcal{Y})$$
$$\mathcal{Z} \supseteq f_{(1)}^{-1}(\mathcal{X} \cap \mathcal{Y})$$

In general, a collection of set constraints does not always have a unique smallest solution. For example consider the constraint $\mathcal{X} \cup \mathcal{Y} = a$ which has two minimal solutions: one that maps X to $\{a\}$ and $\mathcal{Y}$ to the empty set, and the other that maps X to the emtpy set and $\mathcal{Y}$ to $\{a\}$. For certain kinds of program analysis, it is natural to consider sub-classes of set constraints for which least models always exist. For example, consider constraints of the form $\mathcal{X} \supseteq se$ where $\mathcal{X}$ is a set variable and se is a set expression that does not use complementation. Such constraints always have a least solution. Somewhat more general are the *definite* set constraints, which have the form $a \supseteq se$ where a is a set expression that is "atomic" in the sense that it is constructed solely from set variables and function symbols, and se is a set expression that does not use complementation. A collection of definite set constraints is such that whenever it has a solution, it will in fact have a least solution. Further, it can be shown that this solution is *regular* in the sense that every variable is a regular set, that is, a set accepted by a nondetermistic tree automaton.

2.2 A Brief History

The use of set constraints for analysis of programs dates back to the early works by Reynolds [29] (who presents an analysis for a first-order functional language), and Jones and Muchnick [22] (who present an analysis for a simple imperative language). In both of these works, the set constraints used are quite simple: the only set operations employed are union and projection (there are no intersections or quantified expressions). We say more about these applications in the next subsection.

The general calculus of set constraints, as defined above, was first formalized and studied in a general setting in [17]. This work also presented a decision procedure for the class of definite set constraints (recall that definite constraints do not contain the complement symbol, and are restricted to the form $a \supseteq se$ where the set expression a contain only variables and function symbols). This procedure further provides an explicit representation of the least model of a (satisfiable) collection of definite set constraints. [17] also posed decidability of the satisfiability problem for general set constraints as an open question.

Later, [1] proved the decidability of a different, and incomparable, class: the *positive* set constraints. These are defined simply to be set constraints not involving projection. This procedure reduces the constraints into a simpler form. When reduction terminates without detecting inconsistency, the resulting constraints are evidently satisfiable. Note that satisfiable positive set constraints do not always have a least model. Subsequently, [9] provided an alternative procedure using tree automata techniques. Starting with Rabin's result [28] that the theory of k-successors is decidable, they generalized the Rabin automaton to accomodate positive set constraints. They further showed that satisfiable positive constraints always have a regular solution (all variables are assigned a regular set), and a minimal and maximal regular solution.

While the class of definite constraints and the class of positive classes are not comparable, the work [5] proved decidability of a class subsuming the two. Briefly, the set constraints considered here are the positive ones, extended to allow projections in a restricted way. The importance of this work probably lies more in the technique used: it is proved that set constraints can be written into equivalent formulas in the *monadic class*, that is, first-order formulas with unrestricted quantification, but no function symbols and only monadic predicate symbols. The transformation is simple and elegant, and gave rise to complexity results on set constraints based on similar results in the monadic class.

The next step was taken by [10], who proved that *negative* set constraints, ie. the extension to positve constraints with negations of subset relationships such as $se_1 \not\subseteq se_2$, remains decidable. Once again, tree automata techniques were used here. An alternative procedure was then given by [4], by reduction to a number-theoretic decision problem. Subsequently, [6] used the abovementioned translation of set constraints to the monadic class to provide a straightforward procedure for deciding negative set constraints. Note that none of these works on negative constraints deal with projections.

In summary, the state of the art for the set constraint decision problem is largely determined by the reduction to the monadic class of formulas. The main question remains how to deal with (unrestricted) projection. At the time of writing, we have verbal communication [26] indicating that the proof in [6] can be extended to solve this problem. Thus the question of whether the general set constraint problem is open, now becomes open!

2.3 Applications

Early works Two important early works are by Jones and Muchnick [22] and Reynolds [29]. In [22], an analysis is described for an imperative language with LISP-like data structures. The essence here is the construction of set constraints corresponding to a program that capture the flow of values from one variable to another as the program is executed. However, the set constraints here are restricted so that they can be solved by a fairly straightforward algorithm. In particular, the set constraints do not contain a notion of intersection, and their only operation is projection (corresponding to decomposition of data structures). Hence they are not expressive enough to capture a number of important components of programs. For example all information about the conditions in conditional statements is completely omitted. Further, information relating to well definedness of expressions is ignored (for example, after a statement $X = car(Y)$, it must be the case that Y is of the form $cons(\cdots)$ because otherwise the program would have terminated with an error).

In contrast, the earlier paper [29] used set constraints to compute data type definitions for program variables in a first order functional language. The constraints used are similar to those used in [22]. Again the only set operation of the constraints is projection, and so the program approximations obtained can be considerably inaccurate.

In summary, the set constraints used in these early works are simple, but the program approximations that they define are not very accurate. These works viewed set constraints as a tool for obtaining information about the program, and the constraints themselves incorporate a number of *ad hoc* approximations in addition to ignoring inter-variable dependencies. As a result, there is no simple connection between the program and its approximation. This particular shortcoming is one of the motivations for set-based analysis, discussed later in this paper.

Logic Programs The use of set constraints for the bottom-up analysis of logic programs was first considered in [25]. The set constraints in this relatively early work were rather specialized and used a form of approximation called *tuple-distributive* closure (hereafter just called *closure*). This closure, which was subsequently used in some later works, has the effect of enlarging a set of terms S into S^* as follows:

$$S^\star \stackrel{\text{def}}{=} \{c : c \text{ is a constant in } S\} \ \cup \ \bigcup_{f \in \Sigma} f\left((f_{(1)}^{-1}(S))^\star, \dots, (f_{(arity(f))}^{-1}(S))^\star\right)$$

where $f(S_1, \dots, S_n)$ denotes the set $\{f(s_1, \dots, s_n) : s_i \in S_i\}$ and $f_{(i)}^{-1}(S)$ denotes the set $\{s_i : f(s_1, \dots, s_n) \in S\}$. Thus for example, closing the set $\{f(a, b), f(c, d)\}$ produces $\{f(a, b), f(a, c), f(b, d), f(c, d)\}$. The set constraints used in [25] are like the general ones defined above, except that the union operation is interpreted to be the closure of the union of sets.

A different approach to approximation starts from the (bottom-up) fixpoint operator T_P of a program P, and the approximate meaning of a program is obtained by imposing closure on each iteration of the operator. For example, [32] defined the operator $Y_P(S) \stackrel{\text{def}}{=} (T_P(S))^*$ and the approximate meaning of the program is the least fixpoint $lfp(Y_P)$ of Y_P (which is always larger than the exact meaning, $lfp(T_P)$). In [16], a more accurate operator τ_P was used. (Roughly, Y_P ignores inter-argument dependencies, while τ_P ignores only inter-variable dependencies.) A more recent work [8] used the closure operators (in conjunction with another approximation technique called widening) to define and compute a program approximation.

The relationship between these closure-based fixpoint operators and set constraints was described in [18]. One result is that the models of the set constraints in [25], essentially correspond to the fixpoints of Y_P. A similar result was that the other fixpoint operator τ_P corresponded to certain formulas obtained from the program. These formulas are similar to but more general than set constraints. The main point here was that the least fixed-point of τ_P provided a more accurate and intuitive notion of approximation, and importantly, the approximation is decidable. It is open as to whether $lfp(Y_P)$ is decidable.

Functional Programs The general approach of [22, 29] has been extended by [21] to deal with higher-order functions. This approach has been further developed for binding time analysis [24], garbage collection [20] and globalization of function parameters [30]. One presentational difference in these works is the use of various extensions of regular grammars instead of constraints.

Subsequently, a number of set constraint approaches have been developed for the analysis of higher-order functional languages (see, for example, [27, 12, 2, 3, 13]). Perhaps the most developed of these approaches are those by [12, 13] and [2, 3]. The former starts with an operational semantics, and develops a set-based analysis for this semantics. The constraints that arise are briefly sketched in Section 3.3. In the latter, a denotational model of the program inspires the extraction of "type constraints", which are essentially set constraints (involving intersection and complement but not projection) over a domain of downward closed sets of finite elements (essentially the "ideal" model of types). We note that both works include a mechanism for reasoning about non-emptiness of sets (these are called "conditional types" in [3]).

Sorted Unification Broadly, sorted unification is the problem of unifying two terms in the context of a sort theory, the latter imposing constraints on the values that certain variables can take. The sort theory is typically presented as a sort signature, indicating the hierarchical arrangement of the various sorts, together with a specification on the sorts of the various function symbols. For example,

$$\{even \subseteq int, \quad odd \subseteq int, \quad succ : odd \longrightarrow even, \quad succ : even \longrightarrow odd\}$$

specifies that the sorts *even* and *odd* both belong to *int*, that the function *succ* maps an even integer into an odd one, and vice versa. Such constraints can be naturally specified in set constraints:

$$Int = Odd \cup Even, \quad Odd = 0 \cup succ(Even), \quad Even = 0 \cup succ(Odd)$$

In general, sorted unification is decidable only when the sort theory is restricted in some way. In the literature, a typical restriction is that the sorts are regular sets. In [31], a restricted class of set constraints is used to represent the sort theory, and a new sorted unification algorithm is presented. This work shows that further development in set constraints may be useful for sorted unification.

3 Set-Based Analysis

The basic approach of set-based program analysis starts with some description of the operational semantics. Typically, such a description involves environments, which describe the values that each variable may assume at runtime. The next step is a systematic replacement of environments into *set environments*, which map variables into sets of values, as opposed to a single value. This fundamental step gives rise to the notion of a set-based semantics of a program. Next, the set-based semantics is reduced to a set constraint problem, and finally, the set constraints are solved.

In this paper, we will not go through this process in much formal detail. These details can be found in [12]. Instead, we will show by examples how set constraints indeed model the desired approximation from program fragments.

In the following examples, we shall use a simple imperative programming language with basic facilities for data structure creation (e.g. cons and nil for list creation) and data destructuring/projection (e.g. car and cdr for list destructuring). Consider the statement X := cons(Y, X). To model this statement, set variables are introduced to collect the values of the variables X and Y just before and just after the statement (we suppose that these are the only program variables of interest). Let $\mathcal{X}_1$ and $\mathcal{Y}_1$ be the set variables to collect the values of X and Y just before execution of the statement, and let $\mathcal{X}_2$ and $\mathcal{Y}_2$ be the set variables for just after statement execution. Now, the values for X just after execution of the statement include all values $cons(v_y, v_x)$ such that $v_x \in \mathcal{X}_1$ and $v_y \in \mathcal{Y}_1$, and so we write $\mathcal{X}_2 \supseteq \{cons(v_y, v_x) : v_x \in \mathcal{X}_1, v_y \in \mathcal{Y}_1\}$, which is abbreviated by $\mathcal{X}_2 \supseteq cons(\mathcal{Y}_1, \mathcal{X}_1)$. In contrast, the values for Y just after execution of the statement are exactly those before execution, and so we write the constraint $\mathcal{Y}_2 \supseteq \mathcal{Y}_1$. Hence, from the above program statement, we construct two set constraints: $\mathcal{X}_2 \supseteq cons(\mathcal{Y}_1, \mathcal{X}_1)$ and $\mathcal{Y}_2 \supseteq \mathcal{Y}_1$. Note that for this example, we could have replaced $\supseteq$ by $=$ and written the equations $\mathcal{X}_2 = cons(\mathcal{Y}_1, \mathcal{X}_1)$ and $\mathcal{Y}_2 = \mathcal{Y}_1$. However, for a number of reasons, it is somewhat more convenient to use inequalities rather than equalities[3].

Similarly, for the statement X := cdr(X) we construct the two constraints $\mathcal{X}_2 \supseteq cdr(\mathcal{X}_1)$ and $\mathcal{Y}_2 \supseteq \mathcal{Y}_1$, where $cdr(\mathcal{X}_1)$ abbreviates $\{v_2 : cons(v_1, v_2) \in \mathcal{X}_1\}$, and $\mathcal{X}_1, \mathcal{Y}_1, \mathcal{X}_2, \mathcal{Y}_2$ are as before. In general, the use of sets to reason about a program leads to an approximation of the program's actual behaviour. This is because the use of sets ignores dependencies between variable values. For example, consider the following program

```
X := car(W);
Y := cdr(W);
W := cons(X, Y);
```

Let $W_i, \mathcal{X}_i$ and $\mathcal{Y}_i$, $i = 1..4$, be the set variables introduced to collect the values of W, X and Y just before the first statement, just before the second statement, just before the third statement, and just after the third statement respectively. Constructing constraints as before yields:

$W_2 \supseteq W_1$	$W_3 \supseteq W_2$	$W_4 \supseteq cons(\mathcal{X}_3, \mathcal{Y}_3)$
$\mathcal{X}_2 \supseteq car(W_1)$	$\mathcal{X}_3 \supseteq \mathcal{X}_2$	$\mathcal{X}_4 \supseteq \mathcal{X}_3$
$\mathcal{Y}_2 \supseteq \mathcal{Y}_1$	$\mathcal{Y}_3 \supseteq cdr(W_2)$	$\mathcal{Y}_4 \supseteq \mathcal{Y}_3$

Now, suppose that at the start of the program, the variable W is either the list $[1, 2]$ or the list $[3, 4]$. Then the set for $\mathcal{X}_2$ (and $\mathcal{X}_3$) is $\{1, 3\}$, and the set for $\mathcal{Y}_3$ is $\{[2], [4]\}$. Hence, the set for W_4 is $\{[1, 2], [3, 4], [1, 4], [3, 2]\}$. In contrast, the only possible values for W after execution of the third statement are $[1, 2]$ and $[3, 4]$.

The key property of the constraints constructed from a program is that any solution of the constraints conservatively approximates the operational semantics of the program. This means that to obtain a safe approximation of the program, it is sufficient to construct a solution to the constraints. The constraint solving process will typically compute the minimum solution to the constraints since this is the most accurate approximation (described by the constraints).

In summary for this subsection, set constraints can be constructed to approximate the execution of a program by first introducing set variables to capture the

---

[3] In particular, the construction of set constraints is simpler in the presence of statements that change the flow of control.

values of the program variables at each program point, and then writing constraints between these set variables to approximate the relationships between these variables that are inherent in the program. In effect, the construction of constraints reduces the problem of analyzing the program to the problem of reasoning about set constraints.

3.1 Imperative Programs

The example imperative programs considered above do not illustrate how conditional statements and recursion are handled, and these are probably the most interesting aspects of the analysis. In particular, recursion introduces the possibility of infinite sets of values. Consider the following program

$$X := cons(a, cons(b, cons(c, cons(d, nil))));$$
$$Y := nil;$$

$$while(car(X) \neq c) \; do$$
$$Y := cons(car(X), Y);$$
$$X := cdr(X);$$

where a, b, c and d are constants. After execution of this program, X is $cons(c, cons(d, nil))$ and Y is $cons(b, cons(a, nil))$; in other words the program reverses the initial segment of X up until the first occurrence of c. The markers Ⓐ, Ⓑ, Ⓒ and Ⓓ indicate points in the program (note that Ⓓ indicates the point at the end of the program). Corresponding to this program, we can construct the following constraints.

$$\mathcal{X}^A \supseteq cons(a, cons(b, cons(c, cons(d, nil)))) \qquad \mathcal{X}^C \supseteq cdr(\mathcal{X}^B)$$
$$\mathcal{Y}^A \supseteq nil \qquad\qquad\qquad\qquad\qquad\qquad\quad \mathcal{Y}^C \supseteq cons(car(\mathcal{X}^B), \mathcal{Y}^B)$$
$$\mathcal{X}^B \supseteq \mathcal{X}^A \cap \overline{cons(c, \top)} \qquad\qquad\qquad \mathcal{X}^D \supseteq \mathcal{X}^A \cap cons(c, \top)$$
$$\mathcal{Y}^B \supseteq \mathcal{Y}^A \qquad\qquad\qquad\qquad\qquad\quad \mathcal{Y}^D \supseteq \mathcal{Y}^A$$
$$\mathcal{X}^B \supseteq \mathcal{X}^C \cap \overline{cons(c, \top)} \qquad\qquad\qquad \mathcal{X}^D \supseteq \mathcal{X}^C \cap cons(c, \top)$$
$$\mathcal{Y}^B \supseteq \mathcal{Y}^C \qquad\qquad\qquad\qquad\qquad\quad \mathcal{Y}^D \supseteq \mathcal{Y}^C$$

The set expression $\overline{cons(c, \top)}$ (the complement of the set denoted by $cons(c, \top)$) is the set of all values v such that $car(v)$ differs from c. In general, it is useful to introduce a restricted form of complementation in the constraints used to analyze imperative programs. However, these uses are always sufficiently limited that the constraints obtained are still "monotonic". The minimum solution of the above constraints is given by the following mapping:

$$\mathcal{X}^A \mapsto \{cons(a, cons(b, cons(c, cons(d, nil))))\}$$
$$\mathcal{Y}^A \mapsto \{nil\}$$
$$\mathcal{X}^B \mapsto \{cons(a, cons(b, cons(c, cons(d, nil)))), \ cons(b, cons(c, cons(d, nil)))\}$$
$$\mathcal{Y}^B \mapsto list_{a,b}$$
$$\mathcal{X}^C \mapsto \{cons(b, cons(c, cons(d, nil))), \ cons(c, cons(d, nil))\}$$
$$\mathcal{Y}^C \mapsto non\text{-}nil\text{-}list_{a,b}$$
$$\mathcal{X}^D \mapsto \{cons(c, cons(d, nil))\}$$
$$\mathcal{Y}^D \mapsto list_{a,b}$$

where $list_{a,b}$ denotes the set of all lists constructed from a and b, and $non\text{-}nil\text{-}list_{a,b}$ denotes the set of all non-empty lists constructed from a and b.

3.2 Logic Programs

The construction of set constraints for logic programs is similar to that for imperative programs. However, for logic programs, there is a choice for the underlying operational semantics used in the analysis. We begin by illustrating the construction of constraints corresponding to a bottom-up execution. Again we introduce a set variable for each program variable. We also introduce set variables Ret_p, for each predicate p, to collect the set of "return" values for that predicate. Consider the following logic program and constraints constructed to model the bottom-up semantics of the program.

$$
\begin{array}{ll}
\mathsf{p(X) :- q(X), r(X).} & Ret_p \supseteq p(\mathcal{X}) \\
\mathsf{q(a).} & \mathcal{X} \supseteq q_{(1)}^{-1}(Ret_q) \cap r_{(1)}^{-1}(Ret_r) \\
\mathsf{q(b).} & Ret_q \supseteq q(a) \cup q(b) \\
\mathsf{r(b).} & Ret_r \supseteq r(b) \cup r(c) \\
\mathsf{r(c).} &
\end{array}
$$

The minimum solution of these constraints maps Ret_p into $\{p(b)\}$, maps $\mathcal{X}$ into $\{b\}$, maps Ret_q into $\{q(a), q(b)\}$, and maps Ret_r into $\{r(b), r(c)\}$. Now, consider constructing constraints corresponding to a top-down left-to-right execution of the program starting from the goal ?- $p(t)$ where t is either a, b, c or d. The main change here is the introduction of set variables $Call_p$, for each predicate p, to collect the set of "calls" to that predicate. The program points Ⓐ, Ⓑ and Ⓒ respectively denote the points just before execution of $q(X)$, just before execution of $r(X)$ and just after execution of $r(X)$.

$$Call_p \supseteq p(a \cup b \cup c \cup d)$$
$$Ret_p \supseteq p(\mathcal{X}^C)$$

p(X) :- Ⓐ, q(X), Ⓑ, r(X), Ⓒ.
q(a).
q(b).
r(b).
r(c).

$$\mathcal{X}^A \supseteq p_{(1)}^{-1}(Call_p)$$
$$\mathcal{X}^B \supseteq p_{(1)}^{-1}(Call_p) \cap q_{(1)}^{-1}(Ret_q)$$
$$\mathcal{X}^C \supseteq p_{(1)}^{-1}(Call_p) \cap q_{(1)}^{-1}(Ret_q) \cap r_{(1)}^{-1}(Ret_r)$$
$$Call_q \supseteq q(\mathcal{X}^A)$$
$$Ret_q \supseteq (q(a) \cup q(b)) \cap Call_q$$
$$Call_r \supseteq r(\mathcal{X}^B)$$
$$Ret_r \supseteq (r(b) \cup r(c)) \cap Call_r$$

The minimum solution of these constraints maps $Call_p$ into $\{p(a), p(b), p(c), p(d)\}$, Ret_p into $\{p(b)\}$, $\mathcal{X}^A$ into $\{a, b, c, d\}$, $\mathcal{X}^B$ into $\{a, b\}$, $\mathcal{X}^C$ into $\{b\}$, $Call_q$ into $\{q(a), q(b), q(c), q(d)\}$, Ret_q into $\{q(a), q(b)\}$, $Call_r$ into $\{r(a), r(b)\}$, and Ret_r into $\{r(b)\}$. As a third alternative, consider constructing constraints corresponding to a top-down parallel execution of the program starting from the same goals. The program points Ⓐ, Ⓑ and Ⓒ respectively denote the points just before execution of $q(X)$, just before execution of $r(X)$ and just after execution of the entire body of the first rule.

$$Call_p \supseteq p(a \cup b \cup c \cup d)$$
$$Ret_p \supseteq p(\mathcal{X}^C)$$

p(X) :- Ⓐ, q(X), Ⓑ, r(X), Ⓒ.
q(a).
q(b).
r(b).
r(c).

$$\mathcal{X}^A \supseteq p_{(1)}^{-1}(Call_p)$$
$$\mathcal{X}^B \supseteq p_{(1)}^{-1}(Call_p)$$
$$\mathcal{X}^C \supseteq p_{(1)}^{-1}(Call_p) \cap q_{(1)}^{-1}(Ret_q) \cap r_{(1)}^{-1}(Ret_r)$$
$$Call_q \supseteq q(\mathcal{X}^A)$$
$$Ret_q \supseteq (q(a) \cup q(b)) \cap Call_q$$
$$Call_r \supseteq r(\mathcal{X}^B)$$
$$Ret_r \supseteq (r(b) \cup r(c)) \cap Call_r$$

The minimum solution of these constraints maps $Call_p$ into $\{p(a), p(b), p(c), p(d)\}$, Ret_p into $\{p(b)\}$, $\mathcal{X}^A$ and $\mathcal{X}^B$ into $\{a, b, c, d\}$, $\mathcal{X}^C$ into $\{b\}$, $Call_q$ into $\{q(a), q(b), q(c), q(d)\}$, Ret_q into $\{q(a), q(b)\}$, $Call_r$ into $\{r(a), r(b), r(c), r(d)\}$, and Ret_r into $\{r(b), r(c)\}$.

Observe that in all three examples, the use of set constraints has lead to an exact analysis, and that the sets obtained were finite. Neither observation holds in general, as is illustrated by the following bottom-up analysis example:

p(f(X), f(Y)) :- p(X, Y).
p(a,b).

$$Ret_p \supseteq p(f(\mathcal{X}), f(\mathcal{Y})) \cup p(a, b)$$
$$\mathcal{X} \supseteq p_{(1)}^{-1}(Ret_p)$$
$$\mathcal{Y} \supseteq p_{(2)}^{-1}(Ret_p)$$

In the least model of the constraints, Ret_p is mapped into the set $\{p(a, b)\} \cup \{p(f^i(a), f^j(b)) : i \geq 1, j \geq 1\}$, and this set contains elements such as $p(f(a), f(f(b)))$ which are not part of the program's (exact) meaning.

So far, we have made no mention of variables that appear in the head of a rule and not in the body of a rule. Such variables can take on any value. Hence they are modeled using the $\top$ constant, as illustrated in the following example.

$$
\begin{array}{ll}
& Ret_p \supseteq p(\mathcal{X}, \mathcal{Y}) \\
\text{p(X, Y) :- q(X).} & \mathcal{X} \supseteq q_{(1)}^{-1}(Ret_q) \\
\text{q(a).} & \mathcal{Y} \supseteq \top \\
& Ret_q \supseteq q(a)
\end{array}
$$

We conclude this discussion of the analysis of logic programs by noting that the accuracy of the information obtained using set constraints can be improved by using more complex set operators. For example, consider the following program and its (bottom-up) set constraints:

$$
\begin{array}{ll}
\text{p(X, Y) :- q(X, Y), r(X, Y).} & Ret_p \supseteq p(\mathcal{X}, \mathcal{Y}) \\
\text{q(a, b).} & \mathcal{X} \supseteq q_{(1)}^{-1}(Ret_q) \cap r_{(1)}^{-1}(Ret_r) \\
\text{q(b, a).} & \mathcal{Y} \supseteq q_{(2)}^{-1}(Ret_q) \cap r_{(2)}^{-1}(Ret_r) \\
\text{r(a, a).} & Ret_q \supseteq q(a, b) \cup q(b, a) \\
& Ret_r \supseteq r(a, a)
\end{array}
$$

The minimum solution of these constraints maps Ret_p into $p(a, a)$, $\mathcal{X}$ and $\mathcal{Y}$ into $\{a\}$, Ret_q into $\{q(a, b), q(b, a)\}$, and Ret_r into $\{r(a, a)\}$. Another way of constructing constraints is to introduce quantified set expressions, which have the form $\{X : \exists X_1 \ldots \exists X_m (t_1 \in se_1 \wedge \cdots \wedge t_n \in se_n)\}$ where $X, X_1, \ldots, X_m$ are program variables, $t_1, \ldots, t_n$ are atoms or terms whose variables are from $X, X_1, \ldots X_m$, and $se_1, \ldots, se_n$ are set expressions. The constraints using quantified set expressions that are constructed for the (bottom-up) analysis of the above program are:

$$
\begin{aligned}
Ret_p &\supseteq p(\mathcal{X}, \mathcal{Y}) \\
\mathcal{X} &\supseteq \left\{ X : \exists Y \left(q(X, Y) \in Ret_q \wedge r(X, Y) \in Ret_r \right) \right\} \\
\mathcal{Y} &\supseteq \left\{ Y : \exists X \left(q(X, Y) \in Ret_q \wedge r(X, Y) \in Ret_r \right) \right\} \\
Ret_q &\supseteq q(a, b) \cup q(b, a) \\
Ret_r &\supseteq r(a, a)
\end{aligned}
$$

and the minimum solution of these constraints maps Ret_p, $\mathcal{X}$ and $\mathcal{Y}$ into the empty set, Ret_q into $\{q(a, b), q(b, a)\}$, and Ret_r into $\{r(a, a)\}$. The more complex constraints using quantified expressions not only provide more accurate program approximation, but they are also more faithful to the notion of set-based analysis. In particular, they have closer and much simpler relationship to the underlying operational semantics (see [12, 16] for further details).

3.3 Functional Programs

To analyze functional languages such as Standard ML [23], set constraints must be extended with a mechanism to deal with higher-order functions. In essence, this is achieved by the addition of three new components. First, the set of underlying values is enriched to include a new collection of constants to denote functions. In the following examples, we shall use function identifiers for this purpose; in more formal presentations, it is convenient to use abstractions in an appropriate lambda calculus. Second, for each function constant f, we introduce two set variables $Call_f$ and Ret_f to capture the values on which f is called, and the values that calls to f return, respectively. Third, a new set operator $apply$ is introduced to model function application. The meaning of a set expression $apply(se_1, se_2)$ under a mapping $\mathcal{I}$ is defined as follows:

$$\mathcal{I}(apply(se_1, se_2)) \stackrel{\text{def}}{=} \bigcup_{f \in \mathcal{I}(se_1)} Ret_f, \quad \text{provided } \mathcal{I}(Call_f) \supseteq \mathcal{I}(se_2) \text{ for all } f \in \mathcal{I}(se_1)$$

If the side condition is not met then $\mathcal{I}(apply(se_1, se_2))$ is not defined. The notion of solution of a collection of set constraints is appropriately modified so that $\mathcal{I}$ is a solution of the constraints if it is defined on each set expression and satisfies each constraint. Note that the meaning of this expanded class of set expressions involving $apply$ is somewhat unusual, because now set expressions themselves may impose restrictions on solutions, independent of the constraints in which they appear. Importantly, unique minimum solutions are still guaranteed to exist.

To illustrate the construction of set constraints to analyze function programs, consider the following program and its constraints. The set variable $\mathcal{E}$ is introduced to capture the set of values resulting from program evaluation. The minimum solution of the constraints maps $\mathcal{X}$, $Call_{id}$, Ret_{id}, and $\mathcal{E}$ into $\{c\}$.

```
let fun id X = X
in
    id c
end
```

$$\mathcal{X} \supseteq Call_{id}$$
$$Ret_{id} \supseteq \mathcal{X}$$
$$\mathcal{E} \supseteq apply(id, c)$$

Again, more complex set operators can be introduced to provide more accurate modeling of certain aspects of the language (particularly case statements). See [12, 13] for further details. The complexity of solving the set constraints is $O(n^3)$ [13]. This basic formulation of constraints has been extended to deal with arrays, continuations and exceptions.

3.4 Comparison with Other Analysis Techniques

A key advantage of set-based analysis (and, more generally, the use of set constraints to perform program analysis), in comparison to standard abstract interpretation techniques [7], is that there is no underlying abstract domain. When using an abstract domain, the requirement of "finite ascending chains" is typically required for termination, and this limits the usable abstract domains. A remedy is to use techniques of "narrowing" and "widening". Even so, termination continues to place a fundamental restriction on the accuracy of the treatment of values. Avoiding the use of abstract domains leads to important advantages in terms of accuracy and uniformity. In particular, set-based analysis does not use "depth-limits" or other *a priori* restrictions on the sets of values that can be manipulated. We contend that this reduces the potential for chaotic and unintuitive behaviour.

Another benefit of the simplicity and uniformity of the approximation embedded in set-based analysis is that the analysis is extensible and flexible. In the course of implementing a number of prototype set-based analysis systems, we have observed that modifications to incorporate new features are often straightforward. For example, during the development of a system for the analysis of ML programs, the treatment of continuations, side-effects and exceptions required only minor modifications. There appear to be two reasons for this. First, because set-based analysis has a simple and intuitive definition, it is usually straightforward to determine how to treat new features. Second, because the analysis has a uniform definition, the treatment of one component of a language is largely independent of the treatment of other aspects of the language, and so the analysis can be extended in a modular manner.

Of course, the main limitation of set-based analysis is that all inter-variable dependencies are ignored. Such dependencies can be crucial for some kinds of analysis such as mode analysis (see [19] for a discussion of this issue). In contrast, abstract interpretation techniques can retain a limited amount of information about dependencies (although there is, of course, additional computational cost associated with maintaining information about dependencies). Motivated by this observation, hybrid approaches that combine aspects of set constraints with abstract interpretation have been developed [19].

3.5 Efficiency Issues

It is difficult to quantify a comparison between set-based analysis and standard analysis techniques. While worst case complexity costs can be obtained, it is not clear what conclusions we can draw from these results about the practicality of the various approaches. Moreover, the technology for implementing set constraints is still in its infancy. With this in mind, we now briefly describe results from implementations of set-based analysis for two different languages.

The first deals with analysis of logic programs [11], and computes type, mode and sharing information. This analysis has a worst case exponential complexity. While substantial progress was made during the development of this implementation, the results indicate that we are still some distance from practical analysis of medium to large programs. Currently, top-down analysis of programs of the order of 50 rules can be achieved in a few seconds. As expected, analysis based on bottom-up semantics is considerably cheaper that for top-down semantics. One of the main lessons of this implementation is the expense of solving set constraints involving intersection. Much of the work of the implementation was directed at reducing this cost.

The second implementation effort provides a contrasting experience. This implementation [13] focussed on the analysis of ML programs. The core algorithm for this analysis is $O(n^3)$ on the size of the input program. Typical execution times are in the range of 200–400 lines per second for programs up to several thousand lines in length. The main reason for the substantial difference between the results from the two implementations seems to hinge on the fact that intersection is not used in the constraints generated from ML programs. Based on this observation, we are currently investigating ways of constructing constraints for logic programs that provide similar levels of accuracy, but either eliminate or substantially reduce the use of intersection.

The results from the second implementation out-perform current implementations of comparable abstract interpretation based approaches. There appear to be a number of reasons for this. In set-based analysis there is only one pass over the program text. In essence, this performs a "pre-compilation" of the program into a convenient computation form (set constraints). In contrast, many abstract interpretation systems repeatedly pass over (some representation of) program text during the iterative fixed-point computation. In set-based analysis, all approximation is carried out in the translation to set constraints, and so no approximation operations need to be done during the main computational component of the analysis (solving set constraints). Furthermore, set constraints are inherently more incremental than the iterative fixed-point computations of abstract interpretation. In essence, constraints provide a compact implicit representation of information. This representation supports computation over partial information that is particularly well suited to efficient program analysis. We refer to [15] for a deeper discussion of this issue.

3.6 Extensions

So far we have focussed on the use of set constraints to obtain an approximation of the possible run-time values of variables in a program. However, the basic process of constructing set constraints from a program and then solving these set constraints preserves numerous structural properties of a program. It is therefore possible, with only minor modifications to the set constraint algorithm, to compute approximations to a variety of other program properties. We now illustrate this.

Mode Analysis (for Logic Programs) To adapt set constraints to compute mode information for logic programs, we first change the underlying set of values from the set of all "ground" terms to the set of all terms. Then we replace the constant $\top$ by two new constants *ground* and *any*, which shall denote the set of all *ground* terms and the set of all terms respectively. Finally, we modify the definition of solutions of set constraints to account for these changes. For example, the minimum solution of $\mathcal{X} \supseteq f(ground, any)$ maps $\mathcal{X}$ into the set of all terms of form $f(t_1, t_2)$ such that t_1 is ground. The minimum solution of $\mathcal{X} \supseteq f(ground, any, a) \cap f(any, ground, any)$ maps $\mathcal{X}$ into the set of terms $f(t_1, t_2, a)$ such that t_1 and t_2 are both ground. The constraints generated for mode analysis are essentially unchanged, excepting that any and $ground$ may be used to describe the initial goals. The modifications for solving these new constraints involve steps such as simplifying $ground \cap any$ into $ground$, and $f(any) \cap ground$ into $f(ground)$. See [12, 15] for further details. Note that the constants $ground$ and any behave in essentially the same way as $\top$, and may appear in the output of the algorithm (that is, they may appear in the explicit representations that are computed by the algorithm). For example, when the program

```
app(nil, Y, Y).
app(cons(X', X), Y, cons(X', Z)) :- app(X, Y, Z).
```

is analyzed in the context of the goal ?- app(ground, ground, any), the output of the algorithm relevant to $Call_{app}$ and Ret_{app} is

$$
\begin{aligned}
Call_{app} &= app(ground, ground, any) \\
Ret_{app} &= app(nil, ground, ground) \cup \\
&\quad app(cons(ground, \mathcal{X}), ground, cons(ground, \mathcal{Z})) \\
\mathcal{X} &= nil \cup cons(ground, \mathcal{X}) \\
\mathcal{Z} &= ground \cup cons(ground, \mathcal{Z})
\end{aligned}
$$

Structure Sharing Analysis Structure sharing analysis seeks information of the following form: given two variables, determine whether the bindings of these variables can "share" sub-structures (in the sense that the sub-structures have the same heap location). Such information can be used to determine when data structures can be updated in place or when they can be garbage collected. This kind of analysis may be performed by first giving each occurrence of a function symbol a unique label. Then set constraints are constructed as before, with care to preserve the labels on function symbols – call the resulting constraints *labeled* set constraints. The meaning of these constraints is defined by mapping set expressions into sets of *labeled* terms. We refer to [12, 15] for further details.

Interpreted Function Symbols The set constraints considered so far deal with uninterpreted symbols so as to correspond to the data constructors of the language at hand. For analysis of programs involving operations such as arithmetic, this approach must be generalized. One possibility is to compute descriptions of *how* arithmetic values are obtained. These descriptions are essentially terms built from arithmetic operations and integers. For example, the description of computations for a program variable x might be given by

$$
\mathcal{X} = 0 \cup (\mathcal{X} + 1)
$$

that is, the set of computations $\{0, 0 + 1, (0 + 1) + 1, \ldots\}$. Clearly, the actual values of x are included in the set $\{0, 1, 2, \ldots\}$. [14] describes how this approach can be applied to the problem of removing array bounds checks, and this requires that the analysis also reason about arithmetic tests. An example of the kinds of descriptions that arise in this context is:

$$\mathcal{X} = 0 \cup [LE\ 10](X + 2)$$

where $[LE\ 10]$ is a "restriction" operator that essentially picks those elements from a set that are less than 10 (in general a restriction operator is of the form $[op\ se]$ where op is some arithmetic comparison operation and se is some set expression). The least model of the above equation maps $\mathcal{X}$ into $\{0, 2, 4, 6, 8\}$.

4 Conclusion

The calculus of set constraints was presented, and its history of basic results and applications briefly described. The approach of set-based analysis was then presented in an informal style, with a focus on the breadth of applicability of the technique. The relationship between set constraints and set-based analysis is roughly that the approximation of a program by ignoring inter-variable dependencies can be captured by set constraints. It was then argued that set-based analysis can provide accurate and efficient program analysis.

References

1. A. Aiken and E. Wimmers, "Solving Systems of Set Constraints", *Proc. 7th IEEE Symp. on Logic in Computer Science*, Santa Cruz, pp. 329–340, June 1992.
2. A. Aiken and E. Wimmers, "Type Inclusion Constraints and Type Inference", *Proc. 1993 Conf. on Functional Programming and Computer Architecture*, Copenhagen, pp. 31-41, June 1993.
3. A. Aiken, E. Wimmers and T.K. Lakshman, "Soft Typing with Conditional Types" *Proc. 21st ACM Symp. on Principles of Programming Languages*, Portland, OR, pp. 163–173, January 1994.
4. A. Aiken, D. Kozen and E. Wimmers, "Decidability of Systems of Set Constraints with Negative Constraints", IBM Research Report RJ 9421, 1993.
5. L. Bachmair, H. Ganzinger and U. Waldmann, "Set Constraints are the Monadic Class", *Proc. 8th IEEE Symp. on Logic in Computer Science*, 75–83, 1993.
6. W. Charatonik and L. Pacholski, "Negative Set Constraints: an Easy Proof of Decidability", *Proc. 9th IEEE Symp. on Logic in Computer Science*, 1994, to appear.
7. P. Cousot and R. Cousot, "Abstract Interpretation: A Unified Lattice Model for Static Analysis of Programs by Construction or Approximation of Fixpoints", *Proc. 4th ACM Symp. on Principles of Programming Languages*, Los Angeles, pp. 238–252, January 1977.
8. J. Gallagher and D.A. de Wall, "Fast and Precise Regular Approximations of Logic Programs", *Proc. International Conf. on Logic Programming*, MIT Press, to appear 1994.
9. R. Gilleron, S. Tison and M. Tommasi, "Solving Systems of Set Constraints using Tree Automata", *Proc. 10th Annual Symposium on Theoretical Aspects of Computer Science*, pp. 505–514, 1992.

10. R. Gilleron, S. Tison and M. Tommasi, "Solving Systems of Set Constraints with Negated Subset Relationships", in *Foundations of Computer Science*, 372–380, 1993.

11. N. Heintze, "Practical Aspects of Set-Based Analysis", *Proc. Joint International Conf. and Symp. on Logic Programming*, Washington D.C., MIT Press, pp. 765–779, November 1992.

12. N. Heintze, "Set-Based Program Analysis", Ph.D. thesis, School of Computer Science, Carnegie Mellon University, October 1992.

13. N. Heintze, "Set-Based Analysis of ML Programs", to appear, ACM Conference on Lisp and Functional Programming, 1994.

14. N. Heintze, "Set-Based Analysis of Arithmetic", Carnegie Mellon University technical report CMU-CS-93-221, 20pp., December 1993.

15. N. Heintze, "Set Constraints in Program Analysis", Workshop on Global Compilation, International Logic Programming Symposium, October 1993.

16. N. Heintze and J. Jaffar, "A Finite Presentation Theorem for Approximating Logic Programs", *Proc. 17th ACM Symp. on Principles of Programming Languages*, San Francisco, pp. 197–209, January 1990. (A full version of this paper appears as IBM Technical Report RC 16089 (# 71415), 66 pp., August 1990.)

17. N. Heintze and J. Jaffar, "A Decision Procedure for a Class of Herbrand Set Constraints", *Proc. 5th IEEE Symp. on Logic in Computer Science*, Philadelphia, pp. 42–51, June 1990. (A full version of this paper appears as Carnegie Mellon University Technical Report CMU–CS–91–110, 42 pp., February 1991.)

18. N. Heintze and J. Jaffar, "Semantic Types for Logic Programs" in *Types in Logic Programming*, F. Pfenning (Ed.), MIT Press Series in Logic Programming, pp. 141–155, 1992.

19. N. Heintze and J. Jaffar, "An Engine for Logic Program Analysis", *Proc. 7th IEEE Symp. on Logic in Computer Science*, Santa Cruz, pp. 318–328, June 1992.

20. T. Jensen and T. Mogensen, "A Backwards Analysis for Compile-Time Garbage Collection", *Proc. 3rd European Symp. on Programming*, Copenhagen, LNCS 432, pp. 227–239, May 1990.

21. N. Jones, "Flow Analysis of Lazy Higher-Order Functional Programs", in *Abstract Interpretation of Declarative Languages*, S. Abramsky and C. Hankin (Eds.), Ellis Horwood, 1987.

22. N. Jones and S. Muchnick, "Flow Analysis and Optimization of LISP-like Structures", *Proc. 6th ACM Symp. on Principles of Programming Languages*, San Antonio, pp. 244–256, January 1979.

23. R. Milner, M. Tofte and R. Harper, "The Definition of Standard ML", MIT Press, 1990.

24. T. Mogensen, "Separating Binding Times in Language Specifications", *Proc. Functional Programming and Computer Architecture*, London, ACM, pp. 12–25, September 1989.

25. P. Mishra, "Toward a Theory of Types in PROLOG", *Proc. 1st IEEE Symp. on Logic Programming*, Atlantic City, pp. 289–298, 1984.

26. L. Pacholski, personal communication, March 1994.

27. J. Palsberg and M. Schwartzbach, "Safety Analysis versus Type Inference for Partial Types" Information Processing Letters, Vol 43, pp. 175–180, North-Holland, September 1992.

28. M.O. Rabin, "Decidability of Second-order Theories and Automata on Infinite Trees", *Transactions of the American Math. Society* 141, pp 1 - 35, 1969.

29. J. Reynolds, "Automatic Computation of Data Set Definitions", *Information Processing 68*, pp. 456–461, North-Holland, 1969.

30. P. Sestoft, "Replacing Function Parameters by Global Variables", *Proc. Functional Programming and Computer Architecture*, London, ACM, pp. 39–53, September 1989.

31. T.E. Uribe, "Sorted Unification using Set Constraints", *Proc. 11th Intl. Conf. on Automated Deduction*, D. Kapur (Ed), Springer Verlag Lecture Notes in Computer Science, 1992.

32. E. Yardeni and E.Y. Shapiro, "A Type System for Logic Programs", *Journal of Logic Programming*, Vol. 10, pp. 125 – 153, 1991. (An early version of this paper appears in *Concurrent PROLOG: Collected Papers*, Vol. 2, MIT Press, pp 211 - 244, 1987.)

On the Design of Constraint Satisfaction Problems

Massimo PALTRINIERI [*]

Bull S.A.
Rue Jean Jaurès - B.P. 68
78340 Les Clayes Sous Bois
France

Abstract. The development of a system based on constraint programming includes two main phases: first, the problem to be solved is formulated as a constraint satisfaction problem; then, the formulation is implemented in a constraint-programming language. Constraint-programming research has mainly concentrated on the second phase, by studying powerful declarative languages that automatically propagate the constraints stated in a program. Nevertheless, when developing a solution to a real-world problem, the cost due to the first phase, is often more relevant. This paper addresses the issues of what a model of real-world constraint satisfaction problems should be and how it should be constructed.

1 Introduction

A constraint satisfaction problem (CSP) can be formulated as follows: given a set of variables and a set of constraints that limit the combination of values of the variables, find an assignment of values to the variables such that all the constraints are satisfied.

A large number of problems in many areas of computer science can be viewed as special cases of constraint satisfaction problems (for a survey see [Nad90]). To solve more effectively this type of problems, several constraint-programming languages have been developed (for a survey see [Rot93]). The basic idea of these environments is to provide a declarative language where the programmer just defines variables and constraints, while the propagation engine of the language automatically computes the assignment of values that satisfies the constraints.

The author's Department at Bull developed a constraint-programming industrial environment, Charme [Opl89], and successively a number of real-world applications based on it [Cha94, DAn92, Gos93, MaT89, PMT92]. From these experiences, it emerged that the main cost of a constraint-based application is often due to design, rather than implementation. It was also observed [LeL93] the lack of a methodology to define the model of the problem, possibly in tight collaboration with the end user.

This paper discusses the limitations of the notion of CSP as a model to represent real-world problems and extends it along the object-oriented paradigm to overcome those limitations; then, it outlines desirable features of a design methodology for constraint programming and sketches a design methodology that embodies such features for the extended notion of CSP's; finally, it revisits a classical example where the proposed methodology dramatically reduces the size of the model.

---

[*] Present address: Ecole Normale Supérieure, Département de Mathématiques et d'Informatique, 45 rue d'Ulm - Pavillion P1, 75005 Paris, France. E-mail: palmas@dmi.ens.fr

2 Constraint Satisfaction Problems

A *constraint satisfaction problem* is defined by a set $X_1,..,X_n$ of variables, each associated with a domain $D_1,..,D_n$ respectively, and a set $C_1,..,C_m$ of constraints, i.e., subsets of $D_1 x..x D_n$.

CSP's have extensively been studied to develop various types of consistency algorithms (for a survey, see [Kum92]). Nevertheless, when real-world problems are tackled, CSP's suffer from the following limitations:

1. variables are semantically poor entities
2. the only relations over variables are constraints
3. variables cannot be organized.

1. Entities participating to a problem are usually characterized by more than one feature. For example, a task is characterized by its name, start time, duration, etc. Furthermore, several features can be initially unknown, such as the start time of a task and the machine assigned to it. This is not expressible in CSP's because variables are characterized by just a domain.

2. As a consequence, all the relations of a CSP are over domains, i.e., they are constraints. On the contrary, when solving real-world problems, it is necessary to define other relations (e.g. a given task employs a given resource) and confine the combinatorial component to parts of the problem.

3. When defining a problem, it is often useful to aggregate entities according to some criterion, for instance to organize them into levels of abstraction. This is also not taken into account by CSP's.

Each CSP can be graphically represented as a *constraint graph* in which nodes represent variables and edges represent constraints. In principle, constraint graphs could be employed to model CSP's. In practice, they are untractable for real-world problems, as a consequence of 3.

For instance, to represent a binary global constraint, the number of edges to be drawn grows as the square of the number of nodes, which is untractable when the size of the problem increases considerably. In general, it is possible to conclude that the constraint graph is not appropriate to model CSP's.

3 Enhancing Constraint Satisfaction Problems

To overcome the mentioned limitations, the definition of CSP is enhanced through concepts deriving from the object-oriented paradigm. The main difference is that here objects do not have methods (but just data members) since their state is updated by the constraints.

The solution that we propose relies on *abstraction*, i.e., recognizing similarities and concentrating on them. Abstractions are defined both for variables and constraints following the object-oriented paradigm. This leads to an enhanced model, called *object-oriented constraint satisfaction problem* (OOCSP).

An *attribute* is a feature of some type. Each attribute is associated with a domain, a subset of the attribute's type. An *object* is a collection of attributes. Object attributes correspond to variables in CSP's. The set of attributes of an object defines the *structure* of the object. Objects sharing the same structure are grouped into *classes*. Classes are organized into a *hierarchy*. The structure of a lower class includes that of a higher class.

Associations can be defined over classes, objects, class attributes and object attributes and they are named accordingly. The naming convention is outlined in Table 1 and must be applied from the top to the bottom: if at least a class attribute occurs in the association, then it is a *class constraint*; otherwise, if there is at least an object attribute, then it is a *constraint*; otherwise, if there is at least a class, then it is called a *class relation*; otherwise, if there are just objects, it is a *relation*. Class constraints and class relations are also called *class associations*. Constraints and relations are also called *associations*. Class associations induce associations, i.e., the semantics of classes is defined in terms of objects. Classes, objects, attributes, class associations and associations are only under the control of the user, who can add and remove them. Domains are also under the control of the system, which can automatically refine them, i.e., remove values.

A solution to an OOCSP is an assignment of domain values to object attributes such that all the constraints, including those induced, are satisfied. Each OOCSP can be graphically represented as an *object constraint graph*, as explained in the section 5.

If at least a...	...then the association is a
class attribute	class constraint
object attribute	constraint
class	class relation
object	relation

Tab. 1. Naming convention for associations.

4 Design

By design, we mean the construction of a *model* of the problem, consisting of abstractions and relationships that provide an architecture for implementation.

While it is quite well understood, for traditional software development, what the desirable features of a good design and its resulting model should be, this topic has not been much addressed in the field of constraint programming.

We would like the design of a constraint-based application to be

- problem driven
- methodological
- computer aided
- interactive.

Problem Driven. Design should concentrate on the essence of the problem in exam without influences from tangible components such as a target platform or language. It should be a straightforward activity for domain experts, even with no computer skills.

Methodological. Design should follow a methodology, based on massive successful experiences, aiming at identifying and ordering the main steps of the process.

Computer Aided. Design should be supported by tools that make it more effective and fast while possibly controlling it.

Interactive. Design should facilitate and stimulate the participation of domain experts.

Desirable features of the model yielded by design are

- visual
- compact
- hierarchical
- dynamic
- composable
- modular
- multi purpose
- reusable
- language independent
- executable.

Visual. Intuitive graphical formalisms should be employed to study and define the abstractions and relationships in the model.

Compact. The size of the model should be as small as possible.

Hierarchical. It should be possible to concentrate on different levels of abstraction.

Dynamic. The model should account for frequent changes, for instance because new entities participate to the problem.

Composable. It should be possible to compose models into models of more complex problems.

Modular. It should be possible to break down the problem into consistent modules or views, each focusing on a specific aspect of the problem.

Multi purpose. It should be possible to employ the model to investigate different aspects of the problem, for instance by asking different questions.

Reusable. It should be possible to use the model as a starting point for new models of related problems.

Language independent. The model should be easily implemented in any constraint-programming language.

Executable. It should be possible to automatically generate code in a target constraint-programming language. In such a way, the model could be executed to provide immediate feedback on the problem formulation.

5 Design Methodology

A methodology to design OOCSP's that embodies the features listed in the previous section is here sketched. It is based on classical object-oriented design methodologies (for a survey see [Fow93]), and adapted to the constraint-programming domain. The methodology is made of

- a *notation* to represent the model
- a *process* to construct the model

The notation (see Fig. 1) consists of graphical entities that are combined to generate object constraint graphs, the models of OOCSP's. Dotted boxes denote classes, while solid boxes denote objects. Edges denote associations and directed edges inheritance. Specific icons are also introduced for the most common relations, such as "Has" and "Using".

The process consists of the following four steps:

- identify classes and objects
- identify the semantics of these classes and objects
- identify the associations among these classes and objects
- identify the semantics of these associations.

The purpose of the first step is identifying classes and objects to establish the boundaries of the problem. The purpose of the second step is establishing the features of the abstractions identified at the previous step. The purpose of the third step is identifying the dependencies among abstractions. The fourth step formally specifies, through logical formulae, the meaning of the associations identified in the previous steps. This issue is further discussed in the next section.

The process is incremental and iterative. It is incremental because when new classes, objects or associations are identified, existing classes, objects and associations can be refined and improved. It is iterative, because the definition of new classes, objects and associations often gives new insights on the problem that allow the user to simplify and generalize the design.

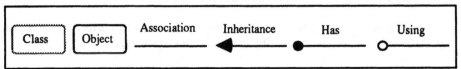

Fig. 1. The notation consists of graphical entities that are combined into object-constraint graphs, the graphical models of OOCSP's.

6 Executable Models

The models of OOCSP's can be directly executed once the edges of the object constraint graph are labeled with logical formulae formalizing the meaning of the associations they represent. Such formulae can be either executed by an interpreter of the object constraint graph, or preprocessed to a target constraint-programming language, not necessarily an object-oriented one. We abstract away from the syntactic details of such a language by taking a multi-sorted first-order logic in which the domain of interpretation for sorts has been fixed.

Formulae are obtained by connecting, through logical connectives, predicate symbols whose arguments are terms, i.e., constants, objects, classes, object attributes and class attributes as well as functions on terms. Class associations, i.e., formulae in which class symbols occur, induce associations, i.e., formulae in which no class symbols occur. They are obtained by replacing each class with its objects or the objects of its derived (through inheritance) classes, in all the possible combinations. A solution is an assignment of domain values to object attributes such that all the formulae, including those induced, are satisfied in the classical sense.

As an example of preprocessing, consider the following class constraint (*Resource*, *Task1* and *Task2* are classes)

$$[Using(Task1, Resource) \wedge Using(Task2, Resource)] \rightarrow$$
$$[Task1.start + Task1.duration \leq Task2.start \quad \vee$$
$$Task2.start + Task2.duration \leq Task1.start]$$

meaning that if two tasks use the same resource then they cannot overlap. Let *T1* and *T2* be objects of class *Task1* and *Task2* respectively and *R* an object of class *Resource*. In the constraint

$$[Using(T1, R) \wedge Using(T2, R)] \rightarrow$$
$$[T1.start + T1.duration \leq T2.start \quad \vee$$
$$T2.start + T2.duration \leq T1.start]$$

no more class symbols occur so it can be handled by traditional constraint languages where object attributes, such as *T1.start*, are variables in the CSP sense.

7 The Bridge Problem

The Bridge Problem [Van89] is a real-life project-planning problem consisting of minimizing the time to build a five-segment bridge (see Fig. 2). The project (see Fig. 3) includes 46 tasks (*A1*, *P1*, etc.) that employ resources (excavator *Ex*, concrete-mixer *CM*, etc.). The constraints of the problem include 31 precedence constraints (execute task *T5* before task *V2*, execute task *M5* before task *T4*, etc.), 77 resource constraints (task *A1* and *A2* cannot overlap because they both employ the excavator, tasks *T2* and *T5* cannot overlap because they both employ the crane, etc.), 60 specific constraints (the time between the completion of task *S1* and the completion of task *B1* is at most 4 days, the time between the completion of task *A4* and the completion of task *S4* is at most 3 days, etc.), for a total of 168 constraints.

The Bridge Problem has been modeled and solved with traditional constraint languages, such as Chip and Charme.

The Chip program [Van89] consists of 55 (Prolog-like) facts defining the data and of 20 (Prolog-like) procedures defining the process. The total size of the program is 90 lines, excluding declarations (35 lines). Data facts define tasks, durations, resources, components, relations and constraints. Process procedures basically iterate over data to set the appropriate constraints. No code concerns constraint propagation since it is taken into account by the language (it is in fact what differentiates Chip from Prolog).

The Charme formulation [Bul91], consists of 5 data (Pascal-like) declarations (arrays and structures) and of 10 (Pascal-like) procedures defining the program. The size of the program is 85 lines, excluding declarations (70 lines). As for the Chip formulation, the program accesses data and sets constraints. Again, no code concerns constraint propagation, as it is built into the language.

Our methodology is now employed to design the Bridge Problem.

Identify Classes and Objects. The basic class of the problem is *Task*. Tasks can be of 14 different types (*Excavation, Foundation*, etc.). Each concrete task is an object, instance of one of such classes. For example, *A1* is an instance of *Excavation, P1* is an instance of *Foundation*, etc. The resources (excavator, concrete-mixer, etc.) are also objects (*Ex, CM*, etc.), instances of the *Resource* class.

Identify the Semantics of These Classes and Objects. Each task is characterized by a *name, start time, duration, component* that it processes, *resource* that it employs and a set of tasks that come *before* it. All these features are attributes of the generic class *Task* and consequently of the 14 derived subclasses. The *start time* is the unknown to be determined, so it is a variable. The initial value is 0..200, meaning that the start time of each task is initially unknown, it will be automatically determined by the system, and it will be included between 0 and 200 days. Resources have no attributes, so their structure is empty.

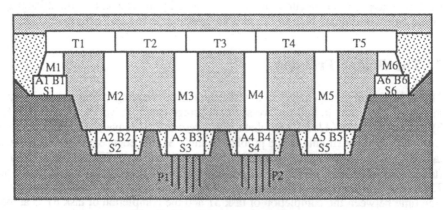

Fig. 2. The five-segment bridge.

Identify the Associations Among These Classes and Objects. The 31 precedence constraints, the 77 resource constraints and the minimality constraint can be expressed as three class constraints, referred to as *Precedence*, *Disjunction* and *Minimal*, respectively. The 60 specific constraints can also be expressed at the class level, with five class constraints referred to as *K1-K5*. Finally, the standard *Using* relation is defined between the classes *Excavation, Piles, Formwork, Foundation, Masonry, Delivery, Positioning* and *Filling*, and the objects *Ex, PD, Ca, CM, Bl, Cr, Cr* and *Cp*, respectively.

Identify the Semantics of These Associations. The semantics of these associations is specified through logical formulae on classes and objects:

Disjunction. $[Using(Task1, Resource) \wedge Using(Task2, Resource)] \rightarrow$
$[Task1.start + Task1.duration \le Task2.start \quad \vee$
$Task2.start + Task2.duration \le Task1.start]$

Precedence. $[Task1.name \in Task2.previous] \rightarrow$
$[Task1.start + Task1.duration < Task2.start]$

Minimal. $Minimal(Stop.start + Stop.duration)$

Using. $Using(Excavation, Ex), Using(Piles, PD), Using(Formwork, Ca),$
$Using(Foundation, CM), Using(Masonry, Bl), Using(Delivery, Cr),$
$Using(Positioning, Cr), Using(Removal, Cp).$

K1. $[Formwork.component = Foundation.component] \rightarrow$
$[Foundation.start + Foundation.duration - 4 \le$
$Formwork.start + Formwork.duration]$

K2. $[Excavation.component = Formwork.component] \rightarrow$
$[Formwork.start - 3 \le Excavation.start + Excavation.duration]$

K3. $Housing.start \le Formwork.start - 6$

K4. $Masonry.start + Masonry.duration - 2 \le Removal.start$

K5. $Delivery.start = Beginning.start + 30.$

The design of the Bridge Problem is complete. The model (see Fig. 4) is ready to be interpreted and executed to determine the start time of the tasks. The model consists of 16 classes, 53 objects, 1 class relation and 8 class constraints. The fact that there are no constraints on objects means that the model is well conceived, because abstraction has been fully exploited to factorize common information. Compared to the Chip (90 lines) and the Charme (85 lines) programs, the textual part of our model consists of 17 lines.

The problem can be designed in other ways. For example, bridge components could be defined as objects, rather than task attributes. It is just a matter of individual perception of the problem. What has to be kept in mind, is that expressing as much as possible at the class level, i.e., exploiting abstraction, is an important target to be pursued, because it reduces the number of constraints producing models that are more compact and clear.

N	Name	Description	Duration	Resource
1	PA	beginning of project	0	-
2	A1	excavation (abutment 1)	4	excavator
3	A2	excavation (pillar 1)	2	excavator
4	A3	excavation (pillar 2)	2	excavator
5	A4	excavation (pillar 3)	2	excavator
6	A5	excavation (pillar 4)	2	excavator
7	A6	excavation (pillar 5)	5	excavator
8	P1	foundation pile 2	20	pile-driver
9	P2	foundation pile 3	13	pile-driver
10	UE	erection of tmp. housing	10	-
11	S1	formwork (abutment 1)	8	carpentry
12	S2	formwork (pillar 1)	4	carpentry
13	S3	formwork (pillar 2)	4	carpentry
14	S4	formwork (pillar 3)	4	carpentry
15	S5	formwork (pillar 4)	4	carpentry
16	S6	formwork (abutment 2)	10	carpentry
17	B1	concrete found. (abutment 1)	1	concrete-mixer
18	B2	concrete found. (pillar 1)	1	concrete-mixer
19	B3	concrete found. (pillar 2)	1	concrete-mixer
20	B4	concrete found. (pillar 3)	1	concrete-mixer
21	B5	concrete found. (pillar 4)	1	concrete-mixer
22	B6	concrete found. (abutment 2)	1	concrete-mixer
23	C1	concrete setting (abutment 1)	1	-
24	C2	concrete setting (pillar 1)	1	-
25	C3	concrete setting (pillar 2)	1	-
26	C4	concrete setting (pillar 3)	1	-
27	C5	concrete setting (pillar 4)	1	-
28	C6	concrete setting (abutment 2)	1	-
29	M1	masonry work (abutment 1)	16	bricklaying
30	M2	masonry work (pillar 1)	8	bricklaying
31	M3	masonry work (pillar 2)	8	bricklaying
32	M4	masonry work (pillar 3)	8	bricklaying
33	M5	masonry work (pillar 4)	8	bricklaying
34	M6	masonry work (abutment 2)	20	bricklaying
35	L	delivery of bearers	2	crane
36	T1	positioning (bearer 1)	12	crane
37	T2	positioning (bearer 2)	12	crane
38	T3	positioning (bearer 3)	12	crane
39	T4	positioning (bearer 4)	12	crane
40	T5	positioning (bearer 5)	12	crane
41	UA	removal of tmp. housing	10	-
42	V1	filling 1	15	Caterpillar
43	V2	filling 2	10	Caterpillar
44	K1	costing point 1	0	-
45	K2	costing point 2	0	-
46	PE	end of project	0	-

Fig. 3. The 46 tasks are characterized by a name, an action they perform, a duration and a resource they employ.

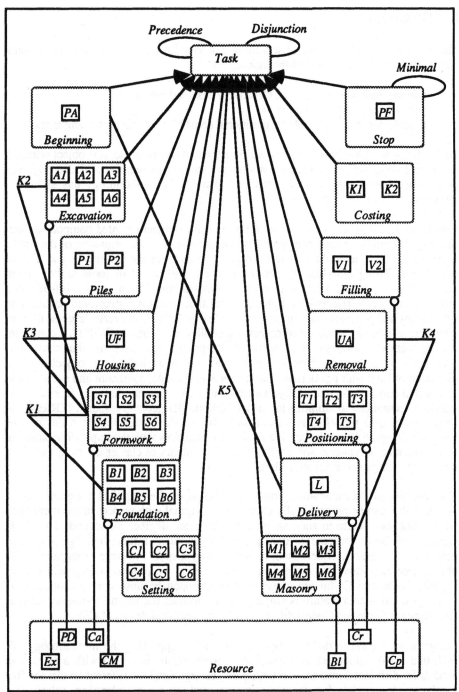

Fig. 4. The Bridge Problem formulated as an OOCSP; 14 classes of specific tasks are derived from the base class *Task*; 7 resources are used to accomplish the tasks as defined by the standard relation *Using*; the 8 class constraints are *Precedence, Disjunction, Minimal, K1, K2, K3, K4, K5.*

8   Discussion

This work originates from the observation, due to industrial experience in developing constraint-based applications, of the lack of

- a framework where CSP's are effectively designed through
- a visual methodology producing
- models directly executable by traditional constraint programming languages.

Such a framework has been sketched and illustrated on an example. It is object oriented, to abstract variables and constraints, and visual, to be more intuitive and effective. The possibility of executing models produced through the methodology has also been discussed.

Constraint-based systems integrating either visual or object-oriented components are: Sketchpad [Sut63], a pioneering visual system developed at the beginning of the sixties allowing the user to build geometric objects from language primitives and certain constraints; ThingLab [Bor79], providing users with a set of tools to help them graphically represent simulations and "experiments" in a constraint-oriented environment; Socle [Har86], an hybrid system that contains a structured partitioning component and a constraint component; Garnet [MGV92], to create large-scale user interfaces combining pre-defined objects into collections; Equate [Wil91], a constraint solving method that obeys the principle of encapsulation, in the sense that constraints do not refer directly to an object's implementation; Cspoo [Kök93], an object-oriented extension of Lisp with pre-defined classes such as variable, constraint and solver; Devi [ThS94], a constraint-based 3D geometric editing environment that uses flexible user-interface techniques to simplify the task of editing 3D geometry; Codm [SRR94], an object-based data model to represent partially-specified information; Kaleidoscope [FBB92], integrating the declarative nature of constraints with the imperative nature of object-oriented languages; Solver [Pug92], a C++ library of classes defining variables, constraints and propagation algorithms.

The objective of the framework proposed in this paper, the graphical design of models of CSP's that can be automatically executed, is original with respect to the mentioned works, but they relate to such an objective at some degree: Sketchpad, ThingLab, Garnet and Devi implement "constraints-for-graphics" rather than "graphics-for-constraints" systems; Kaleidoscope, Solver and Cspoo integrate constraints with objects into imperative constraint languages, whereas we propose a graphical setting; Equate, Socle and Codm are closer to our approach because they are declarative languages, but such a feature is employed for purposes (equation solving for Equate, reasoning for Socle and Codm) different from the graphical design of CSP's.

Future work concerns the development of a tool supporting the methodology. To facilitate the development of applications, it should be provided with a *library of models* for different domains. The library can be organized on different levels: the first level includes models for generic domains, such as project planning, scheduling, finance, resources management, etc.; the second level includes models for more specific domains, such as construction-project management and software-project management for the project planning domain; production scheduling and meeting scheduling for the scheduling domain, etc. To solve a problem, the user selects the appropriate model and customizes it by adding or deleting nodes and edges.

Acknowledgements

This work was partially supported by funding from the Commission of the European Communities as part of the ESPRIT Project 5291, CHIC - Constraint Handling in Industry and Commerce. Many thanks to Y. C. Chan and M. Leconte for reading earlier versions of this paper.

References

[Bor79]   A. Borning, Thinglab: A Constraint-Oriented Simulation Laboratory, *Ph.D. Thesis*, Stanford University, CA, 1979.

[Bul91]   Bull S.A. Ed.: *Manuel Charme First*, Bull Publication No. 95-F2-52GN-REV0, Annexe A, pages 29-49, Paris, France, 1991.

[Cha94]   Y. C. Chan, *Practical Constraint-Based Programming: Solving Problems with the Charme Language*, John Wiley & Sons Publisher, to appear, 1994.

[DAn92]   M. D'Andrea, Scheduling and Optimization in the Automobile Industry, *Lecture Notes in Artificial Intelligence*, vol. 636, G. Comyn, N. E. Fuchs, Ratcliffe (Editors), Springer Verlag, 1992.

[FBB92]   B. Freeman-Benson, A. Borning, Integrating Constraints with an Object-Oriented Language, *Proc. of the 1992 European Conference on Object-Oriented Programming*, June 1992.

[Fow93]   M. Fowler, A Comparison of Object-Oriented Analysis and Design Methods, in *Approaches to Object-Oriented Analysis and Design*, A. Carmichael Ed., Ashgate, 1993.

[Gos93]   V. Gosselin, Train Scheduling Using Constraint Programming Techniques", *Actes 13eme Journée International sur les Systèmes Expert et Leur Application*, Avignon, 1993.

[Har86]   D. R. Harris, A Hybrid Object and Constraint Representation Language, *AAAI-86*, Philadelphia, Pennsylvania, 1986.

[Kök93]   T. Kökény: CSPOO: Un Système à Résolution de Contraintes Orienté Objet, *Réprésentation Par Objet*, La Grande Motte, pages 39-49, July 1993.

[Kum92]   V. Kumar: Algorithms for Constraint Satisfaction Problems: a Survey. *AI Magazine*, 13, 1992, 32-44.

[LeL93]   M. Leconte, F. Leyter, Update Specification of Logic Constraint Programming Methodology, *Deliverable D2.1.2.2*, CHIC Esprit Project 5291, July 1993.

[MaT89]   J. Marcovich, Y. Tourbier, Une Application de la Programmation par Contraintes: Construction de Plans d'Experience Orthogonaux au Sens Strict avec Condor, *Actes des Journées Internationales d'Avignon*, 1989.

[MGV92]   B. A. Myers, D. A. Giuse, B. Vander Zanden, Declarative Programming in a Prototype-Instance System: Object-Oriented Programming Without Writing Methods, *OOPSLA'92*, 184-200, 1992.

[Nad90]   B. Nadel, Some Applications of the Constraint Satisfaction Problem, *Tech. Report* CSC-90-008, Dept. of C.S., Wayne State University, Detroit, MI, 1990.

[Opl89]   A. Oplobedu, Charme: un Langage Industriel de Programmation par Contraintes, *Actes 9eme Journée International sur les Systèmes Expert et Leur Applications*, Vol. 1, 55-70, Avignon, 1989.

[PMT92]   M. Paltrinieri, A. Momigliano, F. Torquati, Scheduling of an Aircraft Fleet, *AAAI Tech. Rep.* SS-92-01. Also as *NASA Tech. Rep.* FIA-92-17, NASA Ames, Moffet Field, CA, USA, 1992.

[Pug92]   J.-F. Puget, Programmation Par Contraintes Orientée Objet, *12th International Conference on AI, ES and NL*, 129-138, Avignon, France, 1992.

[Rot93]   A. Roth, Constraint Programming: A Practical Solution to Complex Problems, *AI Expert*, pages 36-39 Sept. 1993.

[SRR94]   D. Srivastava, R. Ramakrishnan, P. Z. Revesz: Constraint Objects, *Second International Workshop on Principles and Practice of Constraint Programming*, Orcas Island, WA, May 1994.

[Sut63]   I. Sutherland, A Man-Machine Graphical Communication System, *PhD Thesis*, MIT, 1963.

[ThS94]   S. Thennarangam, G. Singh: Inferring 3-dimensional Constraints with DEVI, *Second International Workshop on Principles and Practice of Constraint Programming*, Orcas Island, WA, May 1994.

[Van89]   P. Van Hentenryck: *Constraint Satisfaction in Logic Programming*, The MIT Press, Cambridge, Massachusetts, 1989.

[Wil91]   M. Wilk, Equate: An Object-Oriented Constraint Solver, *OOPSLA '91*, pages 286-298, Phoenix, October 1991.

Experiences with Constraint-based Array Dependence Analysis

William Pugh   David Wonnacott

pugh@cs.umd.edu   davew@cs.umd.edu

Department of Computer Science,
University of Maryland, College Park, MD 20742

Abstract. Array data dependence analysis provides important information for optimization of scientific programs. Array dependence testing can be viewed as constraint analysis, although traditionally general-purpose constraint manipulation algorithms have been thought to be too slow for dependence analysis. We have explored the use of exact constraint analysis, based on Fourier's method, for array data dependence analysis. We have found these techniques can be used without a great impact on total compile time. Furthermore, the use of general-purpose algorithms has allowed us to address problems beyond traditional dependence analysis. In this paper, we summarize some of the constraint manipulation techniques we use for dependence analysis, and discuss some of the reasons for our performance results.

1   Introduction

When two memory accesses refer to the same address, and at least one of those accesses is a write, we say there is a *data dependence* between the accesses. In this case, we must be careful not to reorder the execution of the accesses during optimization, if we are to preserve the semantics of the program being optimized. We therefore need accurate array data dependence information to determine the legality of many optimizations for programs that use arrays. Array dependence testing can be viewed as constraint analysis. For example, in Figure 1, determining whether or not any array element is both written by A[i, j+1] and read by A[100, j], is equivalent to testing for the existence of solutions to the constraints shown on the right of the figure.

```
for i = 1 to n
  for j = i to n
    A[i, j+1] = A[n, j]
```

$1 \leq i_w \leq j_w \leq n$ (write iteration in bounds)
$1 \leq i_r \leq j_r \leq n$ (read iteration in bounds)
$i_w = n$ (first subscripts equal)
$j_w + 1 = j_r$ (second subscripts equal)

Fig. 1. Dependence testing and associated constraints

Since integer programming is an NP-complete problem, ([GJ79]), production compilers employ techniques that are guaranteed to be fast but give conservative answers: they might report a possible solution when no solution exists. We have explored the use of exact constraint analysis methods for array data dependence analysis. We have gone beyond simply checking for satisfiability of conjunctions of constraints to being able to manipulate arbitrary Presburger formulas. This has allowed us to address problems beyond traditional dependence analysis.

In our previous papers [Pug92, PW93a], we have presented timing results for our system on a variety of benchmark programs, and argued that our techniques are not prohibitively slow. In fact, using exact techniques to obtain standard kinds of dependence information requires about 1% − 10% of the total time required by simple workstation compilers that do no array data dependence analysis of any kind.

Our techniques are based on an extension of Fourier variable elimination to integers. Many other researchers in the constraints field [Duf74, LL92, Imb93, JMSY93] have stated that direct application of Fourier's technique may be impractical because of the number of redundant constraints generated. We have not experienced any significant problems with Fourier elimination generating redundant constraints, even though we have not implemented methods suggested [Duf74, Imb93, JMSY93] to control this problem. We believe that our extension of Fourier elimination to integers is much more efficient that described by [Wil76].

In this paper, we summarize some of the constraint manipulation techniques we use for dependence analysis, and discuss some of the reasons for our performance results.

2 The Omega Test

The Omega test [Pug92] was originally developed to check if a set of linear constraints has an integer solution, and was initially used in array data dependence testing. Since then, its capabilities and uses have grown substantially. In this section, we describe the various capabilities of the Omega test.

The Omega test is based on an extension of Fourier variable elimination [DE73] to integer programming. Other researchers have suggested the use of Fourier variable elimination for dependence analysis [WT92, MHL91b] but only as a last resort after exact and fast, but incomplete, methods have failed to give decisive answers. We proved [Pug92] that in cases where the fast but incomplete methods of Lam et al. [MHL91b] apply, the Omega test is guaranteed to have low-order polynomial time complexity.

2.1 Eliminating an Existentially Quantified Variable

The basic operation of the Omega test is the elimination of an existentially quantified variable, also referred to as shadow-casting or projection. For example, given a set of constraints P over x, y and z that define, for example, a dodecahedron, the Omega test can compute the constraints on x and y that define the shadow of the dodecahedron. Mathematically, these constraints are equivalent to $\exists z$ s.t. P. But the Omega test is able to remove the existentially quantified variables, and report the answer just in terms of the free variables (x and y).

Over rational variables, projection of a convex region always gives a convex result. Unfortunately, the same does not apply for integer variables. For example, $\exists y$ s.t. $1 \leq y \leq 4 \wedge x = 2y$ has $x = 2$, $x = 4$, $x = 6$ and $x = 8$ as solutions. Sometimes, the result is even more complicated. For example, the solutions for x in:

$$\exists i, j \text{ s.t. } 1 \leq i \leq 8 \wedge 1 \leq j \leq 5 \wedge x = 6i + 9j - 7$$

are all numbers between 8 and 86 (inclusive) that have remainder 2 when divided by 3, except for 11 and 83.

In general, the Omega test produces an answer in disjunctive normal form: the union of a finite list of clauses. A clause may need to describe a non-convex region. There are two methods for describing these regions:

Stride format The Omega test can produce clauses that consist of affine constraints over the free variables and stride constraints. A stride constraint $c|e$ is interpreted as "c evenly divides e". In this form, the above solution could be represented as:

$$x = 8 \ \vee \ (\ 14 \leq x \leq 80 \wedge 3|(x+1)\ ) \ \vee \ x = 86$$

Projected format Alternatively, the Omega test can produce clauses that consist of a set of linear constraints over a set of auxiliary variables and an affine 1-1 mapping from those variables to the free variables. Using this format, the above solution could be represented as

$$x = 8 \ \vee \ (\exists \alpha \text{ s.t. } 5 \leq \alpha \leq 27 \wedge x = 3\alpha - 1) \ \vee \ x = 86$$

These two representations are equivalent and there are simple and efficient methods for converting between them.

Our Extension of Fourier Elimination to Integers If $\beta \leq bz$ and $az \leq \alpha$ (where a and b are positive integers), then $a\beta \leq abz \leq b\alpha$. If z is a real variable, $\exists z$ s.t. $a\beta \leq abz \leq b\alpha$ if and only if $a\beta \leq b\alpha$. Fourier variable elimination eliminates a variable z by combining together all pairs of upper and lower bounds on z and adding the resulting constraints to those constraints that do not involve z. This produces a set of constraints that has a solution if and only if there exists a real value of z that satisfies the original set of constraints.

In [Pug92] and Figure 2 we show how to compute the "dark shadow" of a set of constraints: a set of constraints that, if it has solutions, implies the existence of an integer z such that the original set of constraints is satisfied. Of course, not all solutions are contained in the dark shadow.

For example, consider the constraints:

$$\exists y \text{ s.t. } 0 \leq 3y - x \leq 7 \wedge 1 \leq x - 2y \leq 5$$

Using Fourier variable elimination, we find that $3 \leq x \leq 27$ if we allow y to take on non-integer values. The dark shadow of these constraints is $5 \leq x \leq 25$. In fact, this equation has solutions for $x = 3, 5 \leq x \leq 27$ and $x = 29$.

In [Pug92] and Figure 2 we give a method for generating an additional sets of constraints that would contain any solutions not contained in the dark shadow. These "splinters" still contain references to the eliminated variable, but also contain an equality constraint (i.e., are flat). This equality constraint allows us to eliminate the desired variable exactly. For the example given previously, the splinters are:

$$\exists y \text{ s.t. } x = 3y \wedge 0 \leq 3y - x \leq 7 \wedge 1 \leq x - 2y \leq 5$$

$$\exists y \text{ s.t. } x + 1 = 3y \wedge 0 \leq 3y - x \leq 7 \wedge 1 \leq x - 2y \leq 5$$

$$\exists y \text{ s.t. } x - 5 = 2y \wedge y \text{ s.t. } 0 \leq 3y - x \leq 7 \wedge 1 \leq x - 2y \leq 5$$

Simplifying these produces clauses in projected form:

$$\exists y \text{ s.t. } x = 3y \wedge 1 \leq y \leq 5$$

$$\exists y \text{ s.t. } x = 3y - 1 \wedge 2 \leq y \leq 6$$

$$\exists y \text{ s.t. } x = 2y + 5 \wedge 5 \leq y \leq 12$$

Eliminate z from C, the conjunction of a set of inequalities
$R = \text{False}$
$C' = $ all constraints from C that do not involve z
$C'' = C$
for each lower bound on z: $\beta \leq bz$
    for each upper bound on z: $az \leq \alpha$
        $C' = C' \wedge a\beta + (a - 1)(b - 1) \leq b\alpha$
        % Misses $a\beta \leq abz \leq b\alpha < a\beta + (a - 1)(b - 1)$
        % Misses $\beta \leq bz < \beta + \frac{(a-1)(b-1)}{a}$
    let $a_{\max} = $ max coefficient of z in upper bound on z
    for $i = 0$ to $((a_{\max} - 1)(b - 1) - 1)/a_{\max}$ do
        $R = R \vee C \wedge \beta + i = bz$
% C' is the dark shadow
% R contains the splinters
% $C' \vee (\exists \text{ integer } z \text{ s.t. } R) \equiv \exists \text{ integer } z \text{ s.t. } C$

Fig. 2. Extension of Fourier variable elimination to integers

2.2 Verifying the Existence of Solutions

The Omega test also provides direct support for checking if integer solutions exist to a set of linear constraints. It does this by treating all the variables as existentially quantified and eliminating variables until it produces a problem containing a single variable; such problems are easy to check for integer solutions. The Omega test incorporates several extensions over a naive application of variable elimination.

2.3 Removing Redundant Constraints

In the normal operation of the Omega test, we eliminate any constraint that is made redundant by any other single constraint (e.g., $x + y \leq 10$ is made redundant by $x + y \leq 5$). Upon request, we can use more aggressive techniques to eliminate redundant constraints. We use fast but incomplete tests that can flag a constraint as definitely redundant or definitely not redundant, and a backup complete test. This capability is used when verifying implications and simplifying formulas involving negation.

We also use these techniques to define a "gist" operator: informally, we say (gist P given Q) is what is "interesting" about P, given that we already know Q. More formally, we guarantee that $((\text{gist } P \text{ given } Q) \wedge Q) \equiv P \wedge Q$ and try to make the set of constraints produced by the gist operator as simple as possible.

2.4 Simplifying Formulas Involving Negation

There are two problems involved in simplifying formulas containing negated conjuncts, such as

$$-10 \leq i + j, i - j \leq 10 \ \wedge \ \neg(2 \leq i, j \leq 8 \wedge 2|i + j)$$

Naively converting such formulas to disjunctive normal form generally leads to an explosive growth in the size of the formula. In the worst-case, this cannot be prevented. But we [PW93a] have described methods that are effective in dealing with these problems for the cases we encounter. One key idea to to recognize that we can transform $A \wedge \neg B$ to $A \wedge \neg(\text{gist } B \text{ given } A)$. Given several negated clauses, we simplify them all this way before choose one to negate and distribute.

Secondly, previous techniques for negating non-convex constraints, based on quasi-linear constraints [AI91], were discovered to be incomplete in certain pathological cases [PW93a]. We [PW93a] describe a method that is exact and complete for all cases.

2.5 Simplifying Arbitrary Presburger Formulas

Utilizing the capabilities described above, we can simplify and/or verify arbitrary Presburger formulas. In general, this may be prohibitively expensive. There is a known lower bound of $2^{2^{o(n)}}$ on the worst case nondeterministic time complexity, and a known upper bound of $2^{2^{2^{O(n)}}}$ on the deterministic time complexity, of Presburger formula verification. However, we have found that we are able to efficiently analyze many Presburger formulas that arise in practice.

For example, our current implementation requires 12 milliseconds on a Sun Sparc IPX to simplify

$$1 \leq i \leq 2n \ \wedge \ 1 \leq i'' \leq 2n \wedge i = i''$$
$$\wedge \ \neg(\ \exists i',j' \text{ s.t. } 1 \leq i' \leq 2n \wedge 1 \leq j' \leq n - 1 \wedge i \leq i' \wedge i' = i'' \wedge 2j' = i'' \ )$$
$$\wedge \ \neg(\ \exists i',j' \text{ s.t. } 1 \leq i' \leq 2n \wedge 1 \leq j' \leq n - 1 \wedge i \leq i' \wedge i' = i'' \wedge 2j' + 1 = i'' \ )$$

to

$$(1 = i = i'' \leq n) \vee (1 \leq i = i'' = 2n) \vee (1 \leq i = i'' \leq 2 \wedge n = 1)$$

Related Work

Other researchers have proposed extensions to Fourier variable elimination as a decision method for array data dependence analysis [MHL91a, WT92, IJT91]. Lam et al. [MHL91a] extend Fourier variable elimination to integers by computing a sample solution, using branch and bound techniques if needed. Michael Wolfe and Chau-Wen Tseng [WT92] discuss how to recognize when Fourier variable elimination may produce a conservative result, but do not give a method to verify the existence of integer solutions. These methods are decision tests and cannot return symbolic answers.

Corinne Ancourt and François Irigoin [AI91] describe the use of Fourier variable elimination for quantified variable elimination. They use this to generate loop bounds that scan convex polyhedra. They extend Fourier variable elimination to integers by introducing floor and ceiling operators. Although this makes their elimination exact, it may not be possible to eliminate additional variables from a set of constraints involving floor and ceiling operators. This limits their ability to check for the existence of integer solutions and remove redundant constraints.

Cooper [Coo72] describes a complete algorithm for verifying and/or simplifying Presburger formulas. His method for quantified variable elimination always introduces disjunctions, even if the result is convex. We have not yet performed a head-to-head comparison of the Omega test with Cooper's algorithm. However, we believe that the Omega test will prove better for quantified variable elimination when the result is convex and better for verification of a formula already in disjunctive normal form. Cooper's algorithm does not require formulas to be transformed into disjunctive normal form and may be better for formulas that would be expensive to put into disjunctive normal form (although our methods for handling negation address this as well).

The SUP-INF method [Ble75, Sho77] is a semi-decision procedure. It sometimes detects solutions when only real solutions exist and it cannot be used for symbolic quantified variable elimination.

H.P. Williams [Wil76] describes an extension of Fourier elimination to integers. His scheme leads to a much more explosive growth than our scheme. If the only constraints involving an eliminated variable x are $L \leq lx$ and $ux \leq U$, his scheme produces $\mathrm{lcm}(l, u)$ clauses, while ours produces

$$1 + \left\lceil \frac{(l-1)(u-1)}{\max(l, u)} \right\rceil$$

clauses. If there are p lower bounds $L_i \leq l_i x$ and q upper bounds $u_j x \leq U_j$, Williams' method produces a formula that, when converted into disjunctive normal form, contains

$$\prod_{1 \leq i \leq p \wedge 1 \leq j \leq q} \mathrm{lcm}(l_i, u_j)$$

clauses, while the number of clauses produced by our scheme is

$$1 + \min \left(\sum_{1 \leq i \leq p} \left\lceil \frac{(l_i - 1)(\max(u_j) - 1)}{\max(u_j)} \right\rceil, \sum_{1 \leq j \leq q} \left\lceil \frac{(\max(l_i) - 1)(u_j - 1)}{\max(l_i)} \right\rceil \right)$$

For example, if the l_i's are $\{1, 1, 1, 2, 3, 5\}$ and the u_j's are $\{1, 1, 3, 7\}$, Williams' method produces

$$23156852670000$$

clauses, while ours produces 12. It is almost certainly possible to improve Williams' method while using the same approach as Williams, but we know of no description of such an improvement.

Jean-Louis Lassez [LHM89, LL92, HLL92] gives an alternative to Fourier variable elimination for elimination of existentially quantified variables. However, his methods work over real variables, are optimized for dense constraints (constraints with few zero coefficients) and are inefficient when the final problem contains more than a few variables since they build a convex hull in the space of variables remaining after all quantified variables have been eliminated.

3 Constraint Based Dependence Analysis

Array dependence testing can be viewed as constraint analysis. Simply testing for the existence of a dependence (as in Figure 1) is equivalent to testing for solutions to a set of constraints.

We can also use constraint manipulation to obtain information about the possible differences in the values of the corresponding index variables at the times of the two accesses (this information can be used to test for the legality of some program transformations). To do so, we introduce variables corresponding to these differences, and existentially quantify and eliminate all other variables. Alternatively, we can choose to eliminate everything but the symbolic constants, and thus determine the conditions under which the dependence exists ([PW92]).

Figure 3 shows a relatively complicated example of constraint-based dependence analysis, from one of the NASA NAS benchmarks. Note that our techniques for eliminating equalities let us reduce both the number of variables and the number of constraints before resorting to Fourier elimination.

Program to be analyzed:

```
for j = 0 to 20 do
  for i = max(-j,-10) to 0 do
    for k = max(-j,-10)-i to -1 do
      for l = 0 to 5 do
        a(l,i,j) = ...a(l,k,i+j)...
```

Constraints before equality substitution:

$\exists j_w, i_w, k_w, l_w, j_r, i_r, k_r, l_r$ s.t.

$$\Delta i = i_r - i_w \wedge \Delta j = j_r - j_w$$
$$\Delta k = k_r - k_w \wedge \Delta l = l_r - l_w$$

$$l_w = l_r \wedge i_w = k_r \wedge j_w = j_r + i_r$$

$$0 \le j_w \le 20$$
$$-10, -j_w \le i_w \le 0$$
$$-j_w - i_w, -10 - i_w \le k_w \le -1$$
$$0 \le l_w \le 5$$

$$0 \le j_r \le 20$$
$$-10, -j_r \le i_r \le 0$$
$$-j_r - i_r, -10 - i_r \le k_r \le -1$$
$$0 \le l_r \le 5$$

Constraints after equality substitution:

$\exists j_r, l_w$ s.t.

$$0 \le l_w \le 5$$
$$0 \le j_r \le 20$$
$$3\Delta j + 2\Delta i + \Delta k \le j_r$$
$$\Delta j \le j_r \le 20 + \Delta j$$
$$2\Delta j + \Delta i \le j_r$$
$$2\Delta j + 2\Delta i + \Delta k \le 10$$
$$1 \le \Delta j + \Delta i + \Delta k$$
$$1 \le \Delta j + \Delta i \le 10$$
$$0 \le \Delta j \le 10$$
$$2\Delta j + \Delta i \le 10$$
$$\Delta l := 0$$

Constraints after eliminating l_w and j_r:

$$2\Delta j + \Delta i \le 10$$
$$0 \le \Delta j \le 10$$
$$3\Delta j + 2\Delta i + \Delta k \le 20$$
$$2\Delta j + 2\Delta i + \Delta k \le 10$$
$$1 \le \Delta j + \Delta i + \Delta k$$
$$1 \le \Delta j + \Delta i \le 10$$
$$\Delta l := 0$$

Fig. 3. Constraint-based dependence analysis

If we extend our constraint manipulation system to handle negated conjunctions of linear constraints, we can include constraints that rule out the dependences that are "killed" by other writes to the array, producing array data flow information ([PW93a]). The analysis tells us the source of the value read at any particular point; standard array data dependence tests just tell us who had previously written to the memory location read at any particular point. We have also found that our use of constraints to represent dependences is useful for other forms of program analysis and transformation ([Pug91, PW93b, KP93]).

4 Experiences

One of the main drawbacks of Fourier's method of variable elimination is the huge number of constraints that can be generated by repeated elimination, many of which could be redundant. Other researchers have found that Fourier's technique may be prohibitively expensive [HLL92, Imb93] for some sets of constraints, and have proposed either alternative methods for projection [HLL92] or methods to avoid generating so many redundant constraints [Imb93].

We have found Fourier's method to be efficient, and do not experience substantial increases in the number of constraints. Our empirical studies have shown that Fourier's method can be used in dependence analysis without a significant impact on total compile time [Pug92, PW93a]. The average time required for memory-based analysis (as in Figure 1) was well under 1 millisecond per pair of references, and the average time for array data flow analysis a few milliseconds. These time trials were measured on a set of benchmarks that includes some of the NASA NAS kernels and some code from the Perfect Club Benchmarks ([B+89]).

We believe this speed is the result of several attributes of the sets of constraints we produce for dependence analysis. First, loop bounds and array subscripts are often either constant or a function of a single variable. If all loop bounds and array subscripts have this form, all of our constraints will involve only one or two variables. Variable elimination is much less expensive within this restricted domain (known as LI(2)), even if we use the general algorithm. The number of constraints generated is bounded by a sub-exponential (though more than polynomial) function, rather than the $2^{n/2}$ of the general case [Cha93, Nel78].

Second, our constraints contain many unit coefficients. When the non-zero coefficients in a sparse set of constraints are all ± 1, projection ends up producing many parallel constraints, which can then be eliminated by our simple test for redundant constraints. Variable elimination in a LI(2) problem with unit coefficients preserves unit coefficients (after dividing through by the GCD of the coefficients). Under such situations, there cannot be more than $O(n^2)$ non-parallel constraints over n variables, and our method needs no more then $O(n^3)$ time to eliminate as many variables as desired [Pug92].

Finally, our constraint sets contain numerous equality constraints. Since we use these constraints to eliminate variables without resorting to projection, they help to keep down the size of the constraint sets that we must manipulate with Fourier's technique.

4.1 Empirical Studies of Dependence Analysis Constraints

We instrumented our system to analyze the types of constraints we deal with during dependence analysis. For each application of the Omega test, we analyzed the constraints that remained (a) after our initial removal of equality constraints and (b) after we had either eliminated all but two variables or run out of quantified variables to eliminate. In doing this analysis, we computed real shadows, as opposed to integer shadows (because the integer shadow may not be a simple conjunct). However, we still performed a number of other operations to rule out non-integer solutions (such as normalizing $2x + 4y \geq 3$ to $x + 2y \geq 2$).

When analyzing a set of constraints, we counted the number of variables, and counted (separately) the number of constraints that involved 1, 2 or 3+ variables. We then eliminated all redundant constraints, and recounted.

We performed these tests over our dataflow benchmark set [PW93a], which includes some of the NASA NAS kernels and some code from the Perfect Club

Averages	when	# vars	kind	# of constraints involving			
				1 var	2 vars	3+ vars	total
	initial	5.6	as given	2.9	3.3	1.4	7.6
			nonredundant	2.0	2.1	0.9	5.0
	final	2.4	as generated	1.8	0.5	0.1	2.4
			nonredundant	1.2	0.3	0.07	1.6

a worst-case (but noncontrived) example encountered in benchmarks	when	# vars	kind	# of constraints involving			
				1 var	2 vars	3+ vars	total
	initial	5	as given	6	5	4	15
			nonredundant	4	2	3	9
	final	3	as generated	2	3	3	8
			nonredundant	1	2	2	5

Fig. 4. Characteristics of constraint sets used in dependence analysis

Benchmarks ([B+89]). In total, we considered 1144 sets of constraints, and obtained the results shown in Figure 4.

Note that our methods always check for parallel constraints and eliminate the redundant one immediately (e.g., given $x + y \leq 5$ and $x + y \leq 10$, the second is eliminated). This can be done in constant time per constraint (through the use of a hash table).

Quite surprisingly, in *none* of the 1144 cases did the number of constraints increase as variables were eliminated (even though we did no elimination of non-parallel redundant constraints).

4.2 Empirical Studies of Random Constraints

To better understand the reasons for our good fortune in avoiding an explosion of constraints, we also studied the behavior of Fourier elimination on sets of random constraints. Figure 5 shows the results of these studies.

In each experiment, we fixed the number of constraints and variables, added one random non-zero to each constraint. When then projected the constraints onto the first two variables, and recorded the maximum number of constraints encountered during the elimination. We then added an additional nonzero coefficient to the original set of constraints, and repeated the projection. We continued doing this until the problem had no non-zeros left. Each line represents the median of 5-21 experiments. The key gives the elimination method used. All experiments shown here had 15 constraints on 5 variables, like the worst-case example from Figure 4.

The top graph compares the effectiveness of Fourier's method and the techniques described by Imbert on sets of constraints in which the non-zero coefficients had random integer values between -10 and +10. Our implementation of Imbert's method [Imb93] of redundant constraint detection uses Theorem 10 of

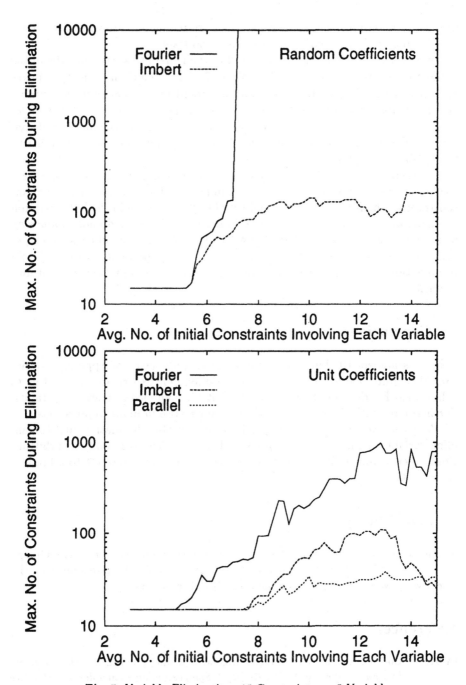

Fig. 5. Variable Elimination: 15 Constraints on 5 Variables

[Imb93] to determine that some constraints are redundant. However, we do not use the more expensive comparison or matrical tests.

Imbert's method is clearly important for problems of this size when the initial number of constraints per variable is above 7. When the initial density is below 5, even Fourier's original technique does not result in an increase in the number of constraints. However, our "worst-case" problem had an average of just under 6 initial constraints per variable, and we saw no increase in the number of constraints. Clearly the sparsity and size of the constraint sets were not sufficient to explain our results.

We therefore re-ran the tests on sets of constraints in which all the non-zero coefficients were ± 1, and included our techniques for detecting parallel redundant constraints. The results of this second set of tests are shown in the bottom graph of Figure 5. Note that the both our techniques and Imbert's do not produce an increase in the number of constraints when the initial number of constraints per variable is below 7. We therefore attribute our observations in Section 4.1 to a combination of constraint set size and sparsity and the high frequency of unit coefficients.

5   Conclusions

Other researchers [HLL92, Imb93] have been quite leary of applying Fourier variable elimination to sets of dense constraints. Our experience has lead us to believe that Fourier's method is quite efficient when applied to sparse constraints. Furthermore, we believe that sparse constraints arise in many applications.

We have extended our work beyond Fourier variable elimination: first to handling variable elimination for integer variables, and then to simplifying arbitrary Presburger formulas. We hope these extensions may be of interest to a broader community.

6   Availability

Technical reports about the Omega test and an implementation of the Omega test are available via anonymous ftp from `ftp.cs.umd.edu:pub/omega` or the world wide web `http://www.cs.umd.edu/projects/omega`.

References

[AI91]   Corinne Ancourt and François Irigoin. Scanning polyhedra with DO loops. In *Proc. of the 3rd ACM SIGPLAN Symposium on Principles and Practice of Parallel Programming*, pages 39–50, April 1991.

[B+89]   M. Berry et al. The PERFECT Club benchmarks: Effective performance evaluation of supercomputers. *International Journal of Supercomputing Applications*, 3(3):5–40, March 1989.

[Ble75] W. W. Bledsoe. A new method for proving certain presburger formulas. In *Advance Papers, 4th Int. Joint Conference on Artif. Intell.*, Tibilisi, Georgia, U.S.S.R, 1975.

[Cha93] Vijay Chandru. Variable elimination in linear constraints. *The Computer Journal*, 36(5):463–472, 1993.

[Coo72] D. C. Cooper. Theorem proving in arithmetic with multiplication. In B. Meltzer and D. Michie, editors, *Machine Intelligence 7*, pages 91–99. American Elsevier, New York, 1972.

[DE73] G.B. Dantzig and B.C. Eaves. Fourier-Motzkin elimination and its dual. *Journal of Combinatorial Theory (A)*, 14:288–297, 1973.

[Duf74] R. J. Duffin. On fourier's analysis of linear inequality systems. *Mathematical Programming Study*, pages 71–95, 1974.

[GJ79] Michael R. Garey and David S. Johnson. *Computers and Intractability: A Guide to the Theory of NP-Completeness*. W.H. Freemand and Company, 1979.

[HLL92] Tien Huynh, Catherine Lassez, and Jean-Louis Lassez. Practical issues on the projection of polyhedral sets. *Annals of mathematics and artificial intelligence*, November 1992.

[IJT91] François Irigoin, Pierre Jouvelot, and Rémi Triolet. Semantical interprocedural parallelization: An overview of the pips project. In *Proc. of the 1991 International Conference on Supercomputing*, pages 244–253, June 1991.

[Imb93] Jean-Louis Imbert. Fourier's elimination: Which to choose? In *PCPP 93*, 1993.

[JMSY93] J. Jaffar, M. J. Maher, P. J. Stuckey, and R. H. C. Yap. Projecting CLP(R) constraints. *New Generation Computing*, 11(3/4):449–469, 1993.

[KP93] Wayne Kelly and William Pugh. A framework for unifying reordering transformations. Technical Report CS-TR-3193, Dept. of Computer Science, University of Maryland, College Park, April 1993.

[LHM89] Jean-Louis Lassez, Tien Huynh, and Ken McAloon. Simplification and elimination of redundant linear arithmetic constraints. In *Proceedings of the North American Conference on Logic Programming*, pages 37–51, 1989.

[LL92] Catherine Lassez and Jean-Louis Lassez. Quantifier elimination for conjunctions of linear constraints via a convex hull algorithm. In Bruce Donald, Deepak Kapur, and Joseph Mundy, editors, *Symbolic and Numerical Computation for Artificial Intelligence*. Academic Press, 1992.

[MHL91a] D. E. Maydan, J. L. Hennessy, and M. S. Lam. Effectiveness of data dependence analysis. In *Proceedings of the NSF-NCRD Workshop on Advanced Compilation Techniques for Novel Architectures*, 1991.

[MHL91b] D. E. Maydan, J. L. Hennessy, and M. S. Lam. Efficient and exact data dependence analysis. In *ACM SIGPLAN'91 Conference on Programming Language Design and Implementation*, pages 1–14, June 1991.

[Nel78] C. G. Nelson. An $o(n^{logn})$ algorithm for the two-variable-per-constraint linear programming satisfiablility problem. Technical Report AIM-319, Stanford University, Department of Computer Science, 1978.

[Pug91] William Pugh. Uniform techniques for loop optimization. In *1991 International Conference on Supercomputing*, pages 341–352, Cologne, Germany, June 1991.

[Pug92] William Pugh. The Omega test: a fast and practical integer programming algorithm for dependence analysis. *Communications of the ACM*, 8:102–114, August 1992.

[PW92] William Pugh and David Wonnacott. Going beyond integer programming with the Omega test to eliminate false data dependences. Technical Report CS-TR-3191, Dept. of Computer Science, University of Maryland, College Park, December 1992. An earlier version of this paper appeared at the SIGPLAN PLDI'92 conference.

[PW93a] William Pugh and David Wonnacott. An evaluation of exact methods for analysis of value-based array data dependences. In *Sixth Annual Workshop on Programming Languages and Compilers for Parallel Computing*, Portland, OR, August 1993.

[PW93b] William Pugh and David Wonnacott. Static analysis of upper and lower bounds on dependences and parallelism. *ACM Transactions on Programming Languages and Systems*, 1993. accepted for publication.

[Sho77] Robert E. Shostak. On the sup-inf method for proving presburger formulas. *Journal of the ACM*, 24(4):529–543, October 1977.

[Wil76] H.P. Williams. Fourier-Motzkin elimination extension to integer programming problems. *Journal of Combinatorial Theory (A)*, 21:118–123, 1976.

[WT92] M. J. Wolfe and C. Tseng. The Power test for data dependence. *IEEE Transactions on Parallel and Distributed Systems*, 3(5):591–601, September 1992.

Set Constraints: Results, Applications and Future Directions

Alexander Aiken

Computer Science Division
University of California, Berkeley
Berkeley, CA 94720-1776
aiken@cs.berkeley.edu

Abstract. Set constraints are a natural formalism for many problems that arise in program analysis. This paper provides a brief introduction to set constraints: what set constraints are, why they are interesting, the current state of the art, open problems, applications and implementations.

1 Introduction

Set constraints are a natural formalism for describing relationships between sets of terms of a free algebra. A set constraint has the form $X \subseteq Y$, where X and Y are *set expressions*. Examples of set expressions are 0 (the empty set), α (a set-valued variable), $c(X, Y)$ (a constructor application), and the union, intersection, or complement of set expressions.

Recently, there has been a great deal of interest in program analysis algorithms based on solving systems of set constraints, including analyses for functional languages [AWL94, Hei94, AW93, AM91, JM79, MR85, Rey69], logic programming languages [AL94, HJ92, HJ90b, Mis84], and imperative languages [HJ91]. In these algorithms, sets of terms describe the possible values computed by a program. Set constraints are generated from the program text; solving the constraints yields some useful information about the program (e.g., for type-checking or optimization).

Set constraints have proven to be a very successful formalism. On the theoretical side, rapid progress has been made in understanding the algorithms for and complexity of solving various classes of set constraints. On the practical side, several program analysis systems based either entirely or partially on set constraint algorithms have been implemented. In addition, the use of set constraints has simplified previously known, but rather complicated, program analyses and set constraints have led directly to the discovery of other, previously unknown, analyses.

Much of the work on set constraints is very recent. Consequently, many of the results are not well known outside of the community of researchers active in the area. The purpose of this paper is to provide a brief, accessible survey of the area: what set constraints are, why they are useful, what is and isn't known about solving set constraints, the important open problems, and likely directions for future work. Section 2 gives definitions of the basic set constraint formalism and some illustrative examples. Section 3 presents a survey of results on the satisfiability, complexity, and solvability of various set constraint problems; open problems are also discussed. In Section 4 a brief, informal description of algorithms for solving systems of set constraints is given; this discussion also points out basic trade-offs between expressive power and computational complexity for various classes of set constraint problems. Section 5 surveys applications of set constraints to program analysis. Section 6 concludes with a discussion of current implementations and likely directions for future work.

2 Set Constraints

Let C be a set of constructors and let V be a set of variables. Each $c \in C$ has a fixed arity $a(c)$; if $a(c) = 0$ then c is a constant. The *set expressions* are defined by the following grammar:

$$E ::= \alpha \,|\, 0 \,|\, c(E_1, \ldots, E_{a(c)}) \,|\, E_1 \cup E_2 \,|\, E_1 \cap E_2 \,|\, \neg E_1$$

In this grammar, α is a variable (i.e., $\alpha \in V$) and c is a constructor (i.e., $c \in C$). Set expressions denote sets of *terms*. A term is $c(t_1, \ldots, t_{a(c)})$ where $c \in C$ and every t_i is a term (the base cases of this definition are the constants). The set H of all terms is the Herbrand universe. An *assignment* is a mapping $V \rightarrow 2^H$ that assigns sets of terms to variables. The meaning of set expressions is given by extending assignments from variables to set expressions as follows:

$$\sigma(0) = \emptyset$$
$$\sigma(c(E_1, \ldots, E_n)) = \{c(t_1, \ldots, t_n) | t_i \in \sigma(E_i)\}$$
$$\sigma(E_1 \cup E_2) = \sigma(E_1) \cup \sigma(E_2)$$
$$\sigma(E_1 \cap E_2) = \sigma(E_1) \cap \sigma(E_2)$$
$$\sigma(\neg E_1) = H - \sigma(E_1)$$

A *system of set constraints* is a finite conjunction of constraints $\bigwedge_i X_i \subseteq Y_i$ where each of the X_i and Y_i is a set expression. A *solution* of a system of set constraints is an assignment σ such that $\bigwedge_i \sigma(X_i) \subseteq \sigma(Y_i)$ is true. A system of set constraints is *satisfiable* if it has at least one solution. The following result was proven first in [AW92]. Simpler proofs have been discovered since [BGW93, AKVW93].

Theorem 1. It is decidable whether a system of set constraints is satisfiable. Furthermore, all solutions can be finitely presented.

It is important to note that the definition of set constraints used here does damage to history. The original formulation of set constraints, due to Heintze and Jaffar [HJ90a], also includes projection operations in the constraint language. However, it is convenient pedagogically to present results as extensions of the definition above. This organization also reflects the manner in which recent research has progressed.

From the definition above, it is easy to see that the set expressions consist only of elementary set operations plus constructors—simply put, it is a set theory of terms. The constraint language is rich enough, however, to describe all of the data types commonly used in programming, and it is this property that makes set constraints a natural tool for program analysis. For example, programming language data type facilities provide "sums of products" data types, which means simply unions of (usually distinct) data type constructors. All such data types can be expressed as set constraints.

Let $X = Y$ stand for the pair of constraints $X \subseteq Y$ and $Y \subseteq X$. Consider the constraint

$$\beta = \text{cons}(\alpha, \beta) \cup \text{nil}$$

If cons and nil are interpreted in the usual way, then the solution of this constraint assigns to β the set of all lists with elements drawn from α. This example also shows that a special operation for recursion is not required in the set expression language—recursion is obtained naturally through recursive constraints.

The set of non-nil lists (with elements drawn from α) can be defined as $\gamma = \beta \cap \neg \text{nil}$, where β is defined as above. The set γ is useful because it describes the proper domain of the function that selects the first element of a list; such a function is undefined for empty lists. This example also illustrates that set constraints can describe proper subsets of standard sums of products data types.

The final example shows a non-trivial set of constraints where some work is required to derive the solutions. Consider the universe of the natural numbers with one unary constructor succ and one nullary constructor zero. Let the system of constraints be:

$$\text{succ}(\alpha) \subseteq \neg \alpha \bigwedge \text{succ}(\neg \alpha) \subseteq \alpha$$

These constraints say that if $x \in \alpha$ (resp. $x \in \neg \alpha$) then $\text{succ}(x) \in \neg \alpha$ (resp. $\text{succ}(x) \in \alpha$). In other words, these constraints have two solutions, one where α is the set of even integers and one where α is the set of odd integers. The solutions are described by the following equations:

$$\alpha = \text{zero} \cup \text{succ}(\text{succ}(\alpha))$$
$$\alpha = \text{succ}(\text{zero}) \cup \text{succ}(\text{succ}(\alpha))$$

Note that the two solutions are incomparable; in general, there is no least solution of a system of set constraints.

3 Results and Open Problems

The set constraint language defined in Section 2 is henceforth called the *basic language*. There are several interesting extensions to the basic language, each of which substantially alters the set constraint problem. Three extensions are discussed in this paper: projections, function spaces, and negative constraints.

For every constructor c of arity n, a family of *projections* $c^{-1}, \ldots, c^{-n}$ can be defined such that

$$\sigma(c^{-i}(E)) = \{t_i | \exists t_1, \ldots, t_n . c(t_1, \ldots, t_n) \in \sigma(E)\}$$

To date, projections are used primarily in set constraint analyses for logic programming languages [HJ90b].

A separate extension is adding sets of functions $X \to Y$ to the set expressions. This is a major change, because it not only enriches the language, but also requires a new domain. The construction of a suitable domain with function spaces is beyond the scope of this paper; somewhat surprisingly, however, given such a domain, set constraint techniques still apply. In an appropriate domain, the meaning of $X \to Y$ is

$$X \to Y = \{f | x \in X \Rightarrow f(x) \in Y\}$$

Function spaces are used primarily in the analysis of functional programming languages [AW93, AWL94].

Finally, negative constraints are strict containments $X \not\subseteq Y$. Negative constraints can express the set of non-solutions of a system of positive constraints:

$$\neg \bigwedge_i (X_i \subseteq Y_i) = \bigvee_i X_i \not\subseteq Y_i$$

Since conjunctions of positive constraints correspond to an existential property (i.e., is any assignment a solution of the constraints) disjunctions of negative constraints can express universal properties (i.e., is every assignment a solution of the constraints) [AKW93, GTT93].

Four proofs of decidability of the satisfiability problem for the basic language are known [AW92, GTT92, BGW93, AKVW93]. Remarkably, each proof is based on completely different techniques. A particularly elegant proof is due to Bachmair, Ganzinger, and Waldmann [BGW93]; their result shows set constraints are equivalent to the *monadic class*, the class of first order formulas with arbitrary quantification but only unary predicates and no function symbols. In addition to satisfiability, constraint resolution algorithms are known that construct explicit representations of the solutions of systems of set constraints for the basic language.

The situation with the various extensions is less clear. Table 1 summarizes the current state of knowledge. The decidability of the satisfiability of set constraints with projections was open for several years [HJ90a] and has only very recently been resolved [CP94b]. Constraint resolution algorithms for restricted forms of the general problem are known [HJ90a, Hei92]; the current state of the art permits the full basic language and restricts only projections [BGW93].

Work on set constraints extended with negative constraints has been motivated in part because it is an intermediate step toward handling projections. To see this, consider the expression $c^{-1}(c(X, Y))$. Note that if $Y = 0$, then

$c(X, Y) = 0$, since constructors function as cross products. Therefore, the meaning of this expression can be characterized as

$$c^{-1}(c(X, Y)) = \begin{cases} 0 \text{ if } Y = 0 \\ X \text{ if } Y \neq 0 \end{cases}$$

Thus, even a restricted form of projection implicitly involves negative constraints ($Y \neq 0$ in the right-hand side above). Three independent proofs of the decidability of set constraints with negative constraints have been discovered [AKW93, GTT93, CP94a]; currently there is only one reported proof of the decidability of set constraints with projections [CP94b]. These are decision procedures only, however, and do not characterize the solution sets.

Problem	Satisfiability	Constraint Resolution
basic	yes	yes
basic with projections	yes	with restrictions
basic with function spaces	yes	with restrictions
basic with negative constraints	yes	?

Table 1. Status of set constraint problems.

Set constraints extended with function spaces have been used to develop very expressive subtype inference systems for functional languages. Currently, constraint solving algorithms for a fairly general class of set constraints with function types are known [AW93, AWL94]. Damm has proven the surprising result that satisfiability of set constraints with function spaces is decidable [Dam94].

Set constraint resolution algorithms can be computationally expensive in general. For the basic problem, deciding satisfiability is NEXPTIME-complete [BGW93] and even if the language is restricted to the set operations over constants satisfiability remains NP-complete [AKVW93]. By restricting the set operations (instead of the arity of constructors) it is possible to achieve polynomial time algorithms for interesting classes of constraints [JM79, MR85, Hei92].

4   Algorithms

At the current time, the literature on set constraint algorithms is very diverse in many dimensions, with a wide variety of notation and algorithmic techniques in use. Unfortunately, no reference provides a systematic introduction to more than a small portion of the body of existing work. This section gives a very brief and relatively informal overview of the basic algorithmic issues in solving systems of set constraints. For a more detailed treatment of the various algorithms, the interested reader should consult sources listed in the bibliography.

All set constraint resolution algorithms have the same basic structure. An initial system of constraints is systematically transformed until the constraints reach a particular syntactic *solved form*. In most cases, the solved form is equivalent to one or more regular tree grammars. More precisely, the final result is a set of equations

$$\alpha = c(X_1, \ldots, X_n) \cup \ldots \cup d(Y_1, \ldots, Y_m)$$

which can viewed equivalently as the productions of a grammar

$$\alpha ::= c(X_1, \ldots, X_n) \mid \ldots \mid d(Y_1, \ldots, Y_m)$$

The language generated by the tree grammar then describes the solution of the constraints.

Unfortunately, this simple explanation of the solutions of set constraints is a bit oversimplified. In reality, set constraints are more general than tree grammars. In the solutions of set constraints, this extra generality appears as "free" variables in the solved form equations. A free variable is one that does not appear on the left-hand side of any equation. Thus, a more accurate description of the solutions of set constraints is that they are tree grammars that may include free variables.

At their core, all set constraint algorithms have two characteristic forms of constraints: transitive constraints and structural constraints. Transitive constraints arise from combining upper and lower bounds on variables:

$$X \subseteq \alpha \wedge \alpha \subseteq Y \Rightarrow X \subseteq Y$$

Because of the need to resolve transitive constraints, most interesting set constraint problems have at least $\mathcal{O}(n^3)$ time complexity.

Structural constraints are constraints between constructor expressions:

$$c(X_1, \ldots, X_n) \subseteq c(Y_1, \ldots, Y_n)$$

In general, there may be many incomparable solutions of such a constraint. For example, because the semantics of a constructor is essentially a cross product, a constructor expression is 0 if any component is 0, and therefore the constraint is satisfied if $X_i = 0$ for any i. Of course, the constraint is also satisfied if $X_i \subseteq Y_i$ for all i. Thus, the complete set of solutions is

$$c(X_1, \ldots, X_n) \subseteq c(Y_1, \ldots, Y_n) \Leftrightarrow X_1 = 0 \vee \ldots \vee X_n = 0 \vee (X_1 \subseteq Y_1 \wedge \ldots \wedge X_n \subseteq Y_n)$$

Searching for a solution of such a constraint requires guessing a disjunct that can be satisfied. This non-deterministic choice increases the complexity of set constraint problems above the complexity of the corresponding tree automata problems. For example, deciding whether the language of one tree automata is a subset of another is complete for EXPTIME [Sei90]; solving a general system of set constraint inclusions is complete for NEXPTIME.

If it is known that the system of constraints under consideration has a least solution and the goal is to compute only the least solution, then it is easy to see that the cases $X_i = 0$ need not be considered and the last case can be chosen deterministically. Thus, more efficient algorithms are possible in the special case that a system of constraints has a least solution.

Finally, the set operators $\cap, \cup$, and $\neg$ play roles very similar to their roles in other logics. There are some distributive laws involving constructors, but these are not surprising:[1]

$$c(X_1,\ldots,X_n) \cap c(Y_1,\ldots,Y_n) = c(X_1 \cap Y_1,\ldots,X_n \cap Y_n)$$

$$c(X_1 \cup Y_1, Z_2,\ldots,Z_n) = c(X_1, Z_2,\ldots,Z_n) \cup c(Y_1, Z_2,\ldots,Z_n)$$

$$\neg c(X_1,\ldots,X_n) = c(\neg X_1, 1,\ldots,1) \cup \ldots \cup c(1,\ldots,1,\neg X_n) \cup$$
$$\bigcup_{d \neq c} d(1,\ldots,1)$$

For set constraint problems with restricted set operations and where the constraints have least solutions, it is possible to design polynomial time algorithms to compute the least solution; for examples, see [JM79, MR85, Hei92, Hei94]. If the set operations are not restricted, then it becomes possible to describe some complex sets of terms very succinctly with set expressions, which raises the computational complexity of constraint resolution to exponential time.

5 Applications

Set constraints have a long history and, in fact, less general formalisms predate the term "set constraints" by many years. The basic language of set constraints is now known to be equivalent to the monadic class of logical formulas [BGW93]; the first decision procedure for the monadic class was given by Löwenheim in 1915 [Lï5]. Within the realm of computer science, Reynolds was the first to develop a resolution algorithm for a class of set constraints [Rey69]. Reynolds was interested in the analysis and optimization of Lisp programs. In this application, set constraints were used to compute a conservative description of the data structures in use at a program point. Using this information, a Lisp program could be optimized by, for example, eliminating run-time type checks where it was provably safe to do so.

Independently of Reynolds, Jones and Muchnick developed a different analysis system for Lisp programs based on solving systems of set equations [JM79]. This analysis was used not only to eliminate dynamic type checks but also to reduce reference count operations in automatic memory management systems based on reference counting. Recently Wang and Hilfinger have proposed another analysis method for Lisp based on set equations [WH92].

---

[1] As written, the law for negation appears to require that the set of all constructors d such that $d \neq c$ can be enumerated and thus the set of constructors must be finite. In fact, this restriction is not necessary, and it is a simple matter to implement negation for infinite sets of constructors.

A different set of applications provide type inference algorithms for functional languages that verify the type correctness of a larger class of programs than the standard Hindley/Milner type system. Mishra and Reddy described a type system based on a set constraint resolution algorithm that could handle considerably more complex constraints than previous algorithms [MR85]. Thatte introduced *partial types* [Tha88], the type inference problem for which, while substantially different from earlier systems, is also reducible a set constraint resolution problem. The most recent work in this area is due to Wimmers and the author [AW93, AWL94], who provide a type inference system that generalizes the results in [MR85, Tha88]. An implementation of this last system is publicly available (see Section 6).

A natural application area for set constraints is the analysis of logic programs. The idea was first explored by Mishra [Mis84]; more recently, this line of work has been well developed in a series of papers by Jaffar and Heintze [HJ90b, HJ90a, HJ92], as well as in Heintze's thesis [Hei92]. Many of the techniques developed in [Hei92] have been fruitfully applied to compile time analysis in other areas, especially the compile-time analysis of ML programs [Hei94].

6 Conclusions and Directions

Interest in set constraints originally arose from the needs of researchers working in program analysis. Currently, there is a lively, continuing interplay between the theoretical and practical efforts in the area. Future work is most likely to proceed along three lines. First, the open problems in Table 1 may be resolved. Second, efforts to apply set constraints to new problems will lead to additional variations on the basic language. Third, there will be additional effort devoted to the efficient implementation of set constraint resolution algorithms. This is likely to include not only new engineering techniques, but also exploration of restricted classes of constraints for which good worst-case complexity results can be obtained.

Besides a number of prototype or special purpose systems, there are currently two substantial, complete set constraint resolution implementations, one by Nevin Heintze at CMU [Hei92] and one by the author and colleagues at IBM. The latter implementation is available by anonymous ftp and comes with a type inference system for a functional language based on solving systems of set constraints [AWL94]. To get this system, retrieve `pub/personal/aiken/Illyria.tar.Z` from the machine `s2k-ftp.cs.berkeley.edu`.

References

[AKVW93] A. Aiken, D. Kozen, M. Vardi, and E. Wimmers. The complexity of set constraints. In *Computer Science Logic '93*, Swansea, Wales, September 1993. To appear.

[AKW93] A. Aiken, D. Kozen, and E. Wimmers. Decidability of systems of set constraints with negative constraints. Research Report RJ 9421, IBM, 1993.

[AL94]   A. Aiken and T.K. Lakshman. Directional type checking of logic programs. In *Proceedings of the 1st International Static Analysis Symposium*, September 1994. To appear.

[AM91]   A. Aiken and B. Murphy. Static type inference in a dynamically typed language. In *Eighteenth Annual ACM Symposium on Principles of Programming Languages*, pages 279–290, January 1991.

[AW92]   A. Aiken and E. Wimmers. Solving systems of set constraints. In *Symposium on Logic in Computer Science*, pages 329–340, June 1992.

[AW93]   A. Aiken and E. Wimmers. Type inclusion constraints and type inference. In *Proceedings of the 1993 Conference on Functional Programming Languages and Computer Architecture*, pages 31–41, Copenhagen, Denmark, June 1993.

[AWL94]   A. Aiken, E. Wimmers, and T.K. Lakshman. Soft typing with conditional types. In *Twenty-First Annual ACM Symposium on Principles of Programming Languages*, pages 163–173, Portland, Oregon, January 1994.

[BGW93]   L. Bachmair, H. Ganzinger, and U. Waldmann. Set constraints are the monadic class. In *Symposium on Logic in Computer Science*, pages 75–83, June 1993.

[CP94a]   W. Charatonik and L. Pacholski. Negative set constraints wtih equality: An easy proof of decidability. In *Symposium on Logic in Computer Science*, July 1994. To appear.

[CP94b]   W. Charatonik and L. Pacholski. Set constraints with projections are in NEXPTIME. In *Foundations of Computer Science*, 1994. To appear.

[Dam94]   F. M. Damm. Subtyping with union types, intersection types and recursive types. In *Proceedings of the International Symposium on Theoretical Aspects of Computer Software*. Springer-Verlag, April 1994. To appear.

[GTT92]   R. Gilleron, S. Tison, and M. Tommasi. Solving systems of set constraints using tree automata. In *Proceedings of the 10th Annual Symposium on Theoretical Aspects of Computer Science*, pages 505–514, 1992.

[GTT93]   R. Gilleron, S. Tison, and M. Tommasi. Solving Systems of Set Constraints with Negated Subset Relationships. In *Foundations of Computer Science*, pages 372–380, November 1993.

[Hei92]   N. Heintze. *Set Based Program Analysis*. PhD thesis, Carnegie Mellon University, 1992.

[Hei94]   N. Heintze. Set-based analysis of ML programs (extended abstract). In *Proceedings of the 1994 ACM Conference on Lisp and Functional Programming*, June 1994. To appear.

[HJ90a]   N. Heintze and J. Jaffar. A decision procedure for a class of Herbrand set constraints. In *Symposium on Logic in Computer Science*, pages 42–51, June 1990.

[HJ90b]   N. Heintze and J. Jaffar. A finite presentation theorem for approximating logic programs. In *Seventeenth Annual ACM Symposium on Principles of Programming Languages*, pages 197–209, January 1990.

[HJ91]   N. Heintze and J. Jaffar. Set-based program analysis. Draft manuscript, 1991.

[HJ92]   N. Heintze and J. Jaffar. An engine for logic program analysis. In *Symposium on Logic in Computer Science*, pages 318–328, June 1992.

[JM79]   N. D. Jones and S. S. Muchnick. Flow analysis and optimization of LISP-like structures. In *Sixth Annual ACM Symposium on Principles of Programming Languages*, pages 244–256, January 1979.

[Lö15]   L. Löwenheim. Über möglichkeiten im relativkalkül. *Math. Annalen*, 76:228–251, 1915.

[Mis84]   P. Mishra. Towards a theory of types in PROLOG. In *Proceedings of the First IEEE Symposium in Logic Programming*, pages 289–298, 1984.

[MR85]   P. Mishra and U. Reddy. Declaration-free type checking. In *Proceedings of the Twelfth Annual ACM Symposium on the Principles of Programming Languages*, pages 7–21, 1985.

[Rey69]   J. C. Reynolds. *Automatic Computation of Data Set Definitions*, pages 456–461. Information Processing 68. North-Holland, 1969.

[Sei90]   H. Seidl. Deciding equivalence of finite tree automata. *SIAM Journal of Computing*, 19(3):424–437, June 1990.

[Tha88]   S. Thatte. Type inference with partial types. In *Automata, Languages and Programming: 15th International Colloquium*, pages 615–629. Springer-Verlag Lecture Notes in Computer Science, vol. 317, July 1988.

[WH92]   E. Wang and P. N. Hilfinger. Analysis of recursive types in Lisp-like languages. In *Proceedings of the 1992 ACM Conference on Lisp and Functional Programming*, pages 216–225, June 1992.

Logic-Based Methods for Optimization *

J. N. Hooker

Graduate School of Industrial Administration, Carnegie Mellon University,
Pittsburgh, PA 15213 USA, email jh38@andrew.cmu.edu

Abstract. This paper proposes a logic-based approach to optimization
that combines solution methods from mathematical programming and
logic programming. From mathematical programming it borrows strategies for exploiting structure that have logic-based analogs. From logic
programming it borrows methods for extracting information that are un-
available in a traditional mathematical programming framework. Logic-
based methods also provide a unified approach to solving optimization
problems with both quantitative and logical constraints.

1 Introduction

The theory and practice of integer and mixed integer programming are based
primarily on polyhedral methods. The thesis of this paper is that one can develop
a parallel theory and practice using logic-based methods.

The basic idea is to replace the essential elements of optimization methods
with logical analogs. The integer variables are regarded as atomic propositions,
and inequality constraints involving them are rewritten as logical formulas. In
a branch-and-cut scheme, discrete relaxations replace the tradition linear programming and Lagrangian relaxations, and they are solved by logic-based algorithms. Logical implications replace cutting planes. In particular, "prime" and
other strong "logic cuts" replace facet-defining cuts. Separating cuts, Gomory
cuts, etc., also have analogs. Much of the theory of cutting planes, duality, etc.,
has a logical counterpart.

This approach can combine some of the problem-solving wisdom accumulated
by mathematical programmers with techniques and insights from constraint programming and logic programming. Most importantly, the optimization community's ways of exploiting structure (strong cutting planes, etc.) carry over into
a logical context. They may also take on greater variety and adaptability when
moved out of the polyhedral context. Strong cuts are traditionally found by
studying the abstract polyhedral structure of a model. But strong logic cuts
can often be found by using one's intuitions about the concrete application of a
model, even in cases where the polyhedron is far too complex to analyze. There
is also a much greater variety of problem relaxations in the logical context.

---

* Supported in part by Office of Naval Research Grant N00014-92-J-1028 and the
Engineering Design Research Center at Carnegie Mellon University, funded by NSF
grant 1-55093.

The logical tradition also makes a key contribution. Logic processing can make more effective use of cuts, once they are discovered, than the traditional mathematical programming methods. A branch-and-bound method typically solves a relaxation of the constraint set generated at a given node of the search tree and may thereby fail to recognize when it is infeasible. An appropriate constraint propagation or logical inference technique may detect infeasibility and avoid the generation of successor nodes. The rapid speedup of propositional satisfiability algorithms over the past few years makes logic processing of this sort increasingly attractive.

So the logic-based methods described here go beyond both mathematical programming and logic programming. They enrich logic programming with strategies for discovering structure that parallel those of mathematical programming. They enrich mathematical programming with methods for extracting information that are supplied by logic and constraint programming.

This paper is a condensation of a longer tutorial on logic-based methods [7]. Its main contributions are to show in general how solution strategies for integer and mixed integer programming can be given logical analogs, and to outline a research program in this direction. To do this it draws on a number of results established elsewhere [6, 8, 9] and presents at least two new results, those of logical duality and the logical analysis of nonbipartite matching problems.

2 Historical Context

If logic-based methods for optimization are so attractive, why have they not gained acceptance already? Actually there is nothing new about them. Hammer and Rudeanu wrote a classic 1968 treatise [5] on boolean methods in operations research. Granot and Hammer [4] showed in 1971 how boolean methods might be used to solve integer programming problems.

Although boolean methods have seen applications (logical reduction techniques, solution of certain combinatorial problems), they have not been accepted as a general-purpose approach to optimization. There seem to be two main reasons for this. One is that they have not been demonstrated to be more effective than branch-and-cut. So there has been no apparent advantage in converting a problem to logical form.

A second reason is that the conversion to a logical problem is itself hard. The most straightforward way to convert an inequality constraint to logical form, for instance, is to write it as an equivalent set of logical clauses. But the number of clauses can grow exponentially with the number of variables in the inequality. Consider for instance the following constraint from a problem in Nemhauser and Wolsey ([11], p. 465).

$$
\begin{aligned}
300x_3 + 300x_4 &+ 285x_5 + 285x_6 + 265x_8 + 265x_9 + 230x_{12} + 230x_{13} \\
&+ 190x_{14} + 200x_{22} + 400x_{23} + 200x_{24} + 400x_{25} + 200x_{26} \\
&+ 400x_{27} + 200x_{28} + 400x_{29} + 200x_{30} + 400x_{31} \le 2700.
\end{aligned} \tag{1}
$$

Barth [1] reports that this constraint expands to 117,520 nonredundant logical clauses, using the
method of Granot and Hammer [4].

So for several years prospects for logic-based methods, as a general approach to optimization, looked bleak. But several factors have recently converged to make them much more attractive. As noted earlier, satisfiability algorithms, a key element of logic-based methods, have improved dramatically. Also it is foolish to expand an inequality constraint into its full logical equivalent. This is analogous to generating all possible cutting planes for an integer programming problem, which is never done. Practical algorithms generate a few "separating cuts," and a closely analogous approach is available in the logical context.

Further, there is a growing trend toward the merger of quantitative and logical elements into a single model, and logic-based methods are a natural approach to solving such models. Purely mathematical models (integer programming, etc.) are often unsuitable for messy problems without much mathematical structure, whereas pure logic models (PROLOG programs, etc.) do not capture the mathematical structure that does exist and are consequently hard to solve. Historically, solution techniques for the two types of models have been unrelated. A technique that solves both opens the door to a wider variety of tractable models.

Logic-based optimization also serves a heuristic function of providing a whole new perspective on optimization problems. In fact, it is in some ways more natural to view a pure integer programming problem as a logical inference problem rather than a polyhedral problem. Similarly, the integer variables of a mixed integer problem can be viewed as artificial devices that can just as well be eliminated.

3   Integer Programming as Logical Inference

A 0-1 inequality $bx \geq \beta$ can be viewed as a logical proposition that is true when the inequality is satisfied. The variables x_j are viewed as atomic propositions that are true when $x_j = 1$ and false when $x_j = 0$. A system of 0-1 inequalities $Ax \geq a$ implies $bx \geq \beta$ when all 0-1 solutions of the former satisfy the latter. Any logical proposition, inequality or otherwise, implied by $Ax \geq a$ is a *logic cut*. The following are obvious but fundamental.

Theorem 1. *An inequality is a valid cut (in the polyhedral sense) for a system of inequalities if and only if it is a logic cut.*

Theorem 2. *Consider an integer programming problem*

$$\min cx \tag{2}$$
$$s.t. \ Ax \geq a$$
$$x_j \in \{0, 1\}, \ all \ j.$$

The optimal value of the objective function is the largest β for which $cx \geq \beta$ is a logic cut.

This fact can be framed as a duality relationship. The following is the *logical dual* of integer programming problem (2).

$$\max \beta \tag{3}$$
$$\text{s.t. } Ax \geq a \text{ implies } cx \geq \beta$$

The optimal value β in (3) is equal to the optimal value of (2). There is a close connection with linear programming duality, which is obtained by replacing $x_j \in \{0,1\}$ with $0 \leq x_j \leq 1$ in (2) and 'implies' with 'implies as a nonnegative linear combination' in (3).

4   A Generic Branch-and-Cut Algorithm

Figure 1 contains a rudimentary logic-based branch-and-cut algorithm (essentially a specialized A*
search) that solves the integer programming problem (2). It combines three strategies that have proved much more effective in combination than when used separately: an enumeration tree, generation of valid separating cuts, and solution of relaxations of the problem.

Fig. 1.

```
Logic-Based Branch-and-Cut Algorithm.
   Set UB=∞.
   Execute Branch(∅,0).
End.

Procedure Branch(S,k)
   If k = 0 then
        the optimal solution is the best found so far
        (infeasible if none found); stop.
   Apply a partial or complete satisfiability algorithm to S.
   If no contradiction is found then
        Find the minimum LB of cx subject to a relaxation of S.
        If LB<UB then:
           Generate separating logic cuts.
           Branch:
               Pick a literal L containing a variable
                  that occurs in S.
               Perform Branch(S ∪ {L}, k + 1).
               Perform Branch(S ∪ {¬L}, k + 1).
   End.
```

Note that the problem is not solved subject to the original constraint set $Ax \geq a$ but to a set S of logic cuts (perhaps logical clauses) for these constraints. The cuts are generated only as needed.

Nodes of the search tree are obtained by branching on the cases $x_j = 1, x_j = 0$. At each node, an optimization problem with a relaxed constraint set is solved to obtain a lower bound on the optimal value of the original problem. If this bound is already greater than the value of a feasible solution obtained earlier, there is no point in generating successor nodes. Classically the relaxations are usually linear (replace $x_j \in \{0, 1\}$ with $0 \leq x_j \leq 1$) or Lagrangean, but a wide variety of discrete relaxations are possible in the logical setting. The simplest is to minimize cx subject to each clause in S separately (a trivial problem) and pick the best bound so obtained.

Finally, logic processing is applied to make explicit some constraints that were only explicit. Traditionally this has been achieved by generating valid inequalities (cuts) with coefficients chosen so that the linear relaxation is as tight as possible, preferably a facet of the convex hull of 0-1 solutions. In a logic-based setting, logic processing can be applied either in the form of a satisfiability algorithm or a cut generation algorithm, or both. The former would normally be an incomplete procedure, such as unit resolution (which happens to be equivalent in deductive power to solving the traditional linear relaxation). The latter would generate *separating* logic cuts, which are those that are violated by the solution just obtained for the current relaxation. Coefficients are no longer relevant, but the logic cuts should be strong (i.e., exclude as many 0-1 solutions as possible).

5   Strong Cuts

The logical analog of a facet-defining cut is a *prime cut*, which is defined with respect to a class C of logical propositions. A prime cut for a system $Ax \geq a$ of inequalities is a logic cut F that is equivalent to any cut in C that is implied by $Ax \geq a$ and implies F. It is a *prime inequality* if C is the set of all inequalities (with integer coefficients and right-hand side).

Useful logic cuts in practice need not and ordinarily would not be prime cuts. But an investigation of of how prime cuts can in principle be generated provides insight into the nature of strong logic cuts.

A fundamental result of integer programming, due to Chvátal [3], says that a finite procedure generates all facet-defining inequalities (the strongest cutting planes) for a 0-1 system $Ax \geq a$. A parallel result can be proved for logic-based programming [6]. Let a *clausal* inequality have the form $ax \geq 1 + n(a)$, where each $a_j \in \{0, 1, -1\}$ and $n(a)$ is the sum of the negative components of a. For instance, the inequality $x_1 + (1 - x_2) \geq 1$, or $x_1 - x_2 \geq 0$, represents the logical clause $x_1 \vee \neg x_2$. A *resolvent* of two clausal inequalities is simply the clausal inequality that represents the resolvent of the corresponding clauses. Let a *diagonal sum* be defined as illustrated by the following example.

$$x_1 + 5x_2 + 3x_3 + x_4 \geq 4$$
$$2x_1 + 4x_2 + 3x_3 + x_4 \geq 4$$
$$2x_1 + 5x_2 + 2x_3 + x_4 \geq 4$$
$$2x_1 + 5x_2 + 3x_3 \qquad \geq 4$$
$$2x_1 + 5x_2 + 3x_3 + x_4 \geq 5$$

The fifth inequality is the diagonal sum of the first four. Note that the first four inequalities are identical except that the diagonal term is reduced by one. Also the right-hand side of the sum is increased by one.

A resolvent can be "generated" from a set S of inequalities if it is a resolvent of two clausal inequalities, each of which is implied by a single inequality of S. A diagonal sum is "generated" in a similar sense. Finally, let a set T of inequalities be *monotone* when T contains all clausal inequalities, and for any given inequality $ax \geq \beta + n(a)$ in T, T contains all inequalities $a'x \geq \beta' + n(a')$ such that $|a'| \leq |a|$ and $0 \leq \beta' \leq \beta$.

Theorem 3. *Let T be a monotone set of inequalities, and let S contain all resolvents and diagonal sums in T in that can be recursively generated from a feasible 0-1 system $Ax \geq a$, up to equivalence. Then every prime inequality for $Ax \geq a$ with respect to T is equivalent to some inequality in S.*

The *rank* of a logic cut (analogous to the Chvátal rank of a polyhedral cut) is the minimum number of iterations of this recursive procedure required to generate the cut.

6 Example: Matching Problems

Logic cuts can be stronger and therefore more useful than facet-defining cuts.[2] A good illustration of this is a nonbipartite matching problem. The augmenting paths traditionally used in the best matching algorithms [11] in effect rely on logic cuts that strictly imply the less useful facet-defining inequalities (odd-set constraints) for the problem.

A matching problem is defined on an undirected graph (V, E) for which each edge in E is given a weight. The edges connect vertices that may be matched or paired, and a *matching* pairs some or all of the vertices. A matching can therefore be regarded as a set of edges, at most one of which touches any given vertex. The *weighted matching problem* is to find a maximum weight matching; i.e., matching that maximizes the total weight of the edges used in the matching.

The matching problem can be written,

$$\max \sum_{e \in E} x_e \qquad (4)$$

---

[2] This section represents joint work with Ajai Kapoor.

$$\text{s.t.} \quad \sum_{e \in \delta(v)} x_e \leq 1, \quad \text{for } v \in V \tag{5}$$

$$x_e \in \{0, 1\}, \quad e \in E,$$

where $\delta(v)$ is the set of edges incident to v. x_e is 1 when e is part of the matching and 0 otherwise.

The convex hull of possible matchings has a particularly simple description. It is based on the fact that a matching for a graph (U, E) with an odd number of vertices can have at most $\frac{|U|}{2}$ edges. So the following *odd set constraints* are valid:

$$\sum_{e \in E(U)} x_e \leq \frac{|U|}{2}, \quad \text{all } U \subset V \text{ with } |U| \geq 3 \text{ and odd}, \tag{6}$$

where $E(U)$ contains the edges in the subgraph of (V, E) induced by U. In fact (5)-(6) define the convex hull of matchings.

For the purposes of logical analysis it is conveninent to reverse the sense of the matching constraints (5) and odd set constraints (6) by replacing variables x_e with $y_e = 1 - x_e$, so that $y_e = 1$ when edge e is absent from the matching.

$$\sum_{e \in \delta(v)} y_e \geq |\delta(v)| - 1, \quad \text{for } v \in V \tag{7}$$

$$\sum_{e \in E(U)} y_e \geq |E(U)| - \frac{|U|}{2},$$

$$\text{all } U \subset V \text{ with } |U| \geq 3 \text{ and odd}. \tag{8}$$

The following is proved in [7].

Theorem 4. *An odd set constraint (7) for a matching problem is a logic cut of rank at most*

$$|E(U)| - \frac{|U|}{2} - 1.$$

Odd set constraints are strictly implied by *augmenting path cuts*. Consider a matching problem on the simple graph of Fig. 6. The odd set constraints (facet-defining cuts) are simply the matching constraints $y_1 + y_2 \geq 1$ and $y_2 + y_3 \geq 1$. They are strictly implied by the augmenting path cut $y_1 + 2y_2 + y_3 \geq 2$, which says that either edge 2 is not in the matching or else edges 1 and 3 are not in the matching.

In general a path of odd length whose edges correspond to $y_{j_1}, \ldots, y_{j_m}$ defines an augmenting path cut,

$$\frac{m-1}{2}y_{j_1} + \frac{m+1}{2}y_{j_2} + \frac{m-1}{2}y_{j_3} + \ldots + \frac{m+1}{2}y_{j_{m-1}}$$
$$+ \frac{m-1}{2}y_{j_m} \geq \frac{(m-1)(m+1)}{2},$$

which says that if the $(m+1)/2$ odd segments belong to a matching, then none of the $(m-1)/2$ even segments may belong to it, and vice-versa.

Fig. 2. A very small matching problem.

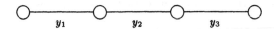

$y_1 \qquad y_2 \qquad y_3$

7 Mixed Integer Programming

Consider a general mixed integer programming (MIP) problem,

$$\min cx + dy \tag{9}$$
$$\text{s.t. } Ax + By \geq a$$
$$y_j \in \{0,1\}, \ j = 1, \ldots, n,$$

A 0-1 point y is *feasible* if (x, y) is feasible for some x. Each 0-1 value of y is associated with a polyhedron $\Pi(y)$ in x-space, namely the set of points satisfying (9) when y is so fixed. The feasible region can therefore be regarded as the union of $\Pi(y)$ over all feasible y.

To write an MIP in logical form, regard the y_j's as atomic propositions.

$$\min cx + dy \tag{10}$$
$$\text{s.t. } y \in Y$$
$$x \in \bigcup_{y \in Y} \Pi(y),$$

Here $y \in Y$ represents a set of logical propositions. (10) is actually more general than (9), due to a theorem of Jeroslow [9, 10]. It states that (10) can be written in the form (9) if and only if the polyhedra $\Pi(y)$ all have the same recession cone.

An MIP in form (10) can be solved by a branch-and cut algorithm that enumerates linear programming constraint sets defining $\Pi(y)$'s, where the enumeration is controlled by the logical propositions $y \in Y$. The enumeration can be markedly accelerated by the use of an expanded sense of logic cuts that obtain in an MIP setting, namely a *nonvalid* logic cut. These may cut off feasible solutions but do not change the optimal solution.

8 An MIP Example

Suppose one wants to decide which of three processing units to install in the processing network of Fig. 3. The units are represented as boxes. Naturally one must install unit 3 if the network is to process anything, and one must install units 1 or 2. Let's suppose in addition that units 1 and 2 should not both be installed. There is a variable cost associated with the flow through each unit, a fixed cost with building the unit, and revenue with the finished product. If x_j's represent flows as indicated in Fig. 13 and y_j's are 0-1 variables indicating which units are installed, the problem has the following MIP model.

Fig. 3. A simple processing network.

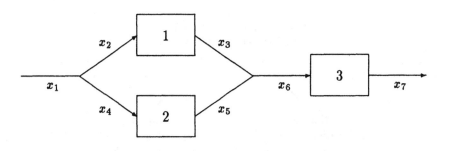

$$\min 3x_3 + 2.8x_5 - 9x_7 + 2x_1 +$$
$$z_1 + z_2 + z_3 \tag{11}$$
$$\text{s.t. } x_1 - x_2 - x_4 = 0 \tag{12}$$
$$x_6 - x_3 - x_5 = 0 \tag{13}$$
$$x_3 - 0.9x_2 = 0 \tag{14}$$
$$x_5 - 0.85x_4 = 0 \tag{15}$$
$$x_7 - 0.75x_6 = 0 \tag{16}$$
$$x_7 \leq 10 \tag{17}$$
$$x_3 - 30y_1 \leq 0 \tag{18}$$
$$x_5 - 30y_2 \leq 0 \tag{19}$$
$$x_7 - 50y_3 \leq 0 \tag{20}$$
$$y_1 + y_2 \leq 1 \tag{21}$$
$$z_1 = 14y_1 \tag{22}$$
$$z_2 = 12y_2 \tag{23}$$
$$z_3 = 10y_3 \tag{24}$$
$$x_j \geq 0, \text{ all } j$$
$$y_1, y_2, y_3 \in \{0, 1\}.$$

Constraints (12)-(13) are flow balance constraints. (14)-(16) specify yields from the processing units. (17) bounds the output. (18)-(20) are "Big M" constraints that prohibit flow through a unit unless it is built. (22)-(24) define the fixed costs.

A conventional branch-and-bound tree for this problem appears in Fig. 4. Note that the optimal solution is to build none of the units.

Fig. 4. Branch-and-bound solution of a small mixed integer programming problem.

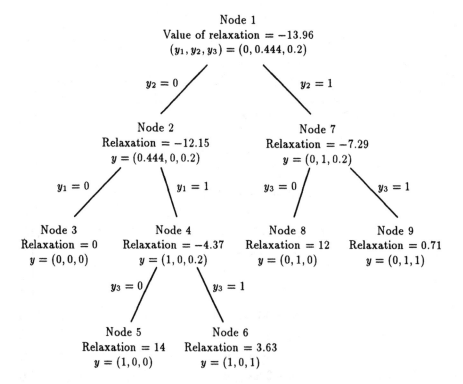

Node 1
Value of relaxation $= -13.96$
$(y_1, y_2, y_3) = (0, 0.444, 0.2)$

$y_2 = 0$ $y_2 = 1$

Node 2
Relaxation $= -12.15$
$y = (0.444, 0, 0.2)$

Node 7
Relaxation $= -7.29$
$y = (0, 1, 0.2)$

$y_1 = 0$ $y_1 = 1$ $y_3 = 0$ $y_3 = 1$

Node 3
Relaxation $= 0$
$y = (0, 0, 0)$

Node 4
Relaxation $= -4.37$
$y = (1, 0, 0.2)$

Node 8
Relaxation $= 12$
$y = (0, 1, 0)$

Node 9
Relaxation $= 0.71$
$y = (0, 1, 1)$

$y_3 = 0$ $y_3 = 1$

Node 5
Relaxation $= 14$
$y = (1, 0, 0)$

Node 6
Relaxation $= 3.63$
$y = (1, 0, 1)$

9 Logic-Based Solution of an MIP

I will now illustrate how logic-based branch-and-bound can solve an MIP problem in logical form. It is convenient to suppose that the objective function of (10) is simply cx. This can be done by introducing a continuous variable z_j for each $d_j \neq 0$, letting the z_j have coefficient 1 in the objective function, and augmenting $\Pi(y)$ with the constraint $z_j = d_j$ whenever $y_j = 1$. The generic algorithm appears in Fig. 5.

Fig. 5.

```
Logic-Based Branch-and-Cut Algorithm for MIP.
   Set UB=∞, y = (u,...,u) (where u =undetermined).
   Execute Branch(∅,y,0).
End.


Procedure Branch(S,k)
   If k = 0 then
      the optimal solution is the best found so far
      (infeasible if none found); stop.
   Apply a partial or complete satisfiability algorithm to
      S, fixing some variables in y if possible.
   If no contradiction is found, then
      Find the minimum LB of cx subject to x ∈ Π(y).
      If LB<UB then:
         Generate separating logic cuts.
         Branch:
            Pick a literal L containing a variable
               that occurs in S.
            Perform Branch(S ∪ {L}, y, k + 1).
            Perform Branch(S ∪ {¬L}, y, k + 1).
End.
```

The example of the previous section is put in logical form as follows. Note first that the objective function is already of the form cx. The set S of logical constraints is simply $\{\neg y_1 \vee \neg y_2\}$, which corresponds to constraint (21). The linear constraint set $\Pi(y)$ consists of constraints (12)-(17), nonnegativity constraints, and the following:

$$
\begin{array}{ll}
x_3 = 0 \text{ if } y_1 = 0, & z_1 = 14 \text{ if } y_1 = 1 \\
x_5 = 0 \text{ if } y_2 = 0, & z_2 = 14 \text{ if } y_2 = 1 \\
x_7 = 0 \text{ if } y_3 = 0, & z_3 = 14 \text{ if } y_3 = 1
\end{array}
\qquad (25)
$$

Note that $\Pi(y)$ is defined even when some components of y are undetermined $(y_j = u)$.

Before solving this example, it is useful to introduce in the next section some additional logic cuts.

10 Nonvalid Logic Cuts

In the context of mixed integer programming it is useful to define a more general sense of logic cut. Let the *graph* G for a mixed integer optimization problem (10) be the set

$$
\{(cx + dy, x, y) \mid y \in Y, x \in \bigcup_{y \in Y} \Pi(y)\}.
$$

The *epigraph* E is

$$\{(z, x, y) \mid (z', x, y) \in G \text{ for some } z' \leq z\}.$$

The *projection* of the epigraph onto the space of continuous variables is

$$\{(z, x) \mid (z, x, y) \in E \text{ for some } y\}.$$

A *logic cut* in the extended sense is a constraint $y \in T$ that, when added to the constraint set of (10), results in the same projected epigraph. The cut is *valid* if

$$\bigcup_{y \in Y} \Pi(y) = \bigcup_{y \in Y \cap T} \Pi(y).$$

A cut can be nonvalid (i.e., cut off feasible values of y), but it never changes the value of the optimal solution.

Some nonvalid logic cuts can be generated for the example of the previous section as follows. Note that it makes no sense to consider a solution in which a unit is installed but carries no flow. Yet such solutions can and do occur in the branch-and-bound tree. Nodes 5 and 8 of Fig. 4 have LP solutions in which the installed unit carries no flow. Computational experience [8, 12] suggests that such superfluous nodes can be very numerous in a branch-and-bound tree.

This situation can be prevented by adding constraints that allow a unit to be installed only if a downstream unit is installed:

$$\neg y_1 \vee y_3 \tag{26}$$
$$\neg y_2 \vee y_3 \tag{27}$$

and only if at least one upstream unit is installed:

$$y_1 \vee y_2 \vee \neg y_3. \tag{28}$$

These are nonvalid logic cuts because they cut off feasible values of (y_1, y_2, y_3). It is shown in [8] that they essentially exhaust the nonvalid logic cuts for such a problem.

Figure. 2 displays the search tree for a logic-based solution of the example that uses (26)-(28). Note that the tree is smaller than the branch-and-bound tree of Fig. 4. The superfluous nodes 5 and 8, as well as other nodes, have been deleted.

Logic-based methods have been applied to MIP models of chemical processing network design problems [8]. They solve larger problems substantially more rapidly than a state-of-the-art MIP solver with preprocessor (OSL), and in some cases solve problems that OSL cannot solve. Logic cuts are also being applied to truss structure design problems with discrete bar sizes [2].

Fig. 6. Logic-based solution of the problem with nonvalid logic cuts.

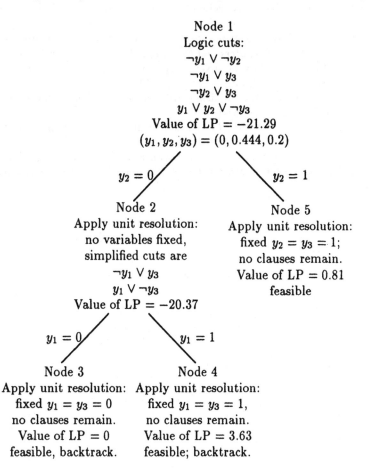

References

1. Barth, P., Linear 0-1 inequalities and extended clauses, manuscript, Max-Planck-Institut für Informatik, W-6600 Saarbrücken, Germany, ca. 1993.
2. Bollapragada, R., O. Ghattas and J. N. Hooker, Logic-based optimization of truss structure design, Carnegie Mellon University, in preparation.
3. Chvátal, V., Edmonds polytopes and a hierarchy of combinatorial problems, *Discrete Mathematics* **4** (1973) 305-337.
4. Granot, F., and P. L. Hammer, On the use of boolean functions in 0-1 linear programming, *Methods of Operations Research* (1971) 154-184.
5. Hammer, P. L., and S. Rudeanu, *Boolean Methods in Operations Research and Related Areas*, Springer Verlag (Berlin, New York, 1968).
6. Hooker, J. N., Generalized resolution for 0-1 inequalities, *Annals of Mathematics and AI* **6** (1992) 271-286.

7. Hooker, J. N., Logic-based methods for optimization: A tutorial, presented at ORSA Computer Science Technical Section meeting, Williamsburg, VA, USA, January 1994.

8. Hooker, J. N., H. Yan, I. E. Grossmann, and R. Raman, Logic cuts for processing networks with fixed costs. *Computers and Operations Research* **21** (1994) 265-279.

9. Jeroslow, R. E., Representability in mixed integer programming, I: Characterization results, *Discrete Applied Mathematics* **17** (1987) 223-243.

10. Jeroslow, R. E., and J. K. Lowe, Modeling with integer variables, *Mathematical Programming Studies* **22** (1984) 167-184.

11. Newhauser, G. L., and L. A. Wolsey, *Integer and Combinatorial Optimization* (Wiley, 1988).

12. Raman, R., and I. E. Grossmann, Relation between MILP modeling and logical inference for chemical process synthesis, *Computers and Chemical Engineering* **15** (1991) 73-84.

Panel Session: Commercial Applications of Constraint Programming

Panelists: David Kurlander, Microsoft Research
Jean-Francois Puget, ILOG Inc.
Jeff Heisserman, Research & Technology, Boeing Computer Services

Organizer: Alan Borning

In addition to presentations of research papers on constraint programming and invited talks, PPCP'94 included a panel session on "Commercial Applications of Constraints." Many researchers in constraint-based languages and systems are interested in seeing the results of their work put to practical use; also, the problems that arise when trying to make such use of constraints can uncover important research questions. The panel was thus a stimulating part of the workshop. Each of the panelists has summarized his panel position for inclusion in the present book.

1   Constraint Technology: Not Ready for Prime Time?

David Kurlander
Microsoft Research
djk@microsoft.com

Though constraint-based systems have existed for over thirty years, they have never made it big in the software market. Here I will discuss why this has been the case, and what must be done to make constraint technology appeal to the mass audience. At Microsoft Research, our charter is to not only develop useful technologies in house, but also to find promising technologies being developed elsewhere, and bring them to the attention of our product groups. Right now there are a number of obstacles that must be overcome before we start putting constraints in our products.

Almost all of Microsoft's products are geared towards the mass market, and our mass market products sell in the hundreds of thousands or millions. Constraints have been featured in niche products from other companies, but there have been few or no major commercial successes for constraints. Why is this? For a product to sell in the millions, it has got to be cheap. When the product is cheap, the software vendor cannot afford to give individual attention to each customer. Right now, users find constraints difficult to work with. I'll explain the many reasons for this momentarily, but unfortunately, users of popular products have to both train themselves, and solve their own problems. They have to be extremely self-sufficient, and provide their own technical support. Further complicating things is that the user base for mass market products includes people with little formal education and technical computer knowledge.

Now there is really a continuum between mass market products and niche products, and a product does not have to sell in the millions to be successful. There have been successes in the CAD industry for constraints, but CAD programs are expensive, CAD users tend to be highly skilled, and they tend to get a higher level of support from their software providers.

I do not want to sound too negative. Microsoft is very interested in constraint technology for a number of applications. First, several of our applications have drawing components. In the future, these disjoint components will be unified, and we would like the drawing editor to be considerably more capable. By incorporating constraints in the editor, we would allow people to create more precisely dimensioned illustrations, and make it easier for people to change a single component of the illustration and have the other components reconfigure as desired.

Microsoft is also building a multimedia authoring environment. We would like to provide constraints to allow the author to specify how objects move in relation to each other, and possibly for temporal sequencing. Recently Microsoft bought SoftImage, which is one of the major vendors of 3D modeling and animation software. There is also interest in adding constraints to their products.

Now the interest from these groups is very tentative, and I wouldn't be surprised if they chose to ignore constraint technology for a while. All three of these groups are interested in using graphical constraints, and there are a number of difficulties that people face when using these constraints.

First, graphical constraints can be hard to specify. It can be very difficult to come up with all the necessary constraints without a great deal of trial and error. When the constraint solver is invoked with a partially specified system, drawings often become degenerate, with vertices unexpectedly becoming coincident or collinear. Also, constraints are often at the wrong abstraction level. For example, the user might think in terms of the desired motion of a mechanism, and not fixed location, fixed distance, and relative rotation constraints.

Second, constraint systems are notoriously difficult to debug. When multiple constraints conflict, there should be a way of indicating which are the problem constraints. Typically there is not. Also it is a challenge to design a visual representation for constraints that does not overly clutter the scene, and is intuitive to the user. A good visual representation is essential to debugging as well as to initial specification.

Finally, graphical constraints become significantly slower to solve as the systems become larger. Furthermore, in some cases, the addition of a single constraint can dramatically slow down the system. We need to develop techniques for accelerating the solving process, and estimating to the user how long the solution might take.

There are two approaches that show promise in reducing the difficulty of declaring constraints and debugging them. We can build systems that automatically infer the constraints that the end user intends, thus simplifying the specification task. We can also encapsulate low-level constraint specifications in higher-level constraint templates. This latter technique simplifies constraint specifications by allowing sets of constraints to be predefined and debugged by experts, and bound to higher-level abstractions.

Actually, one of the most important reasons that we don't see constraints in mass-market products is that few people in industry know much about them. Fairly frequently, I am asked about constraints by people in product groups, but there is no good book that I can point them to. Furthermore, it is rare to find a college computer science course that has more than a single lecture on constraints, and even a single lecture is rare. New constraint practitioners have to learn about the field by collecting and reading an assortment of papers. I asked one of the managers of our multimedia authoring effort why constraints are not in the current architecture. He responded that he hopes to add them, but frankly, nobody in his group has the necessary expertise to design them into a system or implement them. One of the things that would best foster the propagation of constraints into industry would be an excellent textbook, and university courses devoted to the subject.

There are a number of trends that I believe will encourage product developers to take constraints a little more seriously. Faster machines allow users to apply constraints to larger problems, though the algorithmic complexity of most numeric solvers will continue to be somewhat prohibitive. Mass market applications these days are getting better and better, and with each release, developers try to differentiate their products from their competitor's by adding more and more features. Sooner or later, constraints will make it onto the list of features that certain applications must have to be taken seriously. These days, product cycles are getting shorter. This, together with faster computers, will encourage people to use constraint-based development environments.

Perhaps I have been too negative in my assessment of how constraints have faired commercially. Spreadsheet programs and project management software feature very simple constraint capabilities, and have been successful in the marketplace. These programs succeed because they present a relatively straightforward interface to the user, and limitations to the constraint model prevent complexities that would be present in more sophisticated constraint systems.

Such applications suggest that the secret to building successful constraint-based systems is to focus on usability issues. Constraints should be easy to specify and debug. They must have understandable visual representations, and be at an appropriate level of abstraction. They must produce predictable results in a predictable amount of time. As I mentioned before, I believe constraint inferencing and complexity encapsulation to be important for the adoption of graphical constraints in many applications, and their mass market acceptance. Both of these techniques are essentially user interface approaches for dealing with constraint specification. Better constraint coverage in computer science programs will also play a role in enabling more software engineers to incorporate constraints in their systems. I encourage constraint researchers and practitioners to constantly be thinking of the big picture: what can be done to make their work useful, and accessible to large numbers of people. And hopefully then, constraint technology will in fact be ready for prime time.

2 Constraints Are Useful

Jean-Francois Puget
ILOG Inc.
puget@ilog.fr

2.1 Introduction

As a constraint programming tool developer[1], I have a rather simple but extreme position: constraints are useful and are used in quite a lot of different places all over the world. I will demonstrate this using different kind of arguments. First of all, constraints are interesting enough so that some companies are willing to pay for them. This is shown for instance by the fact that several European software companies market constraint programming tools. Second, constraints are useful for a broad class of applications, namely resource allocation. Third, constraints are often the best approach for these problems. Indeed, we will shows a selection of such applications where the use of constraints led to dramatic improvements over the previous situation.

What precedes may sound over optimistic. It is true that, although constraint programming has already some real successes, constraint programming is not yet mature. Indeed, some quite general problems remains unanswered with current techniques. I will review some of them.

2.2 The Market

I will concentrate on the European market since it is the most developed one. In Europe, six constraint programming tools are available from different companies, each of which has achieved significant sales. From the figures given by the vendors, the total sales exceed 1000 development licenses. The table below lists all these tools, with some indication of their origin and the programming language they extend. The reader is referred to [Cras 93] for an independent review of all these tools.

name	company	country	language
ILOG SOLVER	ILOG, BULL	France	C++
CHARME	BULL	France	proprietary (C syntax)
CHIP v4	COSYTEC	France	Prolog
DECISION POWER	ICL	UK	Prolog
SIEMENS PROLOG	SIEMENS	Germany	Prolog
PROLOG III	PROLOGIA	France	Prolog

Most of these tools (CHARME, CHIP v4, DECISION POWER and SIEMENS PROLOG) come from the ECRC's CHIP project [VH 89]. BULL

---

[1] ILOG is a software company that sells ILOG SOLVER, one of the leading constraint programming tools.

has recently agreed to sell ILOG SOLVER under the name BULL SOLVER, thus abandoning new developments on CHARME.

The existence of several competing companies marketing these tools for several years[2] is a good indication of the existence of a real market.

2.3 Resource allocation

The preceding tools are mostly used for resource allocation problems, such as scheduling, time tabling, and routing. In fact the most used part deals with nonlinear finite domain constraints.

To be precise, a *linear constraint* is a weighted sum of constrained variables compared to a constant:

$$\sum_i b_i \times X_i \leq C$$

where X_i denotes a variable, C and b_i denote constants. (Note however that the constraint $X_1 \neq X_2$ is not a linear constraint in general.)

Finite domains constraint deals with problems where the variables must take their values in a given finite set. For instance problems where the variables must take integer variables are the most common type of finite domain problems.

	Constraint Programming resource allocation	Constraints ? design
nonlinear		
linear	Integer programming O.R.	linear programming O.R.
	finite	continuous

The area of problems where constraints can be summarized by the table above. Originally, Operations Research (O.R.) started with the *Simplex* algorithm for solving sets of linear constraints with continuous variables. Subsequently, since most real world problems are finite domain problems, O.R. moved to integer programming, still with linear constraints. Constraint programming with finite domains can be seens as extending this further towards nonlinear constraints. The next move, not yet really successful, would be to handle nonlinear continuous constraints. This would lead to new methods for computer aided design (CAD) for instance.

---

[2] CHARME was launched in 1989, SOLVER in 1991.

2.4 Examples

The following is a selection of some real world applications done with ILOG
SOLVER.

- Long term staff planning [LPMD 94]. Given available staff now, planned
  staffing in 20 years, and recruitment rules, find the right number of people to
  hire each year for each category. This problem is quite large: 10000 variables
  that can take 600 differents values, e.g. between 800 and 1400 and 12000
  constraints. The system routinely solves such problems within 2 minutes.
- Locomotive scheduling for French Railways. The goal is to minimize the
  number of locomotive needed given a set of trains to be pulled.
- Airline crew scheduling. This problem is extremely large. For one month,
  over 3000 crews have to be scheduled. Each crew requires about 6 persons
  to be chosen among 1600, and some quite restrictive work regulations have
  to be followed. This problem is solved using 3000 set variables and about
  30000 integer variables.
- Chemical mixture design for a large chemical company. This problem is a
  linear integer problem. SOLVER proved to be more efficient for this application
  than a state of the art linear programming package (OSL).
- Time tabling for Banque Bruxelles Lambert[J 94]. This application allocates
  manpower for computer maintenance.
- Frequency allocation for French Army. This problem is interesting since it
  is overconstrained. The goal is to allocate frequencies over a network while
  minimizing the violation of interference constraints.
- Production scheduling for a car maker. This is a standard job shop scheduling
  problem. SOLVER was 50 times more efficient than a linear programming
  approach (14 seconds instead of 10 minutes).

These examples shows that constraint programming is already successful.

2.5 Limits

Although successful, constraint programming can still be enhanced. I've selected
the following areas as the one that are the most commonly requested by constraint programmers.

- **Specialized constraints.** Domain specific constraints can be reused for
  similar problems. For instance, limited resource constraints are common to
  all scheduling problems[Lep 94].
- **Over constrained problems.** Current programming techniques are biased
  towards the production of a solution. They are not designed to cope with
  problems where no solution exists. For such problems, one would like to
  know what are the constraints that should be removed in order to obtain a
  solution.

- **Explanations.** Similarly, one would like to know why a solution has been selected, or why such assignment was not possible.
- **Dynamic problems.** Once a problem has been solved, the real problem evolves, and a solution to the new real problem has to be searched. However, it seems intuitively interesting to reuse the solution of the original problem in order to avoid a lot of search effort. This happens clearly for scheduling applications where some replanning must be done when something wrong happens.
- **Optimization.** Many industrial problems are constrained optimization problems rather than constraint satisfaction problems. The standard optimization technique used in constraint programming tools is a kind of depth-first branch and bound that amounts to successively solving problems with tighter and tighter constraints on the cost. Other optimization techniques, such as simulated annealing, should be used when needed.

2.6 Conclusion

Constraint programming is a quite young research area, but (a part of) it has already successfully made its way to end users, as witnessed by the examples given above. However, these first applications shows that some very interesting problems should be studied and solved before constraint programming becomes mature.

References

[Cras 93] Jean-Yves Cras. "A Review of Industrial Constraint Solving Tools." AI Intelligence, Oxford, November 1993.

[Lep 94] C. Le Pape. "Ilog Schedule: A Library for the Development of Constraint-Based Scheduling Systems." To appear.

[J 94] P. Jaques, "Using Constraint Programming for time tabling", *JORBEL journal*, June 1994.

[LPMD 94] C. Lepape, J.F. Puget, C. Moreau and P. Darneaud. "PMFP : The Use of Constraint-Based Programming for Predictive Personnel Management", Proc ECAI'94, Amsterdam, August 1994.

[Pu 92] J.F. Puget, "Object Oriented Constraint Programming for Transportation Problems" Proc of ASTAIR'92, London, November 1992.

[VH 89] P. Van Hentenryck. *Constraint Satisfaction in Logic Programming*, MIT press, 1989.

3 Constraints in Design

Jeff Heisserman
Research & Technology, Boeing Computer Services
heiss@boeing.com

Design and manufacturing covers a broad range of activities, from market analysis, concept development, product definition, manufacturing planning, tooling, and production, to customer support and eventually product disposal. For this discussion, we focus on those aspects of design that constrain the geometric definition of the product. This still requires the consideration of a broad range of perspectives, including the product's function, aesthetics, manufacturability, usage and maintainability.

In order to support geometric design, we are building a variety of new tools that make it possible to produce better designs with less effort and more quickly than is currently possible. These tools automate checking and analysis of designs against design requirements and standards, helping designers maintain the correctness and consistency of the design. Other tools automate some of the more routine design tasks, and support the management of design releases and propagating design changes.

Fig. 1. An automatically generated Queen Anne house.

More sophisticated design tools support the designer in exploring different design possibilities. This includes interactive and automatic generation of designs and design alternatives, supporting the designer with intelligent design editing, and merging different designs — to combine their best properties. Future tools will support design iteration and optimization.

Constraints solving systems are attractive as mechanisms to use in building tools that help in automating design tasks. Constraint solving system have been used as far back as Ivan Sutherland's Sketchpad system. So, why aren't they more prevalent today?

Several problems are evident when applying current constraint solving technology to design problems. Most of the geometric design problems that we encounter have non-linear geometric constraints, e.g. the position and orientation of an object will depend on some angle constraints. They also tend to have both equality and inequality constraints. An example of this is found when bending aircraft hydraulic tubing, the angle of the bend must be greater than a minimum bend angle (in order to cause the material to yield and retain the new shape), and a maximum bend angle (constrained by the geometry of the bending machine).

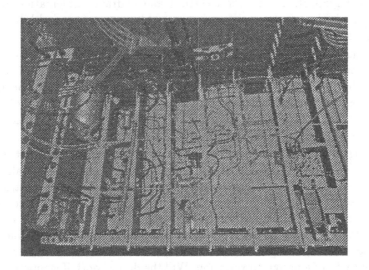

Fig. 2. A wheelwell of a commercial aircraft.

Product	Number of Parts
automobile	20,000
helicopter	45,000
commercial airplane	3,000,000

An additional problem is the sheer quantity of constraints. The complexity of real, commercial products is astonishing. A commercial airplane is composed of about 3,000,000 parts and about 150,000 unique part types. A typical subassembly on an airplane contains 1,000 to 10,000 parts. If we ignore the design constraints that define the geometry and model the interactions between aircraft components, and focus only on the constraints on the position and orientation of the individual components, we still have to solve *millions* of constraints.

Unfortunately, these other constraints do have to be considered, and they often come in forms that may be difficult to handle. A constraint found in aircraft design requires the designer to "maintain a minimum clearance of 0.5 inches between hydraulic tubing and electrical wire bundles." This is a global constraint in the sense that it must be maintained between any tube and wire bundle, but is local geometrically. Another constraint states, "Do not position hydraulic tubing joints so fluid may drip on electrical connectors." These constraints make it difficult to formulate a simple set of constraints that completely describe the problem to be solved.

In addition to the geometric representations, aircraft have a multitude of specialized product representations that are interrelated. A few of these include structural representations (finite element grids), aerodynamics, mechanical function (bond graphs), kinematics, electrical and hydraulic schematics, cabin air (HVAC) and waste system schematics, assembly sequencing, and bills of materials (hierarchical assemblies).

We must also consider the design of the manufacturing process and equipment that is constrained by the aircraft design. The shape and form of tooling is dictated by the aircraft geometry, e.g. jigs and fixtures hold components that are bonded or riveted together, and layup mandrels determine the shape of composite parts. These manufacturing processes impose additional constraints back onto the design of the aircraft.

During the design process, designers will define and attempt to solve many different sets of constraints. Initially, the problems are generally underconstrained. As additional constraints become apparent, these constraints are added — often causing the problem to become overconstrained. Overconstrained problems must be relaxed, or alternative designs must be found. It is important to be able to optimize for some objective criteria, and understand different design trade-offs, e.g. weight vs. cost. It is also important to be able to measure the sensitivity of a design to variation. Will the design work if geometry changes within the expected manufacturing tolerances?

Some commercial CAD systems provide constraint solvers to simplify the creation and manipulation of geometric models. These work quite well in some areas of geometric design — it is quite natural to use geometric constructions for new components based on the geometry of datum points and planes and the geometry of exist components. In these systems, the solvers typically require that the constraints are ordered as directed acyclic graphs (as found in spreadsheets), and require a very conscious effort to order the geometric constraint and operations. Even with these limitations, these systems run out of gas on problems with even one or a small number of very complex parts, or modest sized assemblies.

Many of the hardest problems in design are unrelated to using constraints. Product modeling representations are still quite immature. The data infrastructures that are currently available are generally insufficient. The commercially available geometric modeling tools are still quite fragile.

If constraints are to make a deeper penetration into engineering design, they will need to address a broad range of issues. We need to have better constraint solvers that can handle non-linear geometric equality and inequality constraints. If these cannot be found, then methods are needed that identify the individual constraints that cause solving them to move from a simple task to a difficult (or impossible) task.

Better tools are needed to manage the propagation of change. During design, the product definition is almost always inconsistent. Different abstractions are being used, different amounts of detail are present in different representations and domains, and conflicts are being introduced as different approaches are tried and are left unresolved until the implications are understood. Tools that define boundaries on the effects of changes will be necessary to manage the size and complexity of these constraint problems. It is possible that these mechanisms will look similar to the current engineering release mechanisms.

We need systems that are able to handle underconstrained and overconstrained problems, with effective constraint debugging facilities. Eventually, we will need systems that move easily from constraint satisfaction to constraint optimization.

Author Index

Springer-Verlag
and the Environment

We at Springer-Verlag firmly believe that an international science publisher has a special obligation to the environment, and our corporate policies consistently reflect this conviction.

We also expect our business partners – paper mills, printers, packaging manufacturers, etc. – to commit themselves to using environmentally friendly materials and production processes.

The paper in this book is made from low- or no-chlorine pulp and is acid free, in conformance with international standards for paper permanency.

Lecture Notes in Computer Science

For information about Vols. 1–795
please contact your bookseller or Springer-Verlag

Vol. 833: D. Driankov, P. W. Eklund, A. Ralescu (Eds.), Fuzzy Logic and Fuzzy Control. Proceedings, 1991. XII, 157 pages. 1994. (Subseries LNAI).

Vol. 834: D.-Z. Du, X.-S. Zhang (Eds.), Algorithms and Computation. Proceedings, 1994. XIII, 687 pages. 1994.

Vol. 835: W. M. Tepfenhart, J. P. Dick, J. F. Sowa (Eds.), Conceptual Structures: Current Practices. Proceedings, 1994. VIII, 331 pages. 1994. (Subseries LNAI).

Vol. 836: B. Jonsson, J. Parrow (Eds.), CONCUR '94: Concurrency Theory. Proceedings, 1994. IX, 529 pages. 1994.

Vol. 837: S. Wess, K.-D. Althoff, M. M. Richter (Eds.), Topics in Case-Based Reasoning. Proceedings, 1993. IX, 471 pages. 1994. (Subseries LNAI).

Vol. 838: C. MacNish, D. Pearce, L. Moniz Pereira (Eds.), Logics in Artificial Intelligence. Proceedings, 1994. IX, 413 pages. 1994. (Subseries LNAI).

Vol. 839: Y. G. Desmedt (Ed.), Advances in Cryptology - CRYPTO '94. Proceedings, 1994. XII, 439 pages. 1994.

Vol. 840: G. Reinelt, The Traveling Salesman. VIII, 223 pages. 1994.

Vol. 841: I. Prívara, B. Rovan, P. Ružička (Eds.), Mathematical Foundations of Computer Science 1994. Proceedings, 1994. X, 628 pages. 1994.

Vol. 842: T. Kloks, Treewidth. IX, 209 pages. 1994.

Vol. 843: A. Szepietowski, Turing Machines with Sublogarithmic Space. VIII, 115 pages. 1994.

Vol. 844: M. Hermenegildo, J. Penjam (Eds.), Programming Language Implementation and Logic Programming. Proceedings, 1994. XII, 469 pages. 1994.

Vol. 845: J.-P. Jouannaud (Ed.), Constraints in Computational Logics. Proceedings, 1994. VIII, 367 pages. 1994.

Vol. 846: D. Shepherd, G. Blair, G. Coulson, N. Davies, F. Garcia (Eds.), Network and Operating System Support for Digital Audio and Video. Proceedings, 1993. VIII, 269 pages. 1994.

Vol. 847: A. L. Ralescu (Ed.) Fuzzy Logic in Artificial Intelligence. Proceedings, 1993. VII, 128 pages. 1994. (Subseries LNAI).

Vol. 848: A. R. Krommer, C. W. Ueberhuber, Numerical Integration on Advanced Computer Systems. XIII, 341 pages. 1994.

Vol. 849: R. W. Hartenstein, M. Z. Servít (Eds.), Field-Programmable Logic. Proceedings, 1994. XI, 434 pages. 1994.

Vol. 850: G. Levi, M. Rodríguez-Artalejo (Eds.), Algebraic and Logic Programming. Proceedings, 1994. VIII, 304 pages. 1994.

Vol. 851: H.-J. Kugler, A. Mullery, N. Niebert (Eds.), Towards a Pan-European Telecommunication Service Infrastructure. Proceedings, 1994. XIII, 582 pages. 1994.

Vol. 852: K. Echtle, D. Hammer, D. Powell (Eds.), Dependable Computing – EDCC-1. Proceedings, 1994. XVII, 618 pages. 1994.

Vol. 853: K. Bolding, L. Snyder (Eds.), Parallel Computer Routing and Communication. Proceedings, 1994. IX, 317 pages. 1994.

Vol. 854: B. Buchberger, J. Volkert (Eds.), Parallel Processing: CONPAR 94 – VAPP VI. Proceedings, 1994. XVI, 893 pages. 1994.

Vol. 855: J. van Leeuwen (Ed.), Algorithms – ESA '94. Proceedings, 1994. X, 510 pages.1994.

Vol. 856: D. Karagiannis (Ed.), Database and Expert Systems Applications. Proceedings, 1994. XVII, 807 pages. 1994.

Vol. 857: G. Tel, P. Vitányi (Eds.), Distributed Algorithms. Proceedings, 1994. X, 370 pages. 1994.

Vol. 858: E. Bertino, S. Urban (Eds.), Object-Oriented Methodologies and Systems. Proceedings, 1994. X, 386 pages. 1994.

Vol. 859: T. F. Melham, J. Camilleri (Eds.), Higher Order Logic Theorem Proving and Its Applications. Proceedings, 1994. IX, 470 pages. 1994.

Vol. 860: W. L. Zagler, G. Busby, R. R. Wagner (Eds.), Computers for Handicapped Persons. Proceedings, 1994. XX, 625 pages. 1994.

Vol: 861: B. Nebel, L. Dreschler-Fischer (Eds.), KI-94: Advances in Artificial Intelligence. Proceedings, 1994. IX, 401 pages. 1994. (Subseries LNAI).

Vol. 862: R. C. Carrasco, J. Oncina (Eds.), Grammatical Inference and Applications. Proceedings, 1994. VIII, 290 pages. 1994. (Subseries LNAI).

Vol. 863: H. Langmaack, W.-P. de Roever, J. Vytopil (Eds.), Formal Techniques in Real-Time and Fault-Tolerant Systems. Proceedings, 1994. XIV, 787 pages. 1994.

Vol. 864: B. Le Charlier (Ed.), Static Analysis. Proceedings, 1994. XII, 465 pages. 1994.

Vol. 865: T. C. Fogarty (Ed.), Evolutionary Computing. Proceedings, 1994. XII, 332 pages. 1994.

Vol. 866: Y. Davidor, H.-P. Schwefel, R. Männer (Eds.), Parallel Problem Solving from Nature - PPSN III. Proceedings, 1994. XV, 642 pages. 1994.

Vol 867: L. Steels, G. Schreiber, W. Van de Velde (Eds.), A Future for Knowledge Acquisition. Proceedings, 1994. XII, 414 pages. 1994. (Subseries LNAI).

Vol. 868: R. Steinmetz (Ed.), Multimedia: Advanced Teleservices and High-Speed Communication Architectures. Proceedings, 1994. IX, 451 pages. 1994.

Vol. 869: Z. W. Raś, Zemankova (Eds.), Methodologies for Intelligent Systems. Proceedings, 1994. X, 613 pages. 1994. (Subseries LNAI).

Vol. 870: J. S. Greenfield, Distributed Programming Paradigms with Cryptography Applications. XI, 182 pages. 1994.

Vol. 871: J. P. Lee, G. G. Grinstein (Eds.), Database Issues for Data Visualization. Proceedings, 1993. XIV, 229 pages. 1994.

Vol. 873: M. Naftalin, T. Denvir, M. Bertran (Eds.), FME '94: Industrial Benefit of Formal Methods. Proceedings, 1994. XI, 723 pages. 1994.

Vol. 874: A. Borning (Ed.), Principles and Practice of Constraint Programming. Proceedings, 1994. IX, 361 pages. 1994.